'This powerful collection brings abolitionist thinking to the forefront of social work. It confronts the profession's complicity in colonial and state violence, opening space for urgent debate on justice, liberation and the radical transformation of social work itself.'
Vasilios Ioakimidis, University of West Attica and the International Federation of Social Work

'This groundbreaking text is essential reading for anyone who is concerned about the future trajectory of social work or has questioned whether the profession can authentically make claims to challenging injustice and promoting human liberation. Showcasing the work of a range of critical scholars, this edited collection importantly offers concrete alternatives that address the current gap between the espoused social justice values of social work and the realities of much contemporary practice. Positing a radical rethink of the profession, the book provides a much-needed resource for educators, students and practitioners in the pursuit of a more emancipatory approach to social work.'
Christine Morley, Queensland University of Technology

'Society is increasingly immersed in a toxic brew of Orwellian and Kafkaesque forms of injustice. Into this mix, carceral surveillance melds with irrational, byzantine bureaucracy: a dystopian concatenation that attenuates agency, obviates human rights and objectifies personhood. Into this arena, the theme of abolition in social work takes on a particular purchase as cogently demonstrated in the latest progressive offering from Ian Hyslop and Bob Pease. This edited text makes an original and timely contribution to the reworking of abolitionist practices in social work by championing new visions, possibilities and challenges. I highly commend this publication and its seminal advancement of radical thinking and practice aimed at transforming carceral systems in society.'
Stan Houston, Queen's University Belfast (Emeritus)

'In the context of rising global authoritarianism, social work is at a crossroads – will we resist and shake off the carceral logics and practices that have made our profession a technology of harm and control, or will we dream collectively and enact practices of care, mutuality and solidarity? In *Abolition in Social Work and Human Services: Visions,*

Possibilities and Challenges, contributors wrestle with these questions on an international level. This is a crucial intervention in a discipline that can often be centred on the national or local context and one that speaks to the deep connections and relationships we'll need to create to bring about a future social work rooted in the politics of decolonisation and global liberation.'
**Craig Fortier, Renison University College,
University of Waterloo**

'*Abolition in Social Work and Human Services* interrogates the failure of the social work profession to live up to its own ethics of fighting injustice when it colludes with the state in the oppression and marginalisation of vulnerable and minority populations. From diverse positions and international contexts, the assembled chapters provide responses to this fundamental challenge in ways that are nuanced, practical and revolutionary. By upturning the role of the state, this book expands the horizon of possibility for a praxis of social justice. It is a text I want my students to read.'
Anaru Eketone, University of Otago

'A brilliant collection of work by seminal thinkers in the conversation about abolition in social work. Thought-provoking, intellectually stimulating, rich and grounded in communities' fights to dismantle systems of harm worldwide. A must-read for all social workers and anyone interested in social justice.'
**Jacynta Krakouer, University of South Australia and
The University of Melbourne**

ABOLITION IN SOCIAL WORK AND HUMAN SERVICES
Visions, Possibilities and Challenges

Edited by
Ian Hyslop and Bob Pease

First published in Great Britain in 2025 by

Policy Press, an imprint of
Bristol University Press
University of Bristol
1–9 Old Park Hill
Bristol
BS2 8BB
UK
t: +44 (0)117 374 6645
e: bup-info@bristol.ac.uk

Details of international sales and distribution partners are available at policy.bristoluniversitypress.co.uk

© Bristol University Press 2025

British Library Cataloguing in Publication Data
A catalogue record for this book is available from the British Library

ISBN 978-1-4473-7432-9 hardcover
ISBN 978-1-4473-7433-6 paperback
ISBN 978-1-4473-7434-3 ePub
ISBN 978-1-4473-7435-0 ePdf

The right of Ian Hyslop and Bob Pease to be identified as editors of this work has been asserted by them in accordance with the Copyright, Designs and Patents Act 1988.

All rights reserved: no part of this publication may be reproduced, stored in a retrieval system, or transmitted in any form or by any means, electronic, mechanical, photocopying, recording, or otherwise without the prior permission of Bristol University Press.

Every reasonable effort has been made to obtain permission to reproduce copyrighted material. If, however, anyone knows of an oversight, please contact the publisher.

The statements and opinions contained within this publication are solely those of the editors and contributors and not of the University of Bristol or Bristol University Press. The University of Bristol and Bristol University Press disclaim responsibility for any injury to persons or property resulting from any material published in this publication.

Bristol University Press and Policy Press work to counter discrimination on grounds of gender, race, disability, age and sexuality.

Cover design: Robin Hawes
Front cover image: iStock/tigerstrawberry

This text is written in solidarity with each and every social and human service worker who finds the courage and strength to swim against the tide and challenge structural inequality at work, in public and private institutions and in wider society: abolitionist thinking offers a set of conceptual and practical tools to develop and advance social justice practice.

Contents

Notes on contributors ix

1   The politics of abolition in social work and human services   1
Ian Hyslop and Bob Pease

PART I   The abolitionist critique: foundations and visions

2   Why abolition   25
Dorothy Roberts

3   Social work and the abolitionist movement in the United States   39
Alan J. Dettlaff

4   Abolition and child welfare in England: is another world possible?   52
Anna Gupta

5   Radical reflection plus radical transformation equals revolutionary social work   66
Bindi Bennett and Péta Phelan

6   Punishment disguised as 'help': carcerality in the human services and the role of social work towards abolition   81
Sacha Kendall Jamieson and Lobna Yassine

7   Wither child maltreatment investigations by social workers: a case for abolishing the principal carceral link in the family regulation system   95
Lisa Merkel-Holguin and Ida Drury

PART II   Abolitionist thinking in practice: implications for social justice organising

8   Social work and social justice: the opportunity of an abolitionist lens   113
Ian Hyslop

9   Indigenous child protection in Canada: the insanity of doing it the same way   128
Peter Choate

10   The roadmap to child protection abolition for Māori   142
Kerri Cleaver

11   Prison abolition as a feminist of colour project: lessons from the United States   156
Mimi E. Kim

12	The limits of violence prevention in the non-profit industrial complex: moving beyond the masculinist state *Bob Pease*	164
13	Transformative justice informed community responses to harm: a conversation with Idil Ali, Lauren Caulfield and Anita Thomasson *Anne-lise Ah-fat*	180
14	Dismantling the master's house? Abolition, deradicalisation and social work *Sophie Shall and David McKendrick*	195
15	Harm reduction in the opiate crisis: non-carceral, community-led services and compassion *Donna Baines and Mohamed Ibrahim*	208
16	'They see it as Big Brother watching at all times': lone mothers and their children in Ireland's 'Family Hubs' *Aoife Donohue and Paul Michael Garrett*	221

PART III	**Facing the challenges of abolitionism: critical engagement with the state**	
17	Abolition, decolonisation and public health approaches to child protection: convergence, divergence and the new neoliberalism *Emily Keddell*	239
18	Haunting, abolition and Finnish child welfare *Kris Clarke and Mwenza Blell*	255
19	Beyond 'doing harm' and 'doing nothing': creating generative alternatives to psychiatric carcerality *Emma Tseris*	270
20	Twin births, twin abolitions: abolishing the capitalist, carceral state and the liberal individual – and, with them, conventional social work *John Fox*	284
21	After social work? *Chris Maylea*	299

Index		312

Notes on contributors

Anne-lise Ah-fat is a community organiser and mother of two who lives and works on unceded Wurundjeri Country. She is involved in the Transformative Justice Network, Incendium Radical Library and Infoshop, letter writing prison solidarity network, Radio A and A Transformative Justice Podcast, Healing through Arts, IRL mutual aid, LGBTQIA+ individual and group therapy inside prisons. She is passionate about transformative justice, abolition, community radio and radical libraries. Anne-lise works in grassroots collectives alongside people in prison, in community responses to harm, and in community healing. Her paid role is as a men's family violence practitioner. Anne-lise holds a belief that individual and social transformation can only occur collectively.

Donna Baines is Professor of Social Work, University of British Columbia, Canada. Her work focuses on anti-oppressive and decolonising approaches to theory and practice, paid and unpaid care work, and social policy and austerity. She has published recently in the *British Journal of Social Work*, *Work in the Global Economy* and the 4th edition of *Doing Anti-Oppressive Social Work: Rethinking Theory and Practice* (with N. Clark and B. Bennett, Fernwood Publishing, 2023).

Bindi Bennett (she/her) is a Gamilaraay woman, mother and social worker and is Professorial Research Fellow at the National Centre for Reconciliation, Truth and Justice at Federation University in Australia living and working on the lands of the Jinibara Peoples in Queensland. She is a social justice scholar and activist who is committed to improving and growing cultural responsiveness; re-Indigenising Western spaces; understanding and exploring Indigenous Knowledge Systems in research; and exploring the human–animal bond.

Mwenza Blell is Senior Lecturer in the School of Geography, Politics, and Sociology at Newcastle University, UK. Her research draws from ethnography to examine intransigent and often invisible structures of injustice. Since 2019 she has been working on a research project about reproductive justice in Finland with collaborators Riikka Homanen and Tiia Sudenkaarne.

Peter Choate is Professor of Social Work at Mount Royal University in Alberta, Canada. His particular emphasis is on assessing parenting capacity (with specialties in mental health, domestic violence and child abuse and addictions) as well child and adolescent mental health including maltreatment, neglect and abuse (physical, sexual, emotional), fetal alcohol spectrum disorders (FASD), and the impact of these issues within family systems. He has presented nationally and internationally at various conferences and as a trainer for organisations in these areas. He has also appeared on over 150 occasions as an expert witness in child protection matters. His current research projects include: parents with FASD and the child welfare courts in Canada; the methodology for assessing First Nations parents for child protection and the intersection with social work theory and practice; male experiences as victims of interpersonal violence; and the use of simulation in social work education and interprofessional practice.

Kris Clarke is Professor at the Faculty of Social Sciences at the University of Helsinki, Finland. Her research interests centre on decolonisation, structural social work, LGBTQIA+ issues in social work, and the significance of place and social memory. She teaches structural social work in Finland and is currently working on a study about the history of the AIDS epidemic in Central California.

Kerri Cleaver (Kāi Tahu, Waitaha, Kāti Māmoe) is Senior Lecturer in Social Work at the University of Otago in Aotearoa (New Zealand). Her work has included front-line child protection work, the establishment of the first Kāi Tahu foster system service and working for the Office of the Children's Commissioner. Her research examines experiences of Kāi Tahu women in the care system, preventing removal of Māori children, system devolution and Māori women's perspective of child protection.

Alan J. Dettlaff is a Mexican-American scholar, author and abolitionist. He is currently Professor at the University of Houston Graduate College of Social Work, United States, where he also served as Dean from 2015 to 2022. Alan began his career as a social worker in the family policing system, where he worked as an investigative caseworker and administrator. Today, his work focuses on ending the harm that results from this system. In 2020, he helped to create and launch the upEND movement, a collaborative effort dedicated to abolishing the family policing system and building alternatives that focus on healing and liberation. Alan is author of *Confronting the Racist Legacy of the American Child Welfare System: The Case for Abolition* (Oxford University Press, 2023). He is also co-founding editor of *Abolitionist Perspectives in Social Work*, a peer-reviewed scholarly journal dedicated to developing and disseminating an abolitionist praxis in social work.

Aoife Donohue is a social work practitioner located in the west of Ireland and she has experience of working in the fields of child and family social work and adult services, both nationally and internationally. She has qualifications in social work and social care and has written on the theme of surveillance and its impact on the users of social work and welfare services.

Ida Drury has over 20 years of experience in the human services field, primarily in public child welfare. As Assistant Professor of Paediatrics at the Kempe Centre, United States, she has served multiple consulting and research projects. She currently serves as Kempe's assistant director of workforce development and principal investigator for the Kentucky Alternative Response project. She is a social work educator at Metro State Denver and the University of North Dakota. Prior to joining the Kempe Centre, Ida was a research and data analyst for the Colorado Department of Human Services. In 2009, she served as project director for the Colorado Consortium on Differential Response. Her early career was on the frontline in Minnesota as a child welfare caseworker. Ida's research and expertise are centred on social work education and training, social justice and equity for family and children impacted by the child welfare system, humanising interactions between street-level bureaucrats and citizens, and workforce development that facilitates system transformation.

John Fox is Lecturer in Social Work in the School of Health and Social Development, Deakin University, Australia. As a communist, he explores radical and critical social work theory and practice, collective, materialist, conceptions of the self (such as through the book *Marx, the Body and Human Nature* published by Palgrave Macmillan, 2015) and the development and implementation of pedagogies to promote the embrace of these conceptions in higher education and the broader public (such as through the article 'Adorno in the classroom: How contesting the influence of late capitalism enables the integrated teaching of academic literacies and critical analysis and the development of a flourishing learning community', published by Taylor & Francis Online, 2017).

Paul Michael Garrett is the author of several books and over a hundred articles in international peer-reviewed journals. His most recent books are *Dissenting Social Work: Critical Theory, Resistance and Pandemic* (Routledge, 2021) and *Social Work and Common Sense* (Routledge, 2024). Paul is also an elected member of the prestigious Royal Irish Academy. He has also been a visiting professor in Shanghai and New York and has presented keynote papers at international conferences. An active trade unionist and qualified social worker, he has been employed for two decades as a lecturer at a university in the Republic of Ireland.

Anna Gupta is Professor of Social Work at Royal Holloway University of London, UK. Her research interests include child protection, poverty and inequality; work with Black and minority ethnic children and families; work in the family courts; children in care and adoption; and the Capability Approach and Social Work. Throughout her work is a focus on social justice and human rights, and participatory approaches with people who have had lived experience of social work services. Two of her more recent publications are a co-written book: *Protecting Children: A Social Model* (Bristol University Press, 2018) and a co-edited book: *Unaccompanied Young Migrants: Identity, Care and Justice* (Bristol University Press, 2019). She was Co-investigator on an Economic and Social Research Council-funded project exploring the impact of COVID-19 and racial inequalities on the well-being of Black and Asian families and communities.

Ian Hyslop is Honorary Lecturer with the School of Social Practice, University of Auckland, Aotearoa New Zealand. He holds degrees in law, public policy and a PhD in social work. Ian worked as a statutory social worker for 20 years prior to commencing academic work. His teaching and research interests are primarily concerned with the politics of progressive practice, policy development and social change in liberal capitalist states. His recent book *A Political History of Child Protection: Lessons for Reform from Aotearoa New Zealand* was published by Policy Press in 2022.

Mohamed Ibrahim is Assistant Professor of Social Work, University of British Columbia, Canada. His work focuses on global mental health, health equity, addictions and human rights. His health leadership and clinical work covers over 20 years in the public healthcare system, and refugee and internally displaced settings in Somalia, Kenya and Uganda, as well as in Canada and the United States.

Emily Keddell is Professor of Social and Community Work at the University of Otago – Te Whare Wānanga o Otāgo, Aotearoa (New Zealand). Her research focuses on the social inequities affecting child protection in Aotearoa (New Zealand). Beneath this umbrella, she examines disparities for specific groups, decision-making variability, knowledge interpretation in practice, the use of algorithmic decision tools and the politics of state intervention in family life. Current projects include how to effectively prevent the removal of babies to foster care; how decisions to report to child protection services are made; and a cross-national project examining student social workers' perceptions of risk. Emily was an invited witness to the Waitangi Tribunal hearing investigating inequities for Māori in the Aotearoa New Zealand child protection system and the current Royal Commission into Abuse in State Care. She is a founding member of the *Reimagining Social Work* blog, an associate editor of *Qualitative Social Work*, and a member of the editorial collective of the journal *Aotearoa New Zealand Social Work*.

Notes on contributors

Sacha Kendall Jamieson is Senior Lecturer in Social Work and Policy Studies at the University of Sydney, Australia. She is a qualitative researcher of health equity, carcerality and the moral-political activity of professional work. Sacha has practised as a social worker in acute mental health services and is involved in research on the ethics of involuntary treatment for mental health issues. She is also involved in research projects led by First Nations scholars and Aboriginal Community-Controlled Organisations on the social and emotional wellbeing of First Nations women in prison and post-release, and on the child protection system and upholding First Nations children's rights.

Mimi E. Kim is Associate Professor of Social Work at California State University, Long Beach, United States, and a long-time advocate and activist working on issues of gender-based violence in communities of colour. She is a co-founder of Incite! Women, Transgender and Gender Non-Conforming People of Color Against Violence, a social movement organisation influential in the development of prison abolition feminism. She is currently Co-editor-in-chief of *Affilia: Feminist Inquiry in Social Work*. In 2004, Mimi established Creative Interventions, which promoted collective, community-based and non-criminalising approaches to address and end domestic and sexual violence, an approach known as community accountability and transformative justice. Mimi's research on the historical development of carceral feminism and the contemporary transformative justice movement includes 'The carceral creep: Gender-based violence, race, and the expansion of the punitive state, 1973–1983' (2020) and 'From carceral feminism to transformative justice: Women of color feminism and alternatives to incarceration' (2018). She is currently on a restorative justice pilot project addressing domestic and sexual violence in northern California.

Chris Maylea is a social worker, lawyer and Professor of Law at La Trobe University, Australia. He has practice experience in mental health services as a social worker and manager, and provides advice to government and policy reform bodies. Maylea's work sits at the intersections of health, welfare and the law, and is underpinned by human rights and social justice. He is the author of over 80 peer-reviewed publications and commissioned reports, and is the author of *Social Work and the Law: A Guide for Ethical Practice* (Bloomsbury, 2019). He has conducted evaluations, empirical research and doctrinal and human rights analyses. His work uses co-design approaches, with a focus on promoting the voice of people who use health and welfare services. He previously managed and evaluated mainstream Aboriginal and child and family community mental health services, rehabilitation units and assertive outreach and support services in regional areas.

David McKendrick's research interests lie in the acquisition and application of power and the ways in which particular social policies mobilise authoritarianism, coercive control and urban marginalisation. The role of increasing globalisation and its implications for social work practice has seen a blurring of the lines between emancipatory practice and a form of practice that (along with co-author Dr Jo Finch) David has termed 'securitised safeguarding', often meaning that the very people social workers would be working with to support societal change experience the most oppressive forms of state intervention.

Lisa Merkel-Holguin, Associate Professor, Pediatrics at the Kempe Center at the University of Colorado, and Director of the National Center on Family Group Decision Making, United States, has close to 30 years of experience in identifying, developing and implementing innovative child welfare reforms. Two of these most prominent reforms are family group decision-making and differential response, both which humanise the child welfare system, give professionals the opportunity to build helping relationships with families and organise services to meet their needs, and position families as leaders. Most recently, she launched the Kempe Center's Call to Action to Change Child Welfare, the first international conference of its kind that is encouraging courageous conversations and eliciting solutions that mobilise and recognise child, family and community leadership. As part of this, she is convening an international community of practice that will delve into the challenging issues of racism, sexism, classism, oppression and othering that are deeply embedded in formal child welfare systems across the world.

Bob Pease is Adjunct Professor in the School of Social Sciences at the University of Tasmania and Honorary Professor in the School of Humanities and Social Sciences at Deakin University in Melbourne, Australia. His most recent books are *Facing Patriarchy: From a Violent Gender Order to a Culture of Peace* (Zed Books, 2019), *Post-Anthropocentric Social Work: Critical Posthuman and New Materialist Perspectives* (co-editor, Routledge, 2021), *Undoing Privilege: Unearned Advantage and Systemic Injustice in an Unequal World* (second edition, Zed, 2022), *Posthumanism and the Man Question: Beyond Anthropocentric Masculinities* (co-editor, Routledge, 2023) and *Interconnecting the Violences of Men: Intersections and Continuities in Policy, Research and Activism* (co-editor, Routledge, 2024).

Péta Phelan (she/her) is an Aboriginal person with family connections to the Riverina region of South-West New South Wales, Australia. A queer, cis-woman, with a disability, she is living and thriving as a perpetual guest on the Lands of the Wurundjeri Peoples in Narrm (Melbourne). She is a discipline-specific Rehabilitation Counsellor, mental health professional, social and emotional well-being practitioner, and is currently engaged as a teaching and research academic at La Trobe University in Narrm, Australia. Her academic work is centred in Indigenous social and emotional well-being practice specific to Indigenous, queer and gender diverse disability communities. Her research and practice is deeply embedded in themes and locales of social justice and liberation, with knowledges and practices explored across her work including areas specific to Indigenous, abolitionist, decolonising, queer and gender diverse, feminist, disability/crip, and ecological theories and practices.

Dorothy Roberts is Professor of Law and Sociology at the University of Pennsylvania. She is a highly accomplished academic, award winning author and social activist who is internationally recognised for her ground-breaking work in relation to the impact of race, gender and class discrimination in state social services, particularly in relation to child welfare outcomes. Her work has been germinal in the movement to abolish and reshape the theory and practice of child and family protection services in the US. Her prominent books include *Killing the Black Body: Race, Reproduction, and the Meaning of Liberty* (Pantheon, 1997); *Shattered Bonds: The Color of Child Welfare* (Basic Books, 2001); *Fatal Invention: How Science, Politics, and Big Business Re-create Race in the Twenty-First Century* (The New Press, 2011); and *Torn Apart: How the Child Welfare System Destroys Black Families—and How Abolition Can Build a Safer World* (Basic Books, 2022).

Sophie Shall is a PhD researcher at Glasgow Caledonian University, UK, exploring the circulations of power within the relationship between social work and counter-terrorism policy in the UK. Sophie is interested in the colonial dimensions of social policy and how the entrenchment of white knowledge and dominance continues to shape the experiences of minoritised groups. Using these ideas as a foundation Sophie is also currently writing on Islamophobia within social work and the entanglement of care and control, where systems of 'care' are used to reproduce harms.

Emma Tseris is Senior Lecturer in Social Work and Policy Studies at the University of Sydney, Australia. Her teaching and research interests are in critical mental health scholarship, the intersections between gendered violence and psychiatric discourses, and using creative practices to generate new knowledges about social justice and mental health. Emma is the author of *Trauma, Women's Mental Health and Social Justice: Pitfalls and Possibilities* (Routledge, 2019) and *Psychiatric Oppression in Women's Lives: Creative Resistance and Collective Dissent* (Palgrave, 2024).

Lobna Yassine is Lecturer in Social Work and Policy Studies at the University of Sydney, Australia. Her PhD was a study on risk assessment tools in youth justice, and how these tools neutralise systemic oppressions. Her publications focus on racism and risk assessment tools in youth justice, whiteness and social work collusion, and white superiority in child welfare practices and policies.

1

The politics of abolition in social work and human services

Ian Hyslop and Bob Pease

Introduction

In this edited text, we and our contributors ask whether social work and human services can fundamentally challenge injustice and promote human liberation. We consider the relationship between social work and the liberal capitalist state and contribute to a growing recognition of the oppressive functions associated with social and human services (Ioakimidis and Wyllie, 2023). More importantly, this book begins to develop tangible alternatives for social justice practice by exploring the application of abolitionist theory.

Social work is perpetually fraught with tensions and contradictions. It targets those on the social and economic margins: racialised and gendered populations drawn from the residual working class. The soft-policing of threatening groups has been integral to the functioning of mainstream social work since the late 19th century. Ferguson (2004: 28) identifies social work as 'the decisive bourgeois response' to the disturbing reality of social suffering and fear of social disorder generated by capitalist industrialisation and urbanisation. In this sense, social work can be seen to have served an integrative function in socially and economically stratified societies by mitigating some of the inherent social suffering: effectively saving capitalism from itself (Lorenz, 2017). Abolitionist thinking challenges this perception by arguing that to work within oppressive structures is to collude with social injustice; to effectively become part of a carceral web (Roberts, 2023).

There is a dissonance between the espoused identity of social work and the experience of applied practice. Undergraduate students learn that the aspirational International Federation of Social Workers (2014) definition is fundamentally concerned with human rights and justice. Later, in the austere context of managerialist practice environments, they ponder the gulf between the rhetoric and the reality (Maylea, 2021). After four decades of neoliberal ascendancy across the Anglophone world, it is increasingly clear that conventional social work is, at best, designed to alleviate social suffering rather than challenge structures of oppression. Worse than this, social work has been complicit in widespread social harms over time: explicitly at the behest of authoritarian regimes or less directly through carceral systems administered in the name of care and welfare (Ioakimidis and Trimikliniotis, 2020). Beyond exposing the illusion of beneficence, the chapters assembled in this book also wrestle with the challenge of 'what is to be done?'. Abolitionism provides a means to transcend the disempowering analysis often generated by critical engagement with this question.

The collected chapters coalesce around developing alternative practices and communities of care which actively challenge and change the unequal power relations inscribed within a social order determined by liberal capitalism, coloniality, patriarchy, white supremacy and heteronormativity (Kim, 2018). Given the location and expertise of the various contributors, the focus is on radically reconfiguring responses to the disproportionate suffering visited upon particular population groups within Anglophone/Global North societies. It is recognised, however, that the relative wealth and privilege of such societies is located within a global history of exploitative coloniality, racial capitalism and carceral responses to demonised communities (Baines et al, 2022).

Historical threads

There is a long history of calls for social work to embrace a social justice mandate; to serve rather than 'manage' marginalised populations. This has been a persistent feature of social work literature since the radical Marxist-inspired social work movements of the late 1960s (Galper, 1975; Corrigan and Leonard, 1978; Bailey and Brake, 1980). In part, this radical intent was engendered by the desire to realise the inclusive aspirations of the postwar welfare states. Social work developed as a personal social service supplementing working-class access to health, education, housing and income support: 'Australasia's public health, housing, and education initiatives where part of the same broad political strategy that underpinned the Beveridge scheme in the United Kingdom and the later United States' anti-poverty initiatives of the Kennedy years' (Hyslop, 2012: 413). By contrast, retraction of universal provision and integrated social services over the last four or five decades has led to tightly managed state-sponsored social work that is increasingly focused on policing deviance. This, in turn, has prompted calls to defend social work: to reclaim the discretionary, cooperative and needs-centred practices of the welfare state era (Rogowski, 2020).

The notion of a return to the golden age when social work was a progressive force for social change is problematic for a number of reasons. Such appeals are shaded by graphic revelations across the Anglosphere which illustrate the gross harm caused by social care systems, particularly to Indigenous people/s in the colonial states (Garrett, 2021a). As evidenced by the spate of Inquiry Commissions in Canada, Australia and Aotearoa New

Zealand over the last decade, social work, education and human services have been active and complicit in processes of assimilation, domestication and the proletarianisation of Indigenous peoples: operating at the political intersection of race, class and gendered role ascription within the rubric of capitalism and coloniality (Cox, 2021).

In reality, the promise of the egalitarian welfare state was never a truly inclusive political project and it was relatively short-lived. Social work has a much longer history of carceral practices. In this sense, practice in the contemporary neoliberal era has simply returned to the political trope set in the 19th century: othering and managing excluded people (Parton, 2014). The theoretical heritage of the profession also reflects its relationship to the developing disciplines of social science. An enduring history of backgrounding the structural causes of poverty and inequality in favour of identifying and treating the moral and behavioural pathology of 'problems families' carries disturbing eugenic echoes (Flannagan, 2018; Hyslop, 2022).

Impetus for social justice

There is no shortage of theory and scholarship focused on the relationship between social work and the oppressive social relations which perpetuate injustice (see Pease et al, 2016). The persistent development of anti-oppressive theory for practice is, at least to some degree, fuelled by what Ferguson (2008: 20) identifies as 'the particular societal mandate of going amongst the poor'. Jones (1983: 51) argues that the socialist social work agenda of the late 1960s in the UK was generated, in part, by this positioning: 'There are few state workers such as social workers who inhabit as their primary domain these nether regions of society, and who can gain at first had some insight into problems and circumstances which the state would like to minimise and hide.' This location, at least potentially, provides the opportunity for processes of conscientisation and the radicalisation of practitioners, as evident in the Marxist-inspired radical social work turn (Corrigan and Leonard, 1978). However, the capacity to channel this insight into effective practices of resistance has been largely consumed by 40 years of neoliberal revolution from above.

Apart from the dissonance generated by engaged practice, social work academics have consistently called for 'social work' to explicitly align itself with a social justice mandate; with the interests of the disenfranchised working class, excluded racialised communities and with the political agendas of feminist, anti-capitalist, anti-racist, environmentalist, new left politics and/or other progressive social movements (Dominelli, 2004; Ferguson, 2008: Grey and Webb, 2013; Garrett, 2021a; Baines et al, 2022). Injunctions to recover, reinvent or reimagine the 'social profession' have been prolific and have taken many shapes – from pleas to move from an individual to a structural focus (Mullaly and Dupre, 2018), to developing anti-oppressive (Dominelli, 2004; Baines et al, 2022) or fundamentally critical orientations (Pease et al, 2009). We have also seen pleas for the reform of specific fields of practice to take account of the social inequality generated by rejuvenated neoliberal capitalism, in key areas such as child welfare (Featherstone et al, 2014).

Critical theorising for social work has also been fuelled by broader developments in social theory and social life in recent decades. Like intellectual magpies, pragmatic social work academics are prepared to accommodate conflicting schools of theory if they provide insights into mechanisms of power and social suffering. Older Marxist and feminist understandings of oppressive social relations have been supplemented, modified and contested by postmodern and post-structural analyses of how complex interwoven relations of power produce inequity in the social world (Pease et al, 2016). The notion of intersectionality – multiple overlapping and shifting forms of oppression – has prompted the development of broad and nuanced approaches to just practice under the umbrella concepts of critical (Pease et al, 2016) or anti-oppressive social work (Baines et al, 2022). These theoretical influences have both informed and emerged from social movements, as illustrated in the symbiotic relationship between Black Lives Matter activism and the rejuvenation of abolitionist ideas.

Limitations and the promise of abolitionism

The radical social workers of the 1970s accepted the position of working 'in and against' the state – a contested space where the interests of marginalised groups could be advanced. Critical and anti-oppressive social work theorists largely adopt the same position of working within the contradictions of state structures and institutions: 'If the state is viewed as a constantly changing, unstable, shifting equilibrium of struggles and counter-struggles, it becomes possible for AOP [anti-oppressive] social workers to search for and find spaces in which to resist state oppression and to build new practices, relations and solidarity with others doing likewise' (Baines et al, 2022: 22).

However, abolitionism does not share this conviction. The capacity to implement socially just practice visions within a territory dominated by the liberal state is limited structurally, politically and epistemically (Dimou, 2021; Toraif and Mueller, 2023). Capitalist states are only capable of reform within limited parameters and the current dominant political consensus has stridently adopted the interests of capital over the interests of the working class. Punishment, exclusion and demonisation are all legitimate responses to those unwilling or unable to be self-responsible for the outcomes of structural inequality. Problem populations are compelled to accept the discipline of the market or face the consequences and often social workers become foot-soldiers for repressive institutions. The objective of abolition is not reformist; it is transformational and asks us to lift our eyes towards a wider vision.

Abolitionism: prisons, police and the carceral state

Abolitionism has a long history, dating back to the movement to abolish slavery in the 19th century (Drescher, 2009) through to prison abolition (Davis, 2003) and defunding the police (Purnell, 2021). Angela Davis (2024a) has provided an important bridge between the abolitionist critique of slavery and the contemporary abolitionist critiques of prisons, police and the carceral state. Abolitionist history must also be located in the context of the Black power movement and more recently the Black Lives Matter movement (Brockman, 2024), which argues that prisons and police are part of colonialism, white supremacy and racial capitalism, and must therefore be abolished.

A key element of the abolitionist critique of the criminal justice system is that prisons only address individual perpetrators and are unable to acknowledge structural violence (Surken, 2022). Gendered approaches to violence prevention and child protection which focus on individuals also fail to contextualise violence within the wider apparatuses of the state. An abolitionist critique of violence involves widening understandings beyond interpersonal abuse to encompassing militarist, international, colonial and state violence (McLeod, 2022). From a feminist abolitionist perspective, interpersonal violence is embedded in conditions and systems of structural harm and goes beyond the violence of individual men (Kim, 2018).

Contemporary abolitionism is framed by feminist critiques of the carceral state (Kim, 2020; Davis et al, 2022; Loney-Howes et al, 2024; Kim, Chapter 11, this volume). A number of feminists have noted that feminist-informed violence prevention has become incorporated into the criminal justice response to violence against women (Richie and Martensen, 2020; McLeod, 2022; Davis, 2024b). Termed as 'carceral feminism', the focus is on expectations that the state will protect women from violence. Such a strategy fails to acknowledge the ways in which the state has perpetuated structural violence against women, especially women from marginalised backgrounds (Whalley and Hackett, 2017).

Feminist abolitionists also note the ways in which the carceral state has extended its reach beyond the criminal justice system to influence non-government violence prevention organisations funded by the state (Whalley and Hackett, 2017). Community-based feminist-informed rape crisis centres and women's refuges, originally part of an autonomous women's movement, have, as a result of government funding, increasingly become integrated into what Wilson (2007) refers to as the 'shadow state'. In response, INCITE! (2007)

and other community-based violence prevention organisations (Heiner and Tyson, 2017; Kim, 2021) have emerged to outline an alternative strategy for addressing violence outside of the criminal justice system. Community-based transformative justice strategies and practices are fostered, that go beyond restorative justice which operates within the criminal justice system (Murray et al, 2023).

One of the implications of this critique is that social services are increasingly adopting the logic of the carceral state and replicating the surveillance and control that is present in the criminal justice system (Richie and Martensen, 2020). Kim et al (2024) have referred to social workers as 'soft police', in that they have collaborated in framing those who do not conform to middle-class and white standards of citizenship as deviant and in need of disciplining. In recent times, it has been suggested that social workers could replace or work alongside police in certain recruited fields of policing. However, working with police leads to the further carceralisation of social work rather than humanisation of law enforcement (Rasmussen and Kirk, 2020).

As noted, it is increasingly recognised that social work, throughout its history, has been complicit in the systems that perpetuate colonialism, racism, oppression and structural violence (Vasilios and Wyllie, 2023; Dettlaff, 2024). As we have outlined, many attempts have been made to revitalise and reimagine social work by proposing radical, structural, critical and anti-oppressive approaches to practice. However, all such frameworks have grappled with the contradictions arising from social work's embeddedness within the state. In more recent times, the question has been raised whether social work should be abolished (Maylea, 2021) or whether it is obsolete (Federique, 2024). What do these challenges mean for abolitionist approaches to social work?

Abolitionist approaches to social work

Maylea (2021) has argued that the contradictions within social work are unable to be addressed and that the profession should be abolished. He asserts that the theoretical tensions within social work and the limitations posed by professionalism, along with its unwillingness to atone for historical abuses and inability to respond to contemporary challenges, all mean that the scholarly discipline and professional associations should be dissolved.

Maylea's challenge has elicited critical responses from radical social work theorists (Garrett, 2021b; Whelan, 2022; Brockman, 2024). Garrett (2021b) argues that Maylea's critique risks being weaponised by neoliberal and right-wing critics of social work and instead advocates his concept of dissenting social work to defend what he sees as the progressive aspects of the profession. Whelan (2022) shares Garrett's concern about the call for the abolition of social work aiding the neoliberal agenda and argues for a reckoning with the reality of what social work 'is', as a strategy for developing more progressive alternatives. This would require social work to acknowledge its complicity with colonisation, neoliberalism and the carceral state. Maylea (2021) doubts that such a reckoning is possible. While Brockmann (2024) notes the dangers of a call for the abolition of social work, he reminds readers that it is 'official' state-based social work that Maylea (2021) is referring to, and that this does not address forms of social work outside of the state, such as the 'popular' social work advocated by Lavalette (2019). All of these responses criticise Malyea for not developing a blueprint for a future beyond social work (see Maylea's contribution, Chapter 21, this volume, for his reply).

What does it mean then to talk about abolitionist social work or abolition *in* social work? How does this differ from the abolition of social work, as advocated by Maylea (2021)? Is it simply another radical alternative within official social work? How can social work support the visions of the abolitionist movement? These are questions that this book attempts to address. It is clear from the abolitionist literature in social work that the term abolitionist social work is contested, ranging from supporters of the abolition of the profession to developing forms of abolitionist practice within the profession (Kim and Rasmussen, 2024). So the question is raised whether abolitionist social work is a realistic goal. Kaba (2024) wonders whether abolitionist social work is an oxymoron. Rasmussen and Kirk (2020) argue that social work will be unrecognisable from what it is currently. If it is deprofessionalised, decolonised and disentangled from capitalism, will it still be social work as we know it? (Fortier et al, 2024).

The first important principle, however, shared by all abolitionists, is that social work needs to disengage itself from the carceral state. This means that social workers should not work in prisons, detention centres, police forces or criminal justice settings. It also means that social workers should work against criminalisation and support the abolition of all carceral systems (The Network to Advance Abolitionist Social Work, 2024). This would also require social workers to abandon their involvement in professional associations that are complicit with carceral systems (Murray et al, 2023). Abolitionist social workers would also resist the expansion of carceral institutions into substance abuse treatment, homelessness, mental health, child welfare and schools (Toraif and Mueller, 2023).

Abolitionist perspectives emphasise, and draw inspiration from, decolonisation, deprofessionalisation (The Network to Advance Abolitionist Social Work, 2024) and feminism (Davis et al, 2022). Murray et al (2023) suggest that the practices advocated by Feldman (2022), who calls for a 'disruptive social work', satisfy many of the principles of abolitionism; including collective refusal to cooperate with carceral systems, defiance of carceral rules and policies, mass industrial action, marches and occupations. Abolition is not only about abolishing the military, police and prisons. It is also about conceiving and developing alternative ways of living without oppression and exploitation. Thus it is more than the negation of what is, it is a praxis of building community alternatives to the carceral state. What is important to emphasise in abolitionist approaches to social work is the commitment to building life-affirming relationships and institutions that foster interdependence, mutuality and care outside of colonialism and the carceral state (Beltran et al, 2024; The Network to Advance Abolitionist Social Work, 2024).

What role can abolitionist social workers play in developing these alternatives? Abolitionist social work will be community-centred (Toraif and Mueller, 2023). It will aim to strengthen community organisations and elevate community voices: encouraging mutual aid and informal care networks (Jacobs et al, 2021). Hunter and Wroe (2022) suggest that social workers could facilitate the transfer of resources from the state to community-based care organisations. Pain (2022) explores alternative ways of responding to gender-based violence through commoning and feminist support services. Davis and Fayter (2022) argue that mutual aid is a form of abolitionist praxis. Spade (2020) has written a valuable guide to mutual aid as a strategy for building solidarity and social movements. While being mindful of the ways that mutual aid can be co-opted by neoliberal strategies of privatisation and voluntarism, Spade outlines principles and practices for mobilising people to create social spaces for solidarity and transformative justice.

Bierria et al (2022) argue that part of the process is abolishing the cop within ourselves, in our hearts and in our heads, as this shapes our intimate and communal relationships. Ben-Moshe (2018) talks about this as de-epistemology or letting go of our attachment to specific carceral ways of knowing and opening ourselves up to experiences of disorientation as we question deeply held beliefs. This acknowledges that the carceral systems that we aim to dismantle also live inside of us. If we do not acknowledge this, we will perpetuate forms of domination in our relationships and alternative organisations (Downes, 2019). Federique (2024) explore strategies for forms of care work outside of professional social work. From an abolitionist perspective, care is a political project of mutual aid, political organising and consciousness raising that extends beyond the personal. It is given expression through decolonial and feminist commons where people come together to build social relations based on responsibility, respect, mutuality and reciprocity (Woodly et al, 2021).

Limitations and criticisms of abolitionist approaches

Masson (2020) argues that anti-carceral approaches to violence prevention are at risk of supporting neoliberal privatisation and volunteerism narratives that endorse cuts to public funding. Cuomo (2020) raises the question about the danger of valorising community alternatives to state-based criminal law enforcement, as the 'community' also is shaped by institutional sexism and patriarchy. The community may also collude with perpetrators rather than holding them accountable, or engage in punitive and violent vigilante action (Masson, 2020). Furthermore, many survivors want perpetrators incarcerated because it provides at least a temporary form of safety (McGlynn, 2022). Hassan (2024) says that these tensions and limitations in abolitionism are not necessarily resolvable. But being aware of them allows us to stay uncomfortable and alert to the dangers.

While violence and abuse against women would hopefully be significantly reduced in a less capitalistic and patriarchal society, there would still be criminal harm and violence to address (Kim and Rasmussen, 2024). As noted earlier, most of the forms of abolitionist practice reviewed take place outside of the state and encourage disengagement with the state through mutual aid, commons and transformative justice. Much of this work would seem to require social workers to engage in abolitionist politics beyond their official state-mandated roles and functions, in order to reduce social work's complicity with the carceral state (The Network to Advance Abolitionist Social Work, 2024). What potential is there to practice abolitionist social work within the state?

As canvassed, abolitionists are working to abolish the prison-industrial complex and the wider carceral network of the neoliberal capitalist state. But what does this mean for other functions within what is framed as the welfare state, as in health, mental health, education, housing, income security, childcare and elder care? How are these services connected to the carceral state? Abolitionists disagree about whether the state needs to be completely abolished because of its structural violence and links to carcerality, or whether it is possible to transform the state towards non-carceral, democratised forms of governance (Baines, 2022; Kim and Rasmussen, 2024).

The work of André Gorz (1967) has provided useful reflections about the possibilities of achieving abolition through reforms within the state. Gorz distinguishes between reformist and non-reformist reforms. Reformist reforms, such as shelters, legal changes and professional counselling, are those that reproduce the systems perpetuating social injustice. Non-reformist reforms imagine a horizon beyond the state (Ben-Moshe, 2018) and undermine the dominant social and political order (Akbar, 2023). Spade (2020) develops some questions to differentiate non-reformist reforms from reformist reforms in terms of: whether the work is accountable to those whose interests it aims to serve, whether it avoids dichotomies of 'good' and 'bad', whether it legitimates or undermines carceral systems and whether or not it mobilises affected people for ongoing struggles. Lamble (2022) similarly asks whether it reduces the scope and power of carceral systems, whether it challenges the assumptions underpinning the system and whether it links to a wider vision of social change.

As attested to in this volume, there are living Indigenous knowledges and ways of being that continue to reject the liberal life-world sanctioned and imposed by the capitalist social form. There are a range of communities of interest that dare to imagine and to begin to construct a world that rejects the regulatory functions of the carceral state, and the imperialist heritage of coloniality and racism that constrains the accepted horizon of what is possible locally and globally. The heritage and contemporary manifestations of abolitionist thinking provide a way out of the sociological trap – a way for progressive work in the social to be reimagined and re-enacted outside of the dictates of established power configurations. The chapters in this text explore, as we must, beyond the boundaries of the possible: how we might come to live in alternate ways by embracing practices outside of state-mandated normativity – ways of breaking our chains.

Overview of the book

The book is divided into three parts. Part I outlines the theoretical foundations and vision of the abolitionist critique. Part II explores the implications of abolitionist thinking for social justice organising in specific fields of practice. Part III considers the challenges facing abolitionism, especially arising from critical engagements with the state.

In Chapter 2 of Part I, Dorothy Roberts notes that calls to abolish the child welfare system have provoked questions about the feasibility of dismantling the current system and worries that abolition will put vulnerable children at greater risk of maltreatment. She acknowledges the critiques that despite the clear evidence of harm inflicted by the family policing system, some child welfare experts argue that abandoning the system is dangerous because it is needed to protect children from harm. In this chapter Roberts makes a concise case for abolition of family policing and contests the claims made against it, explaining not only how the family policing system harms children but also why abolishing it is essential to keep children safe.

In Chapter 3, Alan Dettlaff critiques the disjunction between the espoused ethical commitments of the US National Association of Social Workers and the way in which the profession continues to be embedded in systems which perpetuate oppression, including prisons, policing, immigration detention and child welfare. He explores the origins of abolition praxis and examines the discriminatory roots of the US child welfare system, arguing that critics misunderstand or misrepresent the goals and methodology of the abolitionist movement: goals which are, in fact, directly and constructively aligned with the aspirational values of social work. It is argued that social work must not be complicit with structural racism and systemic oppression associated with the carceral state and that steps towards radical social change are both necessary and possible.

Anna Gupta, in Chapter 4, explores the relevance of an abolitionist lens to the challenges facing child protection in the UK, in the aftermath of austerity policies implemented by successive authoritarian neoliberal governments which have increased hardship and reduced support services for many families. She highlights research which has identified both rising numbers and chronic inequalities within the child protection and care systems, disproportionately impacting people living in poverty and some groups of racially minoritised families. In the last decade calls have been made to reimagine and reform the child protection system. However, abolitionist and anti-carceral alternatives have received limited attention. This chapter critically considers the potential for abolitionist thinking to promote the creation of a more socially just and humane child protection system in the English context.

In Chapter 5, Bindi Bennett and Péta Phelan outline how within Australia, social work continues to operate in acquiescence and lockstep with colonial hierarchies. They note that its professionals, performing as agents of the state, are positioned and deployed within the institutions and systems conceived and weaponised to surveil, police and coerce the most marginalised, vulnerable and powerless. Social workers enforce and inflict punishment, harms and further stigmatisation, marginalisation and dehumanisation on those who fail to comply with, or exist outside of, the rigid worldview of coloniality. Against this context, Bennett and Phelan discuss the idea of positioning and learning from, and engaging with, Indigenous peoples to create meaningful, transformative, just and accountable social work.

Sacha Kendall Jamieson and Lobna Yassine, in Chapter 6, argue that in Australia, social workers are inextricably tied to carcerality. They work with police to remove children, to 'manage' people experiencing mental distress, and in response to domestic violence. They also work with children's courts and criminal courts and work with people incarcerated in adult and juvenile prisons. However, despite evidence that carceral institutions are harmful, there is limited discussion among social workers about abolitionism in Australia. In this chapter, the authors argue that if social work is to be anti-oppressive, then it must also be for abolition. Drawing upon examples from their practice, they explore possibilities for social workers to dismantle carceral structures and build practices that shift power to communities.

In Chapter 7, Lisa Merkel-Holguin and Ida Drury exemplify how a kind of carceral logic informs the US child welfare system as evidenced by police-like tactics in child abuse and neglect investigations. This chapter examines these investigations in plain language and as much as possible from a 'family' point of view. Instead of current modalities of investigation, the authors propose a type of non-reformist reform wherein all but the most serious situations are diverted down a pathway known as Circles of Care. Based on restorative justice principles, these circles are designed to provide support for families identified in the system. The focus is on relationship-based assistance rather than carceral tactics. It is argued that this new pathway could constitute a necessary step in dismantling the present-day child welfare system.

Part II begins with Chapter 8, where Ian Hyslop examines the fraught relationship between social work and social justice, arguing that it is unrealistic to assume that social work can be a vehicle for human liberation when it is enmeshed within the unequal relations of power which underpin liberal capitalist societies. A retraction in the capacity of social work to address the consequences of structural inequality is linked with the rise of neoliberal politics. A deeper legacy of regulatory intervention in the lives of excluded populations, particularly in relation to the subjugation of Indigenous peoples, is also considered: the location of social work in the wider schema of capitalist and Western epistemic imperialism. It is argued that abolitionist thinking and methodology is inherently subversive and that it potentially facilitates an ideological and practical reimagining: that there is an 'outside' of liberal capitalist hegemony and that the building of new forms of social justice practice are possible.

In Chapter 9, Peter Choate focuses on the intrusive and destructive nature of child protection intervention into the lives of Indigenous children and their families in Canada. The 'noble' framing of child welfare practice is contrasted with the way in which it became a systematic set of racist state practices designed for the colonisation and assimilation of Indigenous peoples. This legacy translates into the ongoing and significant over-representation in terms of removal from family, culture, land and identity. It is argued that radical change is required. This chapter explores shifting away from legal and practice mechanisms that keep Indigenous children in care, thus ending the insanity of doing it the way we have been for decades, which replicates harm and does not create safety. Government and human service systems must give up power, creating spaces for Indigenous peoples to do what they have known how to do for centuries – look after their own children.

Kerri Cleaver, in Chapter 10, considers abolition and reconstruction of the child protection system for Indigenous Māori in Aotearoa (New Zealand), contending that a flourishing future for Māori can emerge when all mokopuna Māori (Māori children) live in thriving, intact, Māori structures. Centring Māori systems, this chapter critiques the state child protection system and asserts abolitionist aspirations founded on an ethic of restoration protected through legislated Indigenous rights. In Aotearoa, mokopuna account for 68 per cent of children involved with the child protection system, a statistic attributed to the complex web of colonisation, capitalism and neoliberal social service provision. It is argued that, within the context of coloniality and oppressive systems, Māori solutions provide a pathway to radical transformation through Māori social systems, metaphorically represented as the pā harakeke (a powerful intergenerationally protective flax-bush metaphor).

In Chapter 11, Mimi Kim investigates the dynamics of gender, race and class, and the unique role of US feminism in the carceral landscape and emancipatory prison abolitionist movements of the 21st century. She traces how second-wave feminist demands to eradicate gender-based violence coincided with the unprecedented growth of the prison system starting in the 1960s. The passage of the Violence Against Women Act as a part of the Crime Bill of 1994 symbolised feminist anti-violence movement strategies as 'carceral feminism'. Against this context, she documents how the rising anti-policing movement in the late 1990s largely led by people of colour shaped a powerful framework and set of practices that now constitute what is known as prison abolition. In this chapter she draws upon her own involvement in this movement and the implications for social change.

Bob Pease, in Chapter 12, argues that the masculinist state cannot pursue feminist objectives and serve the interests of women and queer and non-binary people, because it is deeply embedded in the reproduction of gender hierarchies and binary gender frameworks. Within this context, Pease interrogates how government-funded programmes that engage men in violence prevention institutionalise masculinity, promote the notion of 'good' men who are protectors of women, devalue the feminine and reproduce the hierarchical gender binary. He outlines an alternative abolitionist approach with men that aims to destabilise their attachment to normative masculinity and heteronormativity, enabling relations of solidarity with women and queer people to foster commoning forms of care, love and justice outside of identity politics and the non-profit industrial complex.

Anne-lise Ah-fat, in Chapter 13, engages in a conversation with three abolitionists to examine the intersections of intimate partner violence and state violence. Through interviews, this chapter challenges liberal anti-violence feminisms, shaped by the conservative state, which promotes carceral responses to harm. The dialogues show how communities, despite their entanglement in these systems, strive to build responses to violence that include reflection and adaptability. They highlight the complexities of sustaining community responses, which prioritise accountability, healing and collective responsibility over punishment. Ah-fat repositions shame as a pathway to ethical reflection and personal transformation, rather than as an instrument of dehumanisation. This approach challenges internalised carceral logics and seeks to ensure that transformative justice informed community responses to harm do not replicate the oppressive systems they aim to dismantle.

Sophie Shall and David McKendrick, in Chapter 14, apply an abolitionist lens to the UK government's PREVENT policy response to the threat of violent extremism. They examine critiques and justifications, exploring the consequences for social work of engaging in this statutory duty. Using key texts, they illustrate how abolitionist perspectives can offer a framework for understanding the ways in which social work is used as a form of policing. It is argued that in the current neoliberal context both professions coalesce around notions of creating and sustaining order. PREVENT is aligned with a violent and coercive carceral logic and connected to the racialised threat of disorder, in contrast to accepted images of social work as inherently liberal and accepting of diversity. This chapter illustrates the potential for abolitionist thought to inform new forms of social work praxis that disrupt and displace what we now know – offering renewed hope for a more equitable world.

In Chapter 15, Donna Baines and Mohamed Ibrahim outline how in British Columbia high levels of drug deaths have led to a public health emergency. While drug users and harm reduction experts have called for supervised consumption, overdose prevention sites, regulated safe supply, testing of illicit drugs, and low barrier, inclusive and supportive social housing, right-wing groups continue to call for further criminalisation and incarceration of those who use drugs. In the context of this division, this chapter draws upon a recent case study to discuss the impact of criminalisation and carceral approaches, and analyses innovative and non-carceral practices around harm reduction and housing. The chapter explores what decriminalisation and anti-carceral approaches means for these marginalised groups of people by meeting people where they are.

In Chapter 16, Aoife Donohue and Paul Michael Garrett focus on how facets of social work and social care are becoming sites where service users experience 'help' in ways that resembles the experience of prisoners. Ireland has a long history of placing 'troublesome' populations in quasi-incarcerative settings; for example, Mother and Baby Homes or Magdalen Institutions for 'unmarried mothers'. This chapter reports on research into social workers' experience of referrals from emergency housing 'Family Hubs', established in 2017. It is clear that these establishments are mostly dealing with marginalised and impoverished mothers subjected to intensive surveillance, monitoring and regulation. Although not condoning the wholesale abolition of social work, the authors' argue that Family Hubs exemplify forms of carceral state intervention that demand abolition. It is concluded that, ultimately, adequately addressing the needs of the women at the centre of this research requires the restructuring of Irish society in a way that redistributes income, wealth and opportunities.

Part III commences with Chapter 17, where Emily Keddell acknowledges the understandings which abolitionist perspectives furnish in relation to contemporarry child protection: that current systems reflect carceral logics of surveillance and punishment, and exacerbate social inequities, while doing little to effectively prevent harm to children. She goes on to critically analyse and compare the solutions promoted by abolitionists with those envisaged within decolonial and public health reform paradigms. Points of commonality are identified in the rejection of individualistic and moralistic approaches, and the promotion of kinship care. Important differences are also noted around what counts as evidence, expert versus community-led development, the recipients of devolution and the operation of coercive powers. It is argued that the threat posed by increasingly right-wing political contexts must draw our attention to points of potential solidarity and shared action, if only in the meantime.

In Chapter 18, Kris Clarke and Mwenza Blell note that representations of Finland often emphasise its ranking as the happiest country and the comprehensiveness of its welfare state. However, they argue that these superficial images are entangled in constructions of universalism that belie the contested heritage of racial hygiene, heteronormativity, white supremacy and classism, which have significantly shaped the field of social work along with notions of Nordic exceptionalism. They argue that social work in Finland is haunted by historical, recent and ongoing trends which serve to undermine the positive representations. In this chapter they develop a specifically abolitionist critique of the system that shows how and why Finnish social work is complicit with carceral policies and practices.

Emma Tseris, in Chapter 19, documents the harms perpetrated within involuntary mental health treatment and outlines a generative approach to decarcerating mental health, rather than simply critiquing the current mental health system. She argues against the anti-carceral response that removing the coercive powers of psychiatry will lead to the large-scale neglect of people experiencing distress. Tseris outlines a strategy to move beyond the dual oppressions of over-surveillance and structural abandonment confronting psychiatrised people. She argues that in response to psychiatric harm, social work must engage in concrete and practical forms of activism to contribute towards politicised, creative and survivor-led alternatives to the carceral status quo.

In Chapter 20, John Fox argues that if the carceral state is to be abolished, so too must the state's ideal subject – the liberal individual. While radical social workers have critiqued the liberal self, they have maintained its foundations: an inner foundation of being. Thus he argues that if social work is to sever its ties with the carceral state, it, too, must abandon those foundations. Marxist and post-anthropocentric theory point to an alternative to the liberal self in which the self is conceived as an ensemble, network or aggregate of relations. Drawing upon autonomist Marxism and commoning, Fox outlines an alternative way of life founded in relational ensembles, and he points to forms of care and interaction that can replace the carceral state and conventional social work.

In the final chapter, Chris Maylea critically examines the role of social work within carceral systems, challenging the assumption that social work can serve as a tool for liberation. Drawing on abolitionist perspectives, he argues that social work, as both a profession and an academic discipline, is inherently tied to oppressive institutions, including involuntary mental health treatment, child removal and various forms of detention. Maylea proposes that the functions of social work be separated into distinct roles that are free from carceral associations. Alternatives such as instructional advocacy and peer work are explored as potential abolitionist practices. He concludes by advocating for the creation of non-carceral forms of support that genuinely embody principles of liberation, community care and self-determination, ultimately calling for a fundamental reimagining of how care and support are provided in society.

Conclusion

The chapters in this book are not exhaustive of the possibilities for abolitionist approaches to social work and human services. We are mindful of the gaps and the voices that are missing from the text. Some significant areas have not been explored in depth. Abolition is key, for example, to imagining and developing a reproductive justice framework. Abolition ecology makes connections between carceral systems and ecological harm. Abolition politics includes efforts to dismantle borders and abolish refugee camps. Abolition is relevant to food justice and poverty alleviation. Our book illustrates just some of the implications of the abolitionist critique for alternative visions in particular fields of practice.

While we have contributors from the United States, Canada, England, Ireland, Scotland, Finland, Australia and New Zealand, and we are privileged to have Indigenous contributors, enabling the exploration of abolition in a range of national contexts, we are also mindful that our collection is restricted to Anglophone countries in the so-called Global North. The countries represented here, while they have different histories, political systems and varied policy contexts, all have solid state institutions. Consequently, we do not explore the implications of an abolitionist approach in countries that are marked by weak state institutions. We are very mindful that the absence of state services and regulatory systems does not, in itself, imply the presence of localised democracy or community empowerment. We are also aware that models of social resilience drawn from the Global South may have application in the development of resistance narratives and alternative forms of community-centred development. Regrettably, an anticipated contribution from Chile, that would have explored these dimensions, did not eventuate.

It is clear also that the contributors bring a diversity of perspectives to abolition and what it means for social work and human services. In fact, it may be more relevant to talk about abolitions in the plural to acknowledge this diversity. It is the richness of these different perspectives that we believe opens up debates about the future of the profession in the face of the current global polycrisis. As the climate emergency and related political frictions deepen, explorations about the recalibration of power and the exercise of non-exploitive ways of human functioning will become critical, if progressive social life is to be sustained. In terms of social justice practice, the visions explored in these chapters begin to chart (and re-chart) conceptual possibilities and practical strategies for a liberationist discipline, and for a profession that accepts the need to challenge and dismantle oppressive power structures. New systems for meeting human need can be built.

We are aware that much of the contemporary political impetus is regressive in a global sense, where the retraction of liberal state institutions exposes the raw power of corporate capital and military domination. We need look no further than the wanton destruction of Palestinian life. While recognising the global stakes and the power of elite interests, we believe that this only increases the need for alternative voices and dissenting actions. This collection makes it clear that alternatives are possible, that resistance strategies can be developed and implemented: that communal human freedom is a goal that can be pursued. In this sense, abolitionist ideas and actions provide fuel for sustainable insurrection.

We hope this book will stimulate further theorising and research and will inspire other social work colleagues to seriously consider abolitionist principles, to reclaim a vision of personal, community and political agency in these critical times: enabling theoretical analysis and practices that transcend carceral social work and the logic of carcerality in the profession.

References

Akbar, A. (2023) 'A horizon beyond legalism: On non-reformist reforms'. Available at: https://lpeproject.org/blog/a-horizon-beyond-legalism-on-non-reformist-reforms/

Bailey, R. and Brake, M. (eds) (1980) *Radical Social Work*, London: Edward Arnold.

Baines, D. (2022) 'Soft cops or social justice activists: Social work's relationship to the state in the context of BLM and neoliberalism', *British Journal of Social Work*, 52(5): 2984–3002.

Baines, D., Clark, N. and Bennett, B. (eds) (2022) *Doing Anti-Oppressive Social Work: Rethinking Theory and Practice* (4th edn), Halifax and Winnipeg: Fernwood Publishing.

Beltran, R., Brown, D., Dunbar, A., Schultz, K and Fernandez, A. (2024) 'Indigenous abolition: A talk story on ideas and strategies for social work practice', in M. Kim, C. Rasmussen and D. Washington Sr (eds), *Abolition and Social Work: Possibilities, Paradoxes and the Practice of Community Care*, Chicago: Haymarket Books, pp 46–64.

Ben-Moshe, L. (2018) 'De-epistemologies of abolition', *Critical Criminology*, 26(3): 341–355.

Bierria, A., Caruthers, J. and Lober, B. (2022) 'Introduction: Making a clearing', in A. Bierria, J. Caruthers and B. Lober (eds), *Abolition Feminisms: Volume 2: Feminist Ruptures Against the Carceral State*, Chicago: Haymarket Books, pp 1–10.

Brockmann, O. (2024) 'Imagining the end of official social work: Thinking beyond the possible and probable', *British Journal of Social Work*, 54(7): 2862–2879.

Corrigan, P. and Leonard, P. (1978) *Social Work Practice Under Capitalism: A Marxist Approach*, London: Macmillan.

Cox, K. (2021) 'The cruel pattern: Early child care and protection and the imposition of settler colonial capitalism in Aotearoa', Master's thesis, University of Auckland, New Zealand. Available at: https://researchspace.auckland.ac.nz/handle/2292/56648

Cuomo, D. (2020) 'Domestic violence, abolitionism and the problem of patriarchy', *Society and Space*. Available at: https://www.societyandspace.org/articles/domestic-violence-abolitionism-and-the-problem-of-patriarchy

Davis, A. (2003) *Are Prisons Obsolete?*, New York: Seven Stories Press.

Davis, A. (2024a) *Abolition: Politics, Practices, Promises. Volume 1*, London: Hamish Hamilton.

Davis, A. (2024b) 'Society for social work and research keynote', in M. Kim, C. Rasmussen and D. Washington Sr (eds), *Abolition and Social Work: Possibilities, Paradoxes and the Practice of Community Care*, Chicago: Haymarket Books, pp 7–18.

Davis, S. and Fayter, R. (2022) 'Mutual aid as abolitionist praxis', in S. Aiken and S. Silverman (eds), *A World Without Cages*, London: Routledge. Available at: https://www.taylorfrancis.com/chapters/edit/10.4324/9781003260868-2/mutual-aid-abolitionist-praxis-simone-weil-davis-rachel-fayter

Davis, A., Dent, G., Meiners, E. and Richie, B. (2022) *Abolition. Feminism. Now.*, London: Hamish Hamilton.

Dettlaff, A. (2024) 'Ending carceral social work', in M. Kim, C. Rasmussen and D. Washington Sr (eds), *Abolition and Social Work: Possibilities, Paradoxes and the Practice of Community Care*, Chicago: Haymarket Books, pp 109–115.

Dimou, E. (2021) 'Decolonizing southern criminology: What can the "decolonial option" tell us about challenging the modern/colonial foundations of criminology?', *Critical Criminology*, 29: 431–456.

Dominelli, L. (2004) *Social Work Theory and Practice for a Changing Profession*, Cambridge: Polity Press.

Downes, J. (2019) 'Re-imagining an end to violence: Prefiguring the worlds we want', in E. Hart, J. Greener and R. Moth (eds), *Resist the Punitive State: Grassroots Struggles Across Welfare, Housing, Education and Prisons*, London: Pluto Press, pp 208–231. Available at: https://oro.open.ac.uk/62033/3/62033.pdf

Drescher, S. (2009) *Abolition: A History of Slavery and Antislavery*, Cambridge: Cambridge University Press.

Featherstone, B., White, S. and Morris, K. (2014) *Reimagining Child Protection: Towards Humane Social Work with Families*, Bristol: Policy Press.

Federique, K. (2024) 'Is social work obsolete?', in M. Kim, C. Rasmussen and D. Washington Sr (eds), *Abolition and Social Work: Possibilities, Paradoxes and the Practice of Community Care*, Chicago: Haymarket Books, pp 79–91.

Feldman, G. (2022) 'Disruptive social work', *British Journal of Social Work*, 52(2): 759–775.

Ferguson, H. (2004) *Protecting Children in Time: Child Abuse, Child Protection and the Consequences of Modernity*, Basingstoke: Palgrave Macmillan.

Ferguson, I. (2008) *Reclaiming Social Work: Challenging Neoliberalism and Practicing Social Justice*, London: SAGE.

Flannagan, K. (2018) '"Problem families" in public housing: Discourse, commentary and (dis)order', *Housing Studies*, 33(5): 684–707.

Fortier, C., Hong-Sing Wong, E. and Rwigema, M. (eds) (2024) *Abolish Social Work (As We Know It)*, Toronto: Between the Lines.

Galper, J. (1975) *The Politics of Social Services*, Englewood Cliffs: Prentice Hall.

Garrett, P.M. (2021a) *Dissenting Social Work: Critical Theory, Resistance and Pandemic*, London: Routledge.

Garrett, P.M. (2021b) '"A world to win": In defence of (dissenting) social work – a response to Chris Maylea', *British Journal of Social Work*, 51(4): 1131–1149.

Gorz, A. (1967) *Strategy for Labor: A Radical Proposal*, Boston: Beacon Press.

Grey, M. and Webb, S. (eds) (2013) *The New Politics of Social Work*, Basingstoke: Palgrave Macmillan.

Hassan, S. (2024) 'Staying in love with each other's survival: Practicing at the intersection of liberatory harm reduction and transformative justice', in M. Kim, C. Rasmussen and D. Washington Sr (eds), *Abolition and Social Work: Possibilities, Paradoxes and the Practice of Community Care*, Chicago: Haymarket Books, pp 143–157.

Heiner, B. and Tyson, S. (2017) 'Feminism and the carceral states: Gender responsive justice and the epistemology of anti-violence', *Feminist Philosophy Quarterly*, 3(1): Article 3. Available at: doi:10.5206/fpq/2016.3.3

Hunter, D. and Wroe, L. (2022) '"Already doing the work": Social work, abolition and building the future from the present', *Critical and Radical Social Work*. Available at: https://doi.org/10.1332/204986021x16626426254968

Hyslop, I. (2012) 'Social work as a practice of freedom', *Journal of Social Work*, 12(4): 404–422.

Hyslop, I. (2022) *A Political History of Child Protection: Lessons for Reform from Aotearoa New Zealand*, Bristol: Policy Press.

International Federation of Social Workers (2014) 'Global definition of social work'. Available at: https://www.ifsw.org/what-is-social-work/global-definition-of-social-work/

INCITE! Women of Color Against Violence (ed) (2007) *The Revolution Will Not Be Funded: Beyond the Non-Profit Industrial Complex*, London: South End Press.

Ioakimidis, V. and Trimikliniotis, N. (2020) 'Making sense of social work's troubled past: Professional identity, collective memory and the quest for historical justice', *British Journal of Social Work*, 50(6): 1890–1908.

Ioakimidis, V. and Wyllie, A. (eds) (2023) *Social Work's Histories of Complicity and Resistance: A Tale of Two Professions*, Bristol: Policy Press.

Jacobs, L., Kim, M., Whitfield, D., Gartner, R., Panichelli, M., Kattari, S., et al (2021) 'Defund the police: Moving towards an anti-carceral social work', *Journal of Progressive Human Services*, 32(1): 37–62.

Jones, C. (1983) *State Social Work and the Working Class*, Basingstoke: Macmillan.

Kaba, M. (2024) 'Foreword', in M. Kim, C. Rasmussen and D. Washington Sr (eds), *Abolition and Social Work: Possibilities, Paradoxes and the Practice of Community Care*, Chicago: Haymarket Books, pp vii–xii.

Kim, M. (2018) 'From carceral feminism to transformative justice: Women-of-color feminism and alternatives to incarceration', *Journal of Ethnic and Cultural Diversity in Social Work*, 27(3): 219–233.

Kim, M. (2020) 'The carceral creep: Gender-based violence, race and the expansion of the punitive state', *Social Problems*, 67: 251–269.

Kim, M. (2021) 'Transformative justice and restorative justice: Gender-based violence and alternative visions of justice in the US', *International Review of Victimology*, 27(2): 162–172.

Kim, M. and Rasmussen, C. (2024) 'Abolition and the welfare state', in M. Kim, C. Rasmussen and D. Washington Sr (eds), *Abolition and Social Work: Possibilities, Paradoxes and the Practice of Community Care*, Chicago: Haymarket Books, pp 92–108.

Kim, M., Rasmussen, C. and Washington Sr, D. (2024) 'Introduction', in M. Kim, C. Rasmussen and D. Washington Sr (eds), *Abolition and Social Work: Possibilities, Paradoxes and the Practice of Community Care*, Chicago: Haymarket Books, pp 1–6.

Lamble, S. (2022) 'Bridging the gap between reformists and abolitionists: Can non-reformist reforms guide the work of prison inspectorates?', *World Prison Brief*. Available at: https://eprints.bbk.ac.uk/id/eprint/48239/

Lavalette, M. (2019) 'Popular social work', in S. Webb (ed) *The Routledge Handbook of Critical Social Work*, London: Routledge, pp 536–549.

Loney-Howes, R., Longbottom, M. and Fileborn, B. (2024) 'Gender-based violence and carceral feminism in Australia: Towards decarceral approaches', *Feminist Legal Studies*. Available at: https://doi.org/10.1007/s10691-024-09546-z

Lorenz, W. (2017) 'Social work education in Europe: Towards 2025', *European Journal of Social Work*, 20(3): 311–321.

Masson, A. (2020) 'A critique of anti-carceral feminism', *Journal of International Women's Studies*, 21(3): 64–76.

Maylea, C. (2021) 'The end of social work', *British Journal of Social Work*, 51(2): 772–789.

McGlynn, C. (2022) 'Challenging anti-carceral feminism: Criminalisation, justice and continuum thinking', *Women's International Forum*, 93: 1–14.

McLeod, A. (2022) 'An abolitionist critique of violence', *The University of Chicago Law Review*, 89(2): 525–556.

Mullaly, B. and Dupre, M. (2018) *The New Structural Social Work: Ideology, Theory, and Practice* (4th edn), Toronto: Oxford University Press.

Murray, B., Copeland, V. and Dettlaff, A. (2023) 'Reflections on the ethical possibilities and limitations of abolitionist praxis in social work', *Affilia*, 38(4): 742–758.

Network to Advance Abolitionist Social Work, The (2024) 'Conceptualizing abolitionist social work', in M. Kim, C. Rasmussen and D. Washington Sr (eds) *Abolition and Social Work: Possibilities, Paradoxes and the Practice of Community Care*, Chicago: Haymarket Books, pp 21–32.

Pain, R. (2022) 'Collective trauma? Isolating and commoning gender-based violence', *Gender, Place and Culture*, 29(12): 1788–1809.

Parton, N. (2014) *The Politics of Child Abuse*, Basingstoke: Macmillan.

Pease, B., Allan, J. and Briskman, L. (eds) (2009) *Critical Social Work: Theories and Practices for a Socially Just World* (2nd edn), London: Routledge.

Pease, B., Goldingay, S., Hosken, N. and Nipperess, S. (eds) (2016) *Doing Critical Social Work: Transformative Practices for Social Justice*, Sydney: Allen and Unwin.

Purnell, D. (2021) *Becoming Abolitionists: Police, Protests and the Pursuit of Freedom*, New York: Verso.

Rasmussen, C. and Kirk, J. (2020) 'Trading cops for social workers isn't the solution to police violence', *Truthout*. Available at: https://truthout.org/articles/trading-cops-for-social-workers-isnt-the-solution-to-police-violence/

Richie, B. and Martensen, K. (2020) 'Resisting carcerality, embracing abolition: Implications for feminist social work practice', *Affilia*, 35(1): 12–16.

Roberts, D. (2023) *Torn Apart: How the Child Welfare System Destroys Black Families – And How Abolition Can Build a Safer World*, New York: Basic Books.

Rogowski, S. (2020) *Social Work: The Rise and Fall of a Profession*, Bristol: Policy Press.

Spade, D. (2020) *Mutual Aid: Building Solidarity During this Crisis (and the Next)*, London: Verso.

Surken, J. (2022) 'How gender-based violence makes prison abolition (un)thinkable: The role of narrations and their setting', *The King's Student Law Review*, 12(1): 77–102.

Toraif, N. and Mueller, J. (2023) 'Abolitionist social work', in D. Bailey and T. Mizrahi (eds), *Encylopaedia of Social Work*, Oxford: Oxford University Press. Available at: https://doi.org/10.1093/acrefore/9780199975839.013.1553

Vasilios, I. and Wyllie, A. (eds) (2023) *Social Work's Histories of Complicity and Resistance: A Tale of Two Professions*, London: Routledge.

Whalley, E. and Hackett, C. (2017) 'Carceral feminisms: The abolitionist project and undoing dominant feminisms', *Contemporary Justice Review*, 20(4): 456–473.

Whelan, J. (2022) 'On your Marx …? A world to win or the dismantlement of a profession? On why we need a reckoning', *British Journal of Social Work*, 52(2): 1168–1181.

Wilson, R. (2007) 'In the shadow of the shadow state', in INCITE: Women of Color Against Violence (ed), *The Revolution Will Not Be Funded: Beyond the Non-Profit Industrial Complex*, London: South End Press, pp 170–187.

Woodly, D., Brown, R., Marin, M., Threadcraft, S., Harris, C., Syedullah, J., et al (2021) 'The politics of care', *Contemporary Political Theory*, 20: 890–925.

PART I

The abolitionist critique: foundations and visions

2

Why abolition

Dorothy Roberts

Introduction

I have written two books about the child welfare system, which were published 21 years apart. The first book, *Shattered Bonds: The Color of Child Welfare* (2001), argued that the stunningly disproportionate entanglement of Black families in the system contributed to the racist subordination of Black people (Roberts, 2001). In *Shattered Bonds*, I stated that we should 'finally abolish' America's destructive child welfare system. The second book, *Torn Apart: How the Child Welfare System Destroys Black Families – And How Abolition Can Build a Safer World* (2022), renews a call for abolition, and argues to completely *replace* the family policing system with a reimagined way of caring for families and keeping children safe (Roberts, 2022).

Three things happened after the publication of *Shattered Bonds* that strengthened my commitment to abolishing the family policing system:

1. I participated in numerous reform efforts to reduce the system's racial disparities, population size and harm, none of which rendered a significant blow to the system's fundamental design;
2. I learned more about the theorising and activism of the prison abolition movement that expanded over the last two decades; and
3. I engaged with parents who experienced family policing, and was inspired by their work to dismantle the system that disrupted their families (Davis, 2005; Kaba and Ritchie, 2022; Just Making a Change for Families, 2023; Movement for Family Power, 2023; Rise Magazine, 2023; UpEND, 2023).

These intersecting developments helped me to envision an abolitionist framework to contest family policing: the only way to stop the destruction caused by family policing is to stop policing families and collectively to support families instead.

In this chapter, I make a case for the abolition of family policing. I explain not only how the family policing system harms children, but also why abolishing it is essential to keep children safe.

Designed to oppress
Targeting marginalised families

The child welfare system cannot be reformed because it is designed to oppress the most marginalised communities in the nation. The child welfare system's purpose is not to support families and improve children's welfare, but rather to *police* families: child welfare agents accuse, investigate, regulate and punish families by relying on their power to forcibly remove children from their homes and separate them from their family caregivers (UpEND, 2023). Most of the families entangled in the system are disenfranchised by their status in unjust hierarchies of race, class, gender, disability and citizenship (Summers, 2013; Edwards et al, 2021). This demography is not an accident: the purpose of terrorising these particular families is to reinforce the very hierarchies that subordinate them.

The massive intervention in Black families is one indicator of the system's unjust aim. There is no question that Black children are over-represented in the family policing system: they comprise a percentage of the foster care population that is nearly double their share of the overall population. More than half of Black children (53 per cent) are subjected to a Child Protective Services (CPS) investigation at some point during their childhoods – almost twice the lifetime prevalence for white children (28.2 per cent) (Kim et al, 2017). About 15 per cent of Indigenous children and 11 per cent of Black children can expect to enter foster care before their eighteenth birthday (Wildeman and Emanuel, 2014). Once taken from their homes, Black children and their families receive inferior services, and are more likely to have their parents' rights terminated (Putnam-Hornstein et al, 2021).

The family-policing system punishes poverty. It is designed to ensnare economically struggling families by equating poverty with child neglect (Milner and Kelly, 2020). Neglect is defined as the failure to meet children's material needs, such as food, housing, clothing, education and medical care. Rather than serving as a defence against a neglect charge, poverty works as an enhancement of parental culpability. Thus, impoverished parents are frequently accused of neglecting their children for the same behaviour that does not trigger an investigation when wealthier parents engage in it, such as using drugs, leaving children unattended and failing to address children's mental health problems. The racist design of the family policing system is facilitated by racial bias at every stage of child welfare decision-making. Studies reveal that hospital staff are more likely to screen Black pregnant patients for drug use and report positive results to child protection authorities, and to evaluate for, diagnose and report child abuse in Black children than white children with similar injuries (Hlavinka, 2023). Research also confirms that caseworkers make racially biased decisions about their investigations of reported abuse and neglect, including requiring less risk of harm to remove Black children from their homes (Rivaux et al, 2008).

Tens of billions of dollars invested in the child welfare system prop up an overall paradigm that relies on destroying families rather than supporting them. Most federal funding for child welfare services becomes available to families only after their children have been placed in state custody, and the money is spent primarily on the costs of family separation. The money federal, state and local governments collectively budget for child welfare services not only skew public policies towards breaking up families; they also facilitate a cabal of private and public enterprises that profit from child removal (Hatcher, 2016).

Foster care is a key mechanism for siphoning money from poor families to state bureaucracies and their corporate partners. Child welfare agencies and the private companies collaborate in what has been referred to as the foster-industrial complex: they profit from families not only by receiving government funds for taking children, but also by extracting payments and property from the very families they break up. Professor Daniel Hatcher calculated the value of assets state agencies take from foster children each year at more than US$250 million (Hatcher, 2016).

The system's racist foundation

The family policing system's oppressive design results from an ideological foundation that was set centuries ago to support white supremacy and colonialism. Family destruction has historically functioned as a chief instrument of group oppression in the United States (Briggs, 2020). Since its inception, the United States has wielded child removal to terrorise, control and destroy racialised populations, and to quash their rebellions against white domination. Enslavers' authority over enslaved children and forced separation of enslaved families were integral to the exploitation of African labour (Mundorff, 2003; Williams, 2012). After the Civil War, white people maintained power, in part, by holding emancipated Black children captive as apprentices to their former enslavers (Fuke, 1988; Zipf, 2005). In the 19th century, the US military weaponised child removal against Native tribes, a policy which later morphed into the federal programme to assimilate Native children by placing them for adoption in white homes (Blackhawk, 2019; Briggs, 2020; Pember, 2019). We can also trace the roots of family policing to the Progressive Era when Elizabethan poor laws placed impoverished European immigrant children to work in local foster homes or on distant farms (Areen, 1975; Trattner, 1989; Rymph, 2017).

From these oppressive historical starting points, child welfare policies have continued to maintain a punitive stranglehold over marginalised communities that are ravaged by economic exploitation, disinvestment and state violence.

Family policing claims to protect children in these communities from harms that it falsely attributes to parental pathologies but are actually created by structural inequities.

Structured to harm
Mass child abuse

Because the family policing system is designed to oppress marginalised communities, it should not be surprising that it harms the children it claims to protect. Foster care is structured to abuse children. The trauma that children experience from being torn from their families is compounded by conditions in foster care that continue to disrupt every aspect of their lives. A major study of mortality statistics between 2003 and 2016 found that the rate of death was higher for children in foster care than children in the general population across every age category, except for children aged 15 to 18 (Chaiyachati et al, 2020). Overall, children in foster care are 42 per cent more likely to die than children who are not in foster care.

In addition to the trauma that investigations and removals inflict on individual children and their families, family policing also causes widespread damage to entire Black communities. In cities across the country, child protection cases tend to be concentrated primarily in Black neighbourhoods, so their damaging effects are felt by all the residents who live there (Roberts, 2008; Fong, 2019). The high rates of child welfare agency involvement in segregated Black neighbourhoods create a uniquely intense relationship between Black families and the child welfare authorities who police them. This awareness of the system's presence creates both fear of state intrusion and suspicion among neighbours, who are seen as potential reporters of each other to child protection services, which negatively influences their relationships both with each other and with the government.

Family surveillance

The child welfare system's policing of families extends far beyond the number of children placed in foster care. As states around the country began to reduce their foster care populations, they simultaneously expanded their invasion into the private lives of families by investigating them and overseeing them with coercive services (Abdurahman, 2021). Although the Fourth Amendment applies to government maltreatment investigations, agencies and courts in effect have created a child welfare exception to the constitutional provisions that pertain to police searches (Ismail, 2023). They treat protecting the privacy of family members as a risk to children, and therefore an excuse to waive constitutional restraints.

Child welfare agencies' extensive multisystem network of mandated reporters combined with their power to pry into a family's personal life give them access to massive amounts of information ordinarily beyond the government's reach. Governments are increasingly employing big databases, computer programming and artificial intelligence to monitor families and make automated decisions about intervening in them (Eubanks, 2018).

For families that are screened into the child welfare system, the next phase of surveillance entails forced compliance with services mandated by agencies and rubber-stamped by judges. The prescribed solutions to the problems struggling families face are a far cry from the material things they need, such as cash, affordable housing, furniture, food, clothing, education and childcare (Lee, 2016; Fong, 2020). Often, the requirements imposed by the permanency plan have nothing to do with their needs at all – like ordering them to attend anger management classes or treatment for drug addiction when they do not have a problem with anger or drugs. Many parents see the forced services as assignments they must complete to get their children back – or to keep them from being taken away – rather than real assistance. Many courts apply a rule that failure to complete the permanency plan is prima facie evidence that children should not be returned home. This heartless edict is reinforced by the Adoption and Safe Families Act's imposition of a 15-month timeframe for agencies to file petitions to terminate parental rights (Guggenheim, 2021). The main reason courts permanently sever family relationships is that parents took too long to jump through the mandated hoops.

The carceral web

The child welfare system not only resembles the criminal legal system in its punitive approach to families; it also operates in tight conjunction with police and prisons. Local child welfare and law enforcement authorities increasingly enter contracts to create various types of collaborations – from sharing information to engaging in common training, cooperating in investigations and jointly responding to reports (Edwards, 2019). Police are a key source of maltreatment reports, and enlisting armed officers for investigations adds extra credibility and terror to caseworkers' threats to remove children. Simultaneously, police officers gain license to enter homes, collect information on families, and remove and detain children with less constitutional restraint because they are acting in the name of child protection. Family policing and criminal law enforcement thus reinforce each other, expanding each system's power to control marginalised communities.

In addition, the child welfare and prison systems intertwine when parents are incarcerated. In 2018, one in ten Black children had a parent in prison, making them six times more likely to have an incarcerated parent than white children (Wakefield and Wildeman, 2013; Harvey, 2020). Incarceration not only makes it extremely difficult, if not impossible, for parents to maintain a relationship with their children, but it is considered by some courts to be a reason to terminate parental rights altogether (Comfort, 2008; Gurusami, 2019). Even when imprisoned parents can keep legal custody of their children, the penalties imposed on formerly incarcerated people create further impediments to maintaining a relationship with their children once they are released from prison. Moreover, foster care criminalises children. Black children placed in foster care are especially vulnerable to arrest, detention and incarceration (Cutuli et al, 2016; Simmons-Horton, 2020). In a 2008 study, economist Joseph Doyle concluded it is unlikely that foster care is effective at preventing children from becoming involved in the criminal punishment system (Doyle Jr., 2008). To the contrary, foster care is a gateway to juvenile detention and prison. The path from foster care to the juvenile justice system is so well-worn that there are labels for children who are caught in both: crossover, dual system, dual status, and dually involved. Equally significant, foster care is structured to increase children's chances of being arrested, prosecuted and detained (Herz et al, 2010). Foster care also pushes children into juvenile detention and jail by causing them to flee (Pergamit and Ernst, 2011). Children who run away may engage in delinquent conduct to survive and may be arrested simply because they fled. Foster care makes children vulnerable to sexual exploitation while they are in care, as well as when they run away (Post, 2015; Steward and Weiser, 2018). To make matters worse, agencies re-victimise sexually exploited foster youth by treating them as criminals (Saar et al, 2015; Watkins, 2018; West, 2019).

Black adolescents and teenagers who enter foster care are also often placed in prison-like settings. In 2021, Think of Us, a research lab founded by former foster youth, issued a report on the dehumanising conditions of these facilities, finding that youth 'frequently compared institutional placements to prison … confined, surveilling, punitory, restrictive, and degrading' (Fathallah and Sullivan, 2021).

Family policing defenders

Needed to protect?

Despite the clear evidence of harm inflicted by the family policing system, some child welfare experts argue that abandoning the system is dangerous because it is needed to protect children from harm. They cast the trauma inflicted by child welfare investigations and family separations, and the dismal outcomes of foster placement, either as unavoidable costs of protecting children from worse maltreatment at home or as aberrational flaws of a beneficial system that can be fixed.

Ironically, those who object to abolition often point to the *failure* of the CPS to keep children safe as evidence of its necessity. They claim that cases of children killed by their parents despite being 'known to the system' show that more children could be saved if agencies worked harder at policing families. But ratcheting up investigations and removals causes 'foster care panics' that unnecessarily overwhelm agencies, making it harder to address cases of severe abuse, and have failed to reduce family violence (National Coalition for Child Protection Reform, 2021). A study of child abuse deaths in Texas, for example, found that Texas CPS investigates a greater-than-average proportion of the referrals it receives, yet Texas has one of the highest child fatality rates in the nation (Burstain, 2009: 7). The report recommended reducing poverty and expanding access to proven violence-prevention programmes as more effective at protecting children from lethal abuse than surveilling and separating families.

The faith in the child welfare system to protect children is based less on evidence than on the difficulty many people have in imagining any other way of keeping children safe. Because the United States has relied on family policing to address children's needs, it has promoted the sense that family policing is essential for children's welfare. The state helps to maintain the unequal societal conditions that are the chief causes of harm to children – the very conditions that many people believe necessitate the system's operation.

Erasing racism

Some advocates for maintaining the child welfare system have contested the evidence of the system's racism. A group of prominent child welfare scholars – I call them disparity defenders – contend that the racial disparities in investigations and foster care are based on justifiable reasons for state intervention in Black families. They argue that the disparate numbers do not mean that Black children are over-represented in the child welfare system, but simply reflect Black children's greater need for child welfare services.

Disparity defenders downplay racism in the child welfare system by reducing it to a problem of racially disparate statistics rather than a problem of state repression of Black communities. Although they may recognise societal inequality, they rationalise the system's racial disparities as resulting from the system's efforts to address Black children's greater needs. This view perpetuates the system's foundational ideology of attributing the 'heavy burden of racism' to child maltreatment instead of state intrusion in Black families (Barth et al, 2020). The disparity defenders ignore the system's role in the burden Black children have borne – by destroying their families instead of ending the structural inequities that cause the greatest harms to children.

The necessity of abolition

Family policing not only harms children but its abolition is *necessary* to keep children safe. Family policing works in opposition to efforts to improve children's welfare. Only by abolishing the child welfare system can we build a society that truly cares for children.

Abolition is not abandonment

The argument that abolition will leave children vulnerable to abuse misunderstands what abolition means. Far from abandoning children, abolitionists aim to support families in ways that will keep children safer than family policing. There is a long way to go between our current destructive system, which upholds an unequal society, and an equal society that has no need for a destructive system. But this is a reason to start the joint project of dismantling the system and creating safer communities now, not to lament the hopelessness of the task. Family policing abolitionists are fighting for 'non-reformist reforms' that reduce the power of child welfare agencies to intervene in Black communities (Gilmore, 2007). For example, JMacForFamilies launched the Parent Legislative Action Network (PLAN), which is pushing the New York State Legislature to enact bills that would require Administration for Children's Services (ACS) workers to give parents notice of their right to refuse ACS entrance into their homes without a warrant, change anonymous reporting to confidential reporting, and ban involuntary drug testing of pregnant patients and their newborns and reporting results to ACS. Organisations are also calling on Congress to repeal the 1997 Adoption and Safe Families Act, which accelerated the timeline for termination of parental rights and incentivised states to increase the numbers of adoptions of children in foster care.

As family-policing abolitionists push for nonreformist reforms that shrink the child welfare system, they are also working to strengthen and expand community-based efforts that already exist and to launch new initiatives that support families and care for children (Spade, 2020; Vega and Shaw, 2021). These mutual aid initiatives are an approach to child welfare that is diametrically opposed to family policing: they are caring instead of punitive, voluntary instead of coercive, generous instead of stingy. Mutual aid offers parents concrete goods and assistance to use however they determine will benefit their children, instead of mandating services based on parents' presumed pathologies.

The 'unintended abolition' of family policing in New York City during the COVID-19 pandemic lockdown shows that mutual aid groups can provide effective replacements for child welfare agencies (Arons, 2022). Professor

Anna Arons notes that ACS drastically reduced its operations during the COVID-19 pandemic lockdown in March 2020: 'This system shrunk in almost every conceivable way as mandated reporters retreated, caseworkers adopted less intrusive investigatory tactics, and family courts constrained their operations.' Despite dire warnings that child abuse would sky-rocket because of the agency's inaction, reports of physical and sexual abuse, as well as ACS investigations related to child fatalities, decreased during the period (Arons, 2022: 7). New York City's children remained safe without ACS intervention because the pandemic generated more caring and effective ways to support families. More than 50 mutual aid networks throughout the city sprang into action to provide residents with tangible resources, such as groceries, diapers, childcare and mental health care. Congress also provided cash assistance and extra unemployment benefits to struggling families by passing the CARES Act in April 2020.

Community-based support groups, mutual aid projects and transformative justice processes allow for mass refusal to participate in family policing. They give struggling parents alternatives to relinquishing custody of their children to the CPS as the price of support. In this way, we can start dismantling the child welfare system while we create the conditions that make it obsolete.

Thwarting support

Some readers might ask, 'Why can't we maintain the child welfare system to protect children from maltreatment while we build more community-based support for families?'. Abolishing the system is necessary not only to avoid the harm it causes, but also because its operation interferes with better ways of supporting families and keeping children safe. The tentacles of CPS surveillance spread throughout US society, far beyond the walls of child welfare agencies. Family policing relies on an expansive network of information sharing that spans the school, healthcare, public assistance and law enforcement systems (Raz, 2017). Despite benign intentions, teachers, healthcare workers and social service providers who report concerns about children's welfare to child protection authorities are unlikely to generate a beneficial response. Instead, CPS treats these calls as accusations to be investigated, not requests for support. Mandated reporting therefore drives many family caregivers from the very people and places that otherwise could be well-equipped to support them (Harvey et al, 2021; Fong, 2023).

Missed children

On top of the terror the family policing system inflicts on investigated families, it also harms even more children who escape its reach. Most

US children who are denied adequate housing, nutrition, healthcare and education by racial capitalist policies – by far, the greatest harms to children – are simply ignored by child welfare agencies. Among Western countries, the United States has the highest rate of childhood poverty, invests the least in supporting families, and spends the most on child removal and foster care (Madrick, 2020).

The family policing system embodies a cruel paradox. While it brutally intrudes on too many families, failing to provide them true safety or support, it also overlooks the damaging impact of poverty, racism and patriarchal culture on even more children. Government authorities refuse to meet the needs of families with tangible resources.

By relying on policing families as the way to protect children, the system blocks imagining a society that is safer for children. We need to implement a radical shift in the state's relationship to families by dismantling the current child welfare system and purging family policing's punitive logic. Concurrently, we need to build a safer society by reimagining the very meaning of child welfare and by creating caring ways of supporting families and meeting children's needs. This is not because reforms have failed to keep children safe enough; it is because only by abolishing the child welfare system can we keep children safe.

Acknowledgements

This chapter is an adapted version of an article entitled 'Why abolition', first published in *Family Court Review* (2023), Vol. 61: 229–241. DOI: 10.1111/fcre.12712. It is reproduced with permission of the author and John Wiley and Sons.

References

Abdurahman, J.K. (2021) 'Calculating the souls of Black folk: Predictive analytics in the New York City Administration for Children's Services', *Columbia Journal of Race and Law*, 11(4): 75–110.

Areen, J. (1975) 'Intervention between parent and child: A reappraisal of the state's role in child neglect and abuse cases', *Georgetown Law Journal*, 63(4): 887–889.

Arons, A. (2022) 'An unintended abolition: Family regulation during the COVID-19 crisis', *Columbia Journal of Race and Law*, 12(1): 1–28.

Barth, R., Jonson-Reid, M., Greeson, J., Drake, B., Berrick, J., Garcia, A., Shaw, T. and Gyouko, J. (2020) 'Outcomes following child welfare services: What are they and do they differ for black children?', *Journal of Public Child Welfare*, 14(5): 477–499.

Blackhawk, M. (2019) 'Federal Indian Law as paradigm within public law', *Harvard Law Review*, 132(7): 1787–1877.

Briggs, L. (2020) *Taking Children: A History of American Terror* (1st edn), Oakland, CA: University of California Press.

Burstain, J. (2009) 'Child abuse and neglect deaths in Texas', *Center for Public Policy Priorities*, 16 December, p 7. Available at: http://library.cppp.org/research.php?aid=936&cid=4

Chaiyachati, B., Wood, J., Mitra, N. and Chiayachati, K. (2020) 'All cause mortality among children in the US foster care system, 2003–2016', *JAMA Pediatrics*, 174(9): 896.

Comfort, M. (2008) *Doing Time Together: Love and Family in the Shadow of the Prison*, Chicago: University of Chicago Press.

Cutuli, J.J., Goerge, R.M., Coulton, C., Schretzman, M., Crampton, D., Charvat, B.J., et al (2016) 'From foster care to juvenile justice: Exploring characteristics of youth in three cities', *Child and Youth Services Review*, 67: 84–94.

Davis, A.Y. (2005) *Abolition Democracy: Beyond Empire, Prisons, and Torture* (1st edn), New York: Seven Stories Press.

Doyle Jr., J.J. (2008) 'Child protection and adult crime: Using investigator assignment to estimate causal effects of foster care', *Journal of Political Economy*, 116(4): 746–770.

Edwards, F. (2019) 'Family surveillance: Police and reporting of child abuse and neglect', *RSF: The Russell Sage Foundation Journal of Social Sciences*, 5(1): 50–70.

Edwards, F., Wakefield, S., Healy, K. and Wildeman, C. (2021) 'Contact with child protective services is pervasive but unequally distributed by race and ethnicity in large US counties', *Proceedings of the National Academy of Sciences of the United States of America*, 118(30): e2106272118.

Eubanks, V. (2018) *Automating Inequality: How High-Tech Tools Profile, Police, and Punish the Poor*, New York: St. Martin's Press.

Fathallah, S. and Sullivan, S. (2021) *Away from Home: Youth Experiences of Institutional Placements in Foster Care*, Think of Us. https://www.thinkofus.org/case-studies/away-from-home

Fong, K. (2019) 'Neighborhood inequality in the prevalence of reported and substantiated child maltreatment', *Child Abuse and Neglect*, 90: 13–21.

Fong, K. (2020) 'Getting eyes in the home: Child protective services investigations and state surveillance of family life', *American Sociological Review*, 85(4): 610–638.

Fong, K. (2023) *Investigating Families: Motherhood in the Shadow of Child Protective Services*, Princeton: Princeton University Press.

Fuke, R.P. (1988) 'Planters, apprenticeship, and forced labor: The Black family under pressure in post-emancipation Maryland', *Agricultural History*, 62(4): 57–74.

Gilmore, R.W. (2007) *Golden Gulag: Prisons, Surplus, Crisis, and Opposition in Globalizing California* (1st edn), Berkeley: University of California Press.

Guggenheim, M. (2021) 'How racial politics led directly to the enactment of the Adoption and Safe Families Act of 1997: The worst law affecting families ever enacted by Congress', *Columbia Journal of Race and Law*, 11(3): 711–732.

Gurusami, S. (2019) 'Motherwork under the state: The maternal labor of formerly incarcerated Black women', *Social Problems*, 6(1): 128–143.

Harvey, B., Gupta-Kagan, J. and Church, C. (2021) 'Reimagining schools' role outside the family regulation system', *Columbia Journal of Race and Law*, 11(3): 575–610.

Harvey, S.A. (2020) *The Shadow System: Mass Incarceration and the American Family*, New York: Bold Type Books.

Hatcher, D.L. (2016) *The Poverty Industry: The Exploitation of America's Most Vulnerable Citizens*, New York: New York University Press.

Herz, D.C., Ryan, J.P. and Bilchik, S. (2010) 'Challenges facing crossover youth: An examination of juvenile justice decision-making and recidivism', *Family Court Review*, 48(2): 305–321.

Hlavinka, E. (2023) 'Racial disparity seen in child abuse reporting: Clinician bias suggested for overdiagnosis in certain groups', *MedPage Today*, 5 October. Available at: https://www.medapagetoday.com/meetingcoverage/aap/88958

Ismail, T. (2023) 'Family policing and the Fourth Amendment', *California Law Review*, 111: 1485–1550.

Just Making a Change for Families (2023) *JMacForFamilies*. Available at: www.jmacforfamilies.com/

Kaba, M. and Ritchie, A.J. (2022) *No More Police: A Case for Abolition*, New York: The New Press.

Kim, H., Wildeman, C., Jonson-Reid, M. and Drake, B. (2017) 'Lifetime prevalence of investigating child maltreatment among US children', *American Journal of Public Health*, 107(2): 274–280.

Lee, T. (2016) *Catching a Case: Inequality and Fear in New York City's Child Welfare System*, New Brunswick, NJ: Rutgers University Press.

Madrick, J. (2020) *Invisible Americans: The Tragic Cost of Child Poverty*, New York: Alfred Knopf.

Milner, J. and Kelly, D. (2017) 'It's time to stop confusing poverty with neglect', *The Imprint*, 17 January. Available at: https://imprintnews.org/child-welfare-2/time-for-child-welfare-system-to-stop-confusing-poverty-with-neglect/40222

Movement for Family Power (2023) 'Our vision and values', *Movement for Family Power*. Available at: www.movementforfamilypower.org/indexa

Mundorff, K. (2003) 'Children as chattel: Invoking the Thirteenth Amendment to reform child welfare', *Cardozo Public Law, Policy and Ethics Journal*, 1(1): 131–188.

National Coalition for Child Protection Reform (2021) 'NCCPR issue paper #2: Foster care panics', *National Coalition for Child Protection Reform*, 21 November. Available at: https://nccpr.org/nccpr-issue-paper-2-foster-care-panics/

Pember, M.A. (2019) 'Death by civilization', *The Atlantic*, 8 March. Available at: https://www.theatlantic.com/education/archive/2019/03/traumatic-legacy-indian-boarding-schools/584293/

Pergamit, M.R. and Ernst, M. (2011) *Running Away from Foster Care: Youths' Knowledge and Access of Services*, Darby: DIANE Publishing.

Post, D. (2015) 'Why human traffickers prey on foster-care kids', *City Limits*, 23 January. Available at: https://citylimits.org/2015/01/23/why-traffickers-prey-on-foster-care-kids/

Putnam-Hornstein, E., Ahn, E., Prindle, J., Magruder, J., Webster, D. and Wildeman, C. (2021) 'Cumulative rates of child protection involvement and terminations of parental rights in a California birth cohort, 1999–2017', *American Journal of Public Health*, 111(6): 1157–1163.

Raz, M. (2017) 'Unintended consequences of expanded mandated reporting laws', *American Academy of Pediatrics*, 139(4): e20163511.

Rise Magazine (2023) 'About Rise', *Rise Magazine*. Available at: www.risemagazine.org/about/

Rivaux, S., James, J., Wittenstrom, K., Baumann, D., Sheets, J., Henry, J. and Jeffries, V. (2008) 'The intersection of race, poverty, and risk: Understanding the decision to provide services to clients and remove children', *Child Welfare*, 87(2): 151–168.

Roberts, D. (2001) *Shattered Bonds: The Color of Child Welfare*, New York: Basic Books.

Roberts, D. (2008) 'The racial geography of child welfare: Toward a new research paradigm', *Child Welfare*, 87(2): 125–150.

Roberts, D. (2022) *Torn Apart: How the Child Welfare System Destroys Black Families – And How Abolition Can Build a Safer World*, New York: Basic Books.

Rymph, C. (2017) *Raising Government Children: A History on Foster Care and the American Welfare State*, Chapel Hill, NC: The University of North Carolina Press.

Saar, M.S., Epstein, R., Rosenthal, L. and Vafa, Y. (2015) The Sexual Abuse to Prison Pipeline: The Girls' Story, Washington: Georgetown Law Center on Poverty.

Simmons-Horton, S.Y. (2020) 'A bad combination: Lived experiences of youth involved in the foster care and juvenile justice systems', *Child and Adolescent Social Work Journal*, 38(1): 583–597.

Spade, D. (2020) *Mutual Aid: Building Solidarity During This Crisis (And the Next)*, New York: Verso.

Steward, N. and Weiser, B. (2018) 'Troubled girls were sent to this town to heal. Many were lured into the sex trade instead', *The New York Times*, 13 December. Available at: https://www.nytimes.com/2018/12/13/nyregion/sex-trafficking-hawthorne-cedar-knolls.html

Summers, A. (2013) 'Disproportionality rates for children in foster care', *National Council of Juvenile and Family Court Judges*.

Trattner, W.I. (1989) *From Poor Law to Welfare State: A History of Social Welfare in America*, New York: Free Press.

UpEND (2023) 'Help in NOT on the way: How family policing perpetuates state directed terror', *UpEND*. Available at: https://upendmovement.org/wp-content/uploads/2022/06/upEND-Movement-Help-is-NOT-on-the-Way-06_2022.pdf

Vega, J. and Shaw, B. (2021) 'Expand support for families, but not inside the child welfare system', *The Imprint*, 4 June. Available at: https://imprintnews.org/opinion/expand-support-for-families-but-not-inside-the-child-welfare-system/55650

Wakefield, S. and Wildeman, C. (2013) *Children of the Prison Boom: Mass Incarceration and the Future of American Inequality*, Oxford: Oxford University Press.

Watkins, A. (2018) 'She ran away from foster care. She ended up in handcuffs and leg irons', *The New York Times*, 6 December. Available at: https://www.nytimes.com/2018/12/06/nyregion/foster-children-arrest-warrants-nyc.html

West, C. (2019) 'When running away from home means getting locked up', *The Appeal*, 19 March. Available at: https://theappeal.org/when-running-away-status-offenses-washington-state/

Wildeman, C. and Emanuel, N. (2014) 'Cumulative risks of foster care placement by age 18 for U.S. children, 2000–2011', *PLoS ONE*, 9(3): e92785.

Williams, H.A. (2012) *Help Me to Find My People: The African American Search for Family Lost in Slavery*, Chapel Hill: NC: The University of North Carolina Press.

Zipf, K.L. (2005) *Labor of Incidents: Forced Apprenticeship in North Carolina 1715–1919*, Baton Rouge, LA: Louisiana State University Press.

3

Social work and the abolitionist movement in the United States

Alan J. Dettlaff

Introduction

Social workers are dedicated to challenging injustice and oppression. This core principle, enshrined in the United States National Association of Social Workers' (NASW) Code of Ethics, sets social work apart from other professions. In 2021, the NASW reinforced this commitment in a revision to the Code, stating: 'Social workers must take action against oppression, racism, discrimination, and inequities' (NASW, 2021a). However, throughout its history, social work has been deeply entwined with the systems that are directly responsible for perpetuating oppression, racism, discrimination and inequities, primarily prisons, policing and child welfare. Although the profession's role in these systems has spanned decades with little attention, in recent years it has faced growing questions regarding its complicity in the harm and inequities resulting from these systems. However, the profession has done little to address these questions and, when pressed, has simply ignored them. Given the racist outcomes produced by these systems, how long can a profession that claims social justice as a core value continue to support them? Can social work truly oppose oppression, racism, discrimination and inequities while also supporting and collaborating with the very systems that produce them? Or must social work divest from and work to dismantle these systems to achieve the justice it seeks? This chapter will explore these questions and consider the profession's future should these questions remain unaddressed.

Social work and the carceral state

Despite the profession of social work's stated commitment to social justice, the origins of the profession are rooted in social control. These origins were significantly shaped by the Industrial Revolution of the 1800s. During this period, the United States transitioned from a predominantly rural, agricultural society to an industrialised and urbanised nation. This transformation was accompanied by a substantial wave of immigration, with millions of people from Eastern and Western Europe arriving in the United States. As the Industrial Revolution introduced mass production reliant on a large labour force, newly arrived immigrants became essential to the workforce. These immigrants, in turn, relied heavily on factory jobs to support their families. However, as their dependence on these wages increased, their quality of life often deteriorated.

This rapid industrialisation created substantial economic gains for the societal elites but relied on a workforce living in precarious conditions. With parents working long hours or falling ill due to harsh working conditions, children were often left unattended, roaming the streets in search of food. This situation among the labour class and their children led to various 'social ills' that concerned the elites, who feared these children might organise and engage in crimes threatening their property and the social order. Consequently, addressing the growing number of homeless or unattended children became a pressing issue for the elite class. This is clear in the early writings of Charles Loring Brace, an influential minister in New York, who wrote in in his 1872 treatise, *The Dangerous Classes of New York*:

> Something must be done to meet the increasing crime and poverty among the destitute children of New York ... [who] hardly seem able to distinguish good and evil. ... No one cares for them, and they care for no one. Some live by begging, by petty pilfering, by bold robbery. ... These boys and girls, it should be remembered, will soon form the great lower class of our city. They will influence elections; they may shape the policy of the city; they will assuredly, if unreclaimed, poison society all around them. They will help to form the great multitude of robbers, thieves, vagrants, and prostitutes who are now such a burden upon the law-respecting community. (Brace, 1872: 90–92)

To address his concerns, Brace established a private charity known as the Children's Aid Society and initiated the Orphan Train Movement, a project that relocated over 200,000 children from the streets of New York to families in the rural Midwest, purportedly to 'rescue' them from poverty. Brace believed that placing these children with new families would instil values of hard work and moral instruction, thereby transforming them into productive members of a rapidly growing capitalist society. However, while the movement claimed to be saving poor children, it was more focused on correcting and controlling their behaviours than addressing the root causes of their poverty. This approach laid the foundation for the 'child-saving' movement and the rise of the social work profession in the late 1800s, emphasising the regulation of poor children's behaviours to prevent them from becoming a threat to society.

In his seminal book, *The Child Savers: The Invention of Delinquency*, Anthony M. Platt stated: 'The child savers viewed themselves as altruists and humanitarians dedicated to rescuing those who were less fortunately placed in the social order' (1969: 3). Jane Addams, a leading figure in social work, was one of the most prominent leaders of the child-saving movement. Under Addams' leadership, the child-saving movement aimed to provide services to European immigrant children, intending to mould them into future American citizens. Like the Orphan Trains, the child-saving movement had an aspect of rescuing children from poverty, but its primary focus was on social control and the regulation of the poor. The goal was to instill behaviours deemed necessary for future citizenship. Thus, the emerging social work profession, led by figures like Jane Addams, was built on a model of policing the behaviours of the poor and controlling those behaviours to maintain a social order acceptable to the elite.

In line with these origins, by the dawn of the 20th century, social workers were deeply integrated into law enforcement and carceral systems. This collaboration expanded greatly in the 1970s with the rise of community policing, an approach that seeks to build partnerships between police and community-based organisations, often social service agencies. As part of this approach, social workers were incorporated into police departments to help address social issues such as domestic violence and mental health. This integration led to what is now known as police social work, or the practice of embedding social workers within police departments to coordinate on family issues, domestic violence, mental health and other social concerns.

Similar to their role in policing, social workers have been deeply embedded within the child welfare system since its earliest origins and the profession actively supports and upholds the role of social workers in this system. In fact, through social work education programmes across the country, the profession has made it a professional obligation to increase the number of social workers in the child welfare system. Through federally funded programmes, over 200 schools of social work in 47 states have committed to preparing social workers to enter the child welfare workforce (Cheung, 2024). Further, the NASW recommends that an undergraduate degree in social work be a minimum requirement for all child welfare workers.

While some believe that systems such as policing and child welfare provide needed services, the outcomes of these systems are stark. One in five Black men born in the United States will experience imprisonment in their lifetime, a rate four times higher than that of white men (Ghandnoosh, 2023). Communities of colour face disproportionate surveillance and policing through biased traffic stops, pedestrian searches and drug arrests (Ghandnoosh and Barry, 2023). Consequently, Black Americans are significantly more likely than white Americans to be arrested and incarcerated (Redbird and Albrecht, 2020) and are disproportionately represented in both juvenile and adult prisons (Nellis, 2021; Rovner, 2021). Similar disparities exist in the child welfare system, where more than half of all Black children in the United States will be subject to an investigation by the time they turn 18 (Kim et al, 2017). Once investigated, Black children are forcibly separated from their families and placed in foster care at a rate nearly double that of white children (Yi et al, 2020).

Yet despite these well-known outcomes and social work's stated commitment to social justice, the profession has steadfastly maintained its involvement in these systems, and in some instances, has strengthened this involvement. Today, we exist as a profession with a code of ethics that challenges us to act against injustice and oppression while simultaneously perpetuating injustice and oppression through our involvement in harmful, racist systems. Although many have called on the profession to reconsider social work's support of these systems and to embrace an abolitionist approach towards addressing the harm these systems cause, the profession, as represented by our professional organisations, has ignored these calls. As such, the work of abolition remains largely misunderstood within the profession. Several social work scholars have been overtly critical of those who have advanced abolitionist ideas and have chosen to singularly focus on the dismantling aspects of abolition, using scare tactics to warn of those who will be harmed if abolitionist ideas are implemented. These scholars fundamentally, and perhaps intentionally, misunderstand the true goals of the abolition movement (for example, Barth et al, 2020, 2022; Garcia et al, 2024). Yet, if social work has any intention of being a profession whose actions match our purported values, we must begin to recognise that the goals of this movement – dating back to the original abolitionists – are both the fulfilment and embodiment of the values we aspire to.

The abolition movement in the United States

The theory and practice of abolition hold deep historical origins that shape contemporary thought and strategy, continually evolving over time. Often, abolition is misrepresented as merely 'dismantling' or 'destroying' institutions or systems, neglecting its deeper meaning. Abolition aims not only to dismantle harmful, racist systems but also to forge a new society founded on liberation. Far from an impractical utopian fantasy, abolition is an ongoing process involving continual scrutiny of all forms of oppression, ongoing assessment and adaptations in strategy, and the cultivation of improved relationships with one another.

Crucially, abolition is not bound by a singular, detailed blueprint. Its scope transcends any single strategy, programme or system, advocating for the emancipation of all communities from oppression and violence. Critics often demand a concrete, specific plan, reflecting a white supremacist mindset that seeks prescriptive changes designed by a select few who believe they can erase centuries of oppression with a few well-designed, evidence-based interventions (for example, Garcia et al, 2024). This fixation on a concrete plan not only narrows the discourse but also deflects attention from the systemic and economic transformations necessary for true liberation. Abolitionists reject this and embrace a variety of approaches to bring about a new reality.

In the United States, the abolition movement emerged from the urgent need to confront the cruelty and dehumanisation inflicted upon people of African descent through enslavement. Abolition then, as it does now, arises from acknowledgement that existing circumstances are intolerable, with no possibility for improvements within the confines of the existing system. Abolition does not emerge in response to mere missteps or minor transgressions but rather in response to indefensible and relentless violence and terror at the hands of the state. Early abolitionists recognised that despite attempts by the state to curb the actions of excessively violent enslavers, the institution of slavery remained merciless for Black people. To sustain slavery, enslavers relied on state-sanctioned and persistent violence inflicted on enslaved people. The very structure of the institution necessitated brutality – it was not an aberration but rather a fundamental aspect of its design.

Abolitionists also went beyond merely denouncing the atrocities of slavery and advocating for its abolition; they also advocated for a society where true liberation was attained by all. Near the conclusion of the Civil War in 1863, Frederick Douglass clearly emphasised that the abolitionist movement would not be complete solely with the ending of slavery, stating:

> I am one of those who believe that we should consent to no peace which shall not be an Abolition peace. I am, moreover, one of those who believe that the work of the American Anti-Slavery Society will not have been completed until the black men of the South, and the black men of the North, shall have been admitted, fully and completely, into the body politic of America. I look upon slavery as going the way of all the earth. It is the mission of the war to put it down. But a mightier work than the abolition of slavery now looms up before the Abolitionist. (Douglass, 1863: np)

In this statement, Douglass clearly articulated that the goal of abolition extended beyond the mere cessation of slavery to include efforts towards full equality of formerly enslaved people. Following Douglass, W.E.B. Du Bois further developed the idea of abolition extending beyond the ending of slavery. In his 1935 work, *Black Reconstruction in America 1860–1880*, Du Bois introduced the concept of 'abolition democracy', a vision for the United States where Black Americans were not only free from slavery but also gained the social, economic and political capital to be recognised as equal members of society. Bringing this vision to reality would require the establishment of new institutions, structures and relationships as the means of realising the true goal of abolition – the creation of a racially just society. As Angela Davis (2005) later stated:

> DuBois argued that the abolition of slavery was accomplished only in the negative sense. In order to achieve the *comprehensive* abolition of slavery – after the institution was rendered illegal and black people were released from their chains – new institutions should have been created to incorporate black people into the social order. (Davis, 2005: 91)

Thus, abolition, from its inception, has never been solely concerned with dismantling institutions; rather, its essence lies in the constructive effort of forging a new society grounded in the ideals of freedom and liberation. Though the thinking and efforts of the early abolitionists did not significantly arise again until nearly a century later, the original intentions of their work persist and continue to propel the movement forward.

As in the past, today's abolition movement emerges in response to the intolerable and persistent state-sanctioned violence against Black Americans. Since at least the 1960s, advocates, scholars and those impacted by incarceration have rallied against prisons, condemning not only their deplorable conditions but also challenging the effectiveness of punishment as a means of constructive intervention. Contemporary abolitionists illustrate how prisons are deliberately designed to be harsh and dehumanising, underscoring that the violence and oppression perpetuated by policing and incarceration are not isolated incidents that are remediable through reform.

With the growth of the modern abolition movement and heightened awareness of the harm inflicted on Black Americans by policing and incarceration, activists and scholars are increasingly drawing parallels between the violence and damage inflicted by policing and that perpetrated by the child welfare system. The child welfare system in the United States forcibly separates hundreds of thousands of children from their families annually (U.S. Department of Health and Human Services, 2023). Research spanning decades shows that these separations inflict irreversible harm on children, their parents and their communities. There is also a large body of research documenting the adverse outcomes for children placed in foster care, including poverty, houselessness, lower levels of educational attainment, increased rates of incarceration, and greater likelihood of substance use disorders, bipolar disorders, depression and anxiety (Doyle, 2007, 2008; Warburton et al, 2014; Côté et al, 2018; Hobbs et al, 2021). Since the earliest origins of this system, these outcomes have been disproportionately inflicted on Black children.

Hence, as was true in the past, today's abolition movement arises from the acknowledgement that current conditions are intolerable, and that improvements are not possible within the existing paradigm. Abolitionists understand that despite state efforts to mitigate certain harms brought by our systems of policing, prisons and child welfare, they remain intrinsically violent and harmful to Black people. The systems rely on violence to persist – it is a foundational aspect of their design.

Like the original abolition movement, which aimed not only to abolish slavery but also to establish a society where Black Americans could live free from injustice and oppression, today's abolition movement is not solely about dismantling harmful, racist systems. It is about building a society where the need for such systems becomes obsolete. Abolitionists strive for a society where these systems are no longer required because, collectively, we have cultivated conditions where all children, families and communities can truly thrive. This is the work of abolition. And this is the work that social work should be embracing today.

Wither social work

Although the goals of the abolitionist movement in the United States are wholly consistent with the values and objectives of social work, the profession has not embraced these goals. Rather, social work has deepened its ties with many carceral institutions, even trumpeting its collaborations with harmful systems, while simultaneously virtue-signalling its commitment to social justice. Following the tragic murder of George Floyd and many others at the hands of the police in 2020, many discussions arose on the role of social work in policing and the potential for social work to mitigate some of the racist outcomes of policing through increased collaborations. This provided an opportunity for the profession and its leaders to acknowledge their historical involvement with policing and to take a stand against the racist violence perpetuated by this system. Instead, the chief executive officer of NASW used this opportunity to emphasise the importance of social work collaborations with police, writing in the *Wall Street Journal*:

> Social workers already work alongside and in partnership with police departments across the nation. Strengthening social worker and police partnerships can be an effective strategy in addressing behavioral health, mental health, substance use, homelessness, family disputes and other similar calls to 911 emergency response lines. In fact, social workers are playing an increasingly integral role in police forces, helping officers do their jobs more effectively and humanely and become better attuned to cultural and racial biases. And studies show social

workers help police excel in fulfilling their mission to protect and serve. (McClain, 2020: np)

The murder of George Floyd and the ensuing protests in 2020 have been described by many as a 'racial reckoning' for the United States. If this pivotal moment in our history failed to prompt the social work profession, as led by the NASW, to reassess its support for policing, despite the widespread violence and evidence of harm, it indicates an utter lack of willingness to challenge the dissonance between its actions and its purported values. Today, NASW maintains its support for a reform-oriented approach to policing rather than embracing an abolitionist perspective. This includes endorsing legislative measures like the George Floyd Justice in Policing Act (NASW, 2021b), legislation that is directly opposed by the Movement for Black Lives because of its embrace of reformist strategies that fail to address the broader, systemic issues that contribute to police violence in racialised communities (Associated Press, 2021).

Similarly, the profession has yet to take any meaningful stance on the harm it causes through its support of the child welfare system, although they have taken a performative stance. In their 2021 report, 'Undoing racism through social work: NASW report to the profession on racial justice priorities and action', they include an 'apology statement', wherein they detail a series of harmful actions the profession has participated in over its history, as well as its current practices, including this acknowledgement: 'One of the most persistent challenges to anti-racist practice within social work is the disproportionate impact of the child welfare system on families of color' (NASW, 2021c). In acknowledging this and other harms, the report asserts: 'This is unacceptable, and we need to make amends.' However, these amends are not described. Instead, the report lists various statements, webinars and reformist policy actions supported by the association. Yet notably absent is a commitment to cease the harm and violence currently being perpetuated. Acknowledging harm and offering apologies while continuing the actions that cause harm renders the exercise futile, epitomising a performative response.

On the future of social work

Consistent with social work's origins and underlying philosophy towards individuals experiencing poverty, today much of social work operates under the assumption that families experiencing poverty are individually responsible for their situation and need to be 'treated' through various interventions. This individualisation of causation distracts from the broader societal issues that create poverty and the role of the government in perpetuating it. Instead, the blame for societal problems is placed on individuals while the responsibility for solving these issues is shifted onto social services that focus on self-correction and behaviour modification. This redirection of blame reinforces the ideology that underpins these systems and justifies increasingly punitive interventions by framing historically oppressed individuals and communities as threats to the social order. This reasoning, often termed carceral logic, is exemplified by today's child welfare system (Williams, 2022). Families reported to the system are blamed for the circumstances that brought them to its attention and are then compelled to comply with a series of 'services' aimed at individual self-correction of the behaviours deemed problematic. While these services are mandated, the system provides no solutions to address the broader societal failures that contributed to families' involvement with the system.

In response to this predominant approach of social work, as well as the broader lack of consistency between social work's purported values and its practice, there have been movements to push the profession towards greater alignment and to embrace a true approach to justice seeking. In the 1970s, a faction of social workers began to focus on how poverty and inequality affected their clients' lives. They argued that social workers should not only help individuals function within an unequal society but also work towards building a new society (Bailey and Brake, 1975; Galper, 1976; Corrigan and Leonard, 1978) similar in many ways to the goals of abolitionists. Conceptualised by some as 'radical social work', this movement was borne out of recognition that multiple system failures are the drivers of individuals to social workers, and as such, social workers' primary goals are to dramatically change these systems. Therefore, radical social work can be seen as shifting from an individual, pathologising approach to one that uses a broader structural analysis. It is notable that the practice of radical social work emerged within the context of the state and is described as a means of helping social workers become 'aware of the contradictions' of the practice of social work within the state, while also aiding social workers to 'develop critical action' (Bailey and Blake, 1975: 10). Mitchell et al (1980) conceptualised this as working 'in and against the state'.

Consistent with this view towards social work, some social workers have recently introduced the concept of abolitionist social work into the discourse. This approach largely emerged out of the conversations on social work and police collaborations following the police violence of 2020 and the lack of movement by mainstream social work to reject these collaborations. Toraif and Mueller (2023) describe abolitionist social work as 'a theoretical framework and political project attempting to further the goals of abolitionism more broadly, but specifically within social work as a field and through social workers as practitioners'. Abolitionist social workers envision their practice as part of a broader abolitionist movement for society. They reject the expansion of carceral systems within social services and work to support communities in developing their own responses to social conflict. Like the principles of radical social work, abolitionist social work seeks to move away from pathologising individuals for their circumstances, and instead, aims to dismantle the systems and structures that create these circumstances and build new systems.

Despite momentum towards abolitionist social work, the mainstream profession has not only failed to adopt abolitionist principles but has also rejected calls to end carceral practices within social work. Further, many social workers advocating for an abolitionist perspective within the field have faced both repression and retaliation (Asgarian, 2023). With the mainstream profession actively resisting operating outside of carceral frameworks, this brings into question the future of abolitionist social work. But, perhaps more importantly, there is an argument that social work cannot truly be abolitionist. If social workers function as an extension of the carceral state, perhaps it is social work itself that needs to be abolished (Maylea, 2021).

There is a narrative that exists among some that for social work to become more radical, the profession needs to return to its roots. However, as outlined in this chapter, the roots of social work are deeply entrenched in carcerality, behaviour modification and social control – elements the profession continues to uphold today. Perhaps there is not a path forward. Or perhaps, in line with abolitionist principles, the path forward is the end of what exists today and the creation of something new. This can begin with a more critical analysis and rejection of reformist movements within the profession that often serve to entrench carcerality rather than liberate from it. Often referred to as an analysis of 'reformist reforms vs. abolitionist steps', organisations such as Critical Resistance (2021) and upEND Movement (Pendleton et al, 2022) have provided critical tools for engaging in this analysis.

As abolitionists, we recognise that the social work we aspire to will only emerge through re-creation, and this re-creation can only occur once the existing framework has been eliminated. As abolitionists, we also recognise that although the elites in our profession want to prevent this change from happening, it is within our power to bring about the change we wish to see. As Angela Davis has said, 'You have to act as if it were possible to radically transform the world. And you have to do it all the time'.

References

Asgarian, R. (2023) 'The case for child welfare abolition', *In These Times*. Available at: https://inthesetimes.com/article/child-welfare-abolition-cps-reform-family-separation

Associated Press. (2021) 'Movement for Black Lives opposes George Floyd Justice in Policing Act', *PBS News Hour*. Available at: https://www.pbs.org/newshour/politics/movement-for-black-lives-opposes-george-floyd-justice-in-policing-act

Bailey, R. and Brake, M. (eds) (1975) *Radical Social Work,* New York: Pantheon Books.

Barth, R., Berrick, J.D., Jonson-Reid, M., Drake, B., Greeson, J. and Garcia, A. (2020) 'The research doesn't support child welfare abolition', *The Imprint.* Available at: https://imprintnews.org/opinion/research-black-families-not-support-child-welfare-abolition/47964

Barth, R., Berrick, J.D., Garcia, A.R., Drake, B., Jonson-Reid, M., Gyourko, J.R., et al (2022) 'Research to consider while effectively re-designing child welfare services', *Research on Social Work Practice*, 32(5): 483–498.

Brace, C.L. (1872) *The Dangerous Classes of New York, and Twenty Years' Work Among Them,* New York: Wynkoop and Hallenbeck.

Cheung, M. (2024) 'National survey of IV-E stipends and paybacks', *University of Houston.* Available at: https://uh.edu/socialwork/academics/cwep/title-iv-e/Stipends-Paybacks/

Corrigan, P. and Leonard, P. (1978) *Social Work Practice Under Capitalism: A Marxist Approach,* Basingstoke: Macmillan.

Côté, S.M., Orri, M., Marttila, M. and Ristikari, T. (2018) 'Out-of-home placement in early childhood and psychiatric diagnoses and criminal convictions in young adulthood: A population-based propensity score-matched study', *The Lancet Child and Adolescent Health*, 2(9): 647–653.

Critical Resistance. (2021) 'Reformist reforms vs. abolitionist steps to end imprisonment', *Critical Resistance.* Available at: https://criticalresistance.org/wp-content/uploads/2021/08/CR_abolitioniststeps_antiexpansion_2021_eng.pdf

Davis, A.Y. (2005) *Abolition Democracy: Beyond Empire, Prisons, and Torture,* New York: Seven Stories Press.

Douglass, F. (1863) 'Our work is not done'. Available at: https://rbscp.lib.rochester.edu/4403

Doyle, J.J. (2007) 'Child protection and child outcomes: Measuring the effects of foster care', *American Economic Review*, 97(5): 1583–1610.

Doyle, J.J. (2008) 'Child protection and adult crime: Using investigator assignment to estimate causal effects of foster care', *Journal of Political Economy*, 116(4): 746–770.

Du Bois, W.E.B. (1935) *Black Reconstruction in America 1860–1880,* New York: The Free Press.

Galper, J. (1976) 'Introduction of radical theory and practice in social work education: Social policy', *Journal of Education for Social Work*, 12(2): 3–9.

Garcia, A.R., Berrick, J.D., Jonson-Reid, M., Barth, R.P., Gyourko, J.R., Kohl, P., et al (2024) 'The stark implications of abolishing child welfare: An alternative path towards support and safety', *Child and Family Social Work*, 29(4): 896–908.

Ghandnoosh, N. (2023) 'One in five: Ending racial inequity in incarceration', *The Sentencing Project.* Available at: https://www.sentencingproject.org/reports/one-in-five-ending-racial-inequity-in-incarceration/

Ghandnoosh, N. and Barry, C. (2023) 'One in five: Disparities in crime and policing', *The Sentencing Project*. Available at: https://www.sentencingproject.org/reports/one-in-five-disparities-in-crime-and-policing/

Hobbs, S.D., Bederian-Gardner, D., Ogle, C.M., Bakanosky, S., Narr, R. and Goodman, G.S. (2021) 'Foster youth and at-risk non-foster youth: A propensity score and structural equation modeling analysis', *Children and Youth Services Review*, 126: 106034.

Kim, H., Wildeman, C., Jonson-Reid, M. and Drake, B. (2017) 'Lifetime prevalence of investigating child maltreatment among US children', *American Journal of Public Health*, 107(2): 274–280.

Maylea, C. (2021) 'The end of social work', *British Journal of Social Work*, 51(2): 772–789.

McClain, A. (2020) 'Social workers cooperate with police forces', *Wall Street Journal*. Available at: https://www.wsj.com/articles/social-workers-cooperate-with-police-forces-11592255480

Mitchell, J., Mackenzie, D., Holloway, J., Cockburn, C., Polanshek, K., Murray, N., et al (1980) *In and Against the State*, London: Pluto.

NASW (National Association of Social Workers) (2021a) 'Code of ethics of the National Association of Social Workers'. Available at: https://www.socialworkers.org/About/Ethics/Code-of-Ethics/Code-of-Ethics-English

NASW (2021b) 'On the anniversary of George Floyd's Death, NASW calls for meaningful police reform'. Available at: https://www.socialworkers.org/News/News-Releases/ID/2321/On-anniversary-of-George-Floyds-death-NASW-calls-for-meaningful-police-reform

NASW (2021c) 'Undoing racism through social work: NASW report to the profession on racial justice priorities and action'. Available at: https://www.socialworkers.org/LinkClick.aspx?fileticket=29AYH9qAdXc%3d&portalid=0

Nellis, A. (2021) 'The color of justice: Racial and ethnic disparities in state prisons', *The Sentencing Project*. Available at: https://www.sentencingproject.org/reports/the-color-of-justice-racial-and-ethnic-disparity-in-state-prisons-the-sentencing-project/

Pendleton, M., Dettlaff, A.J. and Weber, K. (2022) 'Framework for evaluating reformist reforms vs. abolitionist steps to end the family policing system', *upEND Movement*. Available at: https://upendmovement.org/framework/

Platt, A.M. (1969) *The Child Savers: The Invention of Delinquency*, Chicago: University of Chicago Press.

Redbird, B. and Albrecht, K. (2020) 'Racial disparity in arrests increased as crime rates declined', *Northwestern Institute for Policy Research*. Available at: https://www.ipr.northwestern.edu/our-work/working-papers/2020/wp-20-28.html

Rovner, J. (2021) 'Racial disparities in youth incarceration persist', *The Sentencing Project*. Available at: https://www.sentencingproject.org/app/uploads/2022/08/Racial-Disparities-in-Youth-Incarceration-Persist.pdf

Toraif, N. and Mueller, J.C. (2023) 'Abolitionist social work', in C. Franklin (ed), *Encyclopedia of Social Work*, New York: Oxford University Press. Available at: https://oxfordre.com/socialwork/display/10.1093/acrefore/9780199975839.001.0001/acrefore-9780199975839-e-1553

U.S. Department of Health and Human Services (2023) 'The AFCARS report: Preliminary FY 2022 estimates as of May 9, 2023'. Available at: https://www.acf.hhs.gov/sites/default/files/documents/cb/afcars-report-30.pdf

Warburton, W.P., Warburton, R.N., Sweetman, A. and Hertzman, C. (2014) 'The impact of placing adolescent males into foster care on education, income assistance, and convictions', *Canadian Journal of Economics*, 471: 35–69.

Williams, E.P. (2022) 'The carceral logic of the family policing system', *upEND Movement*. Available at: https://upendmovement.org/carceral-logic/

Yi, Y., Edwards, F. and Wildeman, C. (2020) 'Cumulative prevalence of confirmed maltreatment and foster care placement for US children by race/ethnicity, 2011–2016', *American Journal of Public Health*, 110(5): 704–709.

4

Abolition and child welfare in England: is another world possible?

Anna Gupta

Introduction

The ways in which a society responds to its most vulnerable children is central to the debate about the relationship between children, families and the state. For many years there has been growing concern among parents, scholars, policy makers and practitioners that child welfare systems across the world, especially those in English-speaking countries like the United States, UK, Australia and New Zealand, are failing to meet the goal of promoting a better and safer society for children and their families. There have been calls to reimagine and reform the child protection system. However, the abolitionist and anti-carceral debates in relation to child welfare and protection that are happening, particularly in the United States, have received limited attention in the UK. This chapter begins with discussion on the current state of the child protection system in the UK, with a focus on England, and then explores the relevance of the abolitionist debates to the UK and possibilities for promoting transformative change. As the term 'child protection' is commonly used in the UK, this is the term most frequently used in this chapter. However, in the United States and other countries 'child welfare' similarly refers to the involvement of statutory services in private family life and so the terms are used interchangeably.

The context of contemporary child protection policy and practice in England

Over the past three decades, the comparative study of how different countries respond to the welfare of children has increased, providing useful frameworks for understanding policy contexts and political influences. Systems in the UK and the United States have been noted to be more authoritarian and child protection orientated than some Nordic and Northern European countries with a more partnership-based family service orientation, although there are shifts in response to social, political, cultural and economic factors (Gilbert et al, 2011; Parton, 2022). Since the public enquiry into the death of Maria Colwell in England in the mid-1970s, the political and media response to the tragic deaths of children from maltreatment by parents or carers have driven calls for more intrusive and carceral responses by social workers and other child welfare professionals. The first decade of the 21st century saw greater funding for universal family support services under the New Labour government. However, the political and media reaction in 2008 to the death of a young child, Peter Connelly (often referred to as 'Baby P'), heralded a marked shift back to a muscular child protection system, focusing on the decisive use of the law to remove children from their birth families. Following the death of Peter Connelly the numbers of children in out of home care increased, with new applications for public law care proceedings rising 36 per cent as compared with the same period in 2008–2009 (CAFCASS, 2012). The numbers have steadily increased over the next 14 years (GOV.UK, 2023).

In 2010 a Conservative-led coalition government come into power and, following on from the global financial crisis, implemented a tranche of public spending cuts in the name of 'austerity' that continued through successive Conservative governments. The individualisation of poverty, deeming it a result of personal deficiencies rather than structural failings, was fuelled by government rhetoric of the 'feckless' underclass combined with media representations of 'shirkers and scroungers', through coverage commonly referred to as 'poverty porn' (Garthwaite, 2016). In relation to child protection, this was reflected in a newly invigorated child rescue project. The then Minister for Education, Michael Gove, stated that: 'We are leaving them to endure a life of soiled nappies and scummy baths, chaos and hunger, hopelessness and despair. These children need to be rescued, just as much as the victims of any other natural disaster' (Gove, 2013). He and others often spoke of the 'rescue' of children to 'loving' adoptive homes, and a need to speed up the process.

Alongside the practical and material reality of diminishing services, the language of family support all but disappeared from the dominant discourse. Until the end of Conservative governments in July 2024 policies and practices largely continued in this direction, with continuing cuts to community-based family and youth services and a refocusing on statutory child protection interventions. The 'small state' ideology of Conservative governments led to more intensive and punitive interventions in the lives of some marginalised groups, that is 'not a deviation from, but a constituent component of, the neo-liberal leviathan' (Wacquant, 2010: 201). The English child protection system, with the blaming of parents for their problems and for harm to their children, irrespective of their psychological needs and social contexts, was a central part of government policy.

In the context of increasing complexity, rising referrals and significantly diminishing resources, a system whose statutory underpinning emphasises the duty to support children to live and thrive in their birth families and communities has become preoccupied with, and overwhelmed by, the regulatory activities of surveillance, investigation and increased use of out of home care. Social work is being increasingly defined as a narrow child protection service. This can be seen as an example of the expansion of the carceral state in which ideology, economic policy and legal initiatives have supported the growth of punitive responses to economically disadvantaged and marginalised communities, with social work adopting the logics of, and progressively building a relationship with, the carceral state (Richie and Martensen, 2020).

The background and social circumstances of children and families

Socioeconomic context

The Department for Education in England does not collect data on the socioeconomic circumstances of children and families involved with the child protection system. However, the Child Welfare Inequalities Project (CWIP) conducted by Bywaters and colleagues showed that deprivation has a marked correlation with contact from the child protection and care systems in the UK. Children living in areas that are among the 10 per cent most deprived are over ten times more likely to be subject to an intervention than children living in least deprived 10 per cent of areas (Bywaters and the Child Welfare Inequalities Project Team, 2020). Other studies have also highlighted the over-representation of children from socioeconomically deprived backgrounds in the child protection and care systems in England. Bilson and Martin (2017) estimate that in the most deprived 20 per cent of neighbourhoods in England almost one child in two will have been referred to Children's Social Care by the age of five. Bennett et al's (2022) study of linked datasets between 2015 and 2020 found that a 1 per cent increase in child poverty was associated with five additional children entering care per 100,000. Internationally there is growing consensus that families' socioeconomic circumstances are not a background issue but should be viewed as a key causal factor in the emergence of child maltreatment. The influence of poverty works directly and indirectly (through parental stress and neighbourhood conditions), and in interaction with other factors, such as domestic violence, mental health and substance abuse (Bywaters et al, 2016). The importance of adequate social protection is noted, as economic crises increase abuse and neglect rates, but compensatory policies, such as welfare payments, mitigate the effects (Bywaters and Skinner, 2022).

How families are identified as possibly abusing or neglecting their children and then responded to is influenced by attitudes and behaviours of managers and practitioners. The evidence suggests that child protection professionals rarely engage effectively with the impact of income, employment and housing conditions, as opposed to more commonly recognised parental problems, such as mental health difficulties. Families' material circumstances are too often seen as just a background factor rather than one which affects all aspects of family life, and is not 'core business' of child protection work (Morris et al, 2018a). Featherstone et al (2018) propose a social model for protecting children; one that moves away from individualised notions of risk from parents' actions or inactions to one that recognises the social determinants of harm, and the economic, social and cultural barriers faced by most of the families concerned, as well as the protective capacities within families and communities and how these can be mobilised. Studies involving the perspectives of parents have repeatedly highlighted the shaming and blaming nature of child protection interventions, especially with a shift from support to surveillance while their material hardship is ignored (Gupta et al, 2018; Morris et al, 2018b). In recent years, there has been increasing interest in parent advocacy programmes in the UK, influenced by initiatives in the United States. Parents with experience of the child protection system support other parents experiencing interventions. Parent activists also work with academics and practitioners to make the system and processes more humane and socially just (Saar-Heiman and Gupta, 2024).

However, the significance of poverty remains contested and largely absent in child protection policy and practices. In England, the most recent review of serious cases argued that, while poverty is a frequent feature, when practitioners focus on family poverty they risk losing sight of the safety of children, either because neglect is 'normalised' in areas of pervasive high deprivation or because professional intervention focuses on practical support to the exclusion of children's broader needs (Dickens et al, 2022). A government-commissioned Review of Children's Social Care (MacAlister, 2022: 10) stated that: 'the weight of evidence showing a contributory causal relationship between income, maltreatment and state intervention in family life is strong enough to warrant widespread acceptance. ... The fact that services can either deepen or alleviate these inequalities should grip us'. However, the review made no recommendations directly relating to addressing the poverty that so many families face.

Racial and ethnic backgrounds

Regarding race and ethnicity, the Department for Education does collect some data for children on child protection plans and out of home care. As of the end of March 2023, children of white ethnicity accounted for 71 per cent of the children looked after, 10 per cent were Mixed or Multiple ethnic groups, 7 per cent Black, African, Caribbean or Black British, 5 per cent were Asian or Asian British, 5 per cent other ethnicities, and ethnicity was not known or not yet recorded for 1 per cent. This indicates an over-representation of children of mixed heritage and to a lesser extent Black children. Children of Asian origin, which in the UK generally refers to children with Indian, Bangladeshi or Pakistani backgrounds, are under-represented (GOV.UK, 2023).

Behind these statistics there is a complex relationship between deprivation, age, race/ethnicity and state intervention that was explored further by the CWIP. While some communities were experiencing much more difficult socioeconomic circumstances than others, such factors were only a partial explanation for differential intervention rates between ethnic groups. Disproportionate numbers of children from Bangladeshi, Pakistani, Caribbean and African backgrounds live in disadvantaged neighbourhoods; however Asian children overall are almost three times less likely to be in care than white children and almost four times less likely than Black children (Bywaters et al, 2019). Children from white and mixed ethnic groups are more likely to enter care for the first time as young children, with Asian and Black children being more likely to enter care for the first time as teenagers (Ahmed et al, 2022). Among 16- and 17-year-olds, one Black Caribbean child in 30 was in care, compared to one in 100 white British children (Bywaters et al, 2019).

There is limited research into racially minoritised families' experiences of the child protection system. Much of the qualitative research does not disaggregate parents' experiences according to race or ethnicity. However, there is some evidence that stereotypes and biases influence decision-making. Okpokiri's (2021) study of Nigerian parents' experiences found that social workers perpetuated the British public's misrecognition of Nigerian parents through uncritical social work practices, to the detriment of the families' well-being. A review of Serious Case Reviews of Black children found that there was a lack of professional interest 'in understanding the salience of race and racism in the children's lives' (Bernard and Harris, 2019). An analysis of Serious Case Reviews involving families subject to immigration controls identified that many families were living in desperate socioeconomic circumstances, but the social determinants of harm and barriers faced by families were substantially under-recognised (Jolly and Gupta, 2024). This exemplifies a child protection system focused on parental behaviours rather than harm to children resulting from structural inequalities and government policies.

In the UK, over the past two decades, there has been an increased awareness of the types of harm adolescents can face in contexts beyond their families. These harms, commonly known as 'extra-familial risks/harms', include sexual and criminal exploitation (GOV.UK, 2018). Inquiries and research studies have highlighted the widespread occurrence of child sexual exploitation (Jay, 2014) and criminal exploitation, including 'county lines', where criminal networks in large cities export drugs to smaller towns using young people to transport, store and deliver the drugs (Wroe, 2021). There has also been growing recognition that the child protection system developed to respond to abuse and neglect within children's families has not been able to respond adequately to children at risk of extra-familial harm. Contextual Safeguarding is an approach developed to expand the reach of child protection systems into a range of social contexts beyond families and to locate extra-familial harm within the field of child welfare, rather than crime reduction and community safety (Firmin, 2017). The increased visibility of adolescents in child welfare systems sounds a promising move away from criminalisation for the harms they have experienced in their communities. However, in policy and practice, the 'risk' discourses of the child protection and youth justice systems perpetuate more punitive state interventions and expand the carceral web in racialised, classed and gendered ways (Koch et al, 2024). This has been particularly highlighted in relation to Black and Asian young people and implicates state social work in racially targeted oppression (Mahdi and Hakak, 2024).

The involvement of the police in multi-agency child safeguarding processes has caused some concern, particularly in relation to adolescents. Vaughn's (2019) research into practices in response to perceived risk of radicalisation highlights how multi-agency work and the sharing of databases can create value-laden judgements and problematic assumptions of vulnerability and risk in relation to Muslim youth. Wroe (2021: 44–45) argues that 'this analysis can be extended to "risk work" with "county lines" affected young people, where dominant norms about gender, race and age intersect to produce subjective assessments of vulnerability and risk'. The young people profiled by multi-agency child protection/safeguarding processes as 'county lines-affected' are disproportionately Black and male and profiled based on police 'intelligence' which needs to be situated within a criminal justice system that has racial disproportionality embedded throughout (Williams, 2018; Wroe, 2021). Safeguarding practice in the context of institutional racism, increased securitisation and surveillance, including in schools, often results in young people being excluded and criminalised instead of having their education and welfare needs addressed. Community organisations, activists and academics in the field of youth work have raised these concerns and are increasingly engaging with the wider policing and prison abolitionist and anti-carceral debates highlighting connections in relation to Black and other racially minoritised young people (Liberty et al, 2024; Koch et al, 2024).

Abolitionist debates in the United States

As already discussed in this chapter, there is much discontent with the current child protection system in England, and calls to rethink the dominant paradigm, where risk-averse services focus on parental pathology rather than the context of families' lives. Similar debates have been occurring in other countries, such as the United States, New Zealand (Keddell et al, 2022) and Canada (Ma, 2021). In the United States, proposals to abolish child protection are currently being debated furiously; however, the abolitionist arguments have not been a feature of the UK debates about the child protection responses to abuse and neglect thought to be caused by parents and carers, with a few exceptions. One example is *Radical Safeguarding* (Johnston and Akay, nd). As mentioned earlier, there is more engagement with these ideas when considering teenagers and harm outside the home, including from state services. There are several possible reasons for the limited consideration of abolitionist ideas, but also opportunities missed by not engaging with these ideas.

There are clear historical, social and political contexts influencing child welfare/protection that are different between the United States and UK. A notable difference is the histories in relation to racialised communities in the two countries, given the legacies of slavery and British colonialism. In the United States the abolitionist debates are largely led by scholars of colour who highlight the disproportionate removal of Black children by child welfare agencies, together with the over-surveillance of Black families that harm personal and community identities and agency (Dettlaff et al, 2020; Roberts, 2022). Although Black and mixed parentage children are over-represented in the child protection and care systems in England, this has not featured significantly in critiques of the child protection system or research agendas, apart from teenagers and extra-familial harm.

Both the UK and United States have high levels of in-country income inequality and low child well-being compared to countries in the Global North (Pickett et al, 2024). Over the last few decades, the welfare state in Britain created in the aftermath of the Second World War has been eroded. Neoliberal approaches, including privatisation of care services, are permeating all aspects of social policy, as in the United States. Debates about the impact of poverty and reasons for children coming into the child protection and care systems have been occurring in the UK, as discussed earlier, and within the abolitionist debates in the United States. Roberts (2022) highlights that the child welfare or 'family policing' system punishes poverty and is designed to ensnare economically struggling families by equating poverty with child neglect, the reason most children are separated from their parents. In the UK child neglect is also the most common reason for children being in the child protection system. Dettlaff et al (2020), however, argue that even controlling for poverty and other factors, studies in the United States have found race remains a significant predictor of disparities. In the UK this is the case for some ages and groups of racially minoritised children.

Both countries have, in the third decade of the 21st century, witnessed the rise of right-wing populism that has led to far right violence. The riots in England in July and August 2024 were targeted mainly at Muslim and refugee communities but affected many racially minoritised people and were fuelled by Islamophobic and anti-migrant rhetoric of politicians supported by the mainstream media. While the violence was shocking, the subsequent large and peaceful anti-racist protests renewed some hope in the possibilities for collective community responses of solidarity and support. When Roberts, the upEND movement and others write about abolishing family policing in the United States, they talk about strengthening communities, reducing the need for removal as a form of intervention and ultimately rendering it obsolete. Connections are made by family policing abolitionists with other abolitionist and anti-carceral approaches to prisons and policing. A chronic lack of trust within marginalised communities towards social workers and the police and persistent failures on the part of policy makers to understand this lack of trust and what might be needed to repair it are features within both societies. Schenwar and Law (2020) argue that both the child welfare and the criminal justice systems exemplify carceral logic in that they both focus on individual pathology and that the authorities must intervene and forcibly prevent the dangerous 'other' from enacting harm, instead of thinking critically about what it means to co-create safety and offer resources to improve people's lives. For social work the increasing involvement with the carceral web of surveillance and control instead of support and prevention, and the blurring of boundaries with the police, impacts on how families and communities experience professional responses (Richie and Martensen, 2020).

However, in the United States there have also been many critics of abolitionist ideas for child welfare. Garcia et al (2024) are deeply critical of the abolitionist approach and instead present a reformist position. They premise their arguments upon 'the assumption that the term "abolition" means complete eradication of federal, state, and local policies and practices related to child protection and out-of-home care services' (Garcia et al, 2024: 2). This binary position does not engage with the 'process of abolition' that harnesses the strengths of families and communities to develop community resources, restorative practices and transformative justice to replace the need for child protection responses (Dettlaff et al, 2020). The reformist approach proposed by Garcia et al (2024) involves increasing preventative family support services, which is what many advocates for change in child protection responses in the UK have been advocating for, with limited success (Featherstone et al, 2021). This raises questions about actions needed to effect meaningful change in the lives of children and families.

Abolitionist futures in the UK?

The need to create more humane and socially just ways of protecting children from harm and promoting their welfare is accepted by many different stakeholders, yet the route to achieving this is contested. While family group conferences, parent advocacy programmes, poverty-aware practice and other initiatives to effect change towards more family inclusive practices can make a difference to individuals and families, the fundamental processes and premises of the child protection system remain. When writing about challenging injustice, Nancy Fraser identifies affirmative strategies: 'remedies aimed at correcting inequitable outcomes of social arrangements without disturbing the underlying framework that generates them', and transformative strategies: 'remedies aimed at correcting inequitable outcomes precisely by restructuring the underlying generative framework' (Fraser, 1995: 82). While affirmative strategies when working with individuals and families are important, transformative strategies are also required, which is consistent with the abolitionist concept of non-reformist reforms (Lamble, 2022).

Although developed in a different context, the abolitionist approach in the United States offers ideas for transformative change in the UK. That our goal is a future where the need for the removal of children from their families and communities is, if not eradicated, significantly reduced is one that needs to frame our debates in ways not hitherto done to any extent. Engagement with scholars and activists from wider abolitionist and anti-carceral initiatives nationally and internationally is necessary to open spaces for debate about the relevance for the child protection system. Building connections with youth work organisations and scholars already engaged in abolitionist approaches to policing and child safeguarding can offer valuable analyses and possible ways to effect change.

As highlighted in the CWIP (Bywaters and the Child Welfare Inequalities Project Team, 2020), children living in areas of deprivation are far more likely to be involved in the child protection system, and clearly effective change for children involves serious attempts to address poverty, income inequality and related issues such as lack of affordable housing. This needs to continue to be advocated for from government, as does effective universal health, education and welfare services. The child protection system cannot be separated from the impacts of wider social policies and a new social contract is urgently needed in Britain after over a decade of austerity policies and divisive anti-immigration rhetoric. Central to constructing a new social settlement will be tackling inequalities and developing more solidaristic and sustainable ways of living together as human beings. The extent to which the Labour government, which came to power in July 2024, is willing or able to make these necessary changes is not known.

Alongside social policies addressing inequalities, more critical debate is required about the ideological underpinnings of our current child protection system. Richie and Martensen (2020) argue that social workers must be part of the movement to resist carceral expansion and that this resistance starts with understanding the role that the child welfare system plays within the broader carceral state. The emphasis on individually generated risks with a corresponding lack of attention to social harms is profoundly problematic. Both Mason (2020) and Wroe (2021) draw attention to social harms, including the (un)intended consequences of state 'harm reduction' services, such as child protection. Their work, which focuses on older children and extra-familial harm, highlights the racialised and classed nature of state interventions, as well as the experiences and the outcomes of such interventions. Featherstone and colleagues (2018; 2021) argue that fundamental questioning of the current framing of child protection is necessary, as is serious engagement with an intersectional analysis of the root causes of harm to children and reasons why they come into the child protection system. However, in England, with a stubbornly resistant individualising frame and risk-averse culture, effecting any change is challenging.

Developing community-based support groups and mutual aid projects are important aspects of abolitionist approaches to child welfare in the United States (Dettlaff et al, 2020). These have also been identified as crucial to rethinking how we can protect children from harm and promote their well-being in the UK. Featherstone et al (2021) argue for a shift from 'expert' professionally led approaches to child protection to a focus on community development of locality-based services and, importantly, co-production of services with young people and their families. Bernard et al (2024: 4) suggest a community cultural wealth perspective to 'shift away from deficit discourses and stereotypes of racially minoritised communities to extend our insights into the socio-cultural, neighbourhood and community-cultural assets that can foster resilience' despite systems of oppression. There are examples of these types of organisations and initiatives in the field of youth work that can be learned from to support different marginalised communities. Liberty et al (2024) describe various anti-racist youth work organisations and initiatives, committed to racial justice, creating safe spaces and advocating for young people, and building collective resistance and solidarity.

Conclusion

While it is not feasible to adopt wholesale abolitionist approaches to child protection from the United States to the UK, given different historical, social and political contexts, there is much that we can reflect upon and learn from, to build upon current debates and initiatives demanding a fundamental rethink of the child protection system in the UK. A starting point is a reframing of the debate from protecting children from harm to how we can promote the flourishing of children within their families and communities (Featherstone et al, 2021). Crucial to this endeavour is a serious questioning of the carceral logics of the current child protection system and the underpinning ideological assumptions and discourses that drive these processes. Important also are social policies at national and local government that address intersecting structural inequalities which frame the lives of so many children and families. Community development, collective strategies and capacity building is crucial, but must include the marginalised voices of adults and children who have experienced services, in dialogue about how we might do things differently. The extent to which transformative change is realistically possible in contemporary Britian is questionable. Yet we must aspire to a better future for all our society's children and their families, which is what abolitionists are striving for.

References

Ahmed, N., James, D., Tayabali, A. and Watson, M. (2022) 'Ethnicity and children's social care', Department for Education. Available at: https://assets.publishing.service.gov.uk/government/uploads/system/uploads/attachment_data/file/1076919/Ethnicity_and_childrens_social_care.pdf

Bennett, D., Schlüter, D., Melis, G., Bywaters, P., Alexiou, A., Barr, B., et al (2022) 'Child poverty and children entering care in England, 2015–20: A longitudinal ecological study at the local area level', *The Lancet Public Health*, 7(6): 496–503.

Bernard, C. and Harris, P. (2019) 'Serious case reviews: The lived experience of Black children', *Child and Family Social Work*, 24: 256–263.

Bernard, C., Gupta, A., Lakhanpaul, M., Sharma, A. and Peres, T. (2024) 'Racially minoritised young people's experiences of navigating COVID-19 challenges: A community cultural wealth perspective', *British Journal of Social Work*, 54(7): 3256–3273.

Bilson, A. and Martin, K.E.C. (2017) 'Referrals and child protection in England: One in five children referred to children's services and one in nineteen investigated before the age of five', *British Journal of Social Work*, 44(3): 793–811.

Bywaters, P. and the Child Welfare Inequalities Project Team (2020) *The Child Welfare Inequalities Project: Final Report*, Nuffield Foundation. Available at: https://www.nuffieldfoundation.org/wp-content/uploads/2019/11/CWIP-Executive-Summary-Final-V3.pdf

Bywaters, P. and Skinner, G. (2022) *The Relationship Between Poverty and Child Abuse and Neglect: New Evidence*, Nuffield Foundation / University of Huddersfield. Available at: https://research.hud.ac.uk/media/assets/document/hhs/RelationshipBetweenPovertyChildAbuseandNeglect_Report.pdf

Bywaters, P., Bunting, L., Davidson, G., Hanratty, J., Mason, W., McCarten, C., et al (2016) *The Relationship Between Poverty, Child Abuse and Neglect: An Evidence Review*, York: Joseph Rowntree Foundation.

Bywaters, P., Scourfield, J., Webb, C., Morris, K., Featherstone, B., Brady, G., et al (2019) 'Paradoxical evidence on ethnic inequities in child welfare: Towards a research agenda', *Children and Youth Services Review*, 96: 145–154.

CAFCASS (2012) 'Three weeks in November ... three years on ...: CAFCASS care applications study'. Available at: https://research.hud.ac.uk/media/assets/document/hhs/RelationshipBetweenPovertyChildAbuseandNeglect_Report.pdf

Dettlaff, A.J., Weber, K., Pendleton, M., Boyd, R., Bettencourt, B. and Burton, L. (2020) 'It is not a broken system, it is a system that needs to be broken: The upEND movement to abolish the child welfare system', *Journal of Public Child Welfare*, 14(5): 500–517.

Dickens, J., Taylor, J., Cook, L., Cossar, J., Garstang, J., Hallett, N., et al (2022) 'Learning for the future: Final analysis of serious case reviews, 2017 to 2019'. Available at: https://assets.publishing.service.gov.uk/government/uploads/system/uploads/attachment_data/file/1123286/Learning_for_the_future_-_final_analysis_of_serious_case_reviews__2017_to_2019.pdf

Featherstone, B., Gupta, A. and Morris, K. (2021) 'Post-pandemic: Moving on from "child protection"', *Critical and Radical Social Work*, 9(2): 151–165.

Featherstone, B., Gupta, A., Morris, K. and White, S. (2018) *Protecting Children: A Social Model*, Bristol: Policy Press.

Firmin, C. (2017) 'Contextual safeguarding: An overview of the operational, strategic and conceptual framework'. Available at: https://uobrep.openrepository.com/bitstream/handle/10547/624844/Contextual-Safeguarding-Briefing.pdf?sequence=2%26isAllowed=y

Fraser, N. (1995) 'From redistribution to recognition? Dilemmas of justice in a "post-socialist" age', *New Left Review*, 212: 68–93.

Garcia, A.R., Berrick, J.D., Jonson-Reid, M., Barth, R.P., Gyourko, J.R., Kohl, P., et al (2024) 'The stark implications of abolishing child welfare: An alternative path towards support and safety', *Child and Family Social Work*, advanced online publication.

Garthwaite, K. (2016) 'Stigma, shame and "people like us": An ethnographic study of foodbank use in the UK', *Journal of Poverty and Social Justice*, 24(3): 277–289.

Gilbert, N., Parton, N. and Skivenes, M. (eds) (2011) *Child Protection Systems: International Trends and Orientation*, New York: Oxford University Press.

Gove, M. (2013) 'Getting it right for children in need, Michael Gove speech to the NSPCC'. Available at: https://www.gov.uk/government/speeches/getting-it-right-for-children-in-need-speech-to-the-nspcc

GOV.UK (2018) 'Working together to safeguard children'. Available at: https://wscp.org.uk/media/1161/working_together_to_safeguard_children.pdf

GOV.UK (2023) 'Children looked after in England including adoptions'. Available at: https://explore-education-statistics.service.gov.uk/find-statistics/children-looked-after-in-england-including-adoptions/2023

Gupta, A., Blumhardt, H. and ATD Fourth World (2018) 'Poverty, exclusion and child protection practice: The contribution of "the politics of recognition and respect"', *European Journal of Social Work*, 21(2): 247–259.

Jay, A. (2014) 'Independent inquiry into child sexual exploitation in Rotherham 1997–2013'. Available at: https://www.rotherham.gov.uk/downloads/file/1407/independent_inquiry_cse_in_rotherham

Johnston, A. and Akay, L. (nd) 'Radical safeguarding: A social justice workbook for safeguarding practitioners', *Maslaha*. Available at: https://www.maslaha.org/Project/radical-safeguarding

Jolly, A. and Gupta, A. (2024) 'Children and families with no recourse to public funds: Learning from case reviews', *Children and Society*, 8(1): 16–31.

Keddell, E., Fitzmaurice, L., Cleaver, K. and Exeter, D. (2022) 'A fight for legitimacy: Reflections on child protection reform, the reduction of baby removals, and child protection decision-making in Aotearoa New Zealand', *Kōtuitui: New Zealand Journal of Social Sciences Online*, 17(3): 378–404.

Koch, I., Williams, P. and Wroe, L. (2024) '"County lines": Racism, safeguarding and statecraft in Britain', *Race and Class*, 65(3): 3–26.

Lamble, S. (2022) 'Bridging the gap between reformists and abolitionists: Can non-reformist reforms guide the work of prison inspectorates?', ICPR. Available at: https://www.icpr.org.uk/news-events/2022/bridging-gap-between-reformists-and-abolitionists-can-non-reformist-reforms-guide

Liberty, Art Against Knives, No More Exclusions, Northern Police Monitoring Project, Joint Enterprise Not Guilty by Association, Release, INQUEST, National Survival User Network, Maslaha and Kids of Colour (2024) 'Holding our own: A guide to non-policing solutions to serious youth violence'. Available at: https://www.libertyhumanrights.org.uk/wp-content/uploads/2023/04/HoldingOurOwn_Digital-DoubleSpreads.pdf

Ma, J. (2021) 'The intersection and parallels of Aboriginal peoples' and racialized migrants' experiences of colonialism and child welfare in Canada', *International Social Work*, 64(6): 901–916.

MacAlister, J. (2022) 'The independent review of children's social care'. Available at: https://webarchive.nationalarchives.gov.uk/ukgwa/20230308122535mp_/https:/childrenssocialcare.independent-review.uk/wp-content/uploads/2022/05/The-independent-review-of-childrens-social-care-Final-report.pdf

Mahdi, R. and Hakak, Y. (2024) 'The impact of the Prevent Agenda on social work: A systematic literature review', *Critical and Radical Social Work*. doi: 10.1332/20498608Y2024D000000046.

Mason, W. (2020) '"No one learned": Interpreting a drugs crackdown operation and its consequences through the "lens" of social harm', *British Journal of Criminology*, 60(2): 382–402.

Morris, K., Mason, W., Bywaters, P., Featherstone, B., Daniel, B., Brady, G., et al (2018a) 'Social work, poverty, and child welfare interventions', *Child and Family Social Work*, 23(3): 364–372.

Morris, K., Featherstone, B., Hill, K. and Ward, M. (2018b) *Stepping Up, Stepping Down: Family Experiences of Multiple Service Use*, London: FRG/Lankelly Chase.

Okpokiri, C. (2021) 'Parenting in fear: Child welfare micro strategies of Nigerian parents in Britain', *British Journal of Social Work*, 51(2): 427–444.

Parton, N. (2022) 'Comparative research and critical child protection studies', *Social Sciences*, 11(4): 156.

Pickett, K., Gauhar, A. and Wilkinson, R. (2024) *The Spirit Level at 15: The Enduring Impact of Inequality*, York: University of York.

Richie, B.E. and Martensen, K.M. (2020) 'Resisting carcerality, embracing abolition: Implications for feminist social work practice', *Affilia*, 35(1): 12–16.

Roberts, D. (2022) *Torn Apart: How the Child Welfare System Destroys Black Families – And How Abolition Can Build a Safer World*, New York: Basic Books.

Saar-Heiman, Y. and Gupta, A. (2024) 'Beyond participation: Parent activism in child protection as a path too transformative change', *Children and Youth Services Review*, 157: 107443.

Schenwar, M. and Law, V. (2020) *Prison by Any Other Name: The Harmful Consequences of Popular Reforms*, New York: The New Press.

Vaughn, L. (2019) '"Doing risk": Practitioner interpretations of risk of childhood radicalisation and the implementation of the HM government PREVENT duty', PhD thesis, University of Liverpool. Available at: https://www.liverpool.ac.uk/people/leona-vaughn/publications

Wacquant, L. (2010) 'Crafting the neoliberal state: Workfare, prisonfare, and social insecurity', *Sociological Forum*, 25(2): 197–220.

Williams, P. (2018) *Being Matrixed: The (Over)policing of Gang Suspects in London*, London: Stopwatch.

Wroe, L.E. (2021) 'Young people and "county lines": A contextual and social account', *Journal of Children's Services*, 16(1): 39–55.

5

Radical reflection plus radical transformation equals revolutionary social work

Bindi Bennett and Péta Phelan

Positionality statement

The authors of this chapter would like to acknowledge it has been written on the unceded sovereign lands of the Jinibara Peoples, and the Wurundjeri Peoples of the Kulin Nations of Australia. We pay respect to First Nations Elders past, present, and future, of all Countries. We write as Aboriginal cisgendered women, who embody varying other identities such as queer, heterosexual, neurodivergent and disabled. We utilise the terminologies Aboriginal, First Nations Peoples and Indigenous.

Introduction

The profession of social work has been conceived, generated and constructed from a Western Eurocentric worldview, founded in the ideologies, orientations and machinations of colonial patriarchy (Yu et al, 2024). Social work claims to be working in collaboration, practice, service and camaraderie, with individuals and communities who experience oppression, marginalisation and social disadvantage. Yet, social work overwhelmingly replicates, reinforces and sustains the very structures and systems that create and perpetuate harms against such individuals and communities in the first place (BlackDeer and Ocampo, 2022).

We encourage social work professionals to interrogate social work theories and practices from standpoints beyond the colonial foundations it was crafted from. We ask how social work can destabilise and disrupt itself, reorient and remodel itself, and commit to transforming in ways that align with the values the profession claims lay at its core (Phelan and Bennett, 2024). We seek to provoke the social work profession, its practitioners, educators and researchers, to get uncomfortable yet active in disturbing, dissenting, disrupting and dismantling the colonial ideologies, machinery and weaponry across social work (Billow, 2003).

Occupying place in the prison-industrial complex

The prison-industrial complex (PIC) is a term used to describe the interconnected matrix of government and private interests that profit from the presence, expansion and maintenance of the carceral system. The PIC includes related industries such as policing, surveillance and incarceration, and extends to any profession that services and benefits these industries (Davis, 2000). This encompasses services such as government agencies, private prison corporations, security firms, construction companies, and suppliers of goods and services to ensure PIC ongoing operations. Considering the size and complexity of the PIC, and the profound requirements to ensure its flourishing across all stages of its functioning, it begins to become clear the level of involvement of a vast range of industries and professions. Social work occupies a place within the complex machinations of this system (Sliva and Samimi, 2018).

The PIC operates on the pursuit of mass (and ever-elevating) incarceration, that perpetuates cycles of punishment and control (Sered, 2019). The PIC leverages, intersects with, and directly benefits from, other systems of oppression such as colonialism, white supremacy, racism, ableism, cis-heterosexism and capitalism. It further entrenches inequalities and contributes to the social disenfranchisement of stigmatised, marginalised, and minoritised populations. Punishment and state-sanctioned violence is prioritised, which perpetuates and sustains cycles of poverty, undermining efforts towards social justice and equity (Bey and Goldberg, 2022).

Carcerality and the PIC are utilised as tools to uphold capitalist interests (Bonds, 2019). Policing and prisons were conceived and weaponised to serve the powerful and wealthy, to protect their assets and private property, and to control and manage their (sub)human resources such as slaves and indentured labour. They have also been deployed by the ruling class, to seize land and natural resources from Indigenous peoples (Walcott, 2021). The criminal justice system policing and carcerality protect the powerful, while suffocating and brutalising the oppressed. The PIC across the world shares remarkable parallels with modern-day slavery, primarily through the exploitation of incarcerated individuals for labour under coercive conditions. It is yet another resource for those in power, manufactured to exploit the bodies and labour of those it has criminalised and ensnared, extracting and reaping profit from their existence, while destroying their lives and communities (Hattery and Smith, 2021).

This disproportionately targets Indigenous populations, communities of colour, those with disabilities and low-income individuals. Through policies like the war on drugs, governments ensure a steady flow of bodies into prisons (Fornili, 2018). This is shown in Australia; for example, from 30 June 2022 to 30 June 2023 Aboriginal and Torres Strait Islander prisoners increased by 7 per cent (950) to 13,852 (Australian Bureau of Statistics, 2024). Aboriginal and Torres Strait Islander prisoners accounted for 33 per cent of all prisoners. In the 31 years since the Royal Commission into Aboriginal Deaths in Custody (1991), in 2022 there had been 516 Indigenous deaths in custody (McAlister and Bricknell, 2022).

Carcerality is a tool of social control, allowing the powerful to accumulate wealth and maintain their dominance while perpetuating the subjugation and exploitation of Indigenous populations. Examples are land possession, as historically marginalised lands are often seized for prison construction or repurposed for profitable ventures. Economic yields incentivise and perpetuate policies that prioritise incarceration over social resourcing and/or community-based alternatives (Kolkey, 2022). Within the PIC, incarcerated individuals are frequently forced to work for little to no pay, often under hazardous conditions, with minimal or no workers' rights protections. This coerced labour financially benefits private corporations and government agencies, contributing to the sustainment and perpetuation of the system (LeBaron, 2018).

This is one system that social work is positioned within. By working within it, social workers are working for it. Social workers employed in correctional facilities or contracted by private prison corporations may experience pressure to prioritise corporate and/or institutional interests over the rights, dignity and well-being of incarcerated individuals. The PIC dehumanises and disenfranchises individuals, stripping them of their autonomy and perpetuates cycles of oppression and exploitation (LeBaron, 2018). The lure of employment opportunities must not undermine the need for a society that upholds human dignity, equality and justice for all.

Abolitionist social work

Parallel to the rise of the modern police force, the accounting bureaucracy and the colonial legal apparatus, the social work profession is a foundational component to the creation, expansion and adaptation of the settler state (Fortier and Hon-Sing Wong, 2019: 437). Colonial control and domination have historically relied on systems of imprisonment and punishment to assert authority and suppress resistance (Saleh-Hanna, 2020). The establishment of prisons, particularly in colonial contexts, served to subjugate Indigenous populations, dissenting voices and marginalised communities. The abolition of state enforcement and control through the leveraging of policing and prisons is deeply intertwined with challenging and dismantling colonial legacies and disrupting systems of oppression, and rethinking and transforming the way we exist.

The impact of imprisonment extends beyond individuals to entire communities, perpetuating cycles of poverty, trauma and social disenfranchisement. Lived-experience abolitionists Kilroy and Lean (2022: 93) describe it as '[t]he giant carceral beast which chews us up and spits us out, only to snag us again and pull us into its great big jaws of death, and crunch and gnaw on our bones, until there is nothing left of us, but dust and memories'. Carceral and prison abolition offers a pathway to address the inequities created by 'the system', by reimagining justice and investing in community-based solutions that prioritise healing and empowerment.

Abolitionist social work is concerned with identifying, interrogating and transforming the ways in which social work and social workers are complicit in supporting or reinforcing carceral institutions, because complicity with these institutions entails maintaining the structures of oppression that depend on these institutions persisting (Bergen and Abji, 2020). Lamusse (2021: 300) states 'prisons are hyper-productive factories of injustice, oppression, immiseration and violence' and alongside punitive policing produce 'immense brutality, violence, racial stratification, ideological rigidity, despair, and waste' (McLeod, 2015: 62).

Social workers espouse a commitment to social justice. Social workers are currently engaged in service provision at the forefront with diverse communities such as working with Indigenous people; those in out-of-home care; people experiencing mental ill-health, cognitive disability and substance abuse; as well as homelessness or unstable housing (McCausland and Baldry, 2023). As such, abolitionist social workers are interested in exploring community-based alternatives.

Abolitionist social workers demand a society that centres and addresses root causes of crime, such as poverty, lack of access to education and healthcare, and systemic racism (Bell, 2021). Abolitionist social work involves reimagining justice as a process that prioritises healing, restoration and accountability rather than punishment and isolation. Additionally, Brown and Schept state that: 'One key contribution of new abolitionist work is the interruption of dominant understandings of crime, law, punishment, safety and accountability, and justice, and the generation of alternative vocabularies and analyses from which to begin to work our way out of the carceral state' (2017: 4).

Complicity

The social work profession is a product of concentrated social power and domination, born as a response to the oppression and violence of industrialist and capitalist ideology and its social promulgation (Hyslop, 2018). This is shown by the profession predominantly being comprised of women, many of whom have been poorly paid in comparison to men in general and their male counterparts (Hodge et al, 2024). The formal profession in Australia evolved in the context of active colonisation and is a tool leveraged in continuing the progress and power of the colonial project (Yu et al, 2024). Watson states that:

> The colonial project is ultimately about justifying the occupation and exploitation of Indigenous Land and the maintenance of unequal relationships between non-native and native; it is of paramount importance that the colonised remain contained as objects of the colonial state. And for the Indigenous, the only trajectory is to become totally absorbed and assimilated into the state. (Watson, 2016: 33)

Social work has been a distinct and critical node of the colonial matrix, playing its role in the upholding and continuation of colonial power. Ironically, it has played on being a benevolent player in the dedicated progression towards social justice through the provision of services, remedies and soothing to the marginalised, disenfranchised and disadvantaged from beyond the confines of the colonial project (Abramovitz, 2012).

Social work has historically been, and remains, a key component of this system, and a horrific example of this in Australia is the Stolen Generation (Yu, 2019), where social work was complicit in the removal of Aboriginal children from their families for assimilation into white society. Australia continues to have Aboriginal children overrepresented in out-of-home care (Australian Institute of Family Studies, 2020). Continued child removal practices are integral components of colonial carceral logics, perpetuating intergenerational trauma and reinforcing systems of coloniser domination. These practices aim to assimilate Aboriginal people into Eurocentric cultures and severe ties to their identities and heritage, dismantle traditional kinship structures, erase cultural practices, and eradicate language, all while maintaining control and domination.

Kilroy declares that 'the legal system in Australia is built on the genocide and dispossession of Aboriginal Peoples. Since invasion, the legal system has operated as a mechanism to order, control, regulate and dispose of Aboriginal lives and bodies' (2018: 264). Social work has a long history of surveilling, policing and disproportionally separating Aboriginal children from their families. Most cases where Aboriginal children are removed also involve colonial enforced structural issues such as poverty which is measured as limited food in the house, limited education opportunities and multiple family members sharing the house and bedrooms. This system punishes oppressed and marginalised victims of oppressive and racist structures while failing to address the root colonial structural causes (Preston, 2021). Social workers have benefited from colonisation and more so if they have the added privilege of being white. They have been overseeing the actioning of government social policies that promote desirable traits and suppressing those deemed undesirable (Gibson, 2015).

To resist complicity with the PIC, social workers must critically examine how their foundational underpinnings, theories, language and practices intersect with systems of oppression, and advocate for systemic change. They should prioritise community-based solutions, abolitionist principles, and the dismantling of structures that perpetuate harm and inequality. We propose engaging in radical reflection, radical transformation and revolutionary social work to assist such action.

Becoming radical

We define radical as challenging existing norms and systems, aiming to address the root causes of injustice, rather than its symptoms and encompassing approaches advocating for deep, comprehensive change. In social work, radicalism critically analyses and challenges power dynamics and structural inequalities, focusing on how systemic issues like capitalism, patriarchy and racism impact individuals and communities. It is grounded in principles of social justice, equality and the empowerment of marginalised groups. It confronts social structures, policies and practices perpetuating inequality and injustice. Radical social work is a practice framework for creating human rights and fairness.

Ioakimidis (2016: np) claims that within social work, 'meaningful practice should always incorporate elements of political action'. Intrinsically, radical social work practitioners must embody the political. Practitioners participate in activism and advocacy to influence policy, elevate awareness of social injustice and progress systemic change. Working in collaboration with individuals and communities centres empowerment by encouraging participation in decision-making and self-determination. It is grounded in collective action, addressing shared issues and building collective power while decentring and attempting to eradicate neoliberal individualism. This involves challenging traditional professional boundaries by collaborating with activists and community organisers. By adopting a holistic approach, broader social, economic and political contexts are interrogated. This is critical to target and address both immediate needs and long-term structural changes.

The term 'radical' is often perceived as 'extremist' or vastly different from the norm. Foundational radical social work scholar Rein (1970: 13) states that 'the search for radicalization of the social work profession has taken two major forms: questioning the role of the professional association and changing the essence of the social worker's professional activity'. The essence of radical social work should be aimed at upholding basic human rights. As social work is still deeply embedded in the paradigms and violence of coloniality, it then becomes necessary to encourage social work and its practitioners to not only consider a level of extremism beyond the current colonial confines of social work practice but welcome it. Regarding radical social work, Ioakimidis (2016: np) further states that 'what really differentiates it from mainstream approaches is its emphasis on action that aims at social change'. Social workers must critically analyse, expose and resist historicised and prevailing discourses which normalise people currently constructed as 'clients' as 'dangerous', 'illegitimate', 'othered' and a 'burden' (Green, 2020: 908). This means that our notion of radical means separating social work from the colony, thus creating an anti-colonial approach to justice.

Radical reflection

> The response to neoliberal approaches to people in need is outrage, but armchair outrage is insufficient for resistance against injustice and breaches of human rights ... The challenge then, is how to transcend from personal outrage to social influence and the rejection of the unacceptable through moral and ethical actions. (Fronek and Chester, 2016: 165)

Thompson (1983) used 'radical reflection' to depict a method that critically analyses a social system from the standpoint of power relations and contradictions within the existing ideology. It is radical because it examines 'the root' of the problem. It is reflective because it involves a process of self-enlightenment and self-understanding of the power relations and social constraints of the ideological system (beliefs, values, and ideas) in which we live and may internalise. It is a social and philosophical method to investigate collective experiences of a social group of people in a system to examine it for limitations and contradictions. Thompson (1983) lists five steps in using the method of radical reflection: (1) bracketing, (2) historical recovery, (3) critique, (4) dialectical imagination, and (5) negotiation. Later articulations of critical reflection and critical reflexivity included social work academics such as Fook (2003), Morley and McFarlane (2019) and Morley (2020).

Many are taught to absorb knowledge without critical engagement (Brock-Petroshius et al, 2022). Social work is at a pivotal point where it needs to resist white supremacy and white privilege by creating professionals able to sit and be comfortable in discomfort while retaining the capacity to act. They must know their own race, culture, power dynamics, values, worldviews and biases and be able to relinquish power and dominance. Continued compliance through ticking boxes maintains the colony. Abolitionist social workers argue that social workers should decentre themselves and their own institutional authority and work to 'elevate community voices, community practices, and community problem solving' (Jacobs et al, 2021: 53). This means they must implement different forms of transformative, restorative and other non-carceral and non-punitive forms of justice within the communities in which they work. bell hooks cautions that this unpacking is not going to be easy and asks that we commit to 'brave space' (Arao and Clemens, 2023). We as social workers must create accountability to the brave space. This includes actions such as: (1) committing to call in versus call out, (2) using human-centred language, (3) seeking understanding, (4) committing to critical, reflective and vulnerable communication, and (5) honouring our collective healing process (Brock-Petroshius et al, 2022: 11).

Tranformative social work relies on critical reflection and consciousness raising as a key to addressing systems of oppression and their impact on social work practice (Morley and O'Connor, 2016). Confronting the whiteness of social work teachers, teachings and practice in Australia is needed. Making sure our students align with social work's social justice foundation is imperative. Creating professionalism based on anti-colonial and anti-racist practices is necessary. We call for a system to ethically measure, evaluate or create values and open-minded curiosity (Sonsteng- Person et al, 2023).

Radical transformation

Social workers must resist reformist advancement, promote non-reformist reforms, and advocate for resources, services, and community-based alternatives to incarceration and child welfare systems, prioritising restorative justice practices. Centring the voices and agency of marginalised communities, and in particular working 'to amplify the voices of those currently or formerly incarcerated in the hope of disrupting their forced silence and disappearance' (Stanley and Spade, 2012: 119), is a critical feature of all aspects of service delivery informed by abolitionist perspectives (Kilroy et al, 2013). Embracing abolitionist principles will transform the social work profession by challenging traditional notions of justice and empowerment, fostering a more equitable and just society rooted in principles of liberation and collective healing. This anti-colonial transformation will not only enhance the effectiveness of social work practice but also contribute to broader movements for social justice and decolonisation.

Social work is intended to be grounded in the ethical principles of social justice, equity and 'do-no-harm', with the ultimate and unceasing pursuit of human liberation. However, it has historically sustained, perpetuated and aligned itself with the paradigms, structures, agenda and machinations of the colony. This complicity has hindered its ethical foundation. Despite its intentions, social work has not yet engaged, either fundamentally or substantively, in the necessary anti-colonial radical, critical and self-reflexive dialogues necessary to examine how it can determinately decolonise itself. Achieving anti-colonial transformation will necessitate some systems becoming obsolete and this requires broad social, economic and political changes (Jacobs et al, 2021).

Social workers cannot facilitate emancipation or the creation of conditions of human flourishing by collaborating with the colony or colonial systems. Among alternatives to punitive and retributive justice models, transformative justice has played a particularly influential role among abolitionist social workers (Brown, 2019). Transformative justice largely emerged from radical women of colour feminist and LGBTQIA+ organisations mobilising for non-carceral responses to domestic and gender-based violence. Rather than rely on a criminal legal system that expands the violence faced by marginalised people, transformative justice models call for community-based responses to interpersonal harm that eschew punishment or retribution for their own sake, identify and seek to repair harms caused by individuals, and recognise the forms of structural violence and oppression in which individual actions occur.

The transformative justice model calls for the radical transformation of those conditions of structural violence as part of a larger project of contesting violence in all its forms (Jacobs et al, 2021). The processes of accountability include an acknowledgement of harm, the consequences of that harm, and a series of actions to repair the harm. Anti-colonial practice calls for creative interventions such as the 'Staircase of Accountability', as an important first step in addressing harm (Murray et al, 2023). Social workers can work to achieve this through (1) exercising critical reflexivity, (2) practising reciprocity and respect for self-determination, (3) embracing 'Other(ed)' ways of knowing, being and doing, and (4) embodying a transformative praxis (Thambinathan and Kinsella, 2021). A transformative praxis will seek wider change in society such as the elimination of poverty, systemic racism and other forms of structural violence. Social workers will then need to commit to the rebuilding of community and creation of the bonds that protect and sustain the new ways of being (Maher, 2021).

Revolutionary social work

> '[D]issenting social work' presents opportunities for a 'neo-social work' that can begin to address the root causes of social problems by combating white supremacy and heteropatriarchy, embracing progressive technologies and critical theories, and collectivising through unionisation and movement building in collaboration with communities and 'user' networks. (Hunter and Wroe, 2024: 315)

Revolution refers to the fundamental disturbance and transformation of societal structures, ideologies or practices, evidenced by substantial shifts in worldviews, values and power dynamics. In professional spheres, revolution expresses the initiation of unsettling and disruptive innovations, transformative paradigm shifts, or radical mutations within an industry, thereby instigating the establishment of novel standards, methodologies or approaches. We deliberately utilise the terminology 'mutate' because we want something either different that may emerge from the old or be completely recreated.

The elements to revolution are deep-seated grievances; mass mobilisation; the rebellion against and overthrow of authority; radical change; transition and consolidation. Revolutions arise from deep grievances and profound dissatisfaction with the existing and pervading political, social or economic order. These are most often in response to long-standing systemic oppression, widespread inequalities and abuses of power. The mobilisation of large segments of the population is a feature and may include diverse social groups. The pivotal intent of revolution is the defeat and/or profound transformation of the existing establishment. This may involve the removal of a ruling elite, the dissolution of institutions or the establishment of entirely new systems of governance. Revolutions pursue fundamental and often radical changes to society, economy and politics, including the redistribution of wealth and resources, the ensuring and expansion of rights and liberties, or the advancement and implementation of new logics, principles and practices.

We have a 'wish list' of some of the things we would like to see:

- Participating in mass refusal; for example, refusing to uphold white supremacist policies present in the professionalisation of appearance and communication.
- Accountability leading into a collective process into a transformative justice social equity-based practice and care.
- Active community involvement in designing and implementing social work responses.
- The cessation of individual and racial pathologisation. This involves the recreation of the language of helping and 'saving'.
- Build real power and voice in Black communities. Power, defined in its most simple form, is the ability of a community to make decisions about the things that affect them (Magill and Clark, 1975).
- Build a pipeline out of poverty.
- Build and support Black leadership.
- Resource sharing (mutual aid) and equitable resources are acquired and distributed.
- Curriculum of truth telling, liberatory visions, and incorporate learning desires of Black peoples.
- Looking at macro interventions: advocacy, social movement participation, advancing abolitionist policy agendas, undermining structural racism.
- Social work profession filled with skilled accountable leaders willing and able to make systemic changes.

Revolutionary approaches pursue profound change and transformation at the very root level of societal structures, norms and power dynamics. This includes genuinely acknowledging, challenging and confronting the entrenched, pervasive and intentionally sustained systems of oppression, inequality and injustice that lie at the core of colonial paradigms. Recognition and acceptance of how the profession of social work is borne from, embedded within, and actively participates within such structural violence is an uncomfortable yet critical first step to disrupt and destabilise the repetition and reproduction of the status quo. It is also vital in the overall dismantling and destruction of the paradigms that generate such injustice in the first place. Rather than simply advocating for incremental reforms within existing frameworks, revolutionary practices aim to uproot and replace oppressive structures with new paradigms rooted in justice, equity and liberation.

Revolutionary practice involves a crucial process of sweeping analysis to expose the complex root causes of social issues and identify pathways for transformative change. Questioning and critiquing underlying assumptions, ideologies, and power relations that sustain systems of oppression, requires humility and the decentring of personal and societal shame, guilt, and fragilities. Only from this positioning, genuine listening to, and centring of, oppressed and marginalised peoples and communities can change occur. Kilroy (2018: 270) states: 'Dismantling racist and capitalist systems and building new institutions to address poverty, homelessness and harm cannot be achieved by one person in one generation. This work is a collective struggle and I believe that a movement for genuine change is possible.'

Conclusion

How does social work truly become compassionate, healing, empathic in solidarity, accountable and empowering? Violence, both interpersonal and structural, must be concurrently confronted to achieve social transformation, rather than the commissioning and utilisation of punishment for social control. Abolition takes an intersectional and structural approach to analysing and dismantling systems of oppression. There is no social justice without true liberation from state-sanctioned violation, abuse, and oppression. This statement, consequently, positions social work in both the uncomfortable and threatening position of de-coupling itself from the state, should it ever wish to achieve the principles, aims and outcomes of its existence.

Social workers need to put themselves – ourselves – on the line in a non-passive stand in solidarity. This requires a substantial self-sacrifice for the needs and justice of others where all benefit. Social work needs to interrogate its shame and fragility and move this to a place where we have a practice where people are feeling well and healthy and then able to make better choices. Social work needs to lean into the fear – and do the changes anyway.

Social work must self-reflect, disturb, and unsettle itself, if the profession and its practitioners are to pursue authentically and robustly, abolition and justice as a whole-of-life approach, understanding that the liberation of community and society, starts with radically transforming ourselves.

References

Abramovitz, M. (2012) 'Theorising the neoliberal welfare state for social work', in J. Midgley, M. Grey and S.A. Webb (eds) *The SAGE Handbook of Social Work*, London: SAGE, pp 33–50.

Arao, B. and Clemens, K. (2023) 'From safe spaces to brave spaces: A new way to frame dialogue around diversity and social justice', in L.M. Landreman (ed) *The Art of Effective Facilitation: Reflections from Social Justice Educators*, New York: Routledge, Taylor and Francis Group, pp 135–150.

Australian Bureau of Statistics (2024) *Prisoners in Australia 2023*, 1 January. Available at: https://www.abs.gov.au/statistics/people/crime-and-justice/prisoners-australia/latest-release

Australian Institute of Family Studies (2020) 'Child protection and Aboriginal and Torres Strait Islander children', *Child Family and Community Resource Sheet*. Available at: https://aifs.gov.au/resources/policy-and-practice-papers/child-protection-and-aboriginal-and-torres-strait-islander

Bell, M. (2021) 'Abolition: A new paradigm for reform', *Law and Social Inquiry*, 46(1): 32–68.

Bergen, H. and Abji, S. (2020) 'Facilitating the carceral pipeline: Social work's role in funneling newcomer children from the child protection system to jail and deportation', *Affilia*, 35(1): 34–48.

Bey, M. and Goldberg, J.A. (2022) 'Queer as in abolition now!', *GLQ*, 28(2): 159–163.

Billow, R.M. (2003) 'Rebellion in group', *International Journal of Group Psychotherapy*, 53(3): 331–351.

BlackDeer, A.A. and Ocampo, M.G. (2022) '# socialworksowhite: A critical perspective on settler colonialism, white supremacy, and social justice in social work', *Advances in Social Work*, 22(2): 720–740.

Bonds, A. (2019) 'Race and ethnicity: Property, race, and the carceral state', *Progress in Human Geography*, 43(3): 574–583.

Brock-Petroshius, L., Mikell, D., Washington, D.M. and James, K. (2022) 'From social justice to abolition: Living up to social work's grand challenge of eliminating racism', *Journal of Ethnic and Cultural Diversity in Social Work*, 31(3–5): 225–239.

Brown, M. (2019) 'Transformative justice and new abolition in the United States', in L.A. Franca and P. Carlen (eds) *Justice Alternatives*, London: Routledge, pp 73–87.

Brown, M. and Schept, J. (2017) 'New abolition, criminology and a critical carceral studies', *Punishment and Society*, 19(4): 440–462.

Davis, A. (2000) 'Masked racism: Reflections on the prison industrial complex', *Indigenous Law Bulletin*, 4(27): 4–7.

Fook, J. (2003) 'Critical social work: The current issues', *Qualitative Social Work*, 2(2): 123–130.

Fornili, K.S. (2018) 'Racialized mass incarceration and the war on drugs: A critical race theory appraisal', *Journal of Addictions Nursing*, 29(1): 65–72.

Fortier, C. and Hon-Sing Wong, E. (2019) 'The settler colonialism of social work and the social work of settler colonialism', *Settler Colonial Studies*, 9(4): 437–456.

Fronek, P. and Chester, P. (2016) 'Moral outrage: Social workers in the Third Space', *Ethics and Social Welfare*, 10(2): 163–176.

Gibson, M.F. (2015) 'Intersecting deviance: Social work, difference and the legacy of eugenics', *British Journal of Social Work*, 45(1): 313–330.

Green, B.A. (2020) 'Drowning in neoliberal lies: State responses towards people seeking asylum', *British Journal of Social Work*, 50(3): 908–925.

Hattery, A. and Smith, E. (2021) *Policing Black Bodies: How Black Lives Are Surveilled and How to Work for Change*, Lanham, MD: Rowman & Littlefield.

Hodge, L., McIntyre, H., Morley, C., Briese, J., Clarke, J. and Kostecki, T. (2024) '"My anxiety was through the roof": The gendered nature of financial stress and its impact on mental health and well-being for women when undertaking social work placements', *Affilia: Feminist Inquiry in Social Work*, 39(3): 499–516.

Hunter, D. and Wroe, L.E. (2024) '"Already doing the work": Social work, abolition and building the future from the present', *Critical and Radical Social Work*, 12(3): 312–329.

Hyslop, I. (2018) 'Social work, capitalism and social justice: Big and small pictures', *Reimagining Social Work in Aotearoa*, 13 August. The RSW Collective. Available at: https://reimaginingsocialwork.nz/2018/08/13/social-work-capitalism-and-social-justice-big-and-small-pictures/

Ioakimidis, V. (2016) A guide to radical social work. *The Guardian*, 24 May. Available at: https://www.theguardian.com/social-care-network/2016/may/24/radical-social-work-quick-guide-change-poverty-inequality

Jacobs, L.A., Kim, M.E., Whitfield, D.L., Gartner, R.E., Panichelli, M., Kattari, S.K., et al (2021) 'Defund the police: Moving towards an anti-carceral social work', *Journal of Progressive Human Services*, 32(1): 37–62.

Kilroy, D. (2018) 'Imagining abolition: Thinking outside the prison bars', *Griffith Review*, 60: 264–270.

Kilroy, D. and Lean, T. (2022) 'The not so easy, simple solution', *Journal of Prisoners on Prisons*, 30(2): 91–95.

Kilroy, D., Barton, P., Quixley, S., George, A. and Russell, E. (2013) 'Decentring the prison: Abolitionist approaches to working with criminalized women', in B. Carlton and M. Segrave (eds) *Women Exiting Prison: Critical Essays on Gender, Post-Release Support and Survival*, Abingdon: Taylor & Francis, pp 156–180.

Kolkey, S. (2022) 'People over profit: The case for abolishing the prison financial system', *California Law Review*, 110(1). Available at: lhttps://www.theguardian.com/social-care-network/2016/may/24/radical-social-work-quick-guide-change-poverty-inequality295

Lamusse, T. (2021) 'Doing justice without prisons: A framework to build the abolitionist movement', *Socialism and Democracy*, 35(2–3): 300–322.

LeBaron, G. (2018) 'Prison labour, slavery, and the state', in J.O.C. Davidson and L. Brace (eds) *Revisiting Slavery and Antislavery: Towards a Critical Analysis*, Germany: Springer International Publishing, pp 151–177.

Magill, R.S. and Clark, T.N. (1975) 'Community power and decision making: Recent research and its policy implications', *Social Service Review*, 49(1): 33–45.

Maher, G. (2021) *A World Without Police: How Strong Communities Make Cops Obsolete*, London: Verso Books.

McAlister, M. and Bricknell, S. (2022) *Deaths in Custody in Australia 2021–2022*, Statistical Report no. 41, Australian Institute for Criminology. Available at: https//www.aic.gov.au/publications/sr/sr41

McCausland, R. and Baldry, E. (2023) 'Who does Australia lock up? The social determinants of justice', *International Journal for Crime, Justice and Social Democracy*, 12(3): 37–53.

McLeod, A.M. (2015) 'Prison abolition and grounded justice', *UCLA Law Review*, 62: 1156–1239.

Morley, C. (2016) Critical reflection and critical social work, in B. Pease, S. Goldingay, N. Hosken and S. Nipperess (eds) *Doing Critical Social Work: Transformative Practices for Social Justice*, Sydney: Allen and Unwin, pp 25–38.

Morley, C. and O'Connor, D. (2016) 'Contesting field education in social work: Using critical reflection to enhance student learning for critical practice', in B. Teater, I. Taylor, M. Bogo and M. Lefevre (eds) *Routledge International Handbook of Social Work Education*, Abingdon: Taylor & Francis, pp 220–231.

Morley, C. and McFarlane, S. (2019) 'Welfare words: Critical social work and social policy', *Critical and Radical Social Work*, 7(2): 277–281.

Murray, B.J., Copeland, V. and Dettlaff, A.J. (2023) 'Reflections on the ethical possibilities and limitations of abolitionist praxis in social work', *Affilia*, 38(4): 742–758.

Phelan, P. and Bennett, B. (2024) 'Privileging Indigenous knowledge and wisdom as feminist social work practitioners', in C. Noble, D. Baines, G. Munoz-Arce, L. Harms-Smith and S. Rasool (eds) *The Routledge International Handbook of Feminisms in Social Work*, Abingdon: Taylor & Francis, pp 55–67.

Preston, S.A. (2021) 'Abolitionist disjuncture: Reducing police violence in frontline social work', *Intersectionalities: A Global Journal of Social Work Analysis, Research, Polity, and Practice*, 9(1): 142–153.

Rein, M. (1970) 'Social work in search of a radical profession', *Social Work*, 15(2): 13–28.

Saleh-Hanna, V. (2020) 'Colonialism, crime, and social control', *Oxford Research Encyclopedia of Criminology and Criminal Justice*. Available at: https://doi.org/10.1093/acrefore/9780190264079.013.560

Sered, D. (2019) *Until We Reckon: Violence, Mass Incarceration, and a Road to Repair*, New York: New Press.

Sliva, S.M. and Samimi, C. (2018) 'Social work and prison labor: A restorative model', *Social Work*, 63(2): 153–160.

Sonsteng-Person, M., Spoth, A.P., Hostetter, R., Akapnitis, I., Barbera, R., Joseph, A., et al (2023) 'A new world cannot be built alone: An abolitionist framework for collective action in social work', *Abolitionist Perspectives in Social Work*, 1(1): 1–21.

Stanley, E.A. and Spade, D. (2012) 'Queering prison abolition, now?', *American Quarterly*, 64(1): 115–127.

Thambinathan, V. and Kinsella, E.A. (2021) 'Decolonizing methodologies in qualitative research: Creating spaces for transformative praxis', *International Journal of Qualitative Methods*, 20: 1–9.

Thompson, J.L. (1983) 'Toward a critical nursing process: Nursing praxis', doctoral dissertation, University of Utah. Available at: https://collections.lib.utah.edu/ark:/87278/s6sj1nh4

Walcott, R. (2021) *On Property: Policing, Prisons, and the Call for Abolition*, Windsor, Canada: Biblioasis.

Watson, I. (2016) 'First Nations and the colonial project', *Inter Gentes*, 1(1): 30–49.

Yu, N. (2019) 'Interrogating social work: Australian social work and the stolen generations', *Journal of Social Work*, 19(6): 736–750.

Yu, N., Morgenshtern, M. and Schmid, J. (2024) 'Social work's colonial past with Indigenous children and communities in Australia and Canada: A cross-national comparison', *Child and Family Social Work*, 29(1): 229–238.

6

Punishment disguised as 'help': carcerality in the human services and the role of social work towards abolition

Sacha Kendall Jamieson and Lobna Yassine

Introduction

Understandings of social workers as 'agents of the state' involved in surveillance and control from positions within the community are not new (Rodger, 1988). In Australia, the settler-colonial context from which we are writing, critiques of social work have proliferated since the 1970s (Mendes, 2009). In the 1990s, coinciding with the emergence of 'postmodern critical social work' approaches emphasising the social-political context of social problems, multiplicity in subjectivities, discourse and critical reflection on professional power (Fook, 1993; Pease and Fook, 1999), two key policy moments occurred: the Report of the Royal Commission into Aboriginal Deaths in Custody 1991 (RCIADIC, 1991) and *Bringing them Home: The Report of the National Inquiry into the Separation of Aboriginal and Torres Strait Islander Children from Their Families* (HREOC, 1997). Both the RCIADIC and *Bringing them Home* demonstrated the state violence perpetrated against Aboriginal and Torres Strait Islander peoples under the law and perversely in the name of 'protection'. Both revealed ongoing colonisation through the government systems that form 'the welfare state', including the criminal legal system and human services where social work practice occurs.

As part of the National Inquiry into the Separation of Aboriginal and Torres Strait Islander Children from their Families, the Australian Association of Social Workers (AASW) submitted an acknowledgement and apology for the profession's complicity in the systemic removal of Aboriginal and Torres Strait Islander children, the 'Stolen Generations' (HREOC, 1997: 253). However, despite this apology, which was followed by the Australian government's National Apology to the Stolen Generations in 2008, and the endorsement of the United Nations Declaration on the Rights of Indigenous Peoples in 2009, out-of-home care rates for Aboriginal and Torres Strait Islander children are almost 12 times that of non-Aboriginal children

(AIHW, 2024). Similarly, although the RCIADIC recommended Aboriginal and Torres Strait Islander people be diverted from prison, Aboriginal and Torres Strait Islander people are incarcerated at 17 times the rate of non-Aboriginal people. This is despite subsequent national policies to end the 'over-representation' of Aboriginal and Torres Strait Islander people in prison (Australian Governments and the Coalition of Aboriginal and Torres Strait Islander Peak Organisations, 2020). This figure is even higher for Aboriginal and Torres Strait Islander women, who are incarcerated at 25 times the rate of non-Aboriginal women (ABS, 2023). Aboriginal and Torres Strait Islander children are 29 times as likely as non-Aboriginal children to be in juvenile detention (AIHW, 2023). In the state of New South Wales (NSW), where our social work practice has taken place, research has shown that the child protection system and criminal legal system are interlocking parts of a carceral net that targets Aboriginal and Torres Strait Islander people (McFarlane, 2010; Gerard et al, 2023).

The AASW has stated its concern for 'a potential creation of a second Stolen Generation' (AASW, 2018) and its commitment to upholding the rights of Indigenous people (AASW, 2020). Yet, there has been no identifiable AASW action on this issue or in response to the RCIADIC, notwithstanding direct calls (Fejo-King, 2011), or the evidence that children in out-of-home care are disproportionately criminalised in the court system (McFarlane, 2018), or the evidence of racist practices of child protection workers (Davis, 2019). The AASW has also professed a commitment to 'prevent and eliminate negative discrimination and oppression against people on the basis of personal, social or background characteristics and to recognise and challenge racism and other forms of oppression' (AASW, 2020: 12). This statement is aligned with 'anti-oppressive practice' (AOP), a critical approach to addressing systemic racism and all forms of structural oppression (Baines, 2017). However, there has not been a concomitant embrace of abolitionist goals, despite alignment between these approaches.

AOP aims to dismantle the structures that produce and reify injustice, raise critical consciousness of the professional practices (social work and other professions) that maintain these structures, and support action with social movements and local communities to promote community well-being and safety. Abolitionism is concerned with the relationship between institutional violence, oppression, criminalisation and carcerality, with the goal of ending the power relations which sustain these processes. While abolitionism, like AOP, is not a unitary approach, there is a shared focus on looking beyond the individual to the context of state violence and dismantling discriminatory and harmful structures and institutions. Drawing on Davis et al (2022), we emphasise that abolition is less about 'dismantling' and more about 'rebuilding', transforming society through the imagining of new, anti-racist and anti-carceral conceptualisations of justice and bringing these to life through practice and political action.

Perhaps statutory social work systems do not permit AOP to be enacted. Perhaps social workers in these systems are unable to see how 'dismantling' is possible and abandon the approach. Perhaps social workers in these systems can do AOP, but there is a white colonial co-option of the approach. For example, a selective application of AOP that equates to reform within colonial systems that perpetuates racist carceral logics. This can also be understood as 'reformist reform', that is, reforms that contribute to maintaining or expanding the carceral state (see Akbar [2023] and Davis [2011] for the distinction between reformist and non-reformist reforms). In this chapter we argue that if social workers are to uphold their commitment to 'preventing and eliminating oppression' (AASW, 2020) and practice in ways that are anti-oppressive, then such social work must also be 'for abolition'. We cannot be advocates for Indigenous rights, anti-racism and anti-violence, for example, and maintain the carceral system. This is antithetical. It deflects from incarceration as a colonial tool for inflicting punishment and harm against Aboriginal and Torres Strait Islander people. It reinforces the role of social workers as agents of surveillance and control, bestowing power that conflicts with our professional values and goals. It obfuscates that colonial government policies, systems and services disguise punishment as help. In the next section we use examples from our practice to illustrate this point.

Sacha

More than a decade ago, Walter et al's (2011) formative article 'How white is social work in Australia?' was published in *Australian Social Work*. During this time, I was employed on a research project led by Aboriginal[1] women on the health and social and emotional well-being of incarcerated Aboriginal mothers in NSW (Sherwood and Kendall, 2013). The project involved interviewing Aboriginal women in six women's prisons in NSW. Professor Juanita Sherwood was leading this work, and I was there as a second researcher/co-facilitator. As a non-Aboriginal, white social work academic, these words from Walter et al's article resonated strongly: 'Enmeshed within the lived unconsciousness of White as normal, entering a raced space not confined to non White races can be deeply unsettling' (2011: 7). Seeing the inside of prisons and listening to incarcerated Aboriginal women's voices, I became acutely aware of my white privileges, my 'social worker identity', and the intersections between them in terms of the opportunities and power bestowed by normative whiteness. I wasn't employed as a social worker at this time. I was in the prisons as a researcher, and so this professional identity was not visible to the women who participated in the research. However, I could identify the presence of social work in the stories they shared. Although women didn't specifically name social workers, every system where social workers are employed was mentioned.

The women's stories drew attention to professional practices that perpetuate and conceal the dominance of white worldviews and privilege. Aboriginal women's stories were accounts of systemic harm and punishment before, during and after prison. The women in this project had endured harmful experiences of racism and discrimination within systems throughout their lives, including but not limited to education, child protection, health, social security (for example, Centrelink), housing and the criminal legal system. Aboriginal mothers who spoke to us explained how they had been denied the opportunity to be a mother, including numerous examples of never being offered support by family and community services and having their babies removed at birth. They explicitly named that another Stolen Generation was occurring (Kendall et al, 2019). This experience was central to women's stories of ill-health and incarceration. In prison, not only was there no support for the trauma and grief of child removal, but women experiencing mental distress were dismissed, ignored and ridiculed. Women shared accounts of being denied healthcare on the basis of racial stereotypes that they were 'drug-chasers' (Kendall et al, 2019, 2020).

I learned through this research that the criminalisation and incarceration of Aboriginal women occurs through a broad, colonial-patriarchal social welfare system of surveillance, control and punishment, of which the criminal legal system is just one part (Baldry and Cunneen, 2014). Health and social services intersect with the carceral system and jointly function to conceal and perpetuate settler-colonialism through child removal and perpetual punishment of mothers. My idea of social workers as 'agents of the state' expanded to encompass an understanding of 'social work as positioned within the carceral state'. My questioning around health and social inequalities changed from 'what are the system barriers and how do we improve accessibility and practices?' to 'how are systems and practices generating harm and how is this intentional and by design?'. In considering these questions over time, this research has informed my critique of the dominant discourse of the health and well-being of incarcerated women in terms of what it generates, what it conceals, who benefits and what social work can do to subvert this. In the remainder of this section, I offer an outline of this critique and make an argument for abolitionism.

The dominant discourse of the health and well-being of women in prison in Australia is a public health discourse of individual disadvantage, vulnerability and unmet needs (for example, Breuer et al, 2021; Lobo and Howard, 2021). This discourse is produced through an almost ubiquitous approach to presenting the issue of women's incarceration that focuses on describing the 'characteristics' of the population. This takes the form of listing physical and mental health conditions, substance use, and social determinants of health including low levels of education, unemployment and homelessness (AIHW, 2020). Incarcerated women are typically compared to incarcerated men by highlighting that their mental health is worse, often 'evidenced' through statistics on higher rates of mental health diagnosis and the prescription of psychiatric medication with disregard for the evidence of how this is highly gendered and pathologising (Lafrance et al, 2013), and by their histories of domestic violence and childhood trauma (AIHW, 2020). Strangely, these two issues are typically discussed separately, even though violence is recognised by the World Health Organization as a social determinant of health.

Incarcerated women's trauma is typically explained via a vulnerability discourse of women in prison as 'victims and offenders' (Stathopoulos and Quadara, 2014). This conceals the structural and state violence that criminalises women, maintaining the image of the state as neutral by excluding the harm caused by institutional violence. Perversely, this also serves to obfuscate the gendered violence that occurs in prisons. Activists and women with lived experience of prison have been outspoken on this issue, calling out institutional practices of control, such as strip-searching, for how they replicate women's past traumatic experiences of gender-based violence and impinge on women's human rights (Kilroy, 2016). Addressing gender-based violence is a current policy priority and the National Plan to End Violence Against Women 2022–2032 (Commonwealth Government, 2022) recognises that incarceration increases women's risk of victimisation on release. However, the strategies for prevention outlined in the national plan do not include strategies for preventing women's incarceration, even though Aboriginal women and abolitionists have been outspoken on this issue (ICRR and Sisters Inside, 2021; Commonwealth of Australia, 2023).

Applying an abolitionist lens, these issues are one and the same. Ending violence against women requires looking at the circumstances of those most affected (Davis, 2024). Resisting the siloing of issues is an important aspect of abolitionism. One way in which to do this is to reveal how dominant political discourses decontextualise and reduce complex and historically bound issues to sustain and expand the prison industry for the benefit (and harm) of particular groups. For example, the NSW Department of Communities and Justice currently espouses 'tough and smart' justice measures as necessary for the 'safety of the community', creating a binary between incarcerated and non-incarcerated people. This is othering, permitting treatment of incarcerated people as lesser citizens. For example, incarcerated people are denied access to healthcare equivalent to that available in the community, as is their right under the United Nations Standard Minimum Rules for the Treatment of Prisoners (the Mandela Rules). One outcome of this is that Aboriginal people in prison are deprived access to Aboriginal community-controlled health services (Kendall et al, 2020). This binary also deflects from how more than half (53.5 per cent) of women incarcerated in NSW are on remand (unsentenced) (BOCSAR, 2024), nearly half (46 per cent) have been previously incarcerated (ABS, 2024), and the vast majority (71 per cent) have a minimum security classification (ABS, 2024). These statistics draw seriously into question the supposed threat that incarcerated women pose to the community and the justification for locking them up.

Prison has a 'criminogenic effect', enmeshing women in the correctional system and other systems of surveillance and control that increases their likelihood of future incarceration (Baldry et al, 2015). Yet, public health discourse constructs women's recidivism as a problem of 'unmet needs' requiring further funding of programmes and interventions delivered by professionals: that is, reform that effectively expands the carceral system. There is a presupposition, supported by biomedical and therapeutic jurisprudence discourses, that professionals are experts who will generate health and justice outcomes, legitimising their carceral role. Politicians and professionals gain from the perpetuation of these discourses.

The reinforcement of professional power, and particularly carceral professional power, should be a critical social work concern. The intersection of biomedical discourse with the law has implications for the interpretation of human rights. Abolitionist social workers can identify and challenge where dominant discourses in policy and law are functioning to impinge on individual and collective rights under the guise of supporting well-being or improving access to treatment. For example, when biomedical constructs of 'addiction' or 'mental illness' result in assessments of capacity, risk and best interests that justify increased use of carceral responses (Seear, 2019).

Lobna

It is impossible to discuss child imprisonment in Australia without putting at the forefront Australia's colonial roots. Today, there is often concern and outrage when a child engages in criminal activity or violence, because it challenges the concept of childhood as a stage of innocence. Yet, childhood innocence is not a universal or shared idea.

When the first fleet invaded Australian shores in 1788, the English 'back home' were developing ideas about the 'nature' of childhood, and the beginning of a recognition of the 'vulnerability' of children. However, the idea of the 'innocence' of childhood was not carried over to Australia in relation to Aboriginal populations. Open colonial warfare disregarded age completely, and it is recorded that Aboriginal children were murdered alongside Aboriginal adults, with the sole purpose of expanding the colony. As Cunneen and White state:

Aboriginal people were murdered because they were Aboriginal: that is, because they were the Indigenous people in possession of the land and because they resisted colonial expansion ... the killing was indiscriminate ... conflict involving the killing of Aboriginal adults and children by punitive parties of Europeans went on at least until the late 1920s in the Northern Territory and Western Australia. (Cunneen and White, 2002: 157)

Meiners (2015: 136) suggests that 'it desperately matters who is viewed (or not) as innocent or disposable', and that '[c]harting racial disproportionality at every level of the juvenile justice system – surveillance, arrest, removal from home, conviction, and sentencing – clearly shows that youth of colour do not have the same access to innocence and are not understood as sensate in the same way that white youth are' (Meiners, 2015: 131).

This account is highly relevant for understandings of Australia's contemporary juvenile justice system where Aboriginal youth are vastly over-represented, and white youth are under-represented. It is important to note that 19th and 20th century recollections and constructions of childhood and juvenile justice systems have tended to exclude non-white populations. Despite this history, and despite the alarming statistics, the incarceration of children and young people, and the over-incarceration of Aboriginal children, penal systems and institutions remain preoccupied with individual pathology.

Social workers can be found across workplaces that enable the carceral state, such as child protection, mental health and youth justice. The employment of social workers in these spaces indicates social work's role in maintaining and replicating carceral logics. I will argue that social work's presence in these institutions is characteristic of a carceral state. Drawing on the specific example of juvenile justice, my aim is to expose how the welfare/carceral intersection is necessary to justify, and neutralise, the punishment of children in Australia.

Armed with carceral logics from criminology, developmental psychology and sociology, the juvenile is constructed in a very specific way. In my previous employment as a juvenile justice counsellor, administering a risk assessment tool to measure 'risk of reoffending' was part-and-parcel of my everyday practice. Measuring risk includes asking several questions that draw on individual and social 'factors', such as homelessness, poverty, family dysfunction, mental health and anti-social attitudes. These risk factors become sites of 'help' and 'support', with the goal of reducing recidivism.

For example, low socioeconomic status is considered a strong risk factor for juvenile crime, so it seems obvious that children are questioned about their living circumstances, such as experiences of homelessness or poverty. Alongside this, the child's family comes under scrutiny, with questions such as 'are there a lot of rules at home?' and 'how are you disciplined?' (Australian Adaptation of Youth Level of Service/Case Management Inventory, Australian Adaptation, 2002). This risk determination process illuminates intersecting problem representations (Bacchi and Goodwin, 2016) that not only imply what the problem is (poor dysfunctional families), but also what the potential solution is (state intervention). Morality, rationality and human essence are expressed in concrete questions, such as 'do you feel you were treated fairly by the police and the court?' and then subsequently 'what's getting in the way? How can we help?' (Australian Adaptation of Youth Level of Service/Case Management Inventory, Australian Adaptation, 2002). In this example, the social worker administering the risk assessment tool is both the judge and the 'helper'.

In this way, both institutions, child protection and youth justice, do not simply intersect, rather they unify. In the absence of interrogation, it might appear that the aim is to 'protect' children from harmful and failed families. However, lifting the gaze to statistics exposes the material effects of a carceral state, shrouded in the language of 'help' and 'protection'. It is no coincidence that Aboriginal children, and children of colour, are over-represented across both so-called child protection and youth justice. In fact, these two institutions in combination pose significant risk for certain children and communities. A study conducted by Colvin et al (2020: 2, 12) demonstrated that out-of-home care (OOHC) and criminalisation overlap: 'between 2014 and 2016, children in OOHC [out-of-home care] were 19 times more likely to be under Juvenile Justice supervision compared with children from the general population. ... Our file reviews showed that 54.5 percent of care children versus 21.4 percent of non-care children had previously been incarcerated'.

In the same study, Colvin et al (2020: 12) also found that: 'Children on a section 28 order became "homeless" while in custody, and sometimes spent lengthy periods in custody, while practically bailed on minor offences because of the lack of a suitable placement ... demonstrate how relatively minor care-based incidents can lead to custody.'

Children on a section 28 are unable to be released on bail if no accommodation is available. There is a dominant discourse, in youth justice practice and research, of antisocial families who produce antisocial children, which distracts from the reality that children are often in a vicious cycle of offending, and are often pushed into homelessness. Although it is imperative that children are protected from circumstances of homelessness, poverty and abuse, carceral discourse invisibilises how the state punishes, individualises and *creates* circumstances of poverty.

Mental health is another intersecting carceral system draped in helping discourse. In Australia, a child can be charged and arrested from the age of ten,[2] and over the past decade, the racialisation of crime has come to light more publicly. For example, in 2016 images of children being forcibly detained in Don Dale Youth Detention Centre in Australia's Northern Territory were brought into the spotlight. African 'gangs' have become a policy focus across Melbourne, South Australia and Queensland. In 2023, rap music was banned from the Easter show, on the basis that it encouraged young Pacific Islander boys to join 'gangs'. In 2024, in NSW, several young Muslim boys are being held in detention on 'terrorism' offences. These examples demonstrate competing notions of 'children', and depending on the colour of the skin, which children are cast as 'dangerous' or 'innocent' remains slippery. Carcerality relies heavily on the illusion of 'help' and 'protection', and social work relies on the illusion of 'helper' to sustain its usefulness. If social work is found in the exact places where carceral logics are present, then perhaps social work is a symptom of oppression.

Discussion

This chapter has argued that social work in Australia is happening in a carceral state. 'Punishment disguised as help' is lodged in discourses of neutrality, where the presence of social workers is used as 'evidence' of an equitable welfare state and access to care. This is how governments can claim the colonial period is over, and that what we see today in terms of inequality is a matter of individual and family dysfunction. Professional 'helpers', such as social workers, come to represent the 'social' response to crime, while effectively contributing to discourses of offending and risk that perpetuate the colonial project and paradoxically undermine social work values. Discourses of 'help', 'protection', 'safety' and 'best interests' position individuals and families front-and-centre in constructions of problems, obscuring the role of carceral systems. Biomedical and child protection discourses that dominate in social work function to invisibilise whiteness, reinforce professional power, legitimise punishment and perpetuate carceral logics.

If social work is to practice *anti*-oppression, an abolitionist reconceptualisation of help and care is required. The examples in this chapter have demonstrated how carcerality is harmful to women and children, and how although social workers may enter these spaces with good intentions, social work is weaponised. Rather than asking how social work can reform what is essentially a colonial project, we should instead begin to ask, how can social work exit and transcend the carceral continuum?

Drawing on our practice experience, social work can make dents in/dismantle inequitable and discriminatory systems and support current meaningful and tangible actions for abolition. For example, in relation to the criminal legal system, we can support the 'Raise the Age' campaign to raise the age of criminal responsibility in all Australian states from 10 to 14 years of age. There is currently no commitment from social work governing bodies in support of this decarceration policy. We can also support the #FreeHer campaign to keep women and girls out of prison, set up by Debbie Kilroy, chief executive officer of Sisters Inside Inc. Social workers in relevant fields can work critically in collaboration with lawyers to advocate for 'defining crime as a social construction and explaining punishment and the rise of the carceral state as products of racial capitalism, settler colonialism and social control, among other forms of subordination' (Morgan, 2021: 607). This can support interpretation of the law in strategic ways to produce outcomes that 'decouple social responses to harm and conflict from the criminal legal system and toward non-punitive and non-carceral systems of accountability and care' (Morgan, 2021: 608). This idea can similarly be applied to working with psychiatrists and others who are empowered by the law to detain people.

Across services, social workers can learn to recognise system harm and actively resist problem constructions, tools and practices that seek to name this as an individual/family problem. They can instead provide an evidence base for the issue as structural, and frame it as a matter of social injustice. For example, critical feminist scholars are already resisting the co-option of trauma discourse when it is used to pathologise women and construct them as 'vulnerable' and in need of surveillance and control (Tseris, 2013, 2019; Thompson, 2021). Social workers more broadly could join this movement. Social workers can prioritise listening to those most affected by violence when constructing their ideas about what safety and justice mean and how social workers can be useful in preventing and responding to violence. Using rights-based frameworks, social workers can delegitimise stigmatising binaries connected to class, race, gender, sexuality and ability. Social workers can resist the co-option of social work by working with individuals, families and communities to promote safety instead of with the police. One strategy within this approach is to make their system knowledge more accessible to communities, shifting power by facilitating access to information so that formal services are not needed. Social workers can also build multidisciplinary alliances across services (for example, mental health, housing, child protection and non-government support services), to enhance access to non-coercive, preventative support and destabilise existing structures.

Beyond formal state-funded programmes, activist campaigns and research, there remain unseen and not-yet-captured practices within communities that have their own preventative practices that minimise carceral harms. Social workers practising within communities are familiar with the informal processes that are currently taking place, such as communities who abstain from contacting the police and instead lean on neighbours, family and kinship networks to restore safety. Social workers can work to legitimise and value the expertise of communities who often play a role in deescalating volatile situations. This is crucial for Aboriginal communities where the presence of police often leads to serious harm or death.

Abolition social work need not be categorised as 'radical' social work, just as help and care are not categorised as 'radical'. Rather, abolition social work could be incorporated into the definition of care. If social work is to remain connected to systems that perpetuate injustice, then it must seek to side with, and fight for, those who are harmfully impacted. This aligns with our espoused commitment to social justice and human rights. This chapter has demonstrated how the places that espouse the discourse of help are the very places where significant harm is occurring. This is an invitation to depart from and transcend carceral social work and prioritise actions that are embedded in collective freedom and care.

Notes

[1] I use the term Aboriginal here, as this was the language used by the researchers and participants in this project.
[2] In Victoria, the age of criminal responsibility has been raised to 12 with the intent to raise it to 14 in 2027.

References

AASW (Australian Association of Social Workers) (2018) *Aboriginal and Torres Strait Islander Issues*, Australian Association of Social Workers. Available at: https://www.aasw.asn.au/about-aasw/aboriginal-and-torres-strait-islander-issues/

AASW (2020) *Australian Association of Social Workers Code of Ethics*. Available at: https://www.aasw.asn.au/about-aasw/ethics-standards/code-of-ethics/

ABS (Australian Bureau of Statistics) (2023) *Prisoners in Australia*. Available at: https://www.abs.gov.au/statistics/people/crime-and-justice/prisoners-australia/latest-release

ABS (2024) *Corrective Services, Australia*. Available at: https://www.abs.gov.au/statistics/people/crime-and-justice/corrective-services-australia/latest-release

AIHW (Australian Institute of Health and Welfare) (2020) *The Health and Welfare of Women in Australia's Prisons*. Cat. no. PHE 281. Canberra: AIHW. Available at: https://www.aihw.gov.au/getmedia/32d3a8dc-eb84-4a3b-90dc-79a1aba0efc6/aihw-phe-281.pdf.aspx?inline=true

AIHW (2023) *Youth Detention Population in Australia 2023*. Available at: https://www.aihw.gov.au/reports/youth-justice/youth-detention-population-in-australia-2023/contents/about

AIHW (2024) *Child Protection Australia 2021–22*. Cat. no. CWS 92. Canberra: AIHW. Available at: https://www.aihw.gov.au/reports/child-protection/child-protection-australia-2021-22/contents/about

Akbar, A. (2023) 'Non-reformist reforms and struggles over life, death, and democracy', *The Yale Law Journal*, 132: 2497–2577.

Australian Adaptation of Youth Level of Service/Case Management Inventory, Australian Adaptation (2002) *NSW Department of Juvenile Justice*. Available at: https://www.nsw.gov.au/legal-and-justice/youth-justice/youth-on-track/program-delivery

Australian Governments and the Coalition of Aboriginal and Torres Strait Islander Peak Organisations (2020) *National Agreement on Closing the Gap (2020)*. Available at: https://www.closingthegap.gov.au/national-agreement

Bacchi, C. and Goodwin, S. (2016) *Poststructural Policy Analysis: A Guide to Practice*, New York: Palgrave.

Baines, D. (ed) (2017) *Doing Anti-oppressive Practice: Social Justice Social Work* (3rd edn), Halifax: Fernwood Publishing.

Baldry, E. and Cunneen, C. (2014) 'Imprisoned Indigenous women and the shadow of colonial patriarchy', *Australian and New Zealand Journal of Criminology*, 47(2): 276–298.

Baldry, E., Carlton, B. and Cunneen, C. (2015) 'Abolitionism and the paradox of penal reform in Australia: Indigenous women, colonial patriarchy, and co-option', *Social Justice*, 41.3(137): 168–189.

BOCSAR (Bureau of Crime Statistics and Research) (2024) *Custody Statistics*. Available at: https://bocsar.nsw.gov.au/statistics-dashboards/custody.html

Breuer, E., Remond, M., Lighton, S., Passalaqua, J., Galouzis, J., Stewart, K., et al (2021) 'The needs and experiences of mothers while in prison and post-release: A rapid review and thematic synthesis', *Health and Justice*, 9: Article 31.

Colvin, E., Gerard, A. and McGrath, A. (2020) *Children in Out-of-home Care and the Criminal Justice System: A Mixed-method Study*, Canberra: Australian Institute of Criminology.

Commonwealth of Australia (2023) *Aboriginal and Torres Strait Islander Action Plan 2023–2025 under the National Plan to End Violence against Women and Children 2022–2032*, Australian Government, Department of Social Services.

Commonwealth Government (2022) *National Plan to End Violence Against Women 2022–2032*, Commonwealth of Australia (Department of Social Services). Available at: https://www.dss.gov.au/ending-violence

Cunneen, C. and White, R. (2002) 'Ethnic minority young people', in C. Cunneen and R. White (eds), *Juvenile Justice: Youth and Crime in Australia*, Melbourne: Oxford University Press, pp 184–207.

Davis, A. (2011) *Are Prisons Obsolete?*, New York: Seven Stories Press.

Davis, A. (2024) 'Society for social work and research keynote 2019', in M. Kim, C. Rasmussen and D. Washington (eds), *Abolition and Social Work, Possibilities, Paradoxes and the Practice of Community Care*, Chicago: Haymarket Books, pp 20–30.

Davis, A., Dent, G., Meiners, E. and Richie, B. (2022) *Abolition. Feminism. Now.*, London: Hamish Hamilton.

Davis, M. (2019) *Family is Culture: Independent Review into Aboriginal Out-of-home care in NSW. Final Report*, Sydney: Family is Culture. Available at: https://bettercarenetwork.org/sites/default/files/2019-11/Family-Is-Culture-Review-Report.pdf

Fejo-King, C. (2011) 'The national apology to the stolen generations: The ripple effect', *Australian Social Work*, 64(1): 130–143.

Fook, J. (1993) *Radical Casework: A Theory of Practice*, St Leonards: Allen and Unwin.

Gerard, A., McGrath, A., Colvin, E. and Gainsford, A. (2023) *Children, Care and Crime: Trauma and Transformation*, London: Routledge.

HREOC (Human Rights and Equal Opportunity Commission) (1997) *Bringing them Home: Report of the National Inquiry into the Separation of Aboriginal and Torres Strait Islander Children from Their Families*, Sydney: Human Rights and Equal Opportunity Commission.

ICRR (Institute for Collaborative Race Research) and Sisters Inside (2021) *The State as Abuser: Coercive Control in the Colony. Joint Submission from Sisters Inside and the Institute for Collaborative Race Research on Discussion Paper 1 of the Women's Safety and Justice Taskforce*. Available at: https://www.womenstaskforce.qld.gov.au/__data/assets/pdf_file/0005/691340/wsjt-submission-sisters-inside-and-institue-for-collaborative-race-research.pdf

Kendall, S., Lighton, S., Sherwood, J., Baldry, E. and Sullivan, E. (2019) 'Holistic conceptualizations of health by incarcerated Aboriginal women in New South Wales, Australia', *Qualitative Health Research*, 29(11): 1549–1565.

Kendall, S., Lighton, S., Sherwood, J., Baldry, E. and Sullivan, E. (2020) 'Aboriginal women's experiences of accessing healthcare in Australian prisons and the limitations of the "equal treatment" principle', *International Journal for Equity in Health*, 19(48): 1–14.

Kilroy, D. (2016) 'Women in prison in Australia', *Current Issues in Sentencing Conference*, 6–7 February. Available at: https://www.njca.com.au/wp-content/uploads/2023/03/Kilroy-Debbie-Women-in-Prison-in-Australia-paper.pdf

Lafrance, M.N., McKenzie-Mohr, S., Marecek, J. and Gavey, N. (2013) 'The DSM and its lure of legitimacy', *Feminism and Psychology*, 23(1): 119–140.

Lobo, J. and Howard, M. (2021) *Women in Prison: An Examination of the Support Needs of Women in Custody with Children*, Corrections Research Evaluation and Statistics, Research Brief No. 4, March 2021, Corrective Services NSW.

McFarlane, K. (2010) 'From care to custody: Young women in out-of-home care in the criminal justice system', *Current Issues in Criminal Justice*, 22(2): 345–353.

McFarlane, K. (2018) 'Care-criminalisation: The involvement of children in out-of-home care in the New South Wales criminal justice system', *Australian and New Zealand Journal of Criminology*, 51(3): 412–433.

Meiners, E.R. (2015) 'Trouble with the child in the carceral state', *Social Justice*, 41(3): 120–144.

Mendes, P. (2009) 'Tracing the origins of critical social work practice', in J. Allan, L. Briskman and B. Pease (eds), *Critical Social Work: Theories and Practices for a Socially Just World* (2nd edn), Crows Nest: Allen and Unwin.

Morgan, J. (2021) 'Lawyering for abolitionist movements', *Connecticut Law Review*, 510: 607–617.

Pease, B. and Fook, J. (eds) (1999) *Transforming Social Work Practice: Postmodern Critical Perspectives*, St Leonards: Allen and Unwin.

RCIADIC (Royal Commission into Aboriginal Deaths in Custody) (1991) Available at: https://www.naa.gov.au/explore-collection/first-australians/royal-commission-aboriginal-deaths-custody

Rodger, J.J. (1988) 'Social work as social control re-examined: Beyond the dispersal of discipline thesis', *Sociology*, 22(4): 563–581.

Seear, K. (2019) *Law, Drugs and the Making of Addiction: Just Habits*, London: Routledge.

Sherwood, J. and Kendall, S. (2013) 'Reframing spaces by building relationships: Community collaborative participatory action research with Aboriginal mothers in prison', *Contemporary Nurse*, 46(1): 83–94.

Stathopoulos, M. and Quadara, A. (2014) *Women as Offenders; Women as Victims: The Role of Corrections in Supporting Women with Histories of Sexual Abuse*, Australian Institute of Family Studies and Corrective Services NSW.

Thompson, L. (2021) 'Toward a feminist psychological theory of "institutional trauma"' *Feminism and Psychology*, 31(1): 99–118.

Tseris, E. (2013) 'Trauma theory without feminism? Evaluating contemporary understandings of traumatized women', *Affilia*, 28(2): 153–164.

Tseris, E. (2019) 'Social work and women's mental health: Does trauma theory provide a useful framework?', *British Journal of Social Work*, 49(3): 686–703.

Walter, M., Taylor, S. and Habibis, D. (2011) 'How white is social work in Australia?', *Australian Social Work*, 64(1): 6–19.

7

Wither child maltreatment investigations by social workers: a case for abolishing the principal carceral link in the family regulation system

Lisa Merkel-Holguin and Ida Drury

Carceral logic, or police-like policy, is deeply embedded in the United States child welfare system, also referred to as the family policing or family regulation system. This chapter seeks to unpack this logic in the child abuse investigation process and proposes a different way of responding to most child maltreatment concerns. We propose a logic of relationships, where the focus of intervention is on accurate and comprehensive assessment, engagement strategies, and provision of supports that meet families' fundamental needs. Empirical research reveals the quality and depth of relationship is the essential ingredient that promotes change. We will demonstrate the way investigations alienate and oppress caregivers, their communities and support networks. We believe the carceral link of 'investigations' in all but sexual abuse and serious physical abuse must be severed. Foundationally, the current oppressive structures within the existing Child Protective Services (CPS) systems must be eliminated for more revolutionary, justice-oriented, ways of working with children and families (Braithwaite, 2021; Merkel-Holguin et al, 2022). We propose, then, a type of non-reformist reform that effectively challenges this heavily embedded and entrenched carceral link.

In the United States, carceral logic infected the design of the child protection system in the 1960s. Kempe and colleagues' seminal Battered Child Syndrome paper (1962) highlighted the 'terrible few' who caused significant harm to children. They defined 'battered child' as a clinical condition in young children who endured serious, chronic, physical abuse from their caregivers. More expansively, however, they also considered evidence of *possible* trauma or neglect as risks for this 'syndrome'. This imposed a medical model that pathologised caregivers and criminalised child maltreatment rather than situating child abuse and neglect as a societal issue (Burton and Montauban, 2021). Advocates and policy makers of the time promoted expansive definitions of child abuse and neglect, ushered in mandated reporting, systematised child abuse investigations, professionalised a new classification of 'social worker', and embedded central registry systems at state and local levels. These structures served to advance the investigation, prosecution and treatment of caregivers as foundational to child protection systems – a foundation that remains cemented in CPS law and policy (Burton and Montauban, 2021) 60 years later. This chapter examines the child abuse and neglect investigation through the lenses of family experience, social work practice and overall (in)efficacy, and highlights the deep carceral logic that permeates these investigations.

Around the year 2008, a now retired Colorado-based child welfare administrator regularly claimed, 'Child Protective Services (CPS) social workers don't do investigations, they conduct family assessments'. This statement may more closely resemble the truth in CPS agencies that implement differential response, a reform strategy where many investigatory tactics are sidelined for a subset of families initially deemed as low to moderate risk based on a CPS hotline report. However, for most families who are the subject of a CPS report, the 'assessment' they experience has the trappings of an 'investigation'. Even though the majority of CPS investigations in the United States are not 'substantiated' or 'founded' and do not result in child removal, there is a growing recognition that CPS investigations cause harm to families and social networks, particularly in low-income communities and communities of colour (Fong, 2019). Softening the language about a CPS worker's initial contact with families, to be more aligned with social work values, is a strategy that propels some of the most powerful myths of the family regulation system.

The myths of supportive assistance and benevolence permeate the lexicon of most child welfare organisations and stakeholders, yet the actual system has deeply embedded carceral-like structures and policies with child-saving ideologies (Bekaert et al, 2021; Roberts, 2022). The structure presents itself as 'help' but is often experienced as coercive and repels parents who need assistance (Pelton, 1998). Across the United States, CPS practice frameworks and policy manuals, developed by professional bureaucrats and actors, describe the system as family-strengths oriented, solution-focused, relationship-based, participatory, culturally responsive and trauma-informed. However, the growing body of literature representing the experiences of children and parents paints a starkly different narrative. Those who experience CPS investigations and family regulation systems, more generally, describe it as punishing, judgement-laden and oppressive (Dumbrill, 2006; Gladstone et al, 2012; Haight et al, 2017). They note the intervention breeds fear and confusion, and results in unrelenting state surveillance over their families with limited, if any, help to address underlying economic hardship. Moreover, when reports are substantiated as abuse or neglect, the irony is that the deemed perpetrator will experience exacerbated long-term economic hardship, as they become ineligible for certain types of employment, oftentimes for many years, if not decades. Parents avoid the CPS, fearing the agency will interpret any problems as 'neglect' resulting in 'intervention consequences they neither sought nor desired' (Pelton, 1998; Fong, 2019). Meanwhile, CPS investigators envisage their role as a civic duty, wielding their power to secure compliance from families (Pryce, 2024) and unleashing authoritarian approaches to direct and control families. The canyon separating how those who construct and deliver the 'service' of an investigation versus those who are on the receiving end couldn't be wider. Unfortunately, this compromises the potential to deliver relevant and family-driven services that could positively impact children and families. Instead, the system upholds its own carceral logic. Pelton (1998) suggested that reforms have ignored how the public child welfare agency perpetuates a punishment and surveillance orientation:

> In most reform proposals, the gateway to services will still be the gateway to accusation, investigation, child removal, and foster care. Even with narrowed definitions of child abuse and neglect, such a common gateway confuses coercion and control with nonjudgmental aid and prevention, deters potential clients, distorts and misdirects funding streams, and inevitably denies clients' due process. (Pelton, 1998: 128)

Pelton's statement, written nearly 30 years ago, reminds us of the perils of reform, and cements our call to non-reformist reform, which in abolitionist terms is a step towards incrementally dismantling the system.

Sometimes those of us who have made a career within the child welfare industry, or the academy that studies the industry, struggle to describe the CPS using plain language. While CPS legislative codes, policies, rules, procedures and practices are continually changed by system bureaucrats and are peppered with jargon, the carceral logic that undergirds CPS investigations is largely unscrutinised. Accordingly, in the following discussion, we attempt to isolate the micro-practices that are embedded in CPS investigations, drawing links to policing and incarceration. In addition, we intentionally use 'straight talk' or language that mirrors how families experience CPS investigations, rather than the strengths-based social work language that the academy or the industry uses to disguise the harm it causes. In doing so, we hope to accentuate the voices of those most impacted by CPS systems and create a chapter that is accessible to audiences outside of the industry.

Reporting and screening

In recent decades across the United States, child welfare agencies' public service campaigns have directed the general public to call a child abuse hotline if they are worried about a child and/or suspect maltreatment. In addition, state-specific yet broad-sweeping mandatory reporting laws require a swathe of professionals (or, in some cases, everyone) to report suspicions of child abuse and neglect to the government, or face significant penalties, including loss of employment or professional licences. Together, these campaigns and laws have resulted in a groundswell of child abuse and neglect reports. A report, however, is only a report until the CPS screening staff decide whether the information meets the legal standard of suspicion for abuse and neglect. In the United States, according to 2022 data, 49.5 per cent of reports, or over two million, become CPS investigations (U.S. Department of Health and Human Services, Administration on Children, Youth and Families, Children's Bureau, 2024).

When CPS screeners are making a decision or CPS intake staff are preparing to launch an investigation, they oftentimes have incomplete or inaccurate information – not only about the allegation, but also the child and family. Characteristics such as race, ethnicity, culture and family norms are often unknown to the reporter and, consequently, to the family regulation agency. Decisions are made based on suspicion of abuse and neglect, which is a bar that varies significantly from jurisdiction to jurisdiction and has done so historically. Wald (1975) decried the common child welfare practice (still common today) of categorising as 'neglect', for the purpose of coercive intervention by CPS agencies, cases involving supposed 'inadequate parenting' which fell short of his proposed measures of severe harm (Pelton, 2016); punishing parents for being poor, not dangerous (Lindsay, 1994). This is where we begin to identify the carceral logic of CPS investigations.

Delving into government databases

One of the first actions taken by CPS personnel, sometimes as early as screening, is to probe the government's civil and criminal databases to gain a 'broader' portrait of the family who will be the subject of investigation. With limited identifying information, and in a matter of seconds, CPS staff gain access to court cases, arrest records, previous CPS cases and their dispositions, demographic information (such as age, household composition, previous addresses), and use of various government benefits such as cash assistance, housing and day care subsidies, and medical insurance. While it is understandable that a CPS investigator might benefit from such information at the onset of their *fact-finding mission*, these data points may be used to build narratives about families and contribute to the ongoing conscious or unconscious pathologising of parents and family systems. Kempe and his colleagues' work (1962) likely contributed to the industry's pathologisation, as it broadly characterised the parents or caregivers who may harm children as psychopaths and sociopaths, and indicated they may be immature, selfish and of low intelligence. In turn, the orientations of child protection investigations resemble inherently biased fact-finding missions that are aligned with the notion of identifying a deficient underclass of abusers. Today's CPS system continues to buy into this distorted picture even though there is sufficient evidence that it is a catchment for those living in poverty. These derogatory stereotypes, along with expansive definitions of child maltreatment, remain deeply embedded in today's child protection laws, policies and practices in the United States, despite the rhetoric of a softer child welfare system.

The system's response to a child abuse report is premised on suspicion, judgement and fear of the unknown. This uncertainty triggers agents to delve even deeper into administrative databases to continue painting a family narrative. The system has far-reaching tentacles and unfettered access to such data – data which can be misconstrued or weaponised against a family when the CPS knocks at their door with information that the family is unaware the CPS has 'on' them. The system actors are adequately prepared, with sanctioned protocols and tools, to unleash the government's response to investigate the allegation, using a range of police tactics; trampling on the Fourth Amendment of the United States, which protects people from unreasonable searches and seizures by the government (Shalleck-Klein, 2023). Some scholars have paralleled child abuse investigation as the equivalent of the police tactic 'stop and frisk', with CPS investigators exercising control over families who have few protections and inflicting abuses of power on marginalised communities (Burrell, 2019). The core purpose of the investigation is not to identify what assistance, support or help a family may need. Rather, the purpose is to determine: did the alleged perpetrator abuse or neglect the alleged victim? When that is the guiding question, carceral logic inevitably pervades the first surprise contact.

Element of surprise

People don't want government officials, and sometimes even neighbours, unexpectedly knocking on their doors or ringing their doorbells. But, just like the police who oftentimes use the element of surprise to capture or arrest their suspect, CPS investigators typically show up unannounced. This is intentional, to catch a family off-guard so that they don't clean up their house, destroy any information or align their stories. Logically it makes sense: if a system is trying to gather evidence about a child abuse and neglect incident, you don't want the evidence destroyed or manipulated. The surprise 'powers up' the position of the government, while putting the family in a powerless, uncertain position. There is an old adage that 'information is power'. There are only two groups of people with power in this equation: the CPS agent and their law enforcement 'partner', if a police assist is requested. They know the rules, processes and policies governing the investigation. Parents are at a significant disadvantage, as they are met immediately, without the benefit of legal counsel, by a government agent asking intrusive questions about their family life. This agent has the authority to forcibly separate the child from their parents, extended family network and community.

Is this police tactic necessary? Given that a high percentage of screened-in maltreatment reports are neglect-related because of poor environmental conditions and families in need of services, here are a few questions to ponder about the element of surprise:

- How does it impact the CPS worker's potential relationship with the parent?
- What if families cleaned or tidied up their house before a CPS investigator arrived?
- How would the dynamics between the family and agency change if the CPS worker called first and set up an appointment to visit?

Collaboration or collusion with police

Roberts (2022) described the child welfare system as one that acts like its criminal counterpart, unsurprisingly because of its origins in slavery, settler colonialism, disgust for the poor, and how it precisely targets marginalised groups. Family regulation agencies have deeply embedded relationships with the police which are leveraged throughout investigation processes, contributing to a carceral web that sweeps unsuspecting suspects into its network of punishment and control.

Notifying parents of their rights

The element of surprise, coupled with the capacity to separate, is bolstered by the fact that in almost all states, CPS workers are not required to notify parents of their rights when they initiate an investigation. For example, do parents have the right to legal counsel, to refuse CPS entry into their home, to not answer the questions of the CPS worker, and/or to deny the CPS worker access to their child? To challenge authoritarian presumptions, leading US advocates and scholars, Joyce McMillan and Dorothy Roberts, are promoting 'know your rights' legislation, whereby CPS workers would be required to notify parents of their rights at the start of an investigation, including the right to an attorney. These are similar to the rights afforded to those charged with crimes, as established by the United States Supreme Court *Miranda* v *Arizona* decision (Urban Matters, 2021). However, in most places where this type of legislation has been introduced as a way to decrease unfair and unnecessary intrusion into family life, legislators, with the support of the child welfare industry, have defeated these legal protections.

The tentacles of the carceral state flourish at the expense of families who live on the margins and in communities that experience a disproportionate level of surveillance.

Intimidation to gain access

When CPS workers do not have a court-issued authorisation to search a family's property, thus violating the Fourth Amendment of the US Constitution, they rely on soft power and intimidation. Shalleck-Klein (2023) noted that one large urban child welfare agency did not obtain court authorisation and entered families' homes unconstitutionally about 99.8 per cent of the time. To gain access to homes, CPS workers adopt a range of coercive tactics, including:

- suggesting cooperation will increase the likelihood that CPS will exit their lives more expeditiously;
- threatening parents that the lack of cooperation will result in the CPS worker returning with the police, or their children being forcibly removed and placed with strangers in foster care;
- misleading parents about the agency's authority; and
- not informing parents of their rights or encouraging them to seek legal counsel.

Parents find themselves in a terrifying, no-win position. Any information voluntarily provided will likely be weaponised as CPS builds their case against them, while simultaneously, refusal to cooperate leaves them vulnerable to more draconian measures that may increase the likelihood of family separation and persistent, targeted surveillance.

The intent to separate

The majority of child abuse and neglect investigations are not classified as requiring an immediate response (within 1–24 hours). As such, CPS staff control their workflow and decide the timing of their initial visits based on policy (for example, a CPS worker may have between two and seven days to 'lay eyes' on the 'victim' child). The guiding procedure mimics carceral logic, separating 'victims' and 'perpetrators' as investigations are launched to gather evidence. This tactic may breed mistrust between the parent and the CPS worker, and between the parent and the child. Rightly or wrongly, the government's CPS agency is not perceived by families as a trusted community partner (Fong, 2019; Pryce, 2024). Parents likely understand the agency's powers to regulate family life and forcibly separate their children from them, their siblings and everything else familiar, which escalates fears and anxieties.

CPS workers attempt to interview children, or the 'alleged victim', without the presence of their 'alleged perpetrators'. This is easier when school is in session as schools are a willing partner, providing space and time for the investigator to interview children. In addition to separately interviewing children, the CPS worker must also have a face-to-face meeting at the home of the parent or caregiver. Because of work schedules or other responsibilities, the CPS worker may struggle to find the parent/caregiver at home during their standard working hours. They may leave a brochure with a telephone number asking the parent to call the agency. Other parents have received knocks at the door late at night, which can be disorienting and traumatising. Sometimes, this type of approach is disproportionate to the response needed because workers are pressured and incentivised via performance metrics to meet response times. No matter how children and parents are contacted, these strategies are designed to separate family members for interviews, which can promote parental resistance and generate parent–child conflict. What if the CPS didn't use the police tactic of separation? Could we imagine interviewing children and parents as a family unit?

'Home visits' gone rogue

Recently, as we have been supporting a state's efforts to design and implement a differential response CPS system, the authors had the opportunity to observe a CPS investigation where the concern that prompted the referral was a bruise on the child's arm. The CPS investigator asked the parent to guide her through the house, so that she could inspect each room. We witnessed the CPS worker moving through the house, looking under beds, lifting up rugs, opening the cupboards and the refrigerator, all while systematically using her government issued phone to take multiple pictures of each room (and even the hallways!). She subsequently uploaded these photos into the state's automated child welfare information system. They will remain in that database until the files are purged, based on state statute. One could argue that photo evidence is necessary in cases of child maltreatment, where criminal charges will be lodged, and a court case will likely ensue. Documenting the home environment at the time of the visit safeguards the worker and agency's decision-making and builds evidence that will be used by the CPS, as the government authorities see fit. But for most child abuse investigations, this is an unethical and unnecessary invasion of family privacy. CPS systems are considered risk-averse (Parton, 2014; Gupta and Blumhardt, 2016) and liability focused. Moreover, they have embraced the impossible and unrealistic goal set by legislative bodies and the general public to prevent all child deaths from maltreatment. As such, CPS systems have procedures that remain firmly grounded in the principle of identifying 'the terrible few', at the expense of the 90 per cent who need support.

Intrusive and irrelevant questioning

In our experience, the type of questioning for families identified for investigation varies across jurisdictions. Questions range from medical contacts such as the child's dentist and pediatrician (even when the allegation is separate from the child's health) to asking about family background with the criminal justice system, housing status past and present, substance use, intimate partner violence, disciplinary practices and other intimate details of family life. Children are interviewed, often at school, and some jurisdictions ask a similar set of questions regardless of allegation, to 'rule out' physical and sexual abuse as well as neglect. Some jurisdictions require pictures be taken of the children during initial interviews as proof the child interview was conducted and for upload into the government's information system. As Fong noted, as part of CPS investigations, government agencies collect 'substantial information about domestic life' – information that is typically unavailable to the state.

Assessing for safety and risk

Generally, all child welfare systems have some method for assessing safety and risk. Two of the most commonly used in the United States have been developed by non-profit organisations. The safety assessment is designed to identify unmitigated actions or potential actions by the caregiver(s) and is used to make decisions about child safety in the home or the need for child placement. Most families subjected to this behavioural assessment are deemed 'safe'. This is in contrast to actuarial risk assessment, which relies on data gleaned from the jurisdiction's past interventions to determine the likelihood that the family will come back to the attention of the child welfare agency based on a series of often static risk factors, like history of poverty and prior involvement. The risk assessment introduces more intrusive questioning and workers don't always understand or explain the reason for their inquiry. This can be viewed as very adversarial and off-putting to the family. The worker's assessment of safety – whether a numeric score or narrative prose – will be used as evidence to undergird the agency's decisions.

Contacting collaterals

In the investigative process, typically CPS workers are required to contact or interview three to four 'collaterals' who may know of, or have a relationship with, the child or family. This may include professionals (teachers, day care providers, medical personnel, mental health clinicians), family members (grandparents, caregivers, spouses, siblings), and those in physical proximity to the child and family, such as neighbours, who may in fact be strangers. At first blush, this is believed to be an imprecise but necessary exercise to gather more information about an incident or contextual factors that led to the child abuse and neglect report. In addition to collateral contacts, CPS workers may ask parents to sign release of information documents, allowing agency access to mountains of information from teachers, therapists, hospitals and others. Ultimately, CPS workers get additional information on which to base their decision. Conversely, for those who are subject of the report, it results in the information and suspicion from an alleged incident being shared with others. This may jeopardise relationships, social support networks and result in parents experiencing more entrenched feelings of isolation, loneliness, shame or fear (Fong, 2019). In essence, when the CPS contacts neighbours of those who they are investigating, it infects communities with feelings of judgement and creates more separation among its members. Those being asked to opine on the child/family situation may find themselves in a predicament – wanting to assist the family, yet often knowing that any information provided could be used as evidence against the family. At its roots, contacting collaterals is a police tactic of 'evidence gathering', a cornerstone element that agencies use to build a case against families.

Is this police tactic necessary? When police investigate a heinous crime, such as murder, we expect them to preserve and interview anyone at the crime scene. However, for most reports, the time CPS workers spend identifying, interviewing and documenting information from collaterals could be repurposed. Instead, the CPS worker would have time to help families access benefits, or services, sort out challenges such as transportation, and connect families with community resources to meet pressing needs. They would encourage families to identify what services they need, rather than imposing services on them, reducing coercive tactics that suppress the voices of parents (Pelton, 2016). In essence, they would be building a trusting and helping relationship with the family, rather than contacting a subset of individuals and focusing on an incident, a strategy others have noted would liberate workers to use their skills and judgement (Featherstone et al, 2017) in ways that are partnership-focused (Bekaert et al, 2021). Just imagine a CPS worker who leads with these questions: 'How can I help?' or 'What do you need?'

Making a decision

At the conclusion of the investigation period, which typically spans 30 to 60 days, there are two decision points of consequence. First, the worker decides whether or not allegations of abuse or neglect are substantiated. Typically, the standard for this determination is 'preponderance of the evidence', or just a greater than 50 per cent likelihood that the maltreatment occurred. If a report of maltreatment is substantiated, caregiver details are placed in the information system as a kind of central registry. This registry will show up in background checks, flagging the caregiver as a perpetrator of maltreatment. This can prevent certain lines of employment for the affected individual, including caregiving jobs in education, childcare and health (Merkel-Holguin et al, 2022). Due to the economic impact of such a decision, caregivers do have the right to appeal and are informed of this right in the closing form letter (that may be delayed by paperwork backlogs on the part of the agency). Appeals are often subject to limits on their timing. In some cases, caregivers only realise the consequences later, as these findings of maltreatment remain for many years, even decades, depending on the state jurisdiction.

The second decision is related to whether or not a family's investigation is opened for ongoing services beyond the investigation. Even in situations where children remain home the entire time, the services provided to the family may be overseen by the court or the threat of court action. Families often find themselves subject to case plans that may closely resemble those of other families regardless of circumstances. Services range from mental health to parenting programmes or substance use treatment, and traditionally have done little to address poverty-related issues that closely associate with neglect. In addition to the requirement of services, families experience a level of surveillance that is unsettling and disruptive to daily life. Parents fear the unknown – a subsequent CPS report, a professional judging a parenting interaction with their child, or some elusive standard that the agency wields as they make decisions to regulate family life.

Sometimes, during this investigatory process, CPS 'help' is often constructed under the disguise of 'voluntary' safety plans, which serve as a non-legally binding custody agreement while the CPS conducts the investigation. Parents are oftentimes coerced into agreeing to these plans, developed by the CPS agents without any judicial review, as the alternative is the threat of placing their children in foster care with strangers. Most parents' worst nightmare – being separated from their children – means that they take the safety plan route, without knowing that they will likely be subjected to CPS regulations and surveillance for the foreseeable future.

Democracies die when their citizens rely on professionals to classify problems and make decisions. That is the case in child protection. Pelton (1998: 127) reminds us that 'an authoritarian relationship between professional and client is needed to maintain the authority and dominance of professional specialties', and the most controlling authority is the power to make decisions. CPS agents, with the assistance of a multidisciplinary team of professionals and courts, render judgements and make decisions with biased, incomplete sets of information. Parents, family members and their communities – those closest to the child and to any challenging situations – are relegated to the sidelines. In essence, they are powerless, as the CPS agents who are considered heroes and child savers make the most consequential decisions about their child and families' lives. Often, they don't even recognise that their decisions have generation-spanning and long-term impacts on health, well-being and the 'connectedness' of these families. Braithwaite's (2002) framework for responsive regulation creates a vision for how the principles of a representative democracy can be revitalised within a CPS context, with governments reflecting on whether a more or less interventionist response is needed for those they seek to regulate. We contend that a lesser response, or one that initially promotes individuals and families' self-regulatory capacities, not only repositions decision-making with parents and within family structures, but also realigns systems to meet community needs.

Could the CPS agent's role be modified, whereby they set aside evidence-building in favour of gathering the child's family and community network to build solutions? Is it possible to imagine CPS workers as activists for social change, who only become major decision makers should their own families become the subject of a CPS report?

An alternative

Unlike some of the more entrenched parts of the child welfare system, the decision to investigate in the first place does have precedent for system reform. Many of the investigative tactics, like unannounced home visits, child interviews and extensive collaterals, are left behind in favour of a response where there is no finding of child maltreatment (and subsequently, no entry into the central registry for impacted caregivers) for a subset of families in a differential response-organised CPS system. This differing approach has led to a myriad of positive outcomes, including enhanced service delivery with more focus on providing useful services, heightened worker job satisfaction, and decreases in subsequent involvement, including out-of-home care (Ender and Hollinshead, 2024). However, we recognise that this non-reformist reform can easily be colonised by the family regulation industry, where a carceral culture dominates and dictates practice. In a system that often wraps itself in the myth of benevolence, yet that steadfastly views investigations as the mechanism to achieve child (and family?) safety, we understand how an abolitionist message is fundamentally challenging: challenging to entrenched capitalism and the profits derived from all the enterprises entangled with child removal and the foster care industry. In a democratic society, it is ethically imperative to replace the lucrative family policing industry in ways that reposition family and community leadership and support their needs. The continued emphasis on investigations as the first government action will not fulfil the promise of supporting families or protecting children; rather, it will result in continued social isolation, fear of the other, weaponisation of social care, fragmentation of families and distrust of the government.

We envision a path to replacing up to 90 per cent of CPS investigations with something we have termed Circles of Care (CoC). The CPS investigator would become a Care Coordinator, replacing the policing tactics with organising strategies. The Care Coordinator would be principally responsible for gathering the parents, children, extended family and fictive kin, resource providers, and other professionals into a CoC. Those who are most vested in the long-term outcome – the child, family and their family/kin network – will be gathered together, to:

- listen to the concerns;
- ask questions;
- understand the help and assistance that can be offered; and
- to make a plan that is responsive, accountable and self-regulatory.

The family protection agency would have the following roles: active family builders to convene the family group; service brokers; and community organisers. Their responsibility would be to bolster family integrity and organise these family groups and their support networks to find solutions that nurture and protect their children. Community connectedness and credibility would be a baseline skill.

We recognise that this vision will require significant changes to public policy and laws, budgets, workforce recruitment and training, practice frameworks, philosophical orientations and day-to-day operations. What we are proposing is a pathway to: help, not surveillance; hope, not harm; family leadership, not professional domination across multiple disciplines; dignity and respect, not judgement and suspicion; and accountability and responsibility, not blame. As a society and as an industry, the harmful impacts and effects that carceral logic has inflicted are graphically evident. For most reports of child maltreatment, it is time to eliminate the unproven child maltreatment investigation that uses various police tactics that have unnecessarily terrorised parents, children, families and communities for generations.

References

Bekaert, S., Paavilainen, E., Schecke, H., Baldacchino, A., Jouet, E., Zabłocka–Zytka, L., et al (2021) 'Family members' perspectives of child protection services, a metasynthesis of the literature', *Children and Youth Services Review*, 128: 106094.

Braithwaite, J. (2002) *Restorative Justice and Responsive Regulation*, New York: Oxford University Press.

Braithwaite, V. (2021) 'Institutional oppression that silences child protection reform'. *International Journal on Child Maltreatment: Research, Policy and Practice*, 1: 49–72.

Burrell, M. (2019) 'What can the child welfare system learn in the wake of the Floyd decision? A comparison of stop-and-frisk policing and child welfare investigations', *CUNY Law Review*, 22(1): 125–147.

Burton, A.O. and Montauban, A. (2021) 'Toward community control of child welfare funding: Repeal the Child Abuse Prevention and Treatment Act and delink child protection from family well-being', *Columbia Journal of Race and Law*, 11(3): 639–680.

Dumbrill, G.C. (2006) 'Parental experience of child protection intervention: A qualitative study', *Child Abuse and Neglect*, 30(1): 27–37.

Ender, K. and Hollinshead, D. (2024) 'Differential response outcomes literature review'. Available at: https://kempecenter.org/wp-content/uploads/2024/09/Differential-Response-Outcomes-Literature-Review-SEPT-2024-1.pdf

Featherstone, B., Robb, M., Ruxton, S. and Ward, M.R.M. (2017) '"They are just good people … generally good people": Perspectives of young men on relationships with social care workers in the UK', *Children and Society*, 31(5): 331–341.

Fong, K. (2019) 'Concealment and constraint: Child protective services fears and poor mothers' institutional engagement', *Social Forces*, 97(4): 1785–1810.

Gladstone, J., Dumbrill, G., Leslie, B., Koster, A., Young, M. and Ismaila, A. (2012) 'Looking at engagement and outcome from the perspectives of child protection workers and parents', *Children and Youth Services Review*, 34(1): 112–118.

Gupta, A. and Blumhardt, H. (2016) 'Giving poverty a voice: Families' experiences of social work practice in a risk-averse child protection system', *Families, Relationships and Societies*, 5(1): 163–172.

Haight, W., Sugrue, E., Calhoun, M. and Black, J. (2017) '"Basically, I look at it like combat": Reflections on moral injury by parents involved with child protection services', *Children and Youth Services Review*, 82: 477–489.

Kempe, C.H., Silverman, F.N., Steele, B.F., Droegmueller, W. and Silver, H.K (1962) 'The battered-child syndrome', *JAMA*, 181(1): 17–24.

Lindsay, D. (1994) *The Welfare of Children*, New York: Oxford University Press.

Merkel-Holguin, L., Drury, I., Gibley-Reed, C., Lara, A., Jihad, M., Grint, K., et al (2022) 'Structures of oppression in the U.S. child welfare system: Reflections on administrative barriers to equity', *Societies*, 12(1): Article 26.

Parton, N. (2014) *The Politics of Child Protection: Contemporary Developments and Future Directions*, Basingstoke: Macmillan.

Pelton, L.H. (1998) 'Four commentaries: How we can better protect children from abuse and neglect', *The Future of Children*, 8(1): 126–129.

Pelton, L.H. (2016) 'Separating coercion from provision in child welfare: Preventive supports should be accessible without conditions attached', *Child Abuse and Neglect*, 51: 427–434.

Pryce, J. (2024) *Broken: Transforming Child Protective Services*, New York: HarperCollins.

Roberts, D. (2022) *Torn Apart: How the Child Welfare System Destroys Black Families – And How Abolition Can Build a Safer World*, Basic Books: New York.

Shalleck-Klein, D. (2023) 'The constitution prohibits unreasonable searches. Child welfare investigators routinely conduct them', *Center for New York City Affairs*. Available at: https://www.centernyc.org/urban-matters-2/the-constitution-prohibits-unreasonable-searches-child-welfare-investigators-routinely-conduct-them

Urban Matters (2021) 'Why a child welfare Miranda rights law is essential: A Q&A with advocate and organizer Joyce McMillan (2021, June 2)', *Center for New York City Affairs*. Available at: https://www.centernyc.org/urban-matters-2/2021/6/2/why-a-child-welfare-miranda-rights-law-is-essential-a-qampa-with-advocate-and-organizer-joyce-mcmillan

U.S. Department of Health and Human Services, Administration on Children, Youth and Families, Children's Bureau (2024) *Child Maltreatment 2022*. Available at: https://www.acf.hhs.gov/cb/data-research/child-maltreatment

Wald, M.S. (1975) 'State intervention on behalf of "neglected" children: A search for realistic standards', *Stanford Law Review*, 27: 985–1040.

PART II

Abolitionist thinking in practice: implications for social justice organising

8

Social work and social justice: the opportunity of an abolitionist lens

Ian Hyslop

Introduction

This chapter considers the relationship between abolition politics and the social work profession. When commitments to just practice within the confines of a structurally unjust order are examined, it is clear that social work is not the social justice project that it purports to be. Pleas for liberationist practice are far from new (Dominelli, 2004; Ferguson, 2008; Grey and Webb, 2013; Garrett, 2021a; Baines et al, 2022). However, this book aims to provide more than another aspirational call for emancipatory social work. I will argue that abolitionist ideas provide practical strategies for developing a theoretically coherent form of social justice practice. This involves thinking and acting outside the confines of liberal capitalism (Wright, 2010, 2019; Toraif and Muller, 2023) and will not produce social work as we know it, but it can deliver an alternate practice worth imagining and enacting.

In neoliberal times, social work is a growing profession, but it is more concerned with surveillance and containment than with troubling the matrix of power in contemporary Anglophone societies (Brockmann, 2024). This chapter will consider the consequences of Maylea's (2021) contention that liberationist social work is a pretense. I will argue that replacing the carceral elements of social work with services which directly serve the needs of oppressed people is not likely to radically change the power relationships which sit at the roots of structural inequality, unless there is a clear recognition of the longer struggle for political emancipation. It is important to name and understand the enemy, and this is where abolitionist analysis is particularly helpful, because it offers an escape from the perception that there is 'no outside' of liberal capitalist hegemony and the carceral state apparatus which governs its boundaries. It reminds us that visions and practices of social justice are possible.

Transformative change involves confronting what it is to be a 'profession' within a structurally oppressive order. Calls to radically reconfigure social work as a social justice profession pay insufficient attention to the embedded nature of oppressive structures: the economic and legal system which underpins liberal capitalism (Kelsey, 2022). Social work, or at least the dominant official professional corpus referred to by Brockmann (2024), is part of this system. Calls for radicalisation are highly problematic when the profession is regulated by the state and employees are constrained from subversive political activity by the master–servant employment relationship (Darroch, 2023). This is a reality which social work writers on the political left have been reluctant to recognise and confront.

The nature of oppression in Western liberal societies is inextricably tied to the capitalist social form. There are material and ideological cracks and contradictions in this edifice (Žižek, 2014), which social workers with critical and radical intent have attempted to exploit over time (Pease et al, 2016). Poverty is the common factor underpinning the problems faced by most social work service users and relative poverty is essential to capitalism (Althusser, 1977; Harvey, 2007). Inequality is a function of the exploitative relationship between capital and labour (Bryer, 1994; Callinicos, 2010). Beyond the social relations of capitalism, there are further structurally entwined forms of oppression; patriarchy, heteronormativity, white supremacy and coloniality. The question is whether a social work that is embedded in such systems can be a force for radical change?

This notion of intrinsic oppression is critical to understanding the abolitionist position. The institutions of liberal capitalist states serve an unjust set of social and economic arrangements. As such, they are fundamentally flawed as vehicles for social justice and must be abolished rather than reformed (Toraif and Mueller, 2023). This critique extends beyond the punitive functions served by the criminal justice system to include the 'carceral' roles of social work and the human services (Silver, 2024). The call to abolish child welfare in the United States applies the reasoning behind the historic rejection of chattel slavery to the racist contemporary processes and outcomes perpetuated by interconnected carceral institutions (Du Bois, 1935; Davis et al, 2022; Roberts, 2023). However, and critically, abolition practice involves more than engineering the collapse of the institutional arrangements which underpin oppression in contemporary society. It entails actively working towards building alternatives (Engler and Engler, 2021; Detlaff, 2023). The following discussion explores the challenges posed to emancipatory practice by examining the relationship between social work, radical social change and the political state, with specific attention to how abolitionist thinking might usefully inform active future resistance to structural inequality.

A conflicted profession

Social work professes to be concerned with the structures which enable or constrain the capacity for individual and collective well-being.

The much referenced International Federation of Social Workers (IFSW, 2014) definition of social work stresses a commitment to human rights and social justice, aligning the profession with the goal of liberation (Ballantyne, 2024). Recent scholarship has cast a shadow over this identity claim, sparking something of an existential crisis, rooted in a less idealised appraisal of contemporary and historic practice (Ioakimidis and Trimikliniotis, 2020). Social workers are embedded in a social, economic and political context in the same way that their 'clients' are. Accordingly, as Featherstone et al (2014: 35–36) have stressed, it is imperative for social work 'to abandon a belief in its essential innocence and to recognise its history under all sorts of highly problematic political regimes'.

Over time, social work has been directly and indirectly engaged with the persecution of marginalised groups (Ioakimidis and Trimikliniotis, 2020) and, even in its helping orientation, has been more concerned with managing the 'problem poor' than with radically changing oppressive structures (Ferguson, 2004; Flannagan, 2018; Hyslop, 2022). In recent decades, social work has become a more domesticated and measured undertaking, as managerial control has tightened (Rogowski, 2020). This taming of autonomy and dissent is consistent with the ascendancy of neoliberal politics. The breadth of social protections for increasingly racialised and precarious working-class communities have eroded as conceptions of the state as a counterweight to economically manufactured inequality have lost political traction (Garrett, 2018). The abolitionist discourse presents a powerful challenge to a profession that is already on the run, fundamentally questioning the function of social and human services in corporate capitalist societies. It also offers invigorating possibilities for social justice work.

Maylea's (2021) polemic call for the moribund profession of social work to be 'pushed into the sea' and Garrett's (2021b) counter-appeal for a re-energised 'dissenting social work', have provoked ongoing controversy (Whelan, 2022; Brockmann, 2024). Maylea (2021) asserts that the emancipatory rhetoric of professional social work bodies amount to little more than the mutterings of a paper tiger. Garrett (2021b) argues that the challenges which confront the social work profession are the result of a potent historical conjuncture: history is not at an end and hope for radical transformation is ongoing. This rhetorical 'end of social work' debate is framed by a range of conceptual and practical challenges, which this chapter sets out to unpick.

Social work has always been a contradictory undertaking and contemporary practice is subject to conflicted political tides (Garrett, 2021a). In the settler-colonial states, disillusionment with state-sponsored social work is not restricted to critics on the political right. It has been fuelled by a growing progressive recognition of the social damage inflicted in the name of 'welfare'. The experience of Indigenous peoples at the hands of the care system has been particularly destructive and unconscionable (Royal Commission of Inquiry into Historical Abuse in State Care and in the Care of Faith-Based Institutions, 2024).

Is the profession hopelessly tied to the governance regimes of liberal capitalist states in the Anglophone context? Alternatively, is there genuine scope for social work to be part of a radical reimagining of social life in these politically turbulent times? As Wallace and Pease (2011: 133) have argued, it is self-evident that mainstream social work is shaped by the political state – since 'social work is a continuous activity, conditioned and dependent upon the context from which it emerges and with which it engages (Harris, 2008, p. 662), changes in welfare regimes will shape the way in which social work is constituted and practiced'. It is clear that the relationship between social work and the state is the crux of the issue at hand.

Mapping the territory

The contradictions which trouble the identity of social work arise from the location of practice; between the state and the marginalised, entangled with the human consequences of economically generated social suffering (Hyslop, 2022). Even though social work is often complicit in redefining the fruits of structural oppression as individual failure, practitioners ingest a daily diet of inequality (Hyslop and Keddell, 2018). Macro-political injustice is mirrored in micro-engagement with people's lives: with the struggles of individuals and families drawn from the underclass poor (Preston, 2021). In this sense, social workers are continually afforded a view beyond the illusions of capitalist social relations. This insight is potentially troublesome to those who have an interest in the status quo and has informed dissenting threads of theory and practice since the radical socialist social work movement of the 1970s (Jones, 1983).

Regardless of this enduring engine of dissent, and equally persistent academic calls for social work to embrace a social justice mandate, social work generally remains a conservative profession intent on remoralising individuals and breaking cycles of deprivation within 'troubled families' (Brockmann, 2024). This is as evident in the contemporary neoliberal social investment policy context of Aotearoa (New Zealand) in the mid-2020s as it was in the receding British welfare state of the late 1970s (Hyslop, 2022). It is captured in Leonard's introduction to Ginsberg's (1979) book, *Class, Capital and Social Policy*: 'At another level, the failure of crude models of individual pathology has led to the invention of an apparently more sophisticated response – the idea of "transmitted deprivation"' (Leonard, in Ginsberg, 1979: ix). Such quasi-eugenic policy orientations screen out structural deprivation. The reality is that social work is too 'close' to the political regime/s of the state to be a consistent force for social justice. Abolitionist critique exposes this dilemma, challenges us to move past it, and offers some tools with which to fashion alternatives.

Welfare politics

At best, social work has functioned historically as part of a social safety net: what Bourdieu (2005) has termed the 'left hand' of the state. At worst, it has been directly involved in the oppression of dehumanised sections of the population (Ioakimidis and Trimikliniotis, 2020). Liberal capitalist states, despite their curated illusions of procedural equality, routinely perform carceral functions in relation to threatening groups (Žižek, 2014). The 19th-century origins of social work are directedly connected to managing the 'underserving' poor (Ferguson, 2004; Parton, 2014a). Arguably, the 'golden age' of social work flowered as a personal social service supplementing the provision of health, education, public housing and income support within the postwar welfare states (Parton, 2014b). The relative autonomy of social workers permitted some engagement with the causes of social disadvantage; or at least the capacity to provide direct assistance to families pushed to the margins by capitalist economics. In Scotland, for example, Brodie et al (2008) describe a unified profession with strategic political influence and an agenda to develop a more equal society. The distribution of funds to striking mine workers is provided as one instance of an explicit alliance with the working class.

My own experience of state social work in Aotearoa in the early 1980s involved routinely dispensing non-recoverable special needs grants to families experiencing financial stress, including support for individuals engaged in industrial action. This sort of unconditional material help can be contrasted with the provision of assistance to surveilled families judged to be in need of services designed to change behaviours. In the mid-1980s, mainstream social workers stood up to the state and influenced the course of social policy development in Aotearoa, when opposition to structural racism first came to dominate professional consciousness (Hyslop, 2022). The capacity to provide material support or to bite the hand that feeds has increasingly narrowed since the neoliberal turn of the late 1980s. Garrett (2018), following Harvey (2005), contrasts the neoliberalism of recent decades with the 'embedded liberalism' of the welfare state. Although the state ultimately functions in the service of capitalism, it is a site of potential contestation between antagonistic class interests (Ginsberg, 1979). However, the ability of the working class to gain concessions from the state has reduced dramatically over 40 years of neoliberal ascendancy. Similarly, privatisation of social services and associated mechanisms of production efficiency, audit and control in the public sector have severely curtailed the social justice agenda of social work, beyond rhetorical commitments (Darroch, 2023).

It is also important to understand that the postwar compromise between the interests of capital and labour was always a reformist political project as opposed to a revolutionary disruption of power relations in class societies. State social work offered a range of support services to a wide group of recipients but it did not have the capacity to significantly disrupt the legal and ideological foundations of the liberal capitalist system, such as individual ownership of private property or the operation of labour markets. Looking back at contested historical processes of political change, Kelsey perceives that systemic reform is possible within proscribed limits: 'The push and pull of these contradictory forces leads to shifts over time, as we have seen in Aotearoa for almost two centuries. Yet, reforms to the colonial state's law have always been adaptations to social and power relations that are defined by western capitalism, colonialism and patriarchy' (Kelsey, 2022: np). Arguably, the conceptual boundaries of Western knowledge and ways of being are as, if not more, far-reaching than the foundational settings of capitalist property relations. In colonial states they are intertwined.

Epistemic justice

Beyond the Marxist critique, abolitionist thinkers focus on intersecting harms situated within entrenched relations of power; patriarchy, heteronormativity and Eurocentricity (Kim, 2020). The furore following the police killing of George Floyd and the associated Black Lives Matter movement coalesces with the legacy of slavery, racial capitalism and the prison-industrial complex. In turn, calls to dismantle the reach of the child welfare system locate 'family policing' within a deep web of white racism (Davis et al, 2022).

The issue of coloniality is critical to understanding the role of social work in the settler states of Aotearoa, Australia, Canada and the United States, although in the latter the logic of elimination – the drive to erase Indigenous peoples – has meant that they are often written out of orthodox histories, even histories of racial oppression (Jacobs, 2018). Dimou (2021) argues that the carceral functions of state institutions emerge from the living legacy of coloniality. It is contended that coloniality underpins the history of modernity and is enabled by Enlightenment reason: an 'episteme', or universal structuring template, that determines the boundaries within which the world can be understood. This refers to the separation of the knowing human subject from 'other' objects observed in the natural world: the Cartesian dualism associated with Descartes (Hyslop, 2012). Human subjects were, and are, classified into hierarchical categories related to race, gender and sexuality. This mechanism is said to enable (and conceal) the negation of 'the other' that is implicit in colonisation. Dimou (2021) argues that the history of genocidal colonial conquest, beginning from the 1400s with the Portuguese and Spanish Empires, was a precursor to the modernist schema of development. Colonialism involves the imposition of Western knowing and has required the erasure of other ways of being and knowing: what Dimou, following de Sousa Santos, refers to as 'epistemicide'. Dimou argues that this global legacy persists as a violent matrix of power which normalises interconnected domains of oppression: knowledge, the economy, subjectivities and authority (see Cleaver, Chapter 10, this volume, for Aotearoa context).

Insight into the economic relations and epistemic structures of power which support contemporary systems of oppression is not necessarily an empowering analysis for social workers when social work is largely controlled by the neoliberal state. However, it does provide insight into what might need to be done in order for social justice practice to be realised; a lens through which to analyse and expand the horizon of possible resistance/s to both capitalism and coloniality. I would argue that to be 'against capitalism' in Aotearoa, or anywhere, is also to be 'against coloniality', given the intersection between class and settler colonial power (Ballantyne, 2024; Silver, 2024).

Child welfare in Aotearoa

The intersection of race and class-based oppression is evidenced in the operation of the statutory social work system over time. The following discussion focuses on the history of child welfare/child protection social work in Aotearoa as an example of the connections between social work and carcerality. This leads to a consideration of future possibilities for social justice practice. In Aotearoa there is a concerted push to decolonise child protection practice, with services (resources and authority) devolved to community and Iwi-based (tribal) organisations (Fitzmaurice-Brown, 2023). Both abolition politics and decolonisation demand radical structural change to the way that authority is situated and exercised in child and family welfare. Efforts to reform statutory social work also provide some telling indications of the degree of change which is 'permissible' within the constitutive boundaries of liberal capitalist governance.

The recent report of the Royal Commission of Inquiry into Historical Abuse in State Care and in the Care of Faith-Based Institutions (2024) catalogues a litany of institutional abuse aimed at punishment and domestication; ultimately a process of violent assimilation. As in comparable colonial states, the percentage of Indigenous children placed in residential institutions during the postwar decades was radically disproportionate to the general population and this imbalance bled into the prison system; a classed and racialised care to prison pipeline:

> After experiencing the extreme rates of State custody of children during the 1970s and up to 1984, in general, this particular cohort

of children grew into the 20–29 year-olds of the 1980s and then the 30–39 year olds of the 1990s. The aging of this birth cohort has been the most significant trigger for rises in the age-specific incidence of imprisonment of Māori men and women, for three decades now. (Cook, 2020: 34)

The historical and contemporary accommodation between the Crown and Māori in Aotearoa is characterised by shifting dynamics of conflict, compromise and resistance (Walker, 2004). Within this relationship there is a fundamental, persistent and generative disconnect between the liberal foundations of postcolonial politics and the communal social fabric of the Māori world (Poata-Smith, 2002; Cleaver, Chapter 10, this volume). The unresolved struggle for justice within the settler-colonial milieu has lent a unique trajectory to state social work reform. In Aotearoa the issue of Indigenous sovereignty is crucial to debates around the future shape of child protection (Cleaver, 2023), as is the question of community devolution and service development.

The role of the state in all of this is ideologically disputed across the established right to centre-left political spectrum (Hyslop, 2022). Although progressive possibilities exist, there are also serious threats posed by the current dominance of hard-right political ideology: the prospect of community-centred solutions amounting to political shorthand for the withdrawal of services, and for tribal empowerment to equate to little more than responsibilisation (Keddell, Chapter 17, this volume). The politics of child welfare is also subject to intense media scrutiny and policy shifts have been volatile for the past decade (Keddell et al, 2022). Tipping points are reached, performative public inquiries are held, legislation is enacted and organisational reform is undertaken, only to be amended or reversed by incoming governments within a three-year political cycle. There is an intensely disputed band of ideological terrain which disguises deeper systemic resistance to policy change that significantly challenges the foundations of power in the colonial capitalist state. The following two examples illustrate this restricted horizon of possibility.

The game-changing 'Puao te Ata Tu (day break) report of the Ministerial Advisory Committee on a Māori Perspective for the Department of Social Welfare' (Ministerial Advisory Committee, 1988) recommended that the state attack racism and deprivation. The Report was endorsed and implemented to a degree by the then Department of Social Welfare rather than adopted across the whole of government. Arguably the most potentially far-reaching recommendation of this report was the establishment of 'Executive Committees', providing direct Māori and other community stakeholder oversight of state social welfare institutions. In abolitionist terms it was a non-reformist reform (Engler and Engler, 2021): 'It was a move towards direct democracy, community accountability and partnership. This soon came to be seen as an inconvenient commitment and was quietly disappeared' (Hyslop, 2022: 94).

A more recent example involved the backlash precipitated by media coverage of the attempted 'uplift' of a newborn baby from a Māori mother in the central North Island city of Hastings in May 2019 (Cleaver, Chapter 10, this volume). This incident exposed the tip of an iceberg of racist practice, and provoked what Keddell et al (2022) describe as a 'fight for legitimacy', where the power of the child protection system was fundamentally challenged. A raft of inquiries were commissioned and an urgent appeal was made to the Waitangi Tribunal (a standing legal entity which makes recommendations regarding harms which may flow from Crown breaches of the 1840 te Tiriti o Waitangi). Two subsequent reports – one produced by a group of Māori leaders assembled under the banner of a pan Māori state-mandated authority, and another produced in two parts by the Office of the Commissioner for Children – recommended radical change to the child protection system.

In the case of the latter report, a process of Māori-driven transformation, 'where Māori lead the transition from a system dominated by state intervention to approaches where whānau, hapū and iwi are the decision makers in all areas relating to the wellbeing of pēpi [babies]', was recommended (Office of the Commissioner for Children, 2020: 108). Similarly, the Waitangi Tribunal called for a transitional authority 'with a clear mandate to design and reform the care and protection system for tamariki Māori, coupled with authority to work in genuine partnership with the Crown to ensure a modified system is properly inplemented' (Wai 2915, 2021: iv)

These recommendations were produced by the watchdog arms of the liberal state; what Althusser (1977) classifies as Ideological State Apparatus. They facilitated a process of 'blood-letting', but the recommended (by Māori for Māori, with the state) transition to Māori authority was not acted upon. Instead, a Māori advisory group was installed, a variety of conceptual practice-focused changes were undertaken and limited service delegation to specific tribal or pan-Māori organisations was stepped up. Much of this work is now threatened, or is being politically redefined, by a populist right-wing coalition government with tightening purse strings and an aversion to autonomous Māori authority.

Redefining reality and possibility

To this point, the discussion has explored a range of key issues. The notion that social work is a moral profession driven by a set of values that places it beyond the machinations of power has been thoroughly debunked in recent times (Ferguson et al, 2018). This illusion obscures the carceral dimensions of modern social work (Silver, 2024). As Maylea (2021) asserts, there are also definitional difficulties when the social justice identity claim of social work is dispersed across such a broad field. Some pockets of practice may be directly concerned with defending human rights and social workers inevitably engage with the lives of people impacted by structural inequality. However, this does not mean that the broader entity known as social work is a social justice profession. Social work is no less politically enmeshed than any other activity. The classification of social work as purely a force for control rather than emancipation is also a potentially misleading simplification. Social work, or at least the insights that social work affords, can be adapted to the cause of social transformation: a different form of social justice work is possible but it 'appears' largely unthinkable or impractical. Abolition challenges this perception.

Žižek (2014) asserts that the illusions which the rubric of liberal politics conspire to maintain are always fragile. The principles of human rights and due process, for example, function to mystify the exploitative foundations of capitalist political economy. The fact that such niceties are routinely backgrounded when they conflict with the logic of commodification, exploitation and profit is what Žižek has termed the 'dirty water' of capitalism. Social work is a fraught occupation because it has a clearer view of these contradictions than other professional service groupings, by virtue of its location between the liberal state and the para-proletariat: those on the precarious edges of the working class (Jones, 1983). The problem is that social workers are not mandated, and effectively are not permitted, to act on this insight. An analysis of the functioning of the liberal capitalist state means that this conclusion is unsurprising. It is also clear that the regulation and control of social work has tightened in recent decades.

In the Anglophone context, the narrative is familiar. The demise of social work as a resistant voice engaged with the interests of the disenfranchised working class is linked with the retraction of the postwar welfare state and the rise of neoliberal administrations preoccupied with the efficient management of problem populations (Rogowski, 2020). As Parton (2014a) has evidenced in England, state-sponsored social work has increasingly metamorphosised into 'muscular' child protection, while generic social services are contracted to private or quasi-private providers and funded, measured and monitored from a distance. I have also argued that the liberal capitalist colonial state is only prepared to tolerate reform within specific ideological parameters. This can be an empowering realisation and is where abolitionism can provide a valuable tool for analysis and action. The system can be disrupted and changed but compromise towards capitalism with a human face is inadequate.

Brockmann (2024) problematises the notion of capitalist 'realism', pointing out that the limits of the possible are perennially defined by the powerful and that to accept such limits is to reinforce the status quo: a rubric inscribed within the boundaries of liberal colonial carcerality (Silver, 2024). In the case of state social work, for example, this inertia of the imagination generates an inability to consider how a child and family welfare system could be built outside of the official 'notify, investigate, assess and intervene' child protection template. Beyond directly intrusive child abuse related practice, child and family social work can be seen to operate as a boundary rider for the colonial carceral liberal project; as exemplified by the preventative supervision/supportive service 'case-work' I engaged with as a state social worker in the early 1980s; surveilling and managing high needs families (whānau). This sort of work continues today in contracted programmes delivered by non-governmental organisation providers; within what is termed the non-profit industrial complex.

This is not a state of affairs that has fallen from the sky. The dominant socioeconomic system and the logic which sustains it is not something that merely 'exists' as a finite realty; it is something that has been made and can therefore be unmade. Ballantyne's (2024) exposition of the anti-capitalist emancipatory social science thinking of Eric Olin Wright (2010, 2019) is very useful in terms of the practical reimagining that is required. Wright (2010) developed a clear analysis of ways and means to challenge and change the hegemony of capitalism in the here and now. There are significant synergies between Wright's methodology and abolitionist thinking; that the future is shaped by our visions 'in the now', and that systems which are inherently harmful should be rejected and replaced. Wright takes a painstakingly logical approach which succeeds in disarming the conviction that nothing can be done. His prescription involves identifying harms, formulating alternatives and taking practical steps towards achieving these. In common with abolitionism, it is recognised that progress may be incremental. The key departure from a reformist agenda is the end goal: that changes must work towards dismantling and replacing carceral systems as opposed to reinforcing or legitimating them.

There are systemic, ideological and practical challenges, but we should not be prepared to accept that social justice workers must be relegated to the current designation of social workers who function as 'trauma cleaners for the system of colonial carceralism' (Silver, 2024: 26). If we are genuinely interested in the pursuit of social justice, social workers and the associations which represent them need to reconceptualise what work can be done to shift the coordinates of an unjust system: abolitionist thinking provides an intellectual tool for this practical struggle in the real world of systemic inequality. If it is accepted that liberal capitalism is an exploitative and unjust system, it becomes necessary to explore the means by which this form of social and economic relations can be fundamentally changed. A reimagining of collective social justice work is required. To do otherwise is to deny the possibility of human freedom and be complicit in the oppression of others and of ourselves.

References

Althusser, L. (1977) *Lenin and Philosophy, and Other Essays* (2nd edn), London: New Left Books.

Baines, D., Clark, N. and Bennett, B. (eds) (2022) *Doing Anti-Oppressive Social Work: Rethinking Theory and Practice* (4th edn), Halifax and Winnipeg: Fernwood Publishing.

Ballantyne, N. (2024) 'Emancipatory social science and anti-oppressive social work: The legacy of Eric Olin Wright', *Aotearoa New Zealand Social Work*, 36(4): 31–45.

Bourdieu, P. (2005) *The Social Structures of the Economy*, Cambridge: Polity Press.

Bryer, R. (1994) 'Why Marx's labour theory is superior to the marginalist theory of value: The case from modern financial reporting', *Critical Perspectives on Accounting*, 5: 313–340.

Brockmann, O. (2024) 'Imagining the end of official social work: Thinking beyond the possible and probable', *British Journal of Social Work*, 54: 2862–2879.

Brodie, I., Nottingham, C. and Plunkett, S. (2008) 'A tale of two reports: Social work in Scotland from social work in the community (1966) to changing lives (2000)', *British Journal of Social Work*, 38(4): 697–715.

Callinicos, A. (2010) *Bonfire of Illusions: The Twin Crises of the Liberal World*, Cambridge: Polity Press.

Cleaver, K. (2023) 'He whare takata: Wāhine Māori reproductive justice in the child protection system', *Aotearoa New Zealand Social Work*, 35(4): 16–30.

Cook, L. (2020) 'A statistical window for the youth justice system: Putting a spotlight on the state custody of generations of Māori', Brief of evidence WAI 2915. Available at: https://forms.justice.govt.nz/search/Documents/WT/wt_DOC_161895442/Wai%202915%2C%20A040(a).pdf

Darroch, J. (2023) 'Political activity and statutory social work in Aotearoa New Zealand: Irreconcilable obligations', PhD thesis, University of Auckland, New Zealand. Available at: https://researchspace.auckland.ac.nz/handle/2292/65498

Davis, A.Y., Dent, G., Meiners, E.R. and Richie, B.E. (2022) *Abolition. Feminism. Now.*, London: Hamish Hamilton.

Detlaff, A. (2023) *Confronting the Racist Legacy of the American Child Welfare System: The Case for Abolition*, New York: Oxford University Press.

Dimou, E. (2021) 'Decolonizing southern criminology: What can the "decolonial option" tell us about challenging the modern / colonial foundations of criminology?', *Critical Criminology*, 29: 431–456.

Dominelli, L. (2004) *Social Work Theory and Practice for a Changing Profession*, Cambridge: Polity Press.

Du Bois, W. (1935) *Black Reconstruction – An Essay Toward a History of the Part which Black Folk Played in the Attempt to Reconstruct Democracy in America, 1860–1880*, New York: Harcourt, Brace and Company.

Engler, M. and Engler, P. (2021) 'Andres Gorz's non-reformist reforms show how we can transform the world today', *Jacobin*, July. Available at: https://jacobin.com/2021/07/andre-gorz-non-reformist-reforms-revolution-political-theory

Featherstone, B., White, S. and Morris, K. (2014) *Reimagining Child Protection: Towards Humane Social Work with Families*, Bristol: Policy Press.

Ferguson, H. (2004) *Protecting Children in Time: Child Abuse, Child Protection and the Consequences of Modernity*, Basingstoke: Palgrave Macmillan.

Ferguson, I. (2008) *Reclaiming Social Work: Challenging Neoliberalism and Practicing Social Justice*, London: SAGE.

Ferguson, I., Ioakimidis, V. and Lavalette, M. (2018) *Global Social Work in a Political Context: Radical Perspectives*, Bristol: Policy Press.

Fitzmaurice-Brown, L. (2023) 'Te rito o te harakeke: Decolonising child protection law in Aotearoa New Zealand', *Victoria University of Wellington Law Review*, 53(4): 507–532.

Flannagan, K. (2018) '"Problem families" in public housing: Discourse, commentary and (dis)order', *Housing Studies*, 33(5): 684–707.

Garrett, P.M. (2018) 'What are we talking about when we talk about "neoliberalism?"', *European Journal of Social Work*, 22(1): 1–13.

Garrett, P.M. (2021a) *Dissenting Social Work: Critical Theory, Resistance and Pandemic*, London: Routledge.

Garrett, P.M. (2021b) '"A world to win": In defence of (dissenting) social work – a response to Chris Maylea', *British Journal of Social Work*, 51(4): 1131–1149.

Ginsberg, N. (1979) *Class, Capital, and Social Policy*, Basingstoke: Macmillan.

Grey, M. and Webb, S. (eds) (2013) *The New Politics of Social Work*, Basingstoke: Palgrave Macmillan.

Harvey, D. (2005) *A Brief History of Neoliberalism*, New York: Oxford University Press.

Hyslop, I. (2012) 'Social work as a practice of freedom', *Journal of Social Work*, 12(4): 404–422.

Hyslop, I. (2022) *A Political History of Child Protection: Lessons for Reform from Aotearoa New Zealand*, Bristol: Policy Press.

Hyslop, I. and Keddell, E. (2018) 'Outing the elephants: Exploring a new paradigm for child protection social work', *Social Science*, 7(7): Article 105.

IFSW (International Federation of Social Workers) (2014) 'Global definition of social work'. Available at: https://www.ifsw.org/what-is-social-work/global-definition-of-social-work/

Ioakimidis, V. and Trimikliniotis, N. (2020) 'Making sense of social work's troubled past: Professional identity, collective memory and the quest for historical justice', *British Journal of Social Work*, 50(6): 1890–1908.

Jacobs, M. (2018) 'Seeing like a settler colonial state', *Modern American History*, 1(2): 257–270.

Jones, C. (1983) *State Social Work and the Working Class*, Basingstoke: Macmillan.

Keddell, E., Fitzmaurice, L., Cleaver, K. and Exeter, D. (2022) 'A fight for legitimacy: Reflections on child protection reform, the reduction of baby removals, and child protection decision-making in Aotearoa New Zealand', *Kōtuitui: New Zealand Journal of Social Sciences Online*, 17(3): 378–404.

Kelsey, J. (2022) 'Truth to power – the critical legal academic as livensed subversive', Valedictory Address, np. Available at: https://e-tangata.co.nz/reflections/jane-kelsey-truth-to-power-the-critical-legal-academic-as-licensed-subversive/

Kim, M. (2020) 'Anti-carceral feminism: The contradictions of progress and the possibilities of counter-hegemonic struggle', *Affilia*, 35(3): 309–326.

Maylea, C. (2021) 'The end of social work', *British Journal of Social Work*, 51(2): 772–789.

Ministerial Advisory Committee (1988) 'Puao te Ata Tu (day break): The report of the Ministerial Advisory Committee on a Maori Perspective for the Department of Social Welfare', Wellington. Available at: https://www.msd.govt.nz/documents/about-msd-and-our-work/publications-resources/archive/1988-puaoteatatu.pdf

Office of the Commissioner for Children (2020) 'Te Kuku O Te Manawa – Moe ararā! Haumanutia ngā tūpuna mō te oranga ngā tamariki' (Part 2). Available from: https://www.manamokopuna.org.nz/publications/reports/tktm-report-2/

Parton, N. (2014a) *The Politics of Child Protection: Contemporary Developments and Future Directions*, Basingstoke: Macmillan.

Parton, N. (2014b) 'Child protection and politics: Some critical and constructive reflections', *British Journal of Social Work*, 44(7): 2042–2056.

Pease, B., Goldingay, S., Hosken, N. and Nipperess, S. (eds) (2016) *Doing Critical Social Work: Transformative Practices for Social Justice*, Sydney: Allen and Unwin.

Poata-Smith, E.S. (2002) 'The political economy of Māori protest politics, 1968–1995: A Marxist analysis of the roots of Māori oppression and the politics of resistance', PhD thesis, University of Otago. Available via interloan at: https://ourarchive.otago.ac.nz/esploro/outputs/doctoral/The-political-economy-of-M%C4%81ori-protest/9926478585301891

Preston, S.A. (2021) 'Abolitionist disjuncture: Reducing police violence in frontline social work', *Intersectionalities: A Global Journal of Social Work Analysis, Research, Policy, and Practice*, 9(1): 142–153.

Roberts, D. (2023) *Torn Apart: How the Child Welfare System Destroys Black Families – And How Abolition Can Build a Safer World*, New York: Basic Books.

Rogowski, S. (2020) *Social Work: The Rise and Fall of a Profession*, Bristol: Policy Press.

Royal Commission of Inquiry into Historical Abuse in State Care and in the Care of Faith-Based Institutions (2024) 'Whanaketia: Through pain and trauma, from darkness to light', Final Report. Available at: https://www.abuseincare.org.nz/reports/whanaketia/

Silver, E. (2024) 'The possibilities and dissonances of abolitionist social work', *Aotearoa New Zealand Social Work*, 36(4): 19–30.

Toraif, N. and Mueller, J.C. (2023) 'Abolitionist social work', in *Encyclopaedia of Social Work*, New York: Oxford University Press. Available at: https://oxfordre.com/socialwork/display/10.1093/acrefore/9780199975839.001.0001/acrefore-9780199975839-e-1553

Wai 2915 (2021) 'Report of the Waitangi Tribunal – He Pārakeke, He Rito Whakakīkanga Whāruarua'. Available at: https://natlib.govt.nz/records/45969211

Walker, R. (2004) *Ka Whawhai Tonu Mātou – Struggle Without End* (rev edn), Auckland: Penguin.

Wallace, J. and Pease, B. (2011) 'Neoliberalism and Australian social work: Accommodation or resistance?', *Journal of Social Work*, 11(2): 132–142.

Whelan, J. (2022) 'On your Marx …? A world to win or the dismantlement of a profession? On why we need a reckoning', *British Journal of Social Work*, 52(2): 1168–1181.

Wright, E.O. (2010) *Envisioning Real Utopias*, London: Verso.

Wright, E.O. (2019) *How to be an Anticapitalist in the Twenty-First Century*, London: Verso.

Žižek, S. (2014) *From the End of History to the End of Capitalism: Trouble in Paradise*, London: Routledge.

9

Indigenous child protection in Canada: the insanity of doing it the same way

Peter Choate

Introduction

The notion of doing 'social good' dates to the English poor laws in the 16th century and the notion of deserving and undeserving poor. The 19th-century poor houses had missions to service poor industrial workers. They were inspiration for Jane Addams and Ellen Gates Starr to open Hull House in Chicago and begin the settlement houses in the United States. Addams argued for children's rights such as an education rather than having to work to support families. She felt child labour needed to be eradicated (Addams, 1905). Thus, the argument to protect children. In Canada, social work began with home visitors whose mission was to help vulnerable people, spread hope and advocate for social justice (CASW, nd). Clarke and Yellow Bird (2021) observe that such social programmes have been, and are, connected to race and settler-colonialism. The profession of social work continues to be operated through notions of expertise, embodying professional imperialism. In essence, what is the standard against which social work is to be done? What constitutes moral right? Who makes the decisions? Typically, these questions are answered in white, middle-class, Eurocentric views of family.

Child protection (CP) has evolved to be about the power of the state to answer these very questions in the lives of families. It is a power wielded with the noble goal of protecting children from caregiver harm, such as physical and sexual abuse. The scope is typically broad and includes neglect, which is often related to lack of access to social determinants of health (SDH). This is not wilful neglect, but rather the inability to meet housing, physical and basic needs. CP is seen as the answer, as opposed to the state providing SDH.

Thus, the conversation begins with the question of worthy versus unworthy. This connects with assessing good enough parenting and the ability to meet the needs of the child from a Eurocentric perspective, including access to SDH (Choate and Engstrom, 2014). Yet, if Eurocentric society is not prepared to offer the SDH, then removal of children into care becomes the answer. For the family, this becomes an unwinnable circle as they lack access to SDH and thus are not good enough but likely could be if they had SDH. For social work, the inevitable use of power to determine the worthy and the unworthy is intricately linked to the profession and the role of CP, which is not typically empowered to solve the SDH needs (Choate, 2024). In this way CP social workers are enmeshed with discriminatory practice.

Canadian context

In 1891, the first children's aid society was established in Toronto and the first related legislation passed in 1893. The focus on early CP was around poverty and the shelter needs of children. Indigenous peoples were not included in these initiatives (Jennissen and Lundy, 2011). The Constitution Act of 1867 granted legislative jurisdiction to the federal parliament over Indians (the term in use at the time) and lands reserved for Indians. In 1950, the Canadian Association of Social Workers pressed for changes to the Indian Act (1951) as part of a call for the full assimilation of 'Indians' into Canadian society, which is something they have now set out an apology for (CASW, 2019). They also argued that Indigenous children were entitled to the same education that all other Canadian children could access as well as access to all types of social services (Jennissen and Lundy, 2011). In 1951, the Indian Act was amended to give the provinces child welfare jurisdiction on reserves. According to Wilkins (2000), the amendments simply led to the growing presence of CP services on reserve and in the lives of Indigenous peoples. The transition to provincial authority following the 1951 amendments was not smooth. The 1967 Hawthorne Report noted: 'The assumption that Indians were "wards" of the federal government, and that the reserves were federal islands in the midst of provincial territory has had the unfortunate effect that basic provincial welfare activities have ignored and bypasses Indians' (Hawthorne, 1967: 316).

Children removed from family 'on reserve' were not taken for reasons associated with safety but rather for reasons associated with cultural perceptions. As the Truth and Reconciliation Commission (TRC, 2015) documented, child protection became the ongoing agency of assimilation. Had CP authorities of the day understood Indigenous cultural parenting practices, then they would have known the children were not at risk. Rather, the authorities began the long-standing and current practice of imposing Eurocentric parenting and family practices as the required standard (Lindstrom and Choate, 2016; Roxburgh and Sinclair, 2024).

As the provinces took over CP, there was a gradual growth in the number of Indigenous children brought into care. At the time of Hawthorne's 1967 report, the percentage of Indigenous children in CP services care in the four Western provinces, where representation has been historically high, was 39 per cent in British Columbia, 40 per cent in Alberta, 50 per cent in Saskatchewan and 60 per cent in Manitoba. In the 1976–1977 fiscal year it was estimated that just over 19 per cent of all children in care across the country were Indigenous (Hepworth, 1980).

Over-representation grew. The 2021 census data reports that 53.8 per cent of children in care aged 14 years and younger in Canada are Indigenous, yet they represent only 7.7 per cent of the population (Canada, 2023). Looking again at the four western provinces, for all Indigenous children in care, in Manitoba the rate is 91 per cent (Manitoba, 2024), in Saskatchewan 86 per cent (Saskatchewan, 2024), Alberta 76 per cent (Alberta, 2024) and British Columbia 68 per cent (British Columbia, 2024). Quinn et al (2022) observe over-representation in Ontario also continues and Hélie et al (2022) show this also in Québec. Statistics Canada (2016) confirms that this is a national issue. In other words, in the 48-year span between Hawthorne and today, the rates of Indigenous children in care have grown significantly.

If we look more carefully at Alberta, for example, we see that the over-representation is long-standing and not subject to improvement. In other words, these high rates are not abnormal but have rather become standard. In Alberta, the period 2013 to 2024 has seen the rate of Indigenous children in care go from 69 per cent to 77 per cent, despite Indigenous children making up about 10 per cent of the population (Alberta, 2024).

In current research underway, I and colleagues note that these high rates occur despite multiple reports identifying the nature of the problem and the need for change. Recent examples of reports include the Missing and Murdered Indigenous Women and Girls Report (MMIWG, 2019), Truth and Reconciliation Commission (TRC, 2015) and the Royal Commission on Aboriginal Peoples (RCAP, 1996). In Alberta, since 1987, there have been 23 documents and reports highlighting the concerns with Indigenous children receiving services from child protection services along with child advocate reports and fatality inquiries. The problem is known.

Following the 1951 amendments to the Indian Act, services were gradually provided to Indigenous peoples on reserves, but it was under a funding formula supported by the federal government. In 1991, the federal government lifted a moratorium allowing Indigenous nations to operate their own delegated services in accordance with the relevant provincial or territorial legislation. Funding was provided by Canada under a formula known as Directive 20-1 (Canada, 2005) but it was heavily weighted to child removal as opposed to family preservation, thus underfunding prevention work.

As a result of the ongoing funding and service deficiencies, '[o]n February 23, 2007, the First Nations Child and Family Caring Society (FNCFCS) and the Assembly of First Nations filed a human rights complaint at the Canadian Human Rights Commission alleging that the Government of

Canada is providing less child welfare funding to First Nations children' (FNCFCS, 2024). There have been over 40 decisions by the Canadian Human Rights Tribunal (CHRT) since the complaint was filed in 2007, and yet the problem might best be described as still acutely discriminatory and unresolved. The case has been focused on child protection, health and education being funded and delivered in an ongoing discriminatory fashion. Dr Cindy Blackstock, Executive Director of FNCFS, reports that the issues remain unresolved (personal communication, 6 June 2024).

The intergenerational legacy

The intrusion of Canada into the familial lives of Indigenous peoples has a long legacy that includes the establishment of the Indian Residential Schools (IRS) in 1831 in New France, although the term typically refers to the larger scale, assimilative efforts from 1880–1997. Estimates are that 150,000 Indigenous children were removed from their communities into these schools whose goal was not education but assimilation. The schools were largely run by Christian churches whose objective was bridging the children into Christian European ways of life while also alienating them from their family, culture, and spiritual traditions. Abuse was common (TRC, 2015). Attending became mandatory under the *Indian Act*. Children could be, and were, forcibly removed from family and community. This was a continuation of missionary goals that go as far back as the 1600's, believing that the best ways of life were drawn from European family values (RCAP, 1996; TRC, 2015). In addition to the IRS, there were 699 Indian Day Schools in operation from 1880 to 2009 (Lacombe and Pind, 2023). With the phasing out of the schools, Dr Cindy Blackstock has argued that child welfare became the new residential schools (Blackstock, 2007).

Naiomi Metallic, an Indigenous lawyer, stated on 5 December 2022, at the Supreme Court of Canada (SCC) hearings into a constitutional challenge of 'An Act respecting First Nations, Inuit and Métis children, youth and families, 2019': 'It was only in the mid 1960s that Canada succeeded in persuading provinces to extend their child welfare laws on reserves but only on the condition of being fully reimbursed.' She went on to state that 'Dr. Cindy Blackstock ... has noted that negotiating payment for specific services, however, remained highly problematic as that required consent from federal officials v provincial if the child was living on nation' (oral evidence, SCC, 12 December 2022).

As the IRS were phased out, a new period emerged that became known as the '60's Scoop'. This is a time when about 20,000 Indigenous children were taken from their families. When children were taken, they were 'gone' (see following quote). Most were adopted, across Canada but also overseas, and now traced to some 33 countries (RCAP, 1996; TRC, 2015; Rosano, 2017).

> My aunties raised us that if we didn't behave ourselves, she would say the white man will come and take you away, and it was a real-life boogie man because it would happen. So, people would make the drive up from Dauphin into the bush, and all we knew was that if the social workers came you disappeared off the face of the earth and you were never seen again. (Quoted in Choate et al, 2022)

By the late 1970s over 15,000 Indigenous children were apprehended with the vast majority removed from culture, family, land and identity (see following quote) (Hepworth, 1980). Social workers have long been complicit in this work as it was, and is, they who have been acting as the agents of society apprehending and removing Indigenous children (Jennissen and Lundy, 2011; Choate et al, 2021).

> One of my aunts who I didn't know at all, whatsoever, was walking through the friendship centre, looked up and saw my picture and saw my name, Desi, and she just freaked out because – and she realised that I was the lost son. I am the lost son who was taken away in the '70s from the family, and they had been wondering whatever happened to us. (Quote from a 60's Scoop survivor, Desi Lindstrom, used with permission)

Following this period, what became known as the Millennium Scoop has continued the over-apprehension of Indigenous children (RCAP, 1996; TRC, 2015; Foster, 2018). Eurocentric standards of parenting have been the ongoing measure of good parenting but this approach is wrong (Choate et al, 2019) and it is continuing. The number of Indigenous children in care today may be the highest in Canadian history and higher than the number taken in the IRS and 60's Scoop combined (Foster, 2018). The impacts of these multigenerational losses accumulate on the nations and in the communities as well as for the children who were 'gone'. The harm of these removals crosses generations into the present day (see previous quotes and the following quote). One might say that the system is performing exactly as designed, even though it is creating harm.

> But at the same time, it wasn't like I was totally disconnected from my family because I would still go on visits with them. But at that time, it was like when I was in the home I would try to fit in and belong instead of trying to be different and like an outsider and this, I don't know. I would try to belong in that family, so it's kind of like I was wearing a mask at home, but when I would go and visit with my biological family with my mom or my dad or my grandparents it was kind of like I would take that mask off and I'm back to where

I started, what I'm familiar with, back to the same food that I used to eat. I would feel comfort. I would feel love. I would get hugs. I would be told that I was loved. (Quote from a Millennium Scoop child in care, Brandy CrazyBull, used with permission)

The judicial systems reinforce the impacts of colonialism and intergenerational trauma. Perhaps one of the most famous illustrations arose from the SCC decision *Racine* v *Woods* (SCC 1983), which placed Eurocentric understandings of attachment (then called bonding) as a higher priority than connection to culture. Arguments seeking to change how the court sees attachment versus culture have largely been unsuccessful in Alberta, and elsewhere in Canada, which sustains bias against Indigenous cultural identity needs versus attachment. This is seen in the case *URM* (2018 ABPC 116) in Alberta, where the late Judge Cooke-Stanhope stated: 'To be absolutely clear, I reject as unsustainable or unsupportable that the factor of maintaining Indigenous heritage is sufficient reason to ignore attachment theory' (para 138). She added that her rejection was consistent with legislation. Thus, both courts and social work practice combine to sustain colonial CP services (Choate and McKenzie, 2015; Lindstrom and Choate, 2016; Choate and Lindstrom, 2023).

Attempts at settling the past

There have been four class action lawsuits that have served as the basis for some form of settling the past. The first is the Indian Residential Schools Settlement Agreement (IRSSA) (2006). Under the IRSSA, CAD1.9 billion was set aside for all former residents of the schools. Each would receive CAD10,000 for the first year of schooling, and CAD3,000 for each subsequent year (Gallant, 2020), with the average payment being CAD20,000. There was a separate settlement for abuse which led to an average payment of CAD91,000 per claimant (CBC, 2022). An estimated 80,000 survivors have received payments (Canada, 2019). There is a separate agreement for Newfoundland and Labrador as that province did not join the Canadian confederation until 1949: 'Those who boarded at an N.L. residential school for less than five years would receive $15,000, while those who spent more than five years would get $20,000. There were an estimated 750–900 people eligible' (CBC, 2022).

There is also a settlement related to the day scholars who attended IRS but did not stay overnight. They were eligible for a CAD10,000 Day Scholar Compensation Payment (Justice for Day Scholars, 2024; *Canada* v *Gottfriedson*, 2014 FCA 55). In the case of *McLean* v *Canada* (2019 FC 1075), survivors of day schools, which are different from the IRS, have been eligible for compensation because of a class action lawsuit, although it did not cover the totality of the period, given it needed to apply to all survivors. Payments ranged between CAD10,000 and CAD200,000.

The fourth major case was associated with the 60's Scoop survivors who would 'benefit' from a class action lawsuit (*Brown* v *Canada*, 2017 ONSC 251). It was determined that there was systemic discrimination. The court stated:

> The impact on the removed aboriginal children has been described as 'horrendous, destructive, devastating and tragic'. The uncontroverted evidence of the plaintiff's experts is that the loss of their aboriginal identity left the children fundamentally disoriented, with a reduced ability to lead healthy and fulfilling lives. The loss of aboriginal identity resulted in psychiatric disorders, substance abuse, unemployment, violence, and numerous suicides. Some researchers argue that the Sixties Scoop was even 'more harmful than the residential schools'.

Following the decision, survivors who qualified (21,208 were deemed eligible) ended up receiving a payment of CAD25,000. However, class action lawsuits of this nature are largely about compensating victims for harms done and can often trigger traumatic memories. There are several more actions underway. As this data shows, however, these compensatory outcomes are not leading to significant changes for Indigenous peoples intersecting with child welfare.

Various politicians have issued apologies, such as the one offered by Prime Minister Harper in 2008, although, in the following year, he denied Canada had a history of colonialism (Assembly of First Nations of Quebec and Labrador, 2009), thus raising questions of whether the apology was disingenuous. There have been multiple other apologies from churches, provinces and territories and professional associations. Again, these apologies are for past harms but seem to have no discernible impact on current and future outcomes for Indigenous children.

What are we to make of the data?

What are we to make of the politics of the data, given that these apologies do not seem connected to actual change? Clearly the numbers cannot be measures of success unless that is defined as Canadian society needing to make up for the failure of Indigenous communities. This would be a shifting of responsibility away from government and Canadian society onto those whose lives have been managed through colonial policies. This is part of the denialism agenda (Carleton, 2021; Fuller, 2024), which is a form of gaslighting Indigenous peoples and trying to show that the CP services data on Indigenous peoples is not connected to the intergenerational trauma discussed in this chapter.

Redden et al (2020) describe how child welfare data is connected to what is measured, how that is selected, the sociopolitical assumptions that underlie the data and then how it is analysed and made public. The question of data bias enters the discussion particularly when justifying surveillance connected to inequality (Wrennall, 2010). This data can then be used as rationale for continued surveillance and failing to address root issues such as lack of SDH. Data is the measure of outcomes not causation. In the case of Indigenous families, colonial imposed trauma, not healed due to ongoing discrimination as shown in the CHRT decisions, means that that the major factors related to child protection investigations are substance use, mental health, lack of social supports and intimate partner violence (Fallon et al, 2021). It is a circular argument.

Where to from here?

The TRC has made 91 Calls to Action, with its first call being to commit to reducing the number of Aboriginal children in care. The data says no progress has been made since the report was issued in 2015. Indeed, the first five calls were specific to CP services but there is little evidence of meaningful application leading to change (Blackstock, 2022; Jewell and Mosby, 2022).

One major step Canada has taken is the 2019 passing of An Act respecting First Nations, Inuit and Métis children, youth, and families. The bill was subject to constitutional appeal but was upheld unanimously and in its entirety by the SCC (2024 SCC 5). The purpose of the legislation is to provide for the recognition of Indigenous laws regarding child and family services. It provides a pathway for Indigenous peoples to exercise their own jurisdiction, make laws and to administer and enforce those laws. Importantly, the law also established minimum standards for Indigenous children being served by various child welfare authorities across the country. Yet, the application of the law is not properly funded by Canada which is a barrier to large-scale success (Garrett, 2021).

There are a variety of legal implications which are beyond the scope of this chapter. According to Canada, 89 Indigenous Governing Bodies have served notice to exercise their legislative authority. Forty five Indigenous Governing Bodies have requested to enter into coordination agreements with Canada regarding their own laws and 12 have implemented their own laws (Canada, 2025). This is far from a perfect pathway as there remains a great deal of legal uncertainty, particularly given that funding is uncertain. At the same time, there is no reason to expect the existing system can do anything other than continue to yield dismal results. There is an irony in the necessity for the Canadian government to 'legislate' permission for Indigenous-led child protection.

Conclusion

The argument for sustaining the present child protection system relative to Indigenous peoples in Canada is profoundly weak. This is not because those who work within it seek to do harm by carrying on with Eurocentric understandings, it is rather that the system is structured to not do otherwise. Some have argued that child protection can be reformed and restructured. I was involved in such a project in Alberta (MPCI, 2018). It was not able to achieve the sorts of foundational changes that would alter how Indigenous peoples intersected with child welfare. Two important lessons arose from that. The first is the intense political will that major impactful reform requires. The balance of power must change and there are political risks, as, in the transition, errors will occur which the politicians must be willing to manage. The death of even one child that might be attributed to the reforms can lead to political unravelling. The second lesson is that the public, politicians and the media know very little about child protection except through the stories of tragedy. Even throughout the inquiry process, the root story related to the death of one child was never out of sight. The expectation was that reform could stop that from happening. It cannot.

There is a third lesson. Despite court orders and inquiries noted in this chapter, Canada continues to fail in meeting the SDH for Indigenous peoples which have been chronically underfunded. The CHRT (2016) has documented this, as has the TRC (2015) and RCAP (1996). The CHRT showed that Canada has discriminated against its own citizens by failing to provide a comprehensive and effective educational system to Indigenous children living on reserve (Phillips, 2016). This is also true for other SDH such as housing and physical healthcare (Nguyen et al, 2020), mental healthcare (Owais et al, 2022) and food (Batal et al, 2021). This too is not accidental.

Multiple efforts at reform have failed. The evidence is clear that Indigenous people are *not* better off because of these efforts. In my view, there is a need to abolish reform foci on the existing systems and shift dramatically to a focus on space for Indigenous peoples to look after their own children. Former Canadian Health Minister Jane Philpott (2024) and former TRC Commissioner Marie Wilson (2024) make it abundantly clear that Indigenous people know the answers, but politicians leave promises unfulfilled. We are then left with the rather famous saying, the origin of which is unclear, 'Insanity is doing the same things over and over again, expecting a different result.' We know differently but we are not doing differently. Sadly, colonialism is still standing.

References

Addams, J. (1905) 'Child labour legislation: A requisite for industrial efficiency', *Child Labour*, 25: 128–136. Available at: https://journals.sagepub.com/doi/10.1177/000271620502500312

Alberta (2024) 'Child intervention information and statistics summary child intervention information and statistics – 2023–24 fourth quarter (March) update'. Available at: https://open.alberta.ca/publications/child-intervention-information-and-statistics-summary-quarter-update

Assembly of First Nations of Quebec and Labrador (2009) 'Prime Minister Harper denies colonialism in Canada at G20', 29 September. Available at: https://www.newswire.ca/news-releases/prime-minister-harper-denies-colonialism-in-canada-at-g20-538621372.html

Batal, M., Chan, H.M., Fediuk, K., Ing, A., Berti, P.R., Mercille, G., et al (2021) 'First Nations households living on-reserve experience food insecurity: Prevalence and predictors among ninety-two First Nations communities across Canada', *Canadian Journal of Public Health*, 112(Suppl 1): 52–63.

Blackstock, C. (2007) 'Residential schools: Did they really close or just morph into child welfare?', *Indigenous Law Journal*, 6(1): 71–78.

Blackstock, C. (2022) 'Ending racial discrimination in child welfare', in E. Jewell and I. Mosby (eds), *Calls to Action Accountability: A 2022 Status Update on Reconciliation*, Toronto: Yellowhead Institute, pp 17– 20.

British Columbia (2024) 'New position expedites progress in Indigenous child welfare: Updated March 7, 2024'. Available at: https://news.gov.bc.ca/releases/2024CFD0002-000292

Canada (2005) *First Nations Child and Family Services: National Program Manual*. Ottawa: Indian and Northern Affairs Canada. Available at: https://publications.gc.ca/collections/Collection/R2-332-2004E.pdf

Canada (2019) 'Statistics on the implementation of the Indian Residential Schools Settlement Agreement'. Available at: https://www.rcaanc-cirnac.gc.ca/eng/1315320539682/1571590489978

Canada (2025) 'Notices and requests related to An Act Respecting First Nations, Inuit and Metis children, youth and families'. Available at: https://www.sac-isc.gc.ca/eng/1608565826510/1608565862367

Canadian Human Rights Tribunal (2016) 'First Nations Child and Family Caring Society of Canada and others, 2016 CHRT 2'. Available at: https://fncaringsociety.com/i-am-witness/chrt-orders

Carleton, S. (2021) '"I don't need any more education": Senator Lynn Beyak, residential school denialism, and attacks on truth and reconciliation in Canada', *Settler Colonial Studies*, 11(4): 466–486.

CASW (Canadian Association of Social Workers) (nd) 'What is social work?'. Available at: https://www.casw-acts.ca/en/what-social-work

CASW (2019) 'Statement of apology and commitment to reconciliation'. Available at: https://www.casw-acts.ca/files/Statement_of_Apology_and_Reconciliation.pdf

CBC (Canadian Broadcasting Corporation) (2022) 'Residential schools, day schools, day scholars: What you need to know'. Available at: https://www.cbc.ca/news/indigenous/residential-day-schools-scholars-1.6525827

Choate, P. (2024) 'Social work: Its place in determining the worthy and the unworthy – a reflection', in R. Attas, M. Yeo and G. Weasel Head (eds), *New Direction for Teaching and Learning*, in press.

Choate, P. and Lindstrom, G. (2023) 'Challenging systemic bias towards Indigenous mothers arising from colonial and dominant society assessment methodology through a lens of humility', in B. Richardson (ed), *Mothering on the Edge. A Critical Examination of Mothering in the Child Protection System*, Toronto: Demeter Press, pp 153–175.

Choate, P.W. and Engstrom, S. (2014) 'The good enough parent: Implications for child protection', *Child Care in Practice*, 20(4): 368–382.

Choate, P.W. and McKenzie, A. (2015) 'Psychometrics in parenting capacity assessments: A problem for First Nations parents', *First People's Child and Family Review*, 10(2): 31–43.

Choate, P.W., St-Denis, N. and MacLaurin, B. (2022) 'At the beginning of the curve: Social work education and Indigenous content', *Journal of Social Work Education*, 58(1): 96–110.

Choate, P., Bear Chief, R., Lindstrom, D. and CrazyBull, B. (2021) 'Sustaining cultural genocide: A look at Indigenous children in non-Indigenous placement and the place of judicial decision making – a Canadian example', *Laws*, 10(3): 59.

Choate, P., Kohler, T., Cloete, F., CrazyBull, B., Lindstrom, D. and Tatoulis, P. (2019) 'Rethinking Racine v Woods from a decolonizing perspective: Challenging applicability of attachment theory to Indigenous families involved with child protection', *Canadian Journal of Law and Society / Revue Canadienne Droit et Société*, 34(1): 55–78.

Clarke, K. and Yellow Bird, M. (2021) *Decolonizing Pathways Towards Integrative Healing in Social Work*, New York: Routledge.

Fallon, B., Lefebvre, R., Trocmé, N., Richard, K., Hélie, S., Montgomery, H.M., et al (2021) 'Denouncing the continued overrepresentation of First Nations children in Canadian child welfare: Findings from the First Nations/Canadian Incidence Study of Reported Child Abuse and Neglect 2019'. Available at: https://cwrp.ca/publications/denouncing-continued-overrepresentation-first-nations-children-canadian-child-welfare

FNCFCS (First Nations Child and Family Caring Society) (2024) 'Canadian Human Rights Tribunal decisions'. Available at: https://fncaringsociety.com/i-am-witness/chrt-orders

Foster, R. (2018) '"Reimagining" the child welfare system', *Journal of Law and Social Policy*, 28(1): 174–175.

Fuller, K. (2024) 'Residential school denialism, conspiracy theories, and the far-right's genocidal attack against Indigenous peoples', *The Abusable Past*. Available at: https://abusablepast.org/residential-school-denialism-conspiracy-theories-and-the-far-rights-genocidal-attack-against-indigenous-peoples/

Gallant, D.J. (2020) (Update of de Bruin, T., 20 January 2016) 'Indian Residential Schools Settlement Agreement', *Canadian Encyclopedia*. Available at: https://www.thecanadianencyclopedia.ca/en/article/indian-residential-schools-settlement-agreement

Garrett, R. (2021) 'The children parliament left behind: Examining the inequity of funding in an act respecting First Nations, Inuit and Métis children, youth and families', *Canadian Journal of Family Law*, 34(1): 45–78.

Hawthorne, B. (ed) (1967) *A Survey of the Contemporary Indians of Canada: Economic, Political, Educational Needs and Policies* (v.1 and 2), Ottawa: Indian Affairs Branch. Available at: https://caid.ca/HawRep1a1966.pdf

Hélie, S., Trocmé, S., Collin-Vézina, D., Esposito, T., Morin, S. and Saint-Girons, M. (2022) 'First Nations/Quebec incidence study of child maltreatment and serious behaviour problems investigated by Child Protection Services in 2019', Report FN/ QIS-2019, Institut universitaire Jeunes en difficulté. Available at: https://iujd.ca/sites/iujd/files/media/document/FN-QIS-2019-final-report.pdf

Hepworth, H.P. (1980) *Foster Care and Adoption in Canada*, Ottawa: Canadian Council on Social Development.

Jennissen, T. and Lundy, C. (2011) *One Hundred Years of Social Work: A History of the Profession in English Canada*, Waterloo: Wilfred Laurier Press.

Jewell, E. and Mosby, I. (2022) *Calls to Action Accountability: A 2022 Status Update on Reconciliation*, Toronto: Yellowhead Institute.

Justice for Day Scholars (2024) Available at: https://www.justicefordayscholars.com/

Lacombe, B.F. and Pind, J. (2023) 'Digitally mapping the Indian day schools and the RG10 school files series in Canada', *Historical Studies in Education*, 35(2): 55–68.

Lindstrom, G. and Choate, P. (2016) 'Nistawatsiman: Rethinking assessment of Aboriginal parents for child welfare following the Truth and Reconciliation Commission', *First Peoples Child and Family Review*, 11(2): 45–59.

Manitoba (2024) 'Manitoba government signs historic declaration to transfer responsibility for Indigenous child welfare to First Nations', 13 May. Available at: https://news.gov.mb.ca/news/print,index.html?item=63579&posted=2024-05-13

MMIWG (National Inquiry into Missing and Murdered Indigenous Women and Girls) (2019) *Reclaiming Power and Place: The Final Report of the National Inquiry into Missing and Murdered Indigenous Women and Girls*. Available at: https://www.mmiwg-ffada.ca/final-report/

MPCI (Ministerial Panel on Child Intervention) (2018) *Walking as One: Ministerial Panel on Child Intervention's Final Recommendations to the Minister of Children's Services*, Edmonton: GOA. Available at: https://www.alberta.ca/child-intervention-panel

Nguyen, N.H., Subhan, F.B., Williams, K. and Chan, C.B. (2020) 'Barriers and mitigating strategies to healthcare access in Indigenous communities of Canada: A narrative review', *Healthcare*, 8(2): Article 112.

Owais, S., Tsai, Z., Hill, T., Ospina, M.B., Wright, A.L. and Van Lieshout, R.J. (2022) 'Systematic review and meta-analysis: First Nations, Inuit, and Métis youth mental health', *Journal of the American Academy of Child and Adolescent Psychiatry*, 61(10): 1227–1250.

Phillips, R.S. (2016) 'Let's not call in the lawyers: Using the Canadian Human Rights Tribunal decision in First Nations education', *Brock Education Journal*, 25(2): 1–18.

Philpott, J. (2024) *Health for All: A Doctor's Prescription for a Healthier Canada*, Toronto: Signal McClelland and Stewart.

Quinn, A., Fallon, B., Joh-Carnella, N. and Saint-Girons, M. (2022) 'The overrepresentation of First Nations children in the Ontario child welfare system: A call for systemic change', *Children and Youth Services Review*, 139.

RCAP (Royal Commission on Aboriginal Peoples) (1996) *Report of the Royal Commission in Aboriginal Peoples*. Available at: https://www.bac-lac.gc.ca/eng/discover/aboriginal-heritage/royal-commission-aboriginal-peoples/Pages/final-report.aspx

Redden, J., Dencik, L. and Warne, H. (2020) 'Datafied child welfare services: Unpacking politics, economics and power', *Policy Studies*, 41(5): 507–526.

Rosano, M. (2017) 'Interview: Mapping the displacement of 60s Scoop adoptees'. *Canadian Geographic*, 29 November. Available at: https://canadiangeographic.ca/articles/interview-mapping-the-displacement-of-60s-scoop-adoptees/

Roxburgh, S. and Sinclair, M. (2024) 'Colonial constructions: Systemic racism in child welfare practice', *Journal of Social Work*, 24(1): 3–20.

Saskatchewan (2024) 'Child welfare statistics'. Available at: https://www.saskatchewan.ca/residents/family-and-social-support/putting-children-first

Statistics Canada (2016) 'Insights on Canadian society: Living arrangements of Aboriginal children aged 14 and under'. Available at: https://www150.statcan.gc.ca/n1/pub/75-006-x/2016001/article/14547-eng.htm

TRC (Truth and Reconciliation Commission of Canada) (2015) 'Truth and Reconciliation Commission of Canada: Calls to action'. Available at: https://www2.gov.bc.ca/assets/gov/british-columbians-our-governments/indigenous-people/aboriginal-peoples-documents/calls_to_action_english2.pdf Canada

Wilkins, K. (2000) 'Still crazy after all these years: Section 88 of the Indian Act at fifty', *Alberta Law Review*, 38(2): 458–503.

Wilson, M. (2024) *North of Nowhere: Song of a Truth and Reconciliation Commissioner*, Toronto: House of Anansi.

Wrennall, L. (2010) 'Surveillance and child protection: De-mystifying the Trojan horse', *Surveillance and Society*, 7(3/4): 304–324.

10

The roadmap to child protection abolition for Māori

Kerri Cleaver

Ko Aoraki te mauka	Aoraki is my mountain and ancestor
Ko Aparima te awa	Aparima is my river, that carries my people
Ko Takitimu te waka	Takitimu (double-hulled canoe) brought my people here
Nō Kāi Tahu, Kāti Māmoe, Waitaha au	These are my tribes
He uri ahau o te hapū o Te Ruahikihiki	My people descend from Te Ruahikihiki
Ko Kerri Cleaver toku ikoa	I am Kerri Cleaver

I introduce and locate myself to the lands that I reside on, to what settlers named as the South Island of New Zealand but what I know as Te Waipounamu. Being Kāi Tahu (umbrella term for the Māori tribes of Kāi Tahu, Kāti Māmoe and Waitaha) connects me to my responsibilities to ancestors past, present and future. I write through these responsibilities and with my experience as a foster system survivor and social worker.

Introduction

A flourishing future for mokopuna[1] (children) Māori[2] enmeshed in the state child protection system exists when the colonial system is replaced with the safety net of an intact flourishing Māori social structure, represented as the Pā harakeke (metaphorical social support structure). Navigating pathways towards restoration of Māori social structures requires recognition of the destruction of Indigenous child safety systems, exposing the barriers in society and legislation which prevent Māori aspiration and advancement. Child protection abolition for Māori is innately linked to settler colonialism, racism and the attempted erasure of Māori societal safety mechanisms. Through the metaphorical Pā harakeke model, the past and existing tensions and complexities of the Aotearoa (New Zealand) child protection landscape are explored and challenged with a view towards abolition on Māori terms. This chapter draws heavily on the work of Māori academics and activists who have paved the way forward by revitalising and restoring a Māori worldview in the hearts and minds of Māori.

The Pā harakeke

Child protection abolition in the settler colonial Aotearoa context, where Indigenous children remain disproportionately represented in removal rates, necessarily begins with discussing both continued coloniality and the impacts of the colonial project on Indigenous populations. Coloniality imposes, on Indigenous communities, an unceasing adaptive mechanism, responsive to its goals of acquisition, system maintenance, capitalism and personal gain (Trask, 1999; Krakouer, 2023). These sit in opposition to the collective and relational Indigenous social foundations with people and the environment. The stripping of Indigenous social safety nets tests the capacity of Indigenous abolitionist aspirations and necessitates a wider response than child protection itself, ensuring the social fabric is restored. To envision alternatives to child protection systems on Indigenous lands, the underpinning egregious wrongs must be acknowledged in actionable ways that address and redress the inequity they created, focusing on repair; not just fixing problems.

Internationally, the relationship between systemic racism and child protection prefaces discussions of abolition, with attention required to critical analysis of how we would undo the system in ways that avoid replicating the various iterations of the colonial and racist foundation it is built on. Dorothy Roberts (2023) stresses that the relationship between racism and child protection signifies a design to oppress and a resultant carceral web enmeshing child protection and prison systems in active subjugation of marginalised communities. It is this designing to oppress that indicates, as Roberts (2023) states, that the system cannot be reformed as it follows an established theoretical base of the logic of elimination. Reformers theorising with anti-oppressive foundations – critiquing racism, capitalism and the construct of 'parental pathology' – while remaining within Western constructs of family and society, miss opportunities to rethink child protection in its relationship with Indigenous worldviews (Ball and Benoit-Jansson, 2023). Anti-oppressive abolition responses in lands under colonial occupation should first look to Indigenous leadership and the social safety nets and structures held in collective community knowings. Envisioning Māori free from state child protective systems through building and supporting alternatives to parental policing, recognising Māori worldviews of what whānau[3] strengthening systems look like, starts with Māori concepts and the Pā harakeke.

In Māori culture, knowledge, societal expectations and responsibilities are carried through all cultural practices; crafts, dance, song and stories, ensuring societal wisdom is widely known and shared (Walker, 1990). One representation of society, behavioural expectations and obligations, is carried through the interpretation, maintenance and value of the Pā harakeke. The Pā harakeke is metaphorically depictive of the Māori social structure that supports mokopuna, whānau, hapū and iwi.[4] A Pā harakeke is a grouping of multiple fanned flax bushes, native to Aotearoa, which together provide co-operative health and well-being support to each plant. Harakeke (flax) comes in many varieties and was/is a treasured resource for Māori; utilised for basketry, clothing, footwear, fishing, housing, toys, boats and rongoa (Māori medicine). Conceptualising the care and support in a whānau, hapū and iwi structure, the inner new shoots of the flax (rito) represent mokopuna, while outer leaves symbolise parents and extended familial relationships, affording protection to new life as it grows; all sustained in a wider social support structure encapsulated as the multiple bushes (Watson, 2020).

Reliance on intact societal structures of safety to support mokopuna to grow and flourish is central to Māori society with the Pā harakeke signifying this. Prior to colonisation, Māori social structure generally worked well at protecting and nurturing mokopuna, in contrast with patriarchal Western notions of children as chattels rather than rights holders. While acknowledged as imperfect and contextual to the time, infringements on mokopuna rights to health and well-being in Māori society were subject to structured systems of accountability and redress, functioning to ensure the collective kept mokopuna safe from any future harm (Jenkins and Harte, 2011). Practices founded on restoration of relationships and the significance of whakapapa (genealogical connections), with mokopuna cherished and provided for as future ancestors, ensured mokopuna were both physically and emotionally safe.

Within Māori society, wāhine[5] Māori are woven through ancestral creation stories, holding roles of status and authority which are replicated through Māori social structures; holding the space of 'the house of humanity' in our relationship between worlds and in our ability to menstruate and carry life (Murphy, 2013; Mikaere, 2017). While this chapter does not explicitly focus on wāhine and the colonial erasure of our roles and responsibilities, including the targeted disproportionate impact of state child protection on wāhine, the premise throughout the text is that wāhine remain the focal strength, subject of oppression and space of healing in the Pā harakeke (Cleaver, 2023).

Colonising the protection of mokopuna

Drawing on shared Indigenous settler colonial experiences, Blackstock et al (2023) describe Indigenous child removal as part of the duplicity of the colonial agenda, founded on characteristics of violence, control and system maintenance. Disproportionate removal is the outcome of immense social and economic stressors produced in an intergenerational lived experience of legislative, policy, practice and societal discrimination by the colonial state. Indigenous social structures, the place of Indigenous women and innovative developments within Indigenous communities are stretched and broken through the colonial project, while child protective safety nets are wrecked.

Māori, in similar ways to Australian, Canadian and American First Nations, suffered considerable land loss, degraded economic resiliency and cultural ethnocide, consequently negatively shaping the contemporary realities of many Māori today, in what Mason Durie describes as states of languishing (Durie, 2016). The destruction of the Pā harakeke accumulates in negative statistics of poverty, health disparity, poor housing, substance abuse and child removal, all prompting the state to continue to recycle old adages of child rescue and interventionist strategies, justifying continued control of Indigenous futures.

Māori child removal follows a globally practised multi-pronged approach securing continued coloniality through separating Indigenous children from any flourishing futures embedded in Indigenous cultural strength, identity and community. Indigenous nations have experienced child removal approaches through education systems – residential schools, adoption systems – the Stolen Generation, youth incarceration and, more recently, through foster systems (Smith, 2013; Blackstock et al, 2023; Krakouer et al, 2023).

In Aotearoa, the logic of elimination embedded structural inequity across society through the loss of sovereignty over Māori lore/law, education, health, social and ecological sustainability. Early demonstration of colonial intent included pre-natal, post-natal and baby supports being refused by the state to Māori, resulting in 40 per cent of Māori babies under one year dying up to the mid-1890s (Cleaver, 2023). The Native School Act, 1867, separated mokopuna Māori from Māori social systems, denying language, seeking assimilation and shaping Māori as the lower class confined to labour and servitude roles (Smith, 2013). Land dislocation and legislated economic restrictions on Māori forced urbanisation in the post-Second World War period, leading to increased surveillance and incarceration of Māori youth in cities, while parallel adoption systems focused on mass infant removal, with high prevalence through the 1950s and 1960s. Statistician Len Cook's evidence to the Waitangi Tribunal testified to one in four Māori male youth being incarcerated in borstals in the 1960s, places now established as sites of torture and cruelty (Waitangi Tribunal, 2021; Royal Commission of Inquiry into Historical Abuse in State Care and in the Care of Faith-Based Institutions, 2024). As adoption reduced in the 1970s, increases of Māori in the child protection system exponentially grew to the current statistics of 68 per cent and 79 per cent across child protection and youth justice, while Māori make up only 25 per cent of the youth population (Oranga Tamariki Practice Centre, 2024).

The largest Royal Commission Aotearoa has ever had, the Royal Commission of Inquiry into Historical Abuse in State Care and in the Care of Faith-based Institutions, released its final report in July 2024, outlining the failure of the state to keep Indigenous children safe in the child protection system. It is estimated that over 200,000 of the 650,000+ mokopuna in state and faith-based systems were abused while in 'care'. This statistic touches only the edges of impact shared across whānau members intergenerationally from a state child protection system purported to be 'in the best interests' of mokopuna: a statistic that goes to the heart of colonial harm to the Pā harakeke (Royal Commission of Inquiry into Historical Abuse in State Care and Faith-Based Institutions, 2024).

An ethic of restoration: pathways to a flourishing Pā harakeke

Māori restoration of the Pā harakeke presents an alternative to decolonial and devolutionary processes which only address or 'fix' the social, political and legislative determinants of Māori suffering through Western measurements of inequity. Discarding the terminology of 'decolonisation', shifting from coloniser limitations of defining and redefining that restrict and boundary the possibilities of future Indigenous rights, Jackson's 'ethic of restoration' is prefaced on Māori sovereignty; repair and restoration adapted to our contemporary environments (Jackson, 2020). Describing and defining who holds authority in settler-colonial nations is critical to determining abolitionist pathways moving forward in child protection. The risk in bringing forth an ideology of abolition without engaging in processes led and developed by Māori on what the restoration of the Pā harakeke looks like (allowing Māori to define our own 'ethic of restoration') is a recycling of the paternalism of coloniality.

There is a place for both settler and Māori in an ethic of restoration. The settler, as majority, can utilise layered systemic privilege for allyship, disrupting the system internally, doing the emotional labour to carve out space for Māori, focusing on scaffolding knowledge of colonisation in dominated white supremacist spaces to build shared relational responsibilities. This leaves Māori to focus on innovation, repair and restoration rather than being dragged into doing the work of decolonisation, where responsibility firmly resides with non-Māori.

An ethic of restoration shifts us from deficit problem solving towards frameworks that actively sustain well-being and encourage flourishing whānau: the return of the Pā harakeke. Mason Durie's (2016) pathways to flourishing guides how to move Indigenous populations from states of languishing (mauri noho) to a state of flourishing (mauri ora). Divided into four key concepts, the pathways are cultural, family and whānau, environmental and societal. Each pathway provides clarity for child protection abolition and restoration of the Pā harakeke. The first three include the resurgence and intergenerational transfer of language, Indigenous resources and cultural continuity; fostering healthy lifestyles across the lifespan, from mokopuna to elders; and safe, healthy and accessible environments with clean air, water and land. The societal pathway to flourishing includes active participation in society while also addressing the importance of legislation for Indigenous rights that enshrines Indigenous leadership, knowledge and protection.

While Indigenous communities have experienced extreme suffering and many whānau still occupy lived realities described as languishing, there is a steady increase in Indigenous flourishing; in improving tertiary educational outcomes, in language reclamation, elders living longer, and as Indigenous youth populations continue to grow. These examples of mauri ora illustrate a wider potential for Indigenous flourishing, despite the absence of Indigenous rights in legislation. Enforceable legislated Indigenous rights are needed to escalate the slow improvements we are currently seeing, expanding on pockets of success and improving outcomes for Māori whānau in contact with Oranga Tamariki,[6] our state child protection system.

Oranga Mokopuna

King et al (2018) developed 'Oranga Mokopuna' – tackling the issue of legally enforceable mechanisms and the Pā harakeke – merging these into a Māori child rights framework. Oranga Mokopuna links to Durie's mauri ora work, emphasising the importance of Indigenous legal enforcements to achieve a state of flourishing, inclusive of the cultural imperatives of Māori knowing, being and doing.

Oranga Mokopuna conceptualises Māori child rights through the Pā harakeke, situating te Ao Māori (Māori worldview) at the centre of understandings about rights and relationships. Three key principles for mokopuna rights are asserted as whakapapa, mana and whanaungatanga. Whakapapa is described as the genealogical links extending beyond the human to place, cosmology, environment, past, present and future; mana is the authority, sacredness, endorsed obligations and responsibilities; while whanaungatanga is the connected importance of relationships to individual and collective identities (King et al, 2018). King asserts inequities experienced by mokopuna Māori in comparison with non-Māori 'are manifest symptomatology of colonisation, coloniality and racism', embedded in legal frameworks and societal 'needs-based' arguments which are flawed and shift us away from a Māori ideology where mokopuna hold a treasured status (King et al, 2018: 187).

The Oranga Mokopuna framework overlays key legal entitlements on the Pā harakeke, upholding the whakapapa, mana and whanaungatanga rights of mokopuna Māori. In the framework Te Whakaputanga o te Rangatiratanga o Nu Tireni, 1835 (The Declaration of Independence) and Te Tiriti o Waitangi,[7] 1840 (te Tiriti) are provided as the legal instruments of Māori unceded sovereign rights: placed before the United Nation mechanisms – The Convention on the Rights of Children (CRC) and the United Nations Declaration on the Rights of Indigenous Peoples (UNDRIP) – which King et al (2018) argue are only met once te Tiriti rights are upheld. Preferencing Māori rights, beliefs and guiding principles, mokopuna Māori rights are inextricably linked to familial relationships. The starting point for child protection abolitionist calls must be to first prioritise Māori societal and relationship rights: the Pā harakeke.

The benevolence of the state: giving and taking

Crown breaches against te Tiriti, the Pā harakeke and child protection were addressed by the Waitangi Tribunal urgent claim following the media exposé of a Māori baby uplift at a hospital, now coined 'the Hawkes Bay Uplift', in 2019. The final Waitangi Tribunal report (2021), 'He Pāharakeke, He rito, Whakakīkīnga Whāruarua',[8] found poor policy implementation and widespread practice by the state child protection agency, in breach of Article Two of te Tiriti which asserts Māori rights to protect the 'kāinga'[9] (home) and governmental responsibility to actively safeguard Māori authority and care over it (Waitangi Tribunal, 2021). The Tribunal detailed Oranga Tamariki's failure in sharing power, the prevalence of epistemological racism, gatekeeping, inconsistencies in procurement and transactional implementation of the recently introduced (and government accountability to Māori centred) Section 7 AA of the Oranga Tamariki Act, 1989. Identifying the intergenerational devastation child removals had on the kāinga, whānau, hapū and iwi (the Pā harakeke) and mokopuna Māori rights to be Māori, the Tribunal recommended the Crown implement a Transitional Māori Authority to start the transfer of power and services from the state to Māori, acknowledging that internal transformation was unlikely.

The Waitangi Tribunal highlighted funding discrepancies with Māori services being inadequately backed, while non-Māori services residing on stolen Māori lands and leveraging a colonial legacy of privilege, secured contract relationships with the Crown: some spanning over 100 years of entrenched entitlement. The introduction of Section 7 AA into legislation in 2019, was designed to address some of these inequities with the first substantive inclusion of measurable provisions for Māori in the child protection system through Crown/Māori partnerships. Section 7 AA holds the Chief Executive accountable to multiple responsibilities, including partnering and innovating with Māori, reduction and reporting targets for mokopuna Māori in the foster system, and a requirement to embed three principles of mana tamaiti, whakapapa and whanaungatanga through practice and policy. The Oranga Mokopuna framework draws on these principles but asserts fundamental Māori authority to define and determine what these principles look like in practice.

The introduction of Section 7 AA led to the swift design, development and accreditation of whānau care services; services set up through strategic partnerships between Māori and the state to deliver delegated functions of the child protection system. There are now ten Crown/Māori strategic partnerships, with 'by Māori, for Māori' services in Aotearoa providing a variety of initiatives, including caregiver support, whānau group homes, wrap-around, transitions from care and preventative supports.

While these advancements have enabled Māori entry into child protection decision-making and practice, the relational difficulties and hamstrung nature of being held in the master–servant relationship where funding and support is at the whim of the state, remains an ongoing issue. Temporal and restricted organisational endowments to Māori are characterised by Donna Huata as 'theatrical', with Māori running alongside the treasury cart trying to catch a few pennies (Waitangi Tribunal, 2021). This is not the Māori-led transformation asserted in te Tiriti, the Tribunal findings or in an ethic of restoration of the Pā harakeke, but rather system tinkering that upholds the continuation of a Crown-dominated system.

Lewis et al (2023), in common with the findings from the Tribunal, unveiled a range of issues for Māori organisations reliant on Oranga Tamariki; from funding restrictions, state practice resistance and the temporality of relationships based on alignment with state agency practice decisions. The experience for Indigenous aspirations in social service delivery in settler-colonial nations is shared, with Blackstock et al (2023) exposing Canada's slow progress as a function of tightly colonially controlled pathways, where system inaction is justified through lip service and recycled rhetoric, confining the pace and parameters of devolution.

These experiences of state regulation of Indigenous and Māori delivery are consistent with my own personal experience setting up the Ngāi Tahu service, Tiaki Taoka, where the state defined and determined both the pace of devolution and the building of Māori responses, maintaining the assumptive settler colonial right to power and authority. Tiaki Taoka was mandated through our tribal authority, Ngāi Tahu, and designed in our community, but funded and enabled through our Section 7 AA iwi/state partnership. While the success of the partnership is tied to the agreed outcome of 'no Ngāi Tahu children in state care', the ability to deliver to our people on this commitment through the service was/is reliant on early referrals from Oranga Tamariki, transparency, shared agreement on decisions, secure finance and funding to innovate. While director of the service, the inconsistency and at times refusal of the state to satisfy these requirements was evident in all parts of the relationship, and to date key preventive and advocacy services for whānau and cultural pathways to flourishing are unable to be delivered. Tiaki Taoka sits as one Ngāi Tahu response in a hub service model, Te Kāika, developed and led by Donna Matahaere-Atariki. The vision of Te Kāika is to provide outcomes across health and well-being to our people and, where possible, partner with the state if it improves the outcomes for Māori.

Māori child protection services do not sit in isolation from wider tribal strategies and as such do not replicate state child protection services. The difficulty in this is that the state continues to silo and function as it always has, under a Western worldview where holistic well-being remains ignored.

Māori continue to pick up opportunities because to do nothing is to leave our whānau in communities of languishing. Historically, what is offered from one government to the next is always minimal and we are currently witnessing a reductive policy turn – a withdrawal of rights at best and overt oppression at worst. The current coalition government has removed Māori wards (community caretakers), dismantled the Māori health authority (parallel Māori-led health response) and is currently attempting to repeal Section 7 AA, a minimal provision that was hard-won. What is clear is that abolition of the child protection system in terms of restoration of the Pā harakeke in collaboration with governments is always conditional; requiring Māori to draw on strategies for internal resistance, developing services outside of the state when possible.

Roadmap to abolition: Māori styles

Māori contemporary theoretical development in road-mapping a way forward that restores Māori to a place of sovereignty over our own affairs does not silo child protection out as an issue to be solved separately to that of the collective. The work on repairing the Pā harakeke by Māori runs across the societal landscape: language, arts, educational, health and well-being, healing. The decades of work repairing the base of Māori epistemological knowing, ontological being and doing, has created shared co-operative understandings of a social system across Māori, while the diversity and differences of knowledge and practice across iwi and hapū (tribes) is an emerging strength. Conceptual frameworks of the Pā harakeke, Mauri ora and Oranga Mokopuna are examples of the collective knowledge mapping of social structure. These have grown despite government responses and inform a trajectory towards a healthy Pā harakeke.

Restoration of the Pā harakeke strongly underway throughout hapū and iwi, include increasingly engaging with both Māori and non-Māori social well-being initiatives as capacity and capability grows. While 'by Māori, for Māori and of Māori' responses increase, new generations of Māori growing up connected to marae and social structure, with language and culture, are envisioning what a Māori future is. They are taking up roles across society while also designing Māori solutions and demanding te Tiriti rights. Māori futures, currently enmeshed in colonial structures, are being challenged and imagined outside of state control: the end to the colonial agenda is not only visible, but also inevitable.

Alongside theoretical conceptual work, constitutional reform continues to be pursued to enshrine Indigenous rights and accelerate Māori well-being.

In 2019 a government working party, the Declaration Working Group, appointed to respond to the government obligation to UNDRIP, produced a report: 'He Puapua', a 20-year blueprint plan to shift assumptive colonial sovereignty and power from a heavily state-loaded model to one of relational equity (Charters et al, 2019). He Puapua envisioned state compliance with Māori rights held in te Tiriti and UNDRIP, mapping a planned approach to reforming Crown and Māori relationships. It sets out a governance plan to achieve a Māori state of wellness where Māori have control over Māori matters, referred to as a 'rangatiratanga-centric[10] model'. The report is divided into five key sections, with the first addressing leadership rights and the last addressing equity and fairness.

He Puapua challenged the government to reassess its claim of legitimacy to govern, putting forward a process of engagement led and developed in Māori communities, to self-determine planned transfer, and how the relational sharing of power will occur. An abolition agenda, utilising the work undertaken in He Puapua, involves clear steps towards a future that replaces state child protection with localised tribal engagement systems, led from within tribal authorities. Ngāi Tahu, prior to partnering with the state under Section 7 AA, were already engaged in design conversations and had developed key attributes defining a flourishing Ngāi Tahu child. Many other iwi have also invested time and expertise in these conversations and are ready (or have already started) to respond, both within and outside of state structures.

The current social climate in Aotearoa is one where 93 per cent of over 2,000 Māori interviewed in the 'Whakatika' report experienced regular and harmful racism (Tinirau et al, 2021). In this environment, it is unsurprising that He Puapua was silenced by government. The Declaration Working Group's belief that we had reached the necessary maturity as a nation to undertake constitutional and societal transformation was unfortunately misplaced. However, the work completed, outlining a model of three decision-making domains; leadership and authority of Māori; continued governance of the Crown; and a shared sphere of interactive cooperation, details a roadmap, including international examples and guidance, regardless of state readiness.

In the first section focused on leadership, He Puapua draws on the First Nation Canadian example of Nisga Nation, which achieved provisions for self-government, constitutional reform, legislative jurisdiction and locally determined responses, to demonstrate the potential of colonial government releasing control. Nisga Nation now provides a social service wrap-around that includes housing, social welfare supports, education, legal services, and child protection authority and services.

Our own Ngāi Tahu Te Kāika hub model has taken its lead from Turtle Island exemplars of Indigenous-led social and health community organising. These share the philosophy of connection to culture, identity, place and holistic well-being, and the determination to repair Indigenous social structures; the Pā harakeke. While organisations and services, even Indigenous ones, cannot fully repair and restore the social structure for Māori, tribal based organisational structures, like Te Kāika, move us towards restoration. Te Kāika opens the door for disconnected whānau to engage with Māori well-being, including health and healing practices such as rongoa, cultural practices and services developed to utilise the wide plethora of Māori practices.

The He Puapua report section on equity and fairness covers health, housing, and criminal and family justice. The strategies exemplified in this section explore shared duties between Māori and the state, with clarity on who has responsibility and authority. Abolition in the child protection system requires Māori leading and determining solutions while not holding responsibility for solving state-created problems. A shared sphere between the Crown and Māori in solving socioeconomic issues acknowledges Māori expertise and the Pā harakeke, while charging the state with accountability on outcomes. In the He Puapua report, shared development, alongside Māori-led initiatives, addresses needed shifts in state-controlled funding and compliance, away from Oranga Tamariki to Māori care of mokopuna Māori.

Repairing the threads of a social safety net

The threads of harakeke woven through the hands of our ancestors' past, present and future bind Māori together collectively. In our resistance against settler-colonial control over the futures of our mokopuna and through the interdependent relational tribal authority and sovereignty over our kaingā, we continue to move towards a state of flourishing; to mauri ora. Māori, with increasing numbers of allies, have been working for child protection abolition for 184 years in Aotearoa, recognising that this is not about a transfer of a failing system from the state to Māori, nor a step away from our responsibilities to hold our mokopuna at the centre of the Pā harakeke. Māori have been asserting our right to Māori social systems of support and care in our communities in a contemporary reality, 'forever'.

We have taken many steps towards this, through repair of the grounding principles of our social structure, revitalisation of language and culture and our continued defiance of a Western monocultural legal framework that sidelines Māori, iwi and hapū rights and legal protections. The Pā harakeke restoration is the protective safety net that will keep mokopuna free from harm and abuse, prioritising the importance of mokopuna and providing community relational responses. Restoration in a new collaborative model consistent with a nation founded and functioning in partnership under te Tiriti, includes the addressing of disparities of poverty, housing, health and well-being through strengthening the pathways that support Māori ambitions across culture, society, whānau and the environment. To realise a flourishing Pā harakeke at a pace needed to turn the tide of mokopuna Māori entering the child protection system, legislation must protect and enhance the process of moving from mauri noho (languishing) to mauri ora (flourishing), which should draw on the work done by Māori experts, including Oranga Mokopuna and He Puapua.

Aotearoa is not the global golden child of Indigenous relations and advancing human rights. The recognition that we do have has been relentlessly fought for by generations of Māori leaders. The interim measures and spaces that hapū and iwi take up under current minimal provisions and partnerships with the state, such as whānau care services under Section 7 AA, are important on this journey as we build 'by Māori, for Māori and of Māori' responses. These mitigate against the colonial harm currently experienced. But these responses are neither the aspiration, nor the solution; they are merely steps taken on the way towards the vision presented in He Puapua, where decision-making sits in spheres of responsibility: Māori, Crown and a shared space of collaboration. The current risk is that these meagre provisions are being retracted by the coalition government, requiring Māori to again focus on resistance to state violence against the Pā harakeke while still advancing the restoration and mauri ora work.

In Aotearoa and comparable settler states, abolition and anti-racism are inextricably linked. To free mokopuna, our future ancestors, from the shackles of the harmful colonial capitalist state, is to realise the promise of te Tiriti by entrenching legislative protections for Māori which guarantee Māori authority over the kāinga. This process of abolition and rebuilding can achieve restoration of the Pā harakeke. It requires recognising Māori, iwi and hapū governance models, in defined autonomous realms of authority, and working with the settler state in defined shared governance spaces. It is a question of constitutional justice, imagination and political will. Māori will not surrender this aspiration.

Notes

[1] Mokopuna is translated as the blueprint for future generations and is used to talk about babies, children and young people.
[2] Māori is a collective term post-colonisation for the many tribes that exist as independent but interdependent sovereign nations.
[3] Whānau represents familial relationships inclusive of parents, grandparents and extended relationships.
[4] Hapū and iwi are Māori social structures. Hapū is groups of whānau that share ancestry located to an area; iwi is the wider groups of hapū who share a migrational ancestor.
[5] Wāhine refers to Māori women while being a non-binary term inclusive of gender fluidity.
[6] Oranga Tamariki is the state child protection system in Aotearoa, holding a Māori title in name only.

7   Te Tiriti o Waitangi is also known as the Treaty of Waitangi and is the founding document and agreement between Māori tribal leaders and the Crown enabling settlers and all immigrants to live in partnership with Māori in Aotearoa.
8   A Māori whakataukī (proverb) which translates to 'the flax bush contains the centre shoot which will fill the valleys'.
9   The kāinga refers to home, land and community that Māori genealogically connect to.
10   Rangatiratanga is used to refer to Māori leadership and self-determination.

References

Ball, J. and Benoit-Jansson, A. (2023) 'Promoting cultural connectedness through indigenous-led child and family services: A critical review with a focus on Canada', *First Peoples Child and Family Review*, 18(1): 34–59.

Blackstock, C., Libesman, T., King, J., Mathews, B. and Hermeston, W. (2023) 'Decolonizing first peoples child welfare', in C. Curreen, A. Deckert, A. Porter, J. Tuari and R. Webb (eds), *The Routledge International Handbook on Decolonizing Justice*, Abingdon: Routledge, pp 313–323.

Charters, C., Kingdon-Bebb, K., Olsen, T., Ormsby, W., Owen, E., Pryor, J., et al (2019) *He Puapua. Report of the Working Group on a Plan to Realise the UN Declaration on the Rights of Indigenous Peoples in Aotearoa New Zealand*. Available at: https://natlib.govt.nz/records/45416887

Cleaver, K. (2023) 'Theoretical research: He whare takata: Wahine Māori reproductive justice in the child protection system', *Aotearoa New Zealand Social Work*, 35(4): 16–30.

Durie, M. (2016) 'Mauri ora pathways to flourishing', Ngā Pae o te Māramatanga 7th Biennial International Indigenous Research Conference, Auckland, Aotearoa.

Jackson, M. (2020) 'Where to next? Decolonisation and the stories in the land', in R. Kiddle (ed), *Imagining Decolonisation*, Wellington: Bridget Williams Books, pp 133–155.

Jenkins, K. and Harte, H.M. (2011) *Traditional Maori Parenting: An Historical Review of Literature of Traditional Māori Child Rearing Practices in Pre-European Times*, Auckland: Te Kahui Mana Ririki.

King, P., Cormack, D. and Kōpua, M. (2018) 'Oranga mokopuna: A tāngata whenua rights-based approach to health and wellbeing', *Mai Journal*, 7(2): 186–202.

Krakouer, J., Nakata, S., Beaufils, J., Hunter, S.A., Corrales, T., Morris, H., et al (2023) 'Resistance to assimilation: Expanding understandings of First Nations cultural connection in child protection and out-of-home care', *Australian Social Work*, 76(3): 343–357.

Lewis, L., Walker, S., King, P.T., Mackay, H., Talamaivao, N., Anderson, D., et al (2023) 'Koi te matapunenga maianga i te matapuuioio – see the unseen, feel the unfelt, believe in the impossible: Courageous and loving practice in a Māta Waka social service provider', *Indigenous Social Development*, 12(1): 3–27.

Mikaere, A. (2017) *The Balance Destroyed*, Ōtaki: Te Wānanga o Raukawa.

Murphy, N. (2013) *Te Awa Atua: Menstruation in the Pre-Colonial Maori World: An Examination of Stories, Ceremonies and Practices Regarding Menstruation in the Pre-Colonial Māori World*, Whakatane: He Puna Manawa Limited.

Oranga Tamariki Practice Centre (2024) Available at: https://orangatamariki.govt.nz/about-us/performance-and-monitoring/quarterly-report/overview/

Roberts, D. (2023) 'Why abolition', *Family Court Review*, 61(2): 229–241.

Royal Commission of Inquiry into Historical Abuse in State Care and Faith-Based Institutions (2024) *Whanaketia: Through Pain and Trauma, from Darkness to Light*, New Zealand Government. Available at: https://www.abuseincare.org.nz/reports/whanaketia

Smith, L.T. (2013) *Decolonizing Methodologies: Research and Indigenous Peoples*, London: Zed Books.

Tinirau, R., Smith, C. and Haami, M. (2021) *Whakatika, How Does Racism Impact on the Health of Black, Indigenous and/or People of Colour Globally? An International Literature Review for the Whakatika Research Project*, Whanganui: Te Atawhai Charitable Trust.

Trask, H.K. (1999) *From a Native Daughter: Colonialism and Sovereignty in Hawaii* (revised edition), Honolulu: University of Hawaii Press.

Waitangi Tribunal (2021) 'He Pāharakeke, He Rito Whakakīkinga Whāruarua Oranga Tamariki Urgent Inquiry, WAI 2915'. Available at: https://forms.justice.govt.nz/search/Documents/WT/wt_DOC_171027305/He%20Paharakeke%20W.pdf

Walker, R. (1990) *Ka Whawhai Tonu Matou: Struggle Without End*, Auckland: Penguin Books.

Watson, A. (2020) 'Qualitative research: Pa Harakeke as a research model of practice', *Aotearoa New Zealand Social Work*, 32(3): 30–42.

11

Prison abolition as a feminist of colour project: lessons from the United States

Mimi E. Kim

Introduction

The year 2024 marked the 30th anniversary of the landmark US legislation launching public legitimacy of, and accompanying federal dollars funding national strategies to challenge, gender-based violence. Specifically naming domestic and sexual violence as crimes, later joined by stalking and trafficking, the Violence Against Women Act (VAWA) passed in 1994 to accolades from the US feminist anti-violence movement which mobilised to initiate, shape and advocate for the US$1.6 billion bill (42 U.S.C. § 13701). VAWA dramatically expanded resources to an increasingly robust feminist social movement and developing field of human services addressing gender-based violence, funding shelters, advocacy centres and crisis lines that emerged en masse in the 1970s and proliferated throughout the 1980s and 1990s. These formations still constitute the US anti-violence sector that exists today. VAWA also elevated crime control measures and resources to further criminalise and prosecute domestic and sexual violence across largely local and state jurisdictions. Sixty per cent of VAWA 1994 was allotted to law enforcement, setting the course for continued carceral investments through a bill initiated and advanced by feminist social movement forces largely embedded within civil society.

VAWA's passage as part of the Clinton era's Violent Crime Control and Law Enforcement Act of 1994 (Crime Bill of 1994) embodies the twisted neoliberal logic of US governance and acquiescence of an allegedly liberatory feminist social movement to the illusory remedies of the carceral state. As a longtime anti-violence advocate and activist who witnessed and indeed participated in this moment, I have continued to be appalled and fascinated by the continued persistence of the movement's embrace of this carceral logic. My work since the co-founding of the radical feminist of colour social movement organisation, INCITE! Women of Color Against Violence (re-named INCITE! Women, Gender Non-Conforming, and Trans People of

Color Against Violence), has exposed and worked to dismantle the carceral state's enduring hegemonic power. I also remain committed to forging liberatory responses to gender-based and state violence and constructing life-affirming norms, practices and vibrant ecosystems.

Communities of colour and resistance to the carceral state

The US criminal legal system is in large part an outgrowth of settler-colonial and imperialist state violence – from cavalries dedicated to the displacement and genocide of Indigenous people and slave patrols created to maintain slavery and the slave economy upon which this country has been built – to global militarised initiatives of conquest and occupation. Indeed, the migration history of my own family follows the trajectory shaped by imperialist wars. My parents migrated to the United States as a result of the devastation and division of Korea stemming from the Korean War – a war that killed one out of five North Koreans and closed with the installation of a US-backed dictatorship in South Korea. Repressive regimes were finally overturned by the successes of the Korean pro-democracy movement; however, remnants of dictatorial forces and new incarnations of anti-democratic power persist in South Korea (Cumings, 2011). Despite more economically framed narratives of migration – 'seeking a better life for our children' – the conditions so many migrants are fleeing are caused by the ambitions of economic conquest backed by military might, paralleling the dynamics of policing domestically.

The project to both dismantle carceral logics and systems and build liberatory practices and spaces is increasingly known as *prison abolition* (Kaba, 2021). As US abolitionist leader, Mariame Kaba, reminds us, 'everything worthwhile is done with other people' (2021: 178). Indeed, my experience of this evolving prison abolitionist movement recalls its history as one that is grassroots, collective and radically decentralised – driven by and accountable to those most impacted by the oppressive systems that undergird this country and its interlocking global systems. Building the intersecting prison abolitionist and abolition feminist movements has been a decidedly collective and participatory project – largely led by women, femme, transgender/non-binary and queer people of colour; Indigenous people and nations; poor and economically marginalised communities; immigrants of colour and their descendants; people in the street economy; those with disabilities; the very young and those who are ageing. Let there be no doubt that these are the people who are not and have never been served by the US criminal legal system and who are more often its targets. The daily acts of creative resistance and more intentional, long-term political strategising by people striving to survive and thrive in the face of these systems of oppression are what fuel the prison abolitionist/abolition feminist movements – even if many of those who contribute to its creation never use these terms nor perhaps have even heard them.

The carceral creep: feminist anti-violence collaboration with crime control

As I learned of, and also witnessed, the growing collaboration between the US anti-violence movement and law enforcement, accelerating through the late 1970s and 1980s (I entered at the end of the 1980s) and cemented with the passage of VAWA in 1994, I was confounded by the ease with which an emancipatory feminist social movement embraced such an intimate relationship with policing. After all, I was aware that many, though not all, of the early feminist leaders of the 1960s and 1970s were anti-police, anti-military and anti-racist.

One aspect of hegemonic power is the containment of imagination and, therefore, action. I came to understand that it is the folly of liberal reforms in a time of the growing power of policing – law enforcement agents, resources, institutions and the political framework of crime control – that contributed to this rapid alignment between a social movement and the carceral state. Nowhere have the contradictions of emancipation and incarceration been more evident than the US feminist anti-violence movement (Simon, 2007) – built on a logic and set of carceral institutions that have unfortunately been exported globally as a model of liberal, freedom-enhancing progress. Sociologist Elizabeth Bernstein (2005, 2012) coined the term 'carceral feminism' in response to the criminalising and militarised remedies to sex trafficking which built upon the carceral strategies already established and firmly embedded within the anti-violence response.

In my work on what I call the *carceral creep*, my research on the emergence of the US feminist anti-violence movement from 1973 to 1983, before the advent of VAWA, chronicles the ways in which early second-wave feminist demands for protection by law enforcement made sense within a reformist framework (Kim, 2020). However, the result of reformist claims-making were increased ties with and reliance upon policy successes vis-à-vis the criminal legal system. In fact, in the 1970s, the agents of crime control were largely disinterested in the protection of primarily women from the physical and sexual violence of primarily male family members, intimate partners, acquaintances, neighbors, co-workers, and so on (Schechter, 1982; Gee, 1983). In the example of the feminist social movement, this was not a case of the carceral state seeking the acquiescence and collaboration of feminist civil society actors and leaders – at least not in the 1970s and 1980s. Rather, a set of aggressive and subversive feminist social movement actions compelled police and law enforcement compliance with what appeared to be a strident feminist agenda – through successful lawsuits challenging the lack of police response to domestic violence (Gee, 1983), coercive strategies to gain protections through crime legislation and collaborative relationships with police and prosecution, and campaigns to align gender-based violence with the expanding frame of crime (Kim, 2020).

This set of strategies worked to tie feminist social movements to the logic, agents and institutions of crime control – leading to seeming social movement victories that eventually transformed into the subservience of a once powerful feminist social movement into agents of the carceral state. The carceral creep refers to the process in which protest actions and demands for law enforcement protections led to the eventual submission of a once emancipatory feminist leadership to an oppressive and violent masculinist agenda embedded within the carceral state. The dynamics of power and privilege have everything to do with the US feminist choice to follow a 'winning' agenda aligned with an egregiously racist and classist regime of mass or hyper incarceration.

Intersectionality and the dangers of essentialist feminism

Although anti-violence feminists in the late 1960s and 1970s questioned the wisdom of ties to the police as well as state-based alternatives, that is, what was understood as misogynist and racist institutions of mental health and psychiatry, early feminist leaders also insisted that law enforcement was an effective target for social change (Schechter, 1982; Gee, 1983; Kim, 2020). Police disregard for gender-based violence as a 'serious' crime fuelled litigation that charged police departments in Oakland, California and New York City for failing to offer equal protection to women as a class (Gee, 1983). Expanding federal dollars for police, prosecution and prisons that started as early as 1968 under President Johnson and followed by President Nixon opened up law enforcement initiatives that reframed civil unrest as crime control (Murakawa, 2014; Hinton, 2016). An increasing public agenda focused on a 'war on crime' coincided with the emergence of second-wave feminism's attention to domestic and sexual violence. For anti-violence feminists, this opened up opportunities to insist upon gender-based violence as crimes worthy of the attention of law enforcement – a strategy accompanied by the carceral instruments of surveillance, arrest, prosecution and incarceration (Gruber, 2020).

It was critical legal scholar, Kimberlé Crenshaw (1989, 1991), who recognised the inherent racist framing and consequences of the early anti-violence movement's strategies. She enumerated the misguided and, in fact, dangerous consequences of the movement's disregard for the different experiences of gender-based violence among Black and other women of colour as well as the negative consequences of white-defined feminist anti-violence practices and policies on women of colour, including immigrants.

The term *intersectionality*, in fact, first arose as Crenshaw's response to the anti-violence movement and the presumption that the perceptions and experiences of white middle-class woman represent that of all women. The essentialist category of 'women' devoid of a race and class analysis invariably meant 'white'. Despite Crenshaw's warnings, widely circulated among anti-violence advocates and activists, three years after the publication of Crenshaw's groundbreaking 1991 essay on intersectionality, VAWA passed as part of the Crime Bill.

INCITE! and the emergence of abolition feminism

By the late 1990s, a robust anti-carceral movement began to build power in the United States. Although the term *prison abolition* was not in wide circulation at the time, such anti-prison activists as Angela Y. Davis forged the organisation, Critical Resistance, calling together a historic inaugural gathering in 1998 that sparked a cross-racial, multi-sector movement calling not only for reform but for the abolition of prisons (Davis et al, 2022). In 2003, Davis' book entitled *Are Prisons Obsolete?* explicitly asked the question that destabilised the assumed inevitability of prisons with an imagined future in which prisons no longer existed.

Davis, along with an array of feminists of colour across race, class, sexuality and nation joined in a conference two years later. The Color of Violence conference held in 2000 in Santa Cruz, California established the radical feminist of colour organisation, INCITE! Women of Color Against Violence, which centred both gender-based violence and state violence as intersecting systems of oppression endangering and targeting women of colour (INCITE! Women of Color Against Violence, 2006). INCITE!, which at that time framed gender as a binary category, later developed and adopted a non-binary understanding of gender and gender-based violence. Under the umbrella of INCITE! and its following conferences, task forces, publications and campaigns, a broad-based understanding of interpersonal and state violence – and a deeply intersectional understanding of the dynamics of gender, race, class, caste, sexuality, nation, ability/disability, religion and other categories – characterised the politics of those influenced by and forging the rich and expansive activities of INCITE! (INCITE! Women of Color Against Violence, 2006; Kim, 2018).

In particular, local and national projects to redefine gender-based violence/state violence and reimagine practices to end and prevent violence emerged as strategies of *community accountability* and *transformative justice* (Kim, 2018). While the term *abolition feminism* had long been associated with those committed to the abolition of any form of sex work, defined through the exclusive lens of gender-based abuse, the term began to transform to describe a form of feminism committed to the abolition of policing, prisons and carceral practices beyond the institutions of law enforcement (Davis et al, 2022). The term *carceral feminism* became increasingly used to critique conventional and still prevailing anti-violence frameworks, practices and institutions tied to law enforcement (Bernstein, 2005, 2012; Law, 2014). *Abolition feminism*, on the other hand, became increasingly used to identify a liberatory politic and set of strategies aligned with not only the end of gender-based violence (understood at this historical moment beyond a binary understanding of gender) but the end of our reliance upon systems of surveillance, punishment and incarceration (Davis et al, 2022).

In 2022, the publication of *Abolition. Feminism. Now.* was among the first to put the words, abolition feminism, into print though it had been in use in radical feminist activist circles for at least a handful of years. Authored by Angela Y. Davis, Gina Dent, Erica R. Meiners and Beth E. Richie, who all have decades of activism and leadership in what we now understand as the abolition feminist movement, the book chronicles the historical development of abolition feminism and documents the centrality of feminism to an often male-dominated abolitionist movement. They also demand the centrality of abolition to a feminist movement marred by its long history of alignment with the US prison system and contribution to the escalation of mass and hyper incarceration.

The carceral creep redux: the current contradictions of success

As VAWA moves beyond its 30th year, we are now faced with another incarnation of social movement success and its contradictions – this time tied to the mounting influence of abolition feminism. The critique of carceral feminism and the development of abolition feminism as a politic and set of practices has also developed and expanded for over 25 years. In 2022, the Reauthorization of VAWA included what was meant to be a nod to the concerns of abolitionist feminists through the inclusion of a restorative practices initiative, explicitly defined as 'unaffiliated with any civil or criminal legal process' (34 U.S.C.A. §12291(a) (31)). Abolitionist feminists of colour, including myself, vehemently opposed its inclusion into the legislation – refusals that were denied by a liberal feminist insistence that reforms within the Department of Justice, the US institution overseeing the nation's system of law enforcement, could only be a positive endeavour. No amount of protest seemed to dim this optimistic belief in the system. The delusions of law-enforcement-based reform that characterised feminist choices five decades prior appeared to be firmly in place (Kim and Kanuha, 2022).

Though still early in its implementation stage, during the writing of this chapter, history would warn us of the carceral creep – processes less the fault of well-meaning individuals than the result of the embeddedness of reforms within a dominant and inherently violent institution (Kim, 2020).

Critical Resistance has a well-developed visual schema describing what some call reformist reforms versus non-reformist reforms in alignment with prison abolition, built upon the original conceptualisation by French New Left philosopher, André Gorz (Gorz, 1967; Critical Resistance, 2021). Such organisations as the Network to Advance Abolitionist Social Work have adopted these categories to help guide the ways in which social workers can discern social change work that ultimately serves to uphold and legitimise institutions of control and punishment – rather than delegitimise and dismantle them (Kim et al, 2024).

With the growing public familiarity with the term, prison abolition, if not necessarily its tenets, the perils of popularity without the grounding of deep analysis and principled practice pose conditions that can easily dilute abolition to mean just about anything. History would tell us again and again that social change is not a straightforward process. If nothing else, this chapter highlights the counternarratives of those most impacted by violence while also reminding us that the pathway forward is constrained by the limitations of imagination reinforced by the many violences of the market and the neoliberal state. The commodification of abolition into a brand, a book title, an academic course, or a piece of potentially meaningless or even hazardous legislation looms as an ever-present danger. However, the ardent abolitionist is a student of contradictions and their constant and evolving resolutions – not only through study but through knowledge woven together through communities of solidarity, principled practice and reflections on the lessons life offers each day.

References

Bernstein, E. (2005) 'Militarized humanitarianism meets carceral feminism: The politics of sex, rights, and freedom in contemporary antitrafficking campaigns', *Signs*, 36(1): 45–71.

Bernstein, E. (2012) 'Carceral politics as gender justice? The "traffic in women" and neoliberal circuits of crime, sex, and rights', *Theoretical Sociology*, 4: 233–259.

Crenshaw, K. (1989) 'Demarginalizing the intersection of race and sex: A Black feminist critique of antidiscrimination doctrine, feminist theory and antiracist politics', *University of Chicago Legal Forum*, 1989(1): 139–168.

Crenshaw, K. (1991) 'Mapping the margins: Intersectionality, identity politics, and violence against women of color', *Stanford Law Review*, 43(6): 1241–1299.

Critical Resistance. (2021) 'Reformist reforms vs abolitionist steps to end imprisonment'. Available at: https://criticalresistance.org/wpontent/uploads/2021/08/CR_abolitioniststeps_antiexpansion_2021_eng.pdf

Cumings, B. (2011) *The Korean War: A History*, London: Random House.

Davis, A.Y. (2003) *Are Prisons Obsolete?* New York: Seven Stories Press.

Davis, A.Y., Dent, G., Meiners, E.R. and Richie, B.E. (2022) *Abolition. Feminism. Now.*, Chicago: Haymarket Press.

Gee, P. (1983) 'Ensuring police protection for battered women: The Scott vs. Hart suit', *Signs*, 9(3): 554–567.

Gorz, A. (1967) *Strategy for Labor: A Radical Proposal*, New York: Beacon Press.

Gruber, A. (2020) *The Feminist War on Crime: The Unexpected Role of Women's Liberation in Mass Incarceration*, Berkeley: University of California Press.

Hinton, E. (2016) *From the War on Poverty to the War on Crime: The Making of Mass Incarceration in America*, Cambridge, MA: Harvard University Press.

INCITE! Women of Color Against Violence (2006) *The INCITE! Anthology*, Boston: South End Press.

Kaba, M. (2021) *We Do This 'til We Free Us: Abolitionist Organizing and Transforming Justice*, Chicago: Haymarket Press.

Kim, M.E. (2018) 'From carceral feminism to transformative justice: Women-of-color feminism and alternatives to incarceration', *Journal of Ethnic and Cultural Diversity in Social Work*, 27(3): 219–233.

Kim, M.E. (2020) 'The carceral creep: Gender-based violence, race and the expansion of the punitive state, 1973–1983', *Social Problems*, 67(2): 309–326.

Kim, M.E. and Kanuha, K. (2022) 'Restorative justice and the dance with the devil', *Affilia*, 37(2): 189–193.

Kim, M.E., Rasmussen, C.W. and Washington, Sr., D.M. (eds) (2024) *Abolition and Social Work: Possibilities, Paradoxes, and the Practice of Community Care*, Chicago: Haymarket Press.

Law, V. (2014) 'Against carceral feminism', *Jacobin*, 17 October. Available at: https://jacobin.com/2014/10/against-carcerla-feminism/

Murakawa, N. (2014) *The First Civil Right: How Liberals Built Prison America*, New York: Oxford University Press.

Schechter, S. (1982) *Women and Male Violence: The Visions and Struggles of the Battered Women's Movement*, Boston: South End Press.

Simon, J. (2007) *Governing Through Crime: How the War on Crime Transformed American Democracy and Created a Culture of Fear*, New York: Oxford University Press.

12

The limits of violence prevention in the non-profit industrial complex: moving beyond the masculinist state

Bob Pease

Introduction

Feminist anti-carceral social work has emerged in the Global North out of five decades of grappling with the contradictions involved in working in and against the masculinist state. Questions have been raised about whether the masculinist state can pursue feminist objectives and serve the interests of women and queer and non-binary people, given that it is deeply embedded in the reproduction of gender hierarchies and binary gender frameworks (Burstyn, 1983; Brown, 1995; Bumiller, 2008, Pease, 2019). Burstyn (1983) and Brown (1995) use the language of masculinism to identify the pursuit of male dominance within the state through socially constructed and historically shaped modes of masculine power. Whether the state is irredeemably masculinist and patriarchal is a subject of contemporary debate (Pease, 2019).

What is less explored from an abolitionist feminist perspective is the adoption of state policies and programmes to engage men in violence prevention and gender equality. Anti-patriarchal activism by men was originally grounded in allyship with feminists in progressive social movements in civil society before their work was taken over by government-funded services. Men's behaviour change programmes, HeForShe, White Ribbon and the Man Box have all focused on encouraging men to develop alternative healthy masculinities to address 'toxic masculinity', which is seen to be at the heart of men's violence and gender inequality. In this chapter I explore how such policies and programmes implicitly institutionalise dominant masculinity, promote the notion of 'good' men who are protectors of women and reproduce the hierarchical gender and sex binary. I outline an abolitionist approach to violence prevention with men that encourages cis-hetero-men to destabilise their attachment to normative masculinity and manhood and form relations of solidarity with women and queer people to foster commoning forms of care, love and justice that utilise mutual aid to resist and challenge violence (Pain, 2022).

Towards feminist anti-carceral practice

In recent years, we have seen the development of feminist anti-carceral approaches to social work and human services practice (Whalley and Hackett, 2017; Kim, 2020, 2021). Informed by prison abolition politics (Davis, 2003) and abolitionist feminism (Davis et al, 2022), anti-carceral approaches to feminist practice provide alternative visions for violence prevention outside of the criminal justice system. Such approaches are critical of the reliance on state crime control to address men's violence against women because of the failure to acknowledge the extent to which the state is masculinist and repressive, and the lack of recognition of how men's interpersonal violence is embedded in systems that perpetuate structural harm against women (Kim, 2021). The focus on crime control is only able to address interpersonal violence mainly by individual men, or small groups of men, and is unable to address wider structural forms of violence (Surken, 2022).

Increasingly, feminist non-profit agencies are funded and regulated by the state which tends to undermine their social movement principles and priorities (Whalley and Hackett, 2017). Feminist civil society organisations have become subordinated to, and incorporated into, the carceral state. Carcerality is also entrenched in gendered essentialist frameworks that reinforce a biologically framed gender binary and aim to secure neoliberal forms of equality between cisgendered men and women.

Bumiller (2008) illustrates how feminist activists' alliance with the state has led to the redefinition of men's violence against women as a social, medical and legal problem requiring intervention by social workers, public health workers and other professionals who bring their professional language and service responses to addressing the problem. Strategies for working with both victims and perpetrators of violence focus on individualised treatment. Women's shelters and rape crisis centres, originally formed as feminist community organisations raising women's consciousness about the wider problem of patriarchy, came under the 'terrain of the state' as they sought government funding. This has led to a professionalisation and bureaucratisation of services divorced from social movement activism. Furthermore, many organisations not informed by feminism accessed state funding to respond to the problem, contributing to a proliferation of apolitical welfare approaches to men's violence against women. In this context, what are the possibilities for social justice for women under neoliberal forms of governmentality?

Biopolitics of gender

While the concept of gender is frequently used as a progressive framework for understanding the experiences of women, Repo (2016) points out that its origins pre-date its use in feminism. She argues that its historical function as a form of biopolitical governance by politically conservative psychiatrists continues to influence its contemporary use, especially in its appropriation by neoliberal state apparatuses which regulate and de-radicalise feminist ideas. Neoliberal forms of governmentality promote ideal forms of masculinity and femininity which reinforce gendered power relations rather than challenge and resist them. In light of its origins in normalisation projects that reinforced the gender binary, and the way it is currently shaped by the neoliberal state, Repo queries whether the concept of gender can foster emancipatory politically interventions.

Biopolitical analysis sheds light on the current debates about carceral feminism which seek to use criminal sanctions to address violence against women. Sandbeck (2012) argues that carceral feminism is a form of neoliberal biopower that focuses primarily on sovereignty and individual responsibility, enabling new forms of self-governed gendered subjectivity. Expecting the state to protect women from violence fails to acknowledge the ways in which the state has perpetuated structural violence against women, especially women from marginalised backgrounds (Whalley and Hackett, 2017).

While much work has been done on feminism, neoliberalism and governmentality, little attention has been given to the ways that the current masculinity discourse constructs men as ideal self-governed neoliberal subjects (Garlick, 2021; Wolfman et al, 2021). Boucher (2023) has suggested that a governmentality framework allows us to problematise masculinity in men's programmes that aim to rehabilitate manhood. Current discussions about the problem of 'toxic masculinity' and interventions to engage men in creating 'healthy masculinities' closely align with biopolitical and neoliberal ideas about personal responsibility (Mohr, 2019). Psychological strategies to foster healthy masculinity in men which encourage self-discipline and restoration of manhood obscure the impact of institutionalised violence on men's bodies and subjectivities.

One form of governmentality is sex classification, whereby sex designation is inextricably linked to gender identity. While this raises particular problems for trans and non-binary people, it also impacts people whose classification as male or female is consistent with their own sense of gender identity. The gender order itself is a form of governmental rationality because people are unable to constitute themselves outside of gendered norms of biopower (de Souza and Parker, 2020).

Beyond the masculinist state

Feminist engagements with the state face many challenges arising from it being a patriarchally gendered structure dominated by men. Liberal states present themselves in the role of protectors, opening up questions of who protects whom against whom. Brown (1995) argues that the politics of protection and regulation are inescapable in state social policies; those who are subject to the state need to abide by the rules established by the protector. Young (2003) also notes that the state assumes the role of patriarch, encouraging dependence and subordination to ensure protection.

This protector role perpetuates a form of rationalist masculinity where so-called liberal 'good' men are contrasted with abusive and violent 'bad' men (Duriesmith, 2018). Because the state is gendered and patriarchal, it institutionalises a form of dominant masculinity to address what is seen to be the exaggerated masculinity of 'bad' men. The state comes to embody a chivalrous masculinity that espouses respect for women and aims to protect them from abusive men. Chivalrous masculinity is embedded in many state-based and non-government violence prevention programmes.

The White Ribbon Campaign, originally a bottom-up social movement in over 60 countries to engage men in the prevention of violence against women, has become corporatised through government and private trust funding in many countries. The White Ribbon Campaign encourages men to take a pledge 'never to commit, condone or remain silent about violence against women' (European Institute for Gender Equality, nd). White Ribbon focuses on attitudes and behaviours which are seen to perpetuate violence and encourages the development of a softer, violence-free, masculinity (Jordan, 2019). Constructing softer masculinities and manhood perpetuates the gender binary that reproduces gendered inequalities. Men are encouraged to identify as 'good' men who are non-violent. Seymour (2018) argues that in encouraging men to identify with more positive versions of masculinity, White Ribbon undermines the responsibility of all men to challenge their complicity in wider systems of patriarchal dominance.

In HeForShe, a United Nations campaign focused on bringing men into conversations about gender equality (HeForShe, nd), men are also encouraged to take a pledge to be 'a man who is going to stand up for women's rights'. Men are told that 'Real men treat women with dignity and give them the respect they deserve'. The campaign reinforces masculinity by affirming the gender binary and ignoring cultural and structural dimensions of male privilege (Henry-White, 2015). Again, men are encouraged to be 'good men' who are protectors of women but they are not required to take any action to challenge their own privilege. HeForShe reproduces the gender binary by disguising the fluidity of gender identities.

Gender and violence by men are interconnected with the violence of the state. Many states reinforce the gender binary by prioritising masculine men, othering feminine women and denigrating those who do not subscribe to the binary gender framework (Finau, 2019). Brown and Williams (2023) argue that the gender binary itself is a carceral ideology because it locks people into gender identity categories on the basis of their anatomy. They propose that gender policing forms part of the medical-industrial complex, exploring the links between the carcerality of gender and the prison-industrial complex. The abolitionist struggle against the prison system is connected to the tyranny of colonial gender systems. Settler colonialism, white supremacy and patriarchy are linked with the practices of the criminal justice system (Coyle and Schept, 2017). The category of gender itself within colonialism constitutes a type of prison (Bey and Goldberg, 2022).

Most government and non-government organisations currently engaging men in violence prevention in Australia aim at fostering healthy or positive masculinities (Pease, 2021). Men's investment in masculinity is used to engage men, but as Burrell (2018) notes, when referring to similar organisations in the UK, these organisations risk reinforcing notions of manhood that are at the heart of violence. Men are encouraged to disinvest from the most abusive forms of masculinity rather than to explore alternatives to masculinity itself.

Massey (2022), in an analysis of gender training for security sector personnel, demonstrates how liberal notions of protector roles were advanced to reform violent masculinities within the security sector. She interrogates the understanding of gender reproduced through this training and questions the extent to which reformed masculinities, divorced from the wider context of unequal power relations, can address the roots of men's violence against women. McCook (2022) similarly uncovered how violence prevention programmes with men and boys in Australia reinforced masculinity as a binary construct, limiting the options for an understanding of masculine subjectivities beyond the binary. In an ABC television programme in Australia, *Man Up*, one the facilitators of an educational programme for young men commented 'The last thing I want to do is to convince guys not to be men' (cited in Masters, 2017), to emphasise that his aim was to change the way in which men thought about their masculinity rather than to undo it.

Violence prevention in the non-profit industrial complex

Much of the work of engaging men in violence prevention takes place within non-government organisations funded by the state. INCITE (2007) has demonstrated how non-profit organisations have become the most significant sites of violence prevention work. The initiative has shifted from grassroots feminist community-based groups to corporate and state-funded programmes. State funding and regulation of non-profit organisations led to monitoring and control of social justice-based work, the management of dissent, a shift in focus from social activism to service delivery and pressure to emulate hierarchical organisational structures (Smith, 2007).

The non-government social services sector has been framed as the 'non-profit industrial complex', which Rodriguez (2007: 21–22) defines as 'a set of symbolic relationships that link political technologies of state and owning class control with surveillance over public political ideology, including and especially progressive and leftist social movements'. This is a corollary to the prison industrial complex, and the military industrial complex where the non-profit industrial complex functions as what Gilmore (2007) calls the 'shadow state', whereby a series of institutions funded and regulated by the state are used to manage dissent.

While the co-optation of feminist services by the state is well noted, Kivel (2007) further outlines ways in which intervention programmes for violent men have proliferated under state funding to become stand-alone behaviour change programmes disconnected from social activism. As I noted previously (Pease, 2004–2005), such programmes individualise men's violence by disconnecting it from the patriarchal social relations governing men's lives. Consequently, men's violence as a political problem that warranted structural change was reframed as an interpersonal problem to be addressed by therapeutic techniques. Twenty years later, this continues to be the case (McInerney and Archer, 2023).

Towards an abolitionist approach to violence prevention

An abolitionist perspective on the prevention of violence by men requires a recognition of the larger context which perpetuates violence. It means moving beyond an understanding of individually enacted interpersonal violence to encompass structural, administrative, military and planetary violence (McLeod, 2022). While cisgender men's violence against cisgender women is a major problem throughout the world, we need to generate new language and new theories to understand the links between intimate violence, global terrorism (Pain, 2015), and state and international violence (Davis et al, 2022).

Gender-based violence which is equated with violence against ciswomen often neglects structural analyses of gender, where violence is expanded beyond interpersonal acts to acknowledge and address structural and state violence (Applin et al, 2023). Such neglect leads to disconnecting men's interpersonal violence from its patriarchal cultural and structural context, while also neglecting structural violence itself. Price (2012) has noted that the frequently cited power and control wheel originally located men's violence against women within the wider context of patriarchy and the state. However, as the power and control wheel became institutionalised in men's behaviour change programmes, it severed the link between the interpersonal violence of men and the cultural and institutional drivers of men's violence.

Structural violence is perpetuated by the state through use of force by police, abuse and neglect of people who are incarcerated, and through economic, political, legal and religious social structures that prevent people from reaching their potential (Butler, 2022). It is also evident through colonialism and violence against combatants and civilians in wars (Dwyer, 2022) and in technologies of citizen surveillance (Torres, 2018). Slow violence that focuses on environmental harms (Nixon, 2013) is a form of structural violence against the planet. Such structural violence is gendered in that hegemonic masculinity is embedded through the gendered practices and processes of institutions, policies and laws (Crawshaw et al, 2015).

Too often, frameworks of 'gender-based violence', which focus solely on men's interpersonal violence against women, reinscribe the hierarchical gender binary and neglect the role of violence in policing normative gender categories (Mack et al, 2018). While gendered norms are often named as influencing the perpetration of violence, it is rare to see analyses of gender itself as constructed and determined by violence. Shepherd (2008) frames gendered violence as 'the violent reproduction of gender', whereby violence is understood as a site where genders are reproduced. Applin et al (2023) refer to violence against individuals who do not conform to the gender binary as 'patriarchy enhancing', in that such violence perpetuates the borders between cismen and ciswomen and polices people into normative gender categories.

Abolitionists increasingly recognise the relationship between the functioning of the militaristic and carceral state and dominant forms of masculinity. Dacquino et al (2021) identify hegemonic masculinity as a weapon of war, as it arises from the construct of the gender binary, which is itself a violent invention. Acheson (2022) argues that militarism is driven by masculinities that seek security in violence rather than care. Deconstructing masculinities and gender categories should be part of the abolitionist project because they entrap people in hierarchical binaries. Innovating new masculinities will not enable men to celebrate their full humanness. Masculinity is more than a 'man box'; it can be understood metaphorically as a form of 'incarceration' and functions in a parallel way to the prison-industrial complex (Howard, 2020).

Gender abolition and violence prevention

Gender binarism is one of the most fundamental forms of disciplinary power in society (Dvorsky and Hughes, 2008). Liberal feminist attempts to reform patriarchy through educational, economic and political strategies will not be successful because they do not address the quasi-biological gendering of the body. Because patriarchy is upheld by the gender/sex binary, there are calls for gender abolition.

For many feminists and their aspiring allies, gender equality is the means to address the problems associated with men's domination of women (Braunschweig, 2020). In this view, the concept of gender is not understood to inherently embody inequality. Rather, it is seen as socially constructed differences which have only a contingent relationship to power and status. Liberal feminists do not want to get rid of male and female gender categories. They want to make them less rigid and more equal in terms of status and power (Earp, 2021). This is the premise underpinning attempts to reform rigid masculinities and promote affirmative action strategies for women. However, Pineda (2021) argues that the idea that men and women can interact as equals while gender is still in place is fundamentally flawed.

Many abolitionist feminists regard gender equality as an oxymoron (Flores and Storm, 2019; Burgess, 2021; Pineda, 2021). In this view, gender differentiation embodied in the sexual division of labour in relation to paid work and care is inherently exploitative and gender is inherently oppressive. If gender was equal it would no longer be recognisable as gender. Similar to the Marxist analysis of class, where the aim is not to create class equality but rather struggle for a class-less society (Wright, 2012), feminist-informed social movements should aim for a gender-less rather than a gender-equal society. But what does it mean to abolish gender, how do we achieve that and what might the difficulties associated with it be?

Gender abolition means different things to different people. For Pratt (2021), in a gender-less society, sex categories would be decoupled from any socially constructed identities and would be no different from varying blood types. Sex characteristics would become almost insignificant. For Braunschweig (2020), gender abolition would not mean that individuals would be prevented from identifying with masculinity and femininity; so there is no attempt to abolish difference (Hester, 2018). Rather it is that these identities would not be connected to structures of power and people would not be forced into the rigid binary. Wright (2012) emphasises that gender-less society does not mean that everyone would be androgynous. There would still be a diversity of behaviours that are currently identified as masculine and feminine. However, there would not be normative pressure for these traits to be connected to male and female bodies. It is the structural base of gender as a relationship of power that would be abolished. Eventually, however, gender identities would become less important and would wither away.

There is considerable resistance to such a shift in direction in gender politics. The current sex/gender binary fulfils a number of psychological needs of individuals. It provides them with a sense of identity and group belonging and for many people being a man or a woman provides a deep sense of self-worth and embodiment connected to sex categories (Pratt, 2021). Deeply held beliefs in the biological sources of gendered behaviour means that gender identity is naturalised and embedded in people's sense of their own bodies (Lorber, 2021). Cisgender men in particular will resist the destabilising of the category of 'man' because it will threaten their access to power, wealth and status (Morgenroth and Ryan, 2021). Many transgender people also want to identify within the sex/gender binary and it is understandable that some would resist the abolition of gender given that it has provided them with a sense of oppositional identity (Earp, 2021). Also, because gender is incorporated and embedded in culture, law, religion and the state, its abolition would require transformative changes to key foundations in society (Burgess, 2021).

Gender abolition and the state

Just as Brown (1995) identified how a women's rights strategy within the state reinscribed women's subordination by gender, Spade (2015) shows how the exposure of transgender people to gender classification leads to criminalisation, marginalisation and violence. Many writers have argued that subordinated groups seeking affirmation of identity and recognition in the state limit their freedom and reproduce their subordinated status (Brown, 1995; Fraser, 1995; Spade, 2015). Also, the state perpetuates cisgenderism and encourages men to identify with normative masculinity and manhood.

However, notwithstanding the tensions noted, any form of gender abolition will require policy changes within the state, as the state frames and perpetuates gender categories (Pratt, 2021). Eliminating state and government policies that require designation of gender in, for example, drivers' licences, marriage certificates and pension and benefit applications, will be necessary. Spade (2015) refers to gender categorisations in administrative policies and practices as 'administrative violence' in terms of their impact on transgender people and those who do not conform to the gender binary, as they are scrutinised, regulated and violated by identification documents, sex-segregated facilities and healthcare access.

Strategies to deconstruct and abolish gender and the gender binary are at present underdeveloped. However, a number of strategies have been proposed:

- abolish compulsory gender registration in government identity documents (Braunschweig, 2020);
- disrupt the gender/sex binary by affirming genders/sexes beyond the binary (Morgenroth and Ryan, 2021);
- abolish the link between sex and gender (Pineda, 2021);
- explore alternative forms of kinship beyond the family (Lewis, 2022);
- support the political struggles of transgender and non-binary people (de Souza and Parker, 2020);
- encourage cisgender people to loosen their connections to a gender identity (Hearn, 2011; Morgenroth and Ryan, 2021);
- encourage cisgender people to adopt gender-neutral pronouns (Saguy et al, 2019).

All of these strategies, however, need to engage with capitalism, colonialism and the state (Flores and Storm, 2019), and hence should be part of a wider abolitionist politics.

Towards abolitionist practices against men's violences

Abolition is an epistemological and ethical perspective that encourages us to let go of our attachments to carceral ways of knowing (Ben-Moshe, 2018). In disrupting conventional knowledge and deeply embedded certainties, it creates a form of disorientation, requiring new ways of relating to each other outside of disciplinary frameworks (Halle-Erby and Keenan, 2022). Woodly (2020) refers to this as a process of undoing, abolishing parts of ourselves that are constituted by carceral logics through the practice of enacting alternative forms of care. Rodriguez (2019) emphasises that abolition is more than a practice of negation. It is a communally building praxis that aims to reconfigure subjectivity, justice and social formation by challenging masculinist and patriarchal constructions of self-determination and freedom.

We need to develop transformative justice strategies to respond to violence (Kim, 2021; Davis et al, 2022; McLeod, 2022). Pain (2022) outlines how commoning practices, which are usually associated with alternative communities and eco-villages, can create collectivist responses to state and intimate violence. Commoning enables us to rethink the formation of identity beyond self-sufficiency and to abolish subjectivities that are accommodated to the gendered and unequal division of labour (Millner-Larsen and Butt, 2018). In recognition that commoning can also reproduce patriarchal relations and the gender binary, recently we have seen moves to gender and queer commoning practices to ensure that the project of destabilising ruling subjectivities is attentive to gender and sex (Millner-Larsen and Butt, 2018; Perivia, 2023). Our relationships with others are essential to the construction of the self and, consequently, care for others and care for the self are interconnected in commoning (Apostolova and Gauthier-Mamaril, 2018).

From an abolitionist perspective, care is a political project that is beyond the personal. It involves mutual aid, consciousness-raising and organising against violence at both local and international levels (Woodly, 2020). An ethic of care perspective can guide violence prevention not only in the family, but also in the wider international context of terrorism and war (Held, 2008). Challenging men's violence against women in the private sphere is the same project as confronting men's terrorist and military violence in the public sphere.

I have argued previously (Pease, 2019) that fostering an ethic of care in men is an effective strategy to prevent men's violence. An ethic of care is the antithesis of violence as all forms of violence involve a failure to care. By doing emotional care work, practising empathy, becoming ontologically vulnerable and developing care in political solidarity with women and queer people, we can foster caring practices and activism for peace. To foster this ethic of care in men, it is important to engage men emotionally in the consequences of violence. Towards this end, I have utilised antisexist consciousness raising, collective memory work and critical pedagogies in workshops to educate men about patriarchy and the gender binary (Pease, 2012).

Conclusion

As I reflect on 40 years of activism against men's violences, I realise that, although I was unaware of it for much of that time, I was enacting a form of abolitionist politics. By forming activist profeminist men's networks outside of the state, I have encouraged communities of practice to provide opportunities for intellectual analysis and civil society organising, unencumbered by state policy discourses. Through Men Against Sexism, Men Against Sexual Assault, patriarchy awareness workshops, accountability processes, public forums on courageous conversations with men about violence against women, marches and public demonstrations against men's violence and academic and media commentary on the limits of public health frameworks, healthy masculinities and neoliberal policy discourses in addressing violence, I have sought to create spaces which I now recognise as forms of commoning. The aim was to provide an alternative to the discursive framing of violence as an individualised problem amenable to professional intervention and state control. Abolition politics and commoning provide a language to frame and support alternative practices of care, love and solidarity beyond categories of gender and coercive apparatuses of the state.

Acknowledgements

I would like to thank Jeff Hearn, Stephen Burrell and Ian Hyslop for their insightful and constructive comments on an earlier version of this chapter.

References

Acheson, R. (2022) *Abolishing Militarised Masculinities*, Women's League for Peace and Freedom. Available at: https://www.wilpf.org/wp-content/uploads/2022/07/RL_10-Abolishing-militarised-masculinities-AW.pdf

Apostolova, I. and Gauthier-Mamaril, E. (2018) 'Care and the self: A philosophical perspective on constructing masculinities', *Feminist Philosophical Quarterly*, 4(1): 1–5.

Applin, S., Simpson, J-M. and Curtis, A (2023) 'Men have a gender and women are people: A structural approach to gender and violence', *Violence Against Women*, 29(5): 1097–1118.

Ben-Moshe, L. (2018) 'De-epistemologies of abolition', *Critical Criminology*, 26: 341–355.

Bey, M. and Goldberg, J. (2022) 'Queer as in abolition now', *A Journal of Lesbian and Gay Studies*, 28(2): 159–163.

Boucher, L. (2023) 'The proliferation of men's sheds in Australia: The problematisations of masculinity in a neoliberal regime', *Cultural Studies*. Available at: doi.org/10.1080/09502386.2023.2169731

Braunschweig, L. (2020) 'Abolishing gender registration: A feminist defence', *International Journal of Gender, Sexuality and Law*, 76: 76–97.

Brown, W. (1995) *States of Injury: Power and Freedom in Late Modernity*, Princeton: Princeton University Press.

Brown, S. and Williams, A. (2023) 'The prison system is a "gendering killing machine"', *Prism*. Available at: https://prismreports.org/2023/04/06/the-prison-system-is-a-gendering-killing-machine/

Bumiller, K. (2008) *In An Abusive State: How Neoliberalism Appropriated the Feminist Movement Against Sexual Violence*, Durham, NC: Duke University Press.

Burgess, I. (2021) 'Gender abolition: Why it matters', *Cherwell*. Available at: https://www.cherwell.org/2021/10/09/gender-abolition-why-it-matters/

Burrell, S. (2018) 'The contradictory possibilities of engaging men and boys in the prevention of men's violence against women in the UK', *Journal of Gender-Based Violence*, 2(3): 447–464.

Burstyn, V. (1983) 'Masculine dominance and the state', *Socialist Register 1983*, 20: 45–89.

Butler, P. (2022) 'The problem of state violence', *Daedalius*, 151(1): 22–37.

Coyle, M. and Schept, J. (2017) 'Penal abolition and the state: Colonial, racial and gender violences', *Contemporary Justice Review*, 20(4): 399–403.

Crawshaw, P., Scott-Samuel, A. and Stanistreet, D. (2015) 'Masculinities, hegemony and structural violence', *Centre for Crime and Justice Studies*, 102: 20–22.

Dacquino, M., Lude, C., Palmisano, C. and Raddad, G. (2021) *Militarised Masculinities: Identifying Causes, Manifestations and Strategies for Change*, Geneva: Geneva Graduate Institute.

Davis, A. (2003) *Are Prisons Obsolete?* New York: Seven Stories Press.

Davis, A., Dent, G., Meiners, E. and Richie, B. (2022) *Abolition. Feminism. Now.*, Chicago: Hamish Hamilton.

de Souza, E. and Parker, M. (2020) 'Practices of freedom and the disruption of binary genders: Thinking *with* trans', *Organization*, 29(1): 67–82.

Duriesmith, D. (2018) 'Manly states and feminist foreign policy: Revisiting the liberal state as an agent of change', in S. Parashar, A. Tickner and J. True (eds), *Revisiting Gendered States: Feminist Imaginings of the State in International Relations*, Oxford: Oxford University Press, pp 51–68.

Dvorsky, G. and Hughes, J. (2008) *Postgenderism: Beyond the Gender Binary*, IEET Monograph Series, Institute for Ethics and Emerging Technologies.

Dwyer, P. (2022) *Violence: A Very Short Introduction*, Oxford: Oxford University Press.

Earp, B. (2021) 'Abolishing gender', in D. Edmonds (ed), *Future Morality*, Oxford: Oxford University Press, pp 35–49.

European Institute for Gender Equality (nd) *White Ribbon Campaign*. Available at: https://eige.europa.eu/sites/default/files/documents/mh0216314enn.pdf

Finau, E. (2019) 'Axiom of a masculinist state and the gendered avowal: An interdisciplinary discourse', *Newcastle Business School Journal*, 2(1): 48–57.

Flores, E. and Storm, V. (2019) *Gender Accelerationist Manifesto*, independently published.

Fraser, N. (1995) 'From redistribution to recognition? Dilemmas of justice in a "post-socialist" age', *New Left Review*, 212: 68–93.

Garlick, S. (2021) 'Technologies of (in)security: Masculinity and the complexity of neoliberalism', *Feminist Theory*, 24(2): 170–187.

Gilmore, R.W. (2007) 'In the shadow of the shadow state', in INCITE: Women of Color Against Violence (ed), *The Revolution Will Not Be Funded: Beyond the Non-Profit Industrial Complex*, Cambridge: South End Press, pp 4–52.

Halle-Erby and Keenan, H. (2022) 'Learning from abolition: Reconsidering the carceral in educational research methodologies', in A. Tachine and Z. Nicolazzo (eds), *Weaving an Otherwise: In-Relations Methodological Practices*, New York: Routledge.

Hearn, J. (2011). 'The materiality of men, bodies and toward the abolition of "men"', in M. Läubli and S. Sahli (eds), *Männlichkeiten denken: Aktuelle Perspektiven der kulturwissenschaftlichen Masculinity Studies*, Bielefeld: Belefeld University Press, pp 195–216.

HeForShe (nd) 'We are the United Nations global solidarity movement for gender equality', UN Women. Available at: Heforshe.org/en

Held, V. (2008) 'Military intervention and the ethics of care', *The Southern Journal of Philosophy*, 46: 1–20.

Henry-White, J. (2015) 'Gender equality? A transnational feminist analysis of the UN HeForShe campaign as a global "solidarity" movement for men', Master of Arts thesis, University of Missouri-Columbia.

Hester, H. (2018) *Xenofeminism*, Cambridge: Polity Press.

Howard, J. (2020) 'It is a box but it is also a prison: Rethinking conversations on masculinity', Ohio Alliance to End Sexual Violence. Available at: https://oaesv.org/where-we-stand/blog/2020/08/04/it-is-a-box-but-it-is-also-a-prison-rethinking-conversations-on-masculinity/

INCITE: Women of Color Against Violence (ed) (2007) *The Revolution Will Not Be Funded: Beyond the Non-Profit Industrial Complex*, Cambridge: South End Press.

Jordan, A. (2019) *The New Politics of Fatherhood: Men's Movements and Masculinities*, London: Palgrave Macmillan.

Kim, M. (2020) 'The carceral creep: Gender-based violence, race and the expansion of the punitive state', *Social Problems*, 67: 251–269.

Kim, M. (2021) 'Transformative justice and restorative justice: Gender-based violence and alternative visions of justice in the US', *International Review of Victimology*, 27(2): 162–172.

Kivel, P. (2007) 'Social service or social change', in INCITE: Women of Color Against Violence (ed), *The Revolution Will Not Be Funded: Beyond the Non-Profit Industrial Complex*, Cambridge: South End Press, pp 129–149.

Lewis, S. (2022) *Abolish the Family*, London: Verso.

Lorber, J. (2021) *The New Gender Paradox: Fragmentation and Persistence of the Binary*, Cambridge: Polity.

Mack, A., Bershon, C., Laiche, D. and Navaro, M. (2018) 'Between bodies and institutions: Gendered violence as co-constitutive', *Women's Studies in Communication*, 41(2): 95–99.

Massey, R. (2022) 'Reforming masculinity: The politics of gender, race, militarism and security sector reform in the Democratic Republic of Congo', *International Feminist Journal of Politics*, 24(4): 586–607.

Masters, J. (2017) ' "Hey mate!": Intervening the masculinity crisis in ABC's Man Up', Bachelor of Arts honours thesis, University of Sydney.

McCook, S. (2022) ' "So what is good masculinity?": Navigating normativity in violence prevention with men and boys', *Australian Feminist Studies*, 37(111): 37–53.

McInerney, W. and Archer, D. (2023) 'Men's violence prevention and peace education: Drawing on Galtung to explore the plurality of violence(s), peace(s), and masculinities', *Men and Masculinities*, 26(1): 69–90.

McLeod, A. (2022) 'An abolitionist critique of violence', *The University of Chicago Law Review*, 89(2): 525–556.

Millner-Larsen, N. and Butt, G. (2018) 'Introduction: The queer commons', *A Journal of Lesbian and Gay Studies*, 23(4): 399–419.

Mohr, S. (2019) 'The biopolitics of masculinity (studies)', *NORMA: International Journal for Masculinity Studies*, 14(4): 199–205.

Morgenroth, T. and Ryan, M. (2021) 'The effects of gender trouble: An integrative theoretical framework of the perpetuation and disruption of the gender/sex binary', *Perspectives on Psychological Science*, 16(6): 1113–1142.

Nixon, R. (2013) *Slow Violence and the Environmentalism of the Poor*, New York: Harvard University Press.

Pain, R. (2015) 'Intimate war', *Political Geography*, 44: 64–73.

Pain, R. (2022) 'Collective trauma? Isolating and commoning gender-based violence', *Gender, Place and Culture*, 29(12): 1788–1809.

Pease, B. (2004–2005) 'Rethinking profeminist men's behaviour change programs', *Women Against Violence*, 16: 32–40.

Pease, B. (2012) 'The politics of gendering emotions: Disrupting men's emotional investment in privilege', *Australian Journal of Social Issues*, 47(1): 125–142.

Pease, B. (2019) *Facing Patriarchy: From a Violent Gender Order to a Culture of Peace*, London: Zed.

Pease, B. (2021) 'The limits of public health approaches and discourses of masculinities in violence against women prevention', in D. McCallum (ed), *The Palgrave Handbook of the History of Human Sciences*, London: Palgrave Macmillan, pp 1–22.

Perivia, H. (2023) 'Gendering the commons or commoning gender studies? A bibliographic analysis', *Science Po OFCE Working Paper*, N 09/2023.

Pineda, A. (2021) 'Arguments for the abolition of gender', *CMC Senior Theses*, 2764. Available at: https://scholarship.claremont.edu/cmc_theses/2764/

Pratt, M. (2021) 'How to abolish gender', *Student Policy Review*, Harvard Kennedy School. Available at: https://studentreview.hks.harvard.edu/how-to-abolish-gender/

Price, J. (2012) *Structural Violence: Hidden Brutality and the Lives of Women*, New York: State University of New York Press.

Repo, J. (2016) *The Biopolitics of Gender*, Oxford: Oxford University Press.

Rodriguez, D. (2007) 'The political logic of the non-profit industrial complex', in INCITE: Women of Color Against Violence (ed), *The Revolution Will Not Be Funded: Beyond the Non-Profit Industrial Complex*, Cambridge: South End Press, pp 21–40.

Rodriguez, D. (2019) 'Abolition as praxis of human being: A foreword', *Harvard Law Review*, 132(6). Available at: https://harvardlawreview.org/archives/vol-132-no-6/

Saguy, A., Williams, J., Dembroff, R. and Wodak, D. (2019) 'We should all use they/them pronouns … eventually', *Scientific American*. Available at: https://www.scientificamerican.com/blog/voices/we-should-all-use-they-them-pronouns-eventually/

Sandbeck, S. (2012) 'Towards and understanding of carceral feminism as neoliberal power', paper presented at the 2012 Annual Conference of the Canadian Political Science Association, University of Alberta.

Seymour, K. (2018) '"Stand up, speak out and act": A critical reading of Australia's White Ribbon campaign', *Australian and New Zealand Journal of Criminology*, 51(2): 293–310.

Shepherd, L. (2008) *Gender, Violence and Security: Discourse as Practice*, London: Zed.

Smith, A. (2007) 'Introduction: The revolution will not be funded', in INCITE: Women of Color Against Violence (ed), *The Revolution Will Not Be Funded: Beyond the Non-Profit Industrial Complex*, Cambridge, South End Press, pp 1–18.

Spade, D. (2015) *Normal Life: Administrative Violence, Critical Trans Politics and the Limits of Law*, Durham, NC: Duke University Press.

Surken, J. (2022) 'How gender-based violence makes prison abolition (un)thinkable: The role of narrations and their setting', *The King's Student Law Review*, 12(1): 77–102.

Torres, G. (2018) 'State violence', in A. Trevino (ed), *The Cambridge Handbook of Social Problems, Volume 2*, Cambridge: Cambridge University Press, pp 381–398.

Whalley, E. and Hackett, C. (2017) 'Carceral feminisms: The abolitionist project and undoing dominant feminisms', *Contemporary Justice Review*, 20(4): 456–473.

Wolfman, G., Hearn, J. and Yeardon-Lee, T. (2021) 'Hollow femininities: The emerging faces of neoliberal masculinities', *NORMA*, 16(4): 217–234.

Woodly, D. (2020) 'The politics of care', lecture at the New School, 18 June.

Wright, E. (2012) 'In defense of genderlessness', in A. En Grosseries and Y. Vanderborght (eds), *Arguing About Justice: Essays for Philippe van Parijs*, Louvain: Presses Universitaires de Louvain, pp 403–413.

Young, I. (2003) 'The logic of masculinist protection', *Signs*, 29(1): 1–25.

13

Transformative justice informed community responses to harm: a conversation with Idil Ali, Lauren Caulfield and Anita Thomasson

Anne-lise Ah-fat

Introduction

In early 2020, the United States experienced one of its most significant uprisings in response to the killing of George Floyd by police. The Minneapolis Third Precinct was burnt down following looting, rioting and protesters forcing police into retreat. The ripples of this uprising were felt here in settler-colonial Australia, where thousands marched in solidarity, as well as to demonstrate against police brutality and Aboriginal deaths in custody on this continent. As social injustice and state-sponsored violence of marginalised communities generates social harm, Aboriginal, Black/Brown, migrant, poor/low-income, disabled, queer/trans and sex worker communities have long recognised and exposed the connections between intimate partner violence and violence enacted by the state. They have offered robust critiques of how liberal anti-violence feminism has been shaped by the state's conservative agenda (Loney-Howes et al, 2024). However, significant and ever-increasing state investment in carceral responses to family violence have amplified family violence policing – propagating a thinking that violence can be addressed through greater state intervention. In contrast, radical anti-violence activists view intimate partner violence as interconnected with capitalism, white supremacy, gender hegemony and colonisation; highlighting that state interventions disproportionately harm marginalised communities who encounter barriers to support, punitive state responses, collusion from services and increased criminalisation.

These communities have sought out and developed responses to sexual and family violence with an intention to not replicate acts of domination, exclusion and punishment; but rather to reduce harm and to create spaces for accountability, support and healing (Richie, 2011). Non-state responses to violence have come to be known as transformative justice (Chen et al, 2016; Dixon and Lakshmi Piepzna-Samarasinha, 2020), although many communities do not use this as a label. Transformative justice approaches seek to address family violence and its impacts as well as transform the conditions which enable family violence and sexual assault to occur – prefigurative of a world without prisons. While abolition and transformative justice emerged from radical Black and Indigenous organising in the United States (Rojas et al, 2012), in settler-colonial Australia there is 250-plus years of Aboriginal-led resistance to the violence of colonisation and policing (Spearim, 2021).

As a migrant settler to so-called Australia, my lineages include Creole slaves, Hakka indentured labourer-slaves and slave owners from France and Portugal. I grew up witnessing how my dad was profiled by police – police and the state were not considered sites of safety. After two decades of participating in abolitionist anti-violence organising, transformative justice informed community responses to harm and prison solidarity projects, most of what I read and engage in comes out of the United States – where the terms 'abolition' and 'transformative justice' emerged (Brazzell and Meiners, 2022). While abolition in 2020 went mainstream in unanticipated ways, local stories of abolitionist practice continue to be obscured. The learnings from the United States have been profound and highly valued but I am fuelled by a desire to share stories and trace lineages of on-the-ground practices on this continent. My hope is that in sharing our stories we can contribute to establishing collective memory, capturing what is not always visible, and providing possibilities in paths towards liberation.

Through lived experience and insight, the following interviews with Idil, Loz and Ani explore how transformative justice approaches are applied, the challenges and limits, and the impacts on individuals and communities. Having known and organised alongside Idil, Loz and Ani for many years through participating in shared anti-violence collectives and supporting each other's projects, I interviewed them through video call and collaboratively transcribed and edited their responses. These narratives describe the theoretical underpinnings of transformative justice, as well as practice approaches. Each person interviewed adopts a self-critical approach, considering contradictions and the challenges of implementing non-carceral responses in a world deeply invested in punitive systems. They speak to practices that attempt to decrease the impacts of systemic harm and work towards collective healing. This is a collective invitation to those working to end violence to consider and value strategies that do not rely on state intervention.

Contributors

I am Idil Ali, a proud Somali woman born in Aotearoa. I spent my early childhood in the United States in Minnesota before moving to so-called Australia. I grew up in a predominantly East African Muslim community in the public housing flats in Carlton, and spent significant time in North Melbourne and Flemington through family, the mosque and East African community.

I am Lauren Caulfield, or Loz, and I live and work on unceded Wurundjeri Country. I am a mother, a migrant and a multiracial cis-woman. I am Shan and Mon on my mum's side, from Myanmar, and Irish Romani on my dad's side, from Liverpool. I work at the intersection of interpersonal and state-sanctioned gender violence in both unwaged and community settings. I also coordinate a community-based project that responds to the violence of policing.

I am Anita Thomasson, or Ani, I live in Naarm and have grown up in so-called Australia. My father is English, Irish and Scottish. His family arrived in Queensland in the Rockhampton area, at a time when colonisation was commencing. My mum's side of the family are Macedonian and came to so-called Australia in the 1950s as post-Second World War refugees. I am involved in prison solidarity projects, community radio and Incendium Radical Library Infoshop.

The conversation

Anne-lise: *How would you describe transformative justice informed community responses to harm?*

Loz: Community accountability and transformative justice for me is about a level of individual and collective responsibility for the violence that occurs in our communities. A carceral response to violence assumes that violence is a problem or an issue that will be solved by an outside other – and that that outside other is the state. In order to respond to violence, to intervene and to prevent violence, it involves a thinking that we will empower the state and invest in the state to come in as an external party to moderate that violence and to provide often what's described as accountability but what I see as punishment. What happens in those systems is, rather than transforming or addressing the drivers of violence – the conditions that recruit people into the use of violence – we are instead relying on outsourcing the violence. We bring in an agency that is capable of using its own power-over model, pushing people into punishment systems and then assuming that that will somehow transform violence. But then of course it doesn't, and violence becomes more and more entrenched over time.

Ani: In the context that I've been in, community responses means trying to create alternative pathways of responding to and intervening on family violence, gendered violence, interpersonal violence and sexual assault without the state. My view of what a community response to harm might be is a bit more complex than when I first engaged with these ideas. It's about trying to create safety or support for people who have experienced harm but also about trying to create safety and support for people who have done harm – as well as trying to support people to shift the beliefs that have led them to act in harmful ways. I think now I am interested in how all people can live their lives in some way within community – and how we can shift the conditions that allow violence to occur.

Anne-lise: *How did you get involved with transformative justice informed community responses to harm?*

Idil: Having grown up with my mother, and around her politics, she had a big focus on how we treat people, how we connect with people, and what we foster – which gave me the sense that we have the power to shape our own lives and also other people's lives. From early on, I knew people who caused harm and I knew that that was not all that they were. A lot of kids have a perception of good people and bad people, but the environment I grew up in was the opposite. I was seeing the people who do the bad things also doing the sweetest, kindest and most caring things. I found it ironic because I saw these guys with hammers and machetes, and then the next day they were giving me a dollar for the milk bar. And I was reflecting on the perceptions that people had about my community – that our community was violent – and I remember thinking, there's all these things we can't talk about outside of our communities because if we do, then it's going to fulfil these stereotypes – but we actually do need to sort this shit out.

Loz: Interpersonal and structural violence is often woven through all of our lives and it's the lived experience of violence that has led me to my interest in anti-violence work and in wanting to learn about that and what constitutes an 'effective' response. When I look back across my lifetime and then go back generations, I look at the gender-based violence that was occurring in my own family and communities. When I look back at who and where the sites of safety were, and what it means to be from a refugee family and to be a child of an interracial relationship, I see that those sites of safety were never located with the state because that's not what the state represented. For me, accessing safety has always been about relationships and a nuanced understanding of all the different things that we are experiencing when we are experiencing violence. As I moved into activist and organising communities, some of these ideas became politicised in a particular way. There was an intentionality and a reflectiveness around thinking about why we might choose to take up particular responses and avoid other responses.

Ani: What brought me to community responses to harm was in alternative subcultures. I was 18 and organising around the Stop G20 conferences. Someone I had met and become close with was experiencing violence from a partner and people were wanting to respond. I was part of a group who were having conversations, trying to figure out what to do and how to create spaces of increased safety for survivors. I didn't have any idea of what I was doing and it also felt against the grain of that particular social milieu. At the Stop G20 gathering, Regrette and Kt Spit did a workshop about community responses to sexual violence. Then out of that, they gathered people's names who wanted to keep talking about this stuff. A World Without Sexual Assault collective started from that workshop, which I joined. That is where I met you and also how I got involved in transformative justice work.

Anne-lise: *In your life, what do transformative justice informed community responses to harm look like?*

Idil: When I was growing up, the amount of times people would go to Flemington police station and be outside of the station, saying, 'Let our people go', and we would stay there for hours and call for more and more people. We have such a rich history

A few years ago somebody in our community was stabbed and the other family was saying, 'Why should we let this criminal run free after they have done this to our child?' A lot of the women were cultivating an environment where they were saying, 'How are any of our kids going to be safe if this person's running around stabbing people?' I remember we were in this conversation with these women – it was intergenerational – there were some younger people in the mix, and I remember saying, 'When it's not your kid, they are a criminal and you want them locked up. But when it is your kid, we have to do everything to keep them out of the system. You guys don't actually believe that people should be locked up. If you thought it was something that was going to make them better, then you would be the first to report them. You wouldn't be trying to take them back home. You wouldn't be trying to get them a plane ticket back to Somalia. You wouldn't be doing everything in your power to make sure that they don't get locked up.' Prison is very disconnecting for our communities.

Loz: I was thinking of a friend who disclosed the violence that her partner was using against her. The agreement we made was that a couple of us would be the contact people for safety planning. We had a lot of conversations about her assessment of what was going on and her sense of what would make things safer or riskier. The safety strategy she had been using was quite a nuanced way of removing herself and her child from the situation in times of heightened risk and use of violence but without engaging in naming or calling out that violence. We worked together to put in place a few different plans. It was a pre-agreed system for how to communicate, as her partner had been checking her phone regularly.

On this particular day, she sent a message saying things weren't good, that they were reaching a crisis point and that she needed accompaniment. In community accountability the principle of close accompaniment is important. A couple of us went over to her place and the partner had just left the house. We had a short conversation about what was needed and agreed we would accompany her and her child as they packed up some belongings and left the home. Her objective in that time was to be able to leave the family home without there being an escalation of violence that resulted in injury or harm to herself or her child.

Anne-lise: *What are some of your learnings and challenges with transformative justice and community accountability experiments?*

Idil: I don't have the skillset that is necessary, of knowing who all the families are and how they are connected to each other, because my mum hasn't been in the country for the last nine years. I have some of that knowledge through my friends and other families, but it's not the same as having the cultural richness of family histories that your own parents hold. I think that's important for repair. Whenever something happens to young people, if they have some relationship to each other it's 100 per cent better – nobody's going to call the police, they are going to sort it out themselves, and it's going to be the best outcome. It's even better when they're the same ethnicity. When something happens across ethnicities, you better hope and pray that they're both Muslim, and then hopefully that can be the uniting force. But if they're not Muslims and they're not the same ethnicity, then somebody's calling the police. And that's the thing my people know – the police are about punishment. They're about being punitive.

Ani: In the past when people who caused harm didn't arrive at an accountability conversation with complete realisation, reflection or confession, I judged their response as defensiveness or hostility – as though the person had no interest in taking responsibility. I saw confession as accountability. Now, I think realisation, reflection and accountability might be an end goal of spending time talking through things and I don't expect someone to arrive there initially.

Anne-lise: *What community resources, skills and infrastructure already exist that support conditions for transformative justice informed community responses to harm? And what is missing?*

Loz: In terms of community infrastructure, there are a whole lot of resources, practice approaches, skill shares, community networks where we exchange stories and experiences, and we have our living archives of the work that we're doing so that we keep learning from each other. In Beyond Survival we don't imagine that justice lives in carceral responses – but in recognising that, it doesn't mean that people don't either elect to or are forced to interface with those systems, whether it's a criminal legal process or a family law process. So, our role as community members or a community-based project might be to look at how we can harm-minimise those processes and actually walk alongside people, through and against harmful systems.

Ani: I think of experience, knowledge and information as community resources. There have been times when collectives or groups of people have run regular workshops or events to hold and distribute stories and build connections, and that's where I've learnt a lot. But in my small social world, people are now living more separately. There is less share-housing and community spaces and people are living further apart from each other. There are less spaces for connection, and 'community' is more disconnected or absent. Stuff on the internet and social media is simplified with a lot less information in it, so if that's where people are learning about doing community responses, I think that's going to look different.

Anne-lise: *There is often so much levelled against community responses to harm. What is your thinking around failure?*

Loz: It is humbling work, right? It requires that we engage with failure, with learning out loud and with being willing to reflect on mistakes in such an ongoing way. And that has to be part of our process of building a body of responses. I think one of the things that is so striking in any community-based response is often how much critique and perfectionism is levelled at those responses. I think we can often engage in this idea that we are measuring our responses against this idea of perfection, a utopian future that's free from violence, where everything has been achieved by the one response. Where people are safe, conditions that have recruited people into the use of violence are transformed and where everybody is better off for going through whatever response we're engaged in. I think this is such an unrealistic and unfair way to measure community responses.

It's slippery language, but it would be far more fair to ourselves and to each other to measure our responses against the existing alternatives. So much resourcing has gone into building these punishment systems, and it is going to take a huge body of work and learning, making mistakes, and learning together with generosity over time, to be able to dismantle them and to rebuild and rediscover and reinvest in all of our community-based alternatives. It is incredibly helpful for me to feel permitted to make mistakes. Particularly because it's scary and it's high responsibility work. The material effects of people's safety are significant and there's a weight of responsibility in that.

Ani: I want to complicate ideas of failure. In talking to a friend recently about community responses to harm, the person experiencing violence felt less alone and had support. In a bad moment, there was someone they could call. They felt cared for. For the person who was using violence there were people who believed that they could do things differently and didn't treat them like a pariah. There wasn't the experience of imprisonment or state violence, court processes or family court battles.
And in terms of culture, there has been a big shift in how people navigate and respond to family and sexual violence. People are more open to talking about and addressing violence, and interpersonal violence is considered to be a political problem. I do however have many learnings about ways I participated in actions that replicated state responses. I think exclusion, ostracism, the framing of a person replicated oppressive dynamics. I wish I had done things in different ways and not contributed to cancel culture.

Anne-lise: *How are carceral feminisms and carceral logics showing up in your context and communities?*

Idil: The not-for-profit industrial complex is the hardest thing that we have to deal with. Anybody who's doing great work in our community and anybody who's respected gets swallowed by these organisations. And then they have us doing what they want us to do. It's difficult to explain how detrimental it is. You need these people to help you. You need this funding in order to do anything. It's great for those years that everybody's getting paid, all these programmes are running, but there's no continuity. It just falls apart – and then what?

And our community is being co-opted by the prisons now. They headhunt us. People have to do what they need to do for the check, but it's not abolitionist. The way that youth workers and community workers are being taught the idea that calling the police is about keeping young people safe – we are being inducted into this. And if you don't see an alternative, you get lost in it. The only reason why I felt I had an alternative is because I attended youth programmes where shit used to happen with police and the workers from the community found ways of responding, and when other people called the police, the workers used to protect the young people – they would make it their responsibility to get the young people out of there.

Loz: What we are seeing in so-called Victoria is a huge amount of investment in policing, which means extra recruitment, expansion of weaponry, but also the export of carceral thinking into all kinds of spaces. Police are authorised, endorsed and centred in the family violence service system. What that looks like is a template response to everyone experiencing violence to call police and an assumption that on everybody's safety plan that calling triple zero should be at the centre. This compromises people's capacity to be able to speak frankly about the harm that they're experiencing from police for fear of repercussions. And there can be so much pressure leveraged against people who might not be choosing to call the police because it doesn't represent safety to them.

Ani: While there's been an increase in anti-police sentiment since Black Lives Matter in 2020, I've noticed at the same time there's been an increase in carceral approaches to people. The way I see that playing out is when the social response to somebody who's done harm is that the person should be excommunicated. And anyone who's in connection with that person is seen as enabling or supporting abuse. There's also no sense of when this ends. Someone might hear about something someone did ten years ago, and they continue to be marked as an abuser.

Anne-lise: *Any final thoughts?*

Idil: The cost of living and the way that we're disconnected from each other is making community responses to harm harder and harder. We live in a settler colony and the settler colony is good at passing on fallacies as facts. And as long as we live in this alternate reality where we are keeping up colonisation as if we're not, where those lies are going to continue to be passed on as truths, then our young people will be indoctrinated either into accepting a lie or losing their minds, because it's actually the type of shit that makes you crazy. Considering the amount of resources that were put into destroying people, where are the resources to repair people? There's no concern and they continue to fund the things that harm us.

Loz: How do we engage in these responses in a way that doesn't replicate some of the pressures of the non-profit industrial complex? The pressure of funding cycles, of an environment where services are pitching against each other – there can be this pressure to search for easily marketable victories and to find examples of successes. It's long-term work, and it's intergenerational work. We need to resist the pressure to thin out the nuanced work of these responses into template stories for the purpose of measurement. It's deep and relational work.

Ani: I think we need skills when speaking with people who've used violence. With less of a culture around zines [short for magazine – zines hold a history rooted in radical politics and do-it-yourself publishing], workshops and skill-shares. I don't see these specific skills being developed much anymore. It used to create a sense of possibility – of who we could ask for advice, of who might have something to share, or who could provide support. People are experiencing abuse and they want to do something about it, and they think fuck the cops, and I hate services, and I hate the state. But, who can help – especially in this context of increasing isolation and separation.

Reflections

Transformative justice is an abolitionist framework that recognises police, prisons, child protection, border protection and human services as sites of violence and coercion (Rojas and Naber, 2022). Transformative justice informed community responses to harm express desires for what a world beyond prisons might be. They occur, however, amidst increased atomisation and carceral responses to violence. At its core, this discussion acknowledges the destructive violence perpetuated by the capitalist and white supremacist state, as well as its institutions – as for many communities, relying on police, the criminal legal system or the child removal system is unviable.

In community responses to harm, skills and knowledges about support, healing, intervention and responses to violence are shared, learned and reflected upon. Cultural and familial knowledge is honoured, and stories show how intergenerational and cultural contexts influence responses to harm. Survivor insider knowledges are valued alongside the importance of seeing people beyond their harmful actions. We are, however, deeply entangled in carceral systems. We internalise carceral logics, often replicating the same hierarchical systems we claim to be dismantling. Community responses are therefore not perfect; embracing learning from mistakes is seen as crucial and includes humility, reflection, and adapting and revising approaches as part of building responses to violence. Ideas of failure are problematised, with a recognition that measuring community responses against utopian ideals is unfair – especially when compared to existing carceral responses and systemic harm perpetrated by the state.

The idea of community itself is subject to debate and contestation. The precarity of community is named, strained by violence, material necessity, the fragmentation of poverty, social isolation, overwork and the grip of capitalism. This precarity, disconnection and isolation makes collective action another challenge. Dominant liberal discourses make it difficult for communities to guard against the co-optation of community resources and people by not-for-profits that offer temporary solutions, without sustainability and often tied to the state.

As intimate-partner and sexual violence continues at the conjunction of nation, race, poverty and gender, our movements attempt to build the relationships, skills, principles, practices and infrastructure needed to transform use of violence. The interviews illustrate the complexities of this: of building and sustaining transformative justice informed community responses to harm. They also demonstrate the need for ongoing skill-sharing, storytelling and documentation that builds a collective body of knowledge and practices that support transformative justice approaches. Each interview reveals the imperfections and also the creativity of radical responses to violence that elicit new questions and challenges.

Working with shame: an offering

Some people have caused immense harm to people and to communities – harm that cannot be minimised. Supporting someone to take steps towards accountability involves them recognising the impacts of those harms and working towards meaningful change. There is no blueprint or map for this work and in the journey towards abolition, we spend time imagining, practising and fumbling through our efforts. One of the effects of neoliberalism has been the professionalisation of local skills and knowledges, which often devalues the skills and knowledges that are located within individuals and communities. In the spirit of sharing resources, the following set of questions is designed to support the understanding of how shame manifests in those who cause harm, and how it impacts the ability to engage in accountability.

In my experience of working alongside people who have caused harm in community and service settings, shame is present in many of our conversations and can appear as avoidance, defensiveness, blame, denial and negative self-perceptions. Shame can then be misinterpreted as a lack of interest in accountability. In community, I have noticed the misinterpretation of shame resulting in the isolation and exclusion of people who have caused harm. Our actions mirroring the punishment tactics of the prison-industrial complex – despite our critique of it. Understanding the role of shame is therefore crucial in being able to create spaces conducive to accountability and healing. The hope is that these questions help to reposition shame, reducing barriers to responsibility, humanising people using violence, and enabling them to connect with their preferred selves (Jenkins, 2009).

Externalising shame alongside people who have caused harm

The following questions externalise shame, contextualise it and explore its effects:

- What is it like to think about shame? Why?
- If shame was talking to you, what might it be saying?
- What does the shame make you want to do or say in response?
- Does it have you blaming others?
- What might others notice when this shame is around?
- When this shame is very present, what sorts of things does it try to convince you about yourself? What sorts of things does it try to convince you about others?
- How do you imagine it manages to present such a convincing picture? What influences this thinking? Are there messages you have received that influence this or strengthen it?
- Has there been a time that shame showed up for you and you used it to take steps towards change or accountability? What made that possible? Did anyone help?
- How does the shame affect what is important to you?

- How does shame affect your relationships with others?
- What do you think about these effects? Are they useful for accountability or do they get in the way? Or a bit of both?
- Are there times the shame tries to pull you away from accountability – or pushes you towards it? How?

Re-storying shame

- When was shame useful in taking steps towards accountability or change? And, was this connected to a value you hold or something that is important to you?
- If you are feeling bad/ashamed/not proud, why are you feeling this way?
- Is it touching on something that is important to you? What is that?
- What does this say about you as a person, what you value and what is important to you?
- Who else would know that these values are important to you – that you care about these things? How might they know that?
- Is this something you want to keep talking about or working on, despite these feelings of guilt, shame, defensiveness, and so on? Why is that important to you?

By co-researching and repositioning shame, people are encouraged to consider new possibilities for their lives, as well as exploring the incongruence between their ethical preferences and their actions. In contrast, shaming others is an act of dehumanisation. When a person faces shame, rather than being shamed, we take a stance of radical love. In transformative justice informed community responses to harm we hold both individual and collective responsibility for addressing harms, while recognising our entanglement in carceral systems and thinking. In challenging how we internalise carceral logics, this offering hopes that our accountability and healing work does not perpetuate the very systems we are seeking to transform.

In summary, transformative justice offers a radical anti-capitalist approach for reimagining community responses to harm, emphasising the abolition of police, prisons and the state as institutions that perpetuate violence. It calls for deep reflection on how communities can address harm without relying on carceral systems. Importantly, transformative justice invites us to reposition shame, strengthening the importance of collective responsibility in addressing harm. It compels us to confront our entanglement in carceral logics and resist replicating systems of domination. Community responses to harm within transformative justice are not without challenges, as they exist within a context of increased atomisation, systemic violence and the precariousness of communities shaped by capitalism. However, through skill-sharing, storytelling and a commitment to collective knowledge-building, transformative justice envisions a world without prisons – one where healing and accountability are not defined by punishment but by radical love and care.

References

Brazzell, M. and Meiners, E. (2022) 'Mapping the networks: An opening roundtable on transnational transformative justice', in A. Bierra, J. Caruthers and B. Lober (eds), *Abolition Feminisms Vol. 1: Organizing, Survival, and Transformative Practice*, Chicago: Haymarket Books, pp 263–292.

Chen, C., Dulani, J. and Lakshmi Piepzana-Samarasinha, L. (eds) (2016) *The Revolution Starts at Home: Confronting Intimate Violence Within Activist Communities*, Chico: Ak Press.

Dixon, E. and Lakshmi Piepzna-Samarasinha, L. (eds) (2020) *Beyond Survival: Strategies and Stories from the Transformative Justice Movement*, Chico: Ak Press.

Jenkins, A. (2009) *Becoming Ethical: A Parallel, Political Journey With Men Who Have Abused*, Dorsett: Russell House Publishing.

Loney-Howes, R., Longbottom, M. and Fileborn, B. (2024) 'Gender-based violence and carceral feminism in Australia: Towards decarceral approaches', *Feminist Legal Studies*, 32: 1–23.

Richie, B.E. (2011) 'Foreword', *Social Justice*, 37(4): 12–13.

Rojas, C. and Naber, N. (2022) 'Genocide and "US" domination ≠ liberation, only we can liberate ourselves', in A. Bierra, J. Caruthers and B. Lober (eds), *Abolition Feminisms Vol. 1: Organizing, Survival, and Transformative Practice*, Chicago: Haymarket Books, pp 11–57.

Rojas, C., Bierria, A. and Kim, M. (2012) 'Community accountability: Emerging movements to transform violence', *Social Justice*, 37(4): 1–11.

Spearim, B. (2021) 'Frontier war stories and Aboriginal responses to conflict and harm pre-colonisation', on Radio A and A, by Anne-lise Ah-fat and Anita Thomasson, 19 July. Available at: https://www.3cr.org.au/satelliteskies/episode-202107192300/radio-and-episode-3

14

Dismantling the master's house? Abolition, deradicalisation and social work

Sophie Shall and David McKendrick

Introduction

One rainy Saturday morning my dad tentatively cleared his throat and started, 'Sophie … have you thought about what you'll do when you finish your PhD?' Surprised, I looked up from my coffee and mumbled something about not being sure what was next for me. He turned to me and said, 'I've been thinking … you could maybe work for the Home Office, see if you can make these counter-terrorism policies that you are studying work better and be less problematic?'

Like many others, Sophie's dad is a man of good intentions. Seeing wrongs in the world, and understanding these through the realm of social policy, he is clear that reforms have to be undertaken in order to cultivate a more just society. Abolitionist approaches offer us a different solution; opening up possibilities beyond systems as we currently know them. What would it mean for our counter-terrorism practices to transform into supporting and building communities, instead of enabling punitive preventative and diversionary methods? For a number of people, on account of the myth of security, this might trigger a range of moral, economic and other anxieties. Rather than being comforted by the self-sustaining violence of counter-terrorism policies and its promises to keep us safe, we choose to engage with the tensions inherent in actively trying to imagine, transform and create a different world, free from carceral systems. Such non-reformist reforms seek to eradicate existing power relations and replace them with a focus on meeting people's needs (Gorz, 1987). Abolitionism thereby advances purported social work values of anti-oppressive and anti-racist practice. In exploring the ways that carcerality began with prisons and is now embedded in policing, bordering and social work practice, we argue that reforming a broken system will afford us nothing more than the continued power, violence and legitimacy of the state.

Like most Western countries, Britain has adopted a socio-legal approach to the threat of violent extremism. Designed as a multi-agency apparatus to identify those at risk of radicalisation and provide a de-radicalisation service, the UK government's PREVENT policy is a continuing controversy. Influenced by the terrorist attacks of 9/11 in New York and 7/7 in London and formalised in the 2015 Counter-Terrorism and Security Act, PREVENT requires public servants, including librarians, nurses, teachers and social workers, to be vigilant for signs of radicalisation being exhibited by individuals they are working with. Radicalisation is closely associated with the concept of 'British Values', as the policy stipulates that extremism is 'vocal or active opposition to fundamental British values', defined as 'democracy, the rule of law, individual liberty and mutual respect and tolerance of different faiths and beliefs' (GOV.UK, 2011: 107). In defining these values as 'fundamental' there is a creation of an 'others' category that places people who do not perform these values outside of these accepted beliefs and defines them as a risk to the security of the nation. If someone is identified as in opposition to British Values, a referral can be made to PREVENT and a multi-agency panel that is concerned with reducing risk through a de-radicalisation programme is convened. Social workers are drawn into assessing individuals' risk of radicalisation as well as in interventions aimed to de-escalate this risk. PREVENT provides an opportunity for the state to intervene directly in an invasive manner that is justified as a proportionate response to the threat of violent extremism.

Critics of PREVENT argue it is an authoritarian instrument that pathologises complex issues of race and class while mobilising intensified surveillance of 'suspect' (predominantly) Muslim communities. Its supporters argue for its expansion into what they describe as a pre-criminal space. This chapter explores the consequences for social work of engaging in this statutory duty and the contradictions inherent in this engagement. Using key abolitionist texts, across a range of disciplines, we illustrate how despite best intentions, social workers entering into these collusive, soft-policing roles serve to reinforce and justify a system that is fundamentally flawed. Abolitionist perspectives can offer a framework for the critical appreciation of the ways in which social work is used by the state as a form of policing. While police and social workers claim to have separate roles, in the current neoliberal context both professions coalesce around notions of creating and sustaining order.

We argue that PREVENT emerges from a carceral logic that is both violent and coercive, and is a response to the perceived racialised and classed threat of disorder, contrasting powerfully with accepted images of social work as a profession that sees itself as inherently liberal and accepting of diversity. This chapter uses abolitionist texts to illustrate the potential of abolitionist thought to inform new forms of social work praxis that disrupt and displace what we have come to accept and 'know'. The texts that we explore here provide an opportunity to consider new ways of thinking about the powers available to the state and the opportunity the state has to intervene in the lives of the population. We consider alternatives to the existing settlement between the state and the population that offer renewed hope for fresh understandings and increased hope for a more equitable world.

Are prisons obsolete? Angela Davis

Davis (2003) describes the ways in which the mass expansion of the American carceral system, including prisons, probation services and other alternatives to custody, operates as a replacement for the racialised punishment of African Americans that followed the abolition of chattel slavery. In this chapter we argue that PREVENT operates in a similar way; the state uses narratives of safeguarding, vulnerability and protection to justify expansion of the policy. Here we offer an alternative reading of PREVENT, one that is invasive, harmful and experienced more punitively by different populations, most notably Muslim communities. Prisons and other instruments of punishment have effectively replaced the plantation as the primary location of racialised forms of social control. The carceral system assumes the role of the interlocutor between the state and a section of the population that is constructed as a commodity. Davis (2003) describes a prison–industrial complex as an environment where goods and services are produced at low cost by a racialised population who receive little protection, and the goods produced are then sold on for significant profit. In this way once more, the prison mirrors the slave trade. The economic benefits of the prison system are given primacy over the conditions in which the goods are produced, supporting a system of racial capitalism (Robinson, 2019).

African Americans are historically constructed and understood as devoid of a life that contains opportunities for hope and optimism. Instead their value is seen in economic terms and in their capacity for economic contribution through taxation and labour. Davis (2003) demonstrates how the chains used to contain and punish slaves for the 'crime' of being African American are now replaced by the bars of the prison cell. This replacement is mobilised in a variety of ways that include the social construction of crime using the lens of race, intensified surveillance of densely populated inner city areas and punitive sentencing policies such as 'three strikes and you are out' legislation that sees indeterminate sentences applied to recidivist offenders. This racialised expansion of incarceration serves as a punitive method of regulating and managing the African American population, many of whose families had been previously owned by slave masters and who, through forced labour, made a significant contribution to building the economic security that is enjoyed by those in the American nation who are advantaged.

Davis (1988) argued that rehabilitation was the primary purpose of incarceration for populations who were racially constructed as white. These populations were understood as rights-bearing, worthy of citizenship and in possession of the right to freedom of speech and suffrage. In this iteration the prison represents the 'penitentiary', a place for reflection and rehabilitation, an opportunity for change and, ultimately, a place of hope and the possibility of a better future. Central to this is the belief in the potential for change contained in the white population. The perception is that this racial grouping are agentic and contain a potential for reflection and are, consequently, worthy of optimism and a belief in the capacity for personal change.

The (limited) optimism of the penitentiary is a privilege afforded to some and not others. The mass incarceration of the African American population operates as a continuation of the dynamic of slavery where racial supremacy is maintained and enforced by violence towards, and control over, Black bodies that finds its form in imprisonment, torture and death. To be African American is to be denied the basic human attributes of your white counterparts and consequently to be perceived as unworthy of the opportunity for redemption that rehabilitation offers. In this sense the application of carceral punishment replicates the dynamic of slavery where optimism was reserved for the white population while pessimism and the consignment to a reduced form of existence is associated with the formerly enslaved, and now imprisoned Black population. Imprisonment brings with it a pervasive sense of mortality as well as the very real threat of the death penalty or a period of life imprisonment. The prison, devoid of hope, subjects some of its inhabitants to a regime of hopelessness.

Racism is the defining component of the carceral system (Davis, 2003). In this analysis the racism of the carceral experience is not understood as an error or aberration within the system, but instead it represents a deliberate and premeditated design feature that is the defining characteristic of the carceral experience. The prison forms part of the social, emotional and economic geography of the lives of Black people (Moran, 2015), representing the vehicle through which the experience of hope and despair and the promise of a life after is experienced differentially by those contained within its walls.

The net result of this expansion of the prison and of America's continuing experiment with mass incarceration has, according to both Mauer (1995) and Tucker (2017), seen one in three Black men incarcerated or placed under the direct control of the prison-industrial complex. The activity of mass incarceration brings with it consequences that are both intended and deliberate. The prison becomes a societal institution for the creation and delivery of forms of punishment that are mediated and differentiated by race, offering conditional hope and opportunity for some while immiserating and disappearing others to be incarcerated without optimism, and in some cases, killed.

Davis' (2003) contention is that a system so clearly discriminatory and so obviously designed to reproduce and intensify structural racism is not reformable and the only adequate response is abolition. There can be no possibility for reform and equally there is no opportunity for neutrality. To engage with the system is to provide it with some form of legitimacy that involves the recognition of it as a system worth saving. Commitment to prison reform contains a tacit belief that the system is *reformable* instead of recognising it as a deliberately designed vehicle for the subjugation and disappearance of the African American population and as a modern replacement for chattel slavery (Davis and Rodriguez, 2000).

Carceral logic thus tells us that the only way to ensure safety is to punish those who are deemed to have the potential to cause harm. While many of these 'suspect' individuals do not become incarcerated in the way we traditionally understand this term, they do become subject to control, restrictions, a culture of criminalisation and forms of confinement. As a result, it is possible, if we look closely enough, to discern the proliferation of mechanisms of policing, surveillance and regulation that intersect and crosscut to contribute to the emerging counter-terrorism industrial complex that is represented in the UK PREVENT policy.

Black resistance to British policing: Adam Elliott-Cooper

The carceral system does not begin and end with the prison. To fully appreciate its role we need to explore the ways in which it seeps into mundane and unnoticed aspects of our everyday lives. The coercive arms of the state are, as we demonstrate here, expanding exponentially and involve a variety of agencies and organisations in a repressive logic of carcerality and policing. Gilmore (2022) uses the discipline of geography to explore how the co-constitutive and interlocking elements of the state combine to produce the 'anti-state state', a complex set of structures that are bound together by their oppressive capacity and work together to ensure that the present system of racial capitalism is maintained and enhanced. Schenwar and Law (2020) note the deliberate disadvantage that racialised people face in engaging with systems along with the perceived necessity in complying with particular structures, emphasising the connections between our everyday lives and the space of the prison. In this way the thread of carceral logic that connects the prison to the PREVENT policy is revealed to us. Counter-terrorism policy pivots on the idea that pre-emptive measures are necessary to de-radicalise extremists, who are predominantly racialised as Muslim, in order to protect the public.

Policing is key to this carceral approach. To provide a historical context to British policing, Elliott-Cooper (2021) describes the relationship between military operations in former colonies and the emergence of modern forms of policing. Modern policing emerges from a militarised paradigm and owes its existence to counter-insurgency methods used against Indigenous groups resisting the rule of the British Empire. Elliott-Cooper (2021) describes the significance of the role played by Brigadier General Sir Frank Kitson in quelling colonial insurgencies throughout the empire, including Kenya, Malaya and Northern Ireland. Britain accrued considerable wealth and power by extracting goods and resources from the colonies, including rubber from Malaya, sugar cane from Jamaica and cotton from India. Inevitably this extraction of wealth led to conflict as local populations sought to recover their land and reclaim their resources; insurgencies against the Empire required a response from the colonial power. Kitson understood that effective counter-insurgency methods were key to securing the legitimacy of colonial power.

Kitson developed a strategy to win the 'hearts and minds' of what Hillyard (1993) described as the 'suspect community'. This approach saw the colonial power maintaining its hegemony by pacifying the colonised population. An example of this would be the coloniser supporting infrastructure projects such as schools or internal transport systems in colonised countries (Neocleous, 2014). If the pacification approach proved unsuccessful and unrest continued then the use of violence was the next step. Using the example of Kenya's struggle for liberation from Britain, Elliott-Cooper (2021) demonstrates how counter-insurgency activities that seek to pacify suspect communities are linked to the carceral logic of policing and cannot be separated from the racial capitalism that is the primary function of colonialism.

The emergence of a police force in the United Kingdom borrowed heavily from Kitson's activities in the colonies. This form of consensual policing is positioned as an alternative to oppressive military force, perpetuating a myth that the police are an institution of and for peace (Nijjar, 2022). For Elliott-Cooper (2021), it is these activities that have come to define policing as an expansive exercise in coercion, repression and social control which is experienced more intensively in the Black community and finds its expression in the killings of Mark Duggan, Jean Charles de Menezes and, most recently, Chris Kaba, all of whom were racially minoritised young men living in London.

This intensification of policing initially appears to be underpinned by support and assistance, portrayed as a response to low level criminality or community concerns around issues such as antisocial behaviour or vandalism. Initiatives like this see police partnering with other agencies to engage with local populations in the provision of activities that are classified as 'preventative' or 'diversionary': examples include street football, bike safe schemes and school 'campus cops'. These represent classic 'hearts and minds' counter-insurgency tactics, whereby police are embedded in populations who contain the potential for unrest. Police are deployed to provide resources and support to the population while at the same time extracting information about the ways in which the community operates (Kundnani, 2023).

This form of policing is focused on what is often described as a 'pre-criminal space'. However, as Holmwood and Aitlhadj (2021) point out, this pre-criminal space is in fact a legal space where no laws are being broken. Policing continues to erode this space, mobilising a shift from investigating crime into the personal lives of vulnerable and isolated populations. The implication of this is that freedom to express your opinions and views is now a matter that can be policed. As Elliott-Cooper (2021) explains, these populations and communities are often those whose experience has been formed by colonialism and who find themselves at the sharp end of social and economic policies of austerity. Thus, racial capitalism and its impact continues to be experienced in a violent and coercive way.

Social workers are deeply embedded within this work of carceral policing. Initially the supportive tone of this work might prove seductive, reflecting social work values and a relational ethic of care. For some the notion of prevention and diversion with its emphasis on relationship-based approaches that encourage close working with marginalised populations can provide a sense of comfort (one social worker described this to the author as 'doing proper social work'). However, as Hayes and Kaba (2023) point out, working in this way sees social workers and other professionals such as nurses, teachers and librarians as softening the impact of policing and as complicit in convincing populations that are oppressed to perceive their oppression through a softer lens. Crucially, social work in the UK often gains its legitimacy through the notion of consent, implying that vulnerable individuals and their families have agreed to be part of PREVENT interventions. Rather than consent being informed, it is effectively coerced due to fear around a deeper involvement with counter-terrorism police or the possibility of child removal if parents withhold their consent (Holmwood and Aitlhadj, 2021).

Social workers, either knowingly or otherwise, become a part of a repressive state machine that has at its core a commitment to ensuring the continued dominance of the neoliberal logic of racial capitalism. This logic is mobilised through policies such as PREVENT that purports to be motivated by 'safeguarding' vulnerable individuals and communities but which, in reality, embeds carceral policing in suspect communities that are, more often than not, disadvantaged and peripheral (Kaba, 2021). Without changing the punitive culture embedded in the functions that social workers are asked to carry out, which we can see through the social work role in PREVENT, social work remains implicated in systems and structures of power and represents a form of pluralised policing (Lister, 2006).

(B)ordering Britain: Nadine El-Enany

As argued earlier, in environments where racial capitalism is dominant, systems of ordering and confinement are not just enforced by prison guards and the police. Border agencies and, increasingly, private security companies are also engaged in the work of securing borders which operate within the broader carceral system. While an analysis of race and racialisation is fundamental to Davis' (2003) insights on the development of the prison-industrial complex, narrow penal-centric initiatives in public service, for example, social work, routinely ignore the experiences of wider racialised populations. When predominantly conceptualising carcerality within the remit of criminal justice, border checkpoints, refugee camps and detention centres are forgotten, invisibilising large numbers of racialised populations who are subject to punitive border regimes. Therefore, it is important to understand bordering as a constitutive element of mass incarceration and as perpetuating carceral logics.

El-Enany (2020) examines the way in which Britain's borders are articulated and solidified by immigration laws. She traces a line from the resource capture that defined the colonial era to ongoing dispossession today that renders racialised populations disproportionately vulnerable to expulsion, punishment and rendition. El-Enany (2020) argues that colonial governments experimented with immigration control, and understands this to be the antecedent to current British immigration law. She describes the ways in which this legislation is exercised through racial exclusion, but uses seemingly 'race-neutral' terms to do so (in much the same way as PREVENT has adopted the language of safeguarding to justify its incursion into families and communities). In contrast to common understanding of the law as inherently just, El-Enany (2020) makes it clear that the law is political and in thrall to dominant ideologies of racial capitalism, demonstrating this by reinforcing and legitimising dominant power relations. The history of British subjecthood is replete with instances of hierarchisation between populations, reflecting the dominant anxieties of differing historical periods and allowing for differential proportioning of resources and entitlements.

An example of this is the British Nationality Act of 1948, which aimed to produce a Commonwealth identity, in lieu of the declining Empire. El-Enany (2020) identifies that the primary reason for this Act was to maintain white British supremacy through relationships with the Commonwealth countries, and as a result facilitated postwar migration to the UK, including the Windrush generation. However, British subjecthood has not protected racialised subjects from the 'violence of Britishness' (Ali, 2023). Indeed, in the decades that followed this Act, British politicians have created a range of ways to limit the rights of new arrivals. Throughout the 1960s, 1970s and 1980s a range of immigration laws assisted in the making of modern

Britain, helping the country transition from an empire to a sovereign, bordered nation state. This culminated in the 1981 British Nationality Act, distinguishing between British citizenship and Commonwealth residents. El-Enany (2020) asserts that it is this Act that made Britishness commensurate with whiteness, promoting and propagating white entitlement to wealth and thus representing a significant colonial manoeuvre.

Despite claiming to be a proud multicultural society that treats people as equals, El-Enany (2020: 5) argues that 'racial place making projects like that of bordering Britain ... rely on the institution of racial terror'. Immigration law entrenches state policies and shapes public opinion. This constellation acts as a divider between those seen as the deserving white British citizens and the undeserving racialised immigrants, whose ancestors experienced the plundering of their wealth and resources. We can see this racial terror through the precaritisation of racialised life, where asylum seekers and migrants alike are forced to report to Home Office reporting centres, are frequently detained in immigration detention centres and most recently risk rendition to Rwanda, a result of the Rwanda Bill, despite having no connections with the country. These systems of surveillance, incarceration and removal all function under a carceral logic that limits the movement of bodies, restricting the freedoms of racialised populations who are characterised as uncivilised and undeserving.

El-Enany (2020) focuses on the violence of law and the ongoing implications of colonialism, with particular emphasis on citizenship. She acknowledges that physical borders are bound up in a variety of technologies, for example documentation such as passports and visas can be understood as an extension of the border. PREVENT asks us to look further than these forms of 'everyday bordering' (Yuval-Davis et al, 2019), emphasising substantive over formal citizenship that focuses on social behaviours and cultural dimensions of belonging (Holston, 2007). The approach to managing those at risk of radicalisation follows a pattern of ahistoricism, that refutes the postcolonial environment in which we currently live. Britain's role in the economic and social vandalism of colonialism imposed on other countries is decontextualised. In this way, communities racialised as Muslim are disproportionately referred to PREVENT as a result of displaying personal opinions that do not align with the political and cultural status quo of Britishness as whiteness. Thus, a consequence of racialisation, as part of a process of bordering, is the loss of political agency, with dissent criminalised in the name of national security (Kundnani, cited in Camp and Heatherton, 2016). This type of security is one that delineates belonging, separating insiders from outsiders, and is reflective of a similar logic to that applied when people are incarcerated, separating them from the wider population who remain at liberty. While PREVENT purports to keep the general public safe, the proliferation of mechanisms of surveillance and regulation actually have the opposite effect; allowing for the continual expansion of counter-terrorism technologies.

The policing of families: Jacques Donzelot

Social work practice itself is also grounded in carceral logics. Jacques Donzelot (1979) recognised this in his influential text *The Policing of Families*, asserting that the state's interest in families is deeply political as a result of its role in fabricating social order (Neocleous, 2020). Writing in the context of France in the 20th century, Donzelot (1979) uses historical analysis to focus at a micro level on the ways in which the 'caring professions' act as agents of social control through the surveillance and education of families. He focuses both on the incursion of these professions into private family life as well as the increasing influence of juridical and correctional, or normalising, mechanisms. This form of state intervention was (and is) disproportionately targeted at marginalised families, often living on the periphery of society and seen as risky or dangerous.

Donzelot (1979) argued that the state took on a patriarchal role; subjecting these working-class families to increased surveillance, regulation and inspection. He explained that in contrast to old forms of charity, new modes of allocating assistance were formulated by distinguishing between those who were deemed in genuine poverty and those who instead chose not to work. Donzelot suggested that the purpose of home visits was to make the distinction between the deserving and undeserving, and subsequently threatening, poor. This practice was a policing mechanism, exposing some to a punitive and robust form of intervention while others received a more supportive and encouraging interaction with social workers. Donzelot also observed how social workers along with teachers and neighbours brought the existence of risky families to the attention of the juvenile courts, the institutions that deal with 'irregular children' (1979: 109). These themes are pertinent to PREVENT, which places a statutory duty on a number of professionals to work together, gathering information and monitoring behaviours. They are then required to document this information and 'inform' (Donzelot's language) police teams about anyone who is perceived as risky.

Such professional and philanthropic interventions were initially characterised by support and assistance to those who used services. However, Donzelot (1979) argued that this was deliberately de-politicising, as the relief that was provided to families intended to serve a purpose; it was aimed at rehabilitating the moral failings of the family. This turned social problems into individual ones, offering a punitive model that regulated working-class populations. We can relate this analysis to current de-radicalisation practices, where professionals only provide support insofar as to ensure that people's values remain within the boundaries of what is deemed 'British'. Donzelot also argued against self-aggrandising discourses that implied that social work was a progressive and scientific response to social problems (Pestaña, 2012), choosing instead to see the way in which social workers and doctors use their expert knowledge to exercise power over their patients. Commenting upon case records from juvenile justice and child protection, he established that these professionals turned patients and clients into cases to be dealt with, collating information and classifying service users into categories. This is again reminiscent of contemporary counter-terrorism policy, which has constructed a vague list of indicators of radicalisation, making room for caseworkers' biases in determining risk.

Donzelot (1979) explained that the classification of service users was commonly supplemented by a medical diagnosis, identifying future pathologies. Thus, instead of, for example, addressing the lack of resources available to families, the assumption was that the problem lay with some form of psychological weakness. In this way social workers could identify families who were at risk, predicting behaviours and acting in a preventative manner. Preventative methods prevail today, sweeping larger numbers into this carceral logic (Eubanks, 2018).

The pathologisation of service users also continues to hold dominance, as a result of anxieties regarding welfare and morality. Coppock and McGovern (2014) suggest that characterisations of young Muslim men as 'psychologically vulnerable' to radicalisation legitimises intervention within their lives, despite the invalidity of assumptions that underpin these claims. Wastell and White (2017) detail a similar extensive embracing of weak neuroscience as justifying the surveillance of parents more generally. This surveillance, detailed clearly by Donzelot, holds particular racialised and classed people to account. Such pathologisation, despite purportedly coming from a place of prevention, continues to blame individuals for social problems and ignore issues of poverty, racism and social exclusion.

Increasing the amount of funding directed to counter-terrorism policies such as PREVENT, in service of promoting a less discriminatory practice through social work involvement, is reflective of an attempt at reforming a fundamentally flawed system. When money is taken from community projects, youth groups and housing, to name a few, and diverted into security, societal tensions are exacerbated, leading to anger and desperation. In turn, opportunities for increased criminalisation and an enhanced PREVENT policy are created, further entrenching carceral logics. In this way, through the eyes of Donzelot (1979: 98–99), social work continues to be the 'unchecked expansion of the apparatus of state' which 'is extending its grip on citizens'.

We conclude where we began with Sophie's dad's populist belief that it is possible to reform our way out of policies such as PREVENT. What is missing from this analysis, and what abolitionist thinking helps us to grapple with, is a structural analysis that avoids the pathologisation of individuals and populations but instead pulls back the curtain to reveal the deeply flawed and inherently violent ideology that produces policies like PREVENT. It is the ideology of racial capitalism that emerged from colonialism and used countries in Africa and the Caribbean as its test-bed. The relatively unsophisticated counter-insurgency methods used in the there and then have been modernised and developed and are deployed in the here and now, and are disguised with more acceptable heuristics that conceal their oppressive functions. Abolitionist theory offers a critique of this and at the same time encourages us to look beyond the rhetoric of policies such as PREVENT and to open up possibilities for doing things differently. It encourages us to reimagine pathologised populations as oppressed and as having unmet needs. We are encouraged to think of a world without these structures, one where decision making is localised, where all voices are amplified and all wealth is distributed according to need, not profit. Abolition theory offers an alternative way of seeing and understanding, providing us with renewed hope and optimism for a different world.

References

Ali, N. (2023) *The Violence of Britishness*, London: Pluto Press.

Camp, J. and Heatherton, C. (2016) 'Total policing and the global surveillance empire today: An interview with Arun Kundnani', in J.T. Camp and C. Heatherton (eds) *Policing the Planet: Why the Policing Crisis Led to Black Lives Matter*, New York: Verso, np.

Coppock, V. and McGovern, M. (2014) '"Dangerous minds"? Deconstructing counter-terrorism discourse, radicalisation and the "psychological vulnerability" of Muslim children and young people in Britain', *Children and Society*, 28: 242–256.

Davis, A. (1988) 'Racialized punishment and prison abolition', in J.L. Lott and J.P. Pittman (eds) *A Companion to African American Philosophy*, Oxford: Blackwell, pp 360–368.

Davis, A. (2003) *Are Prisons Obsolete?*, New York: Seven Stories Press.

Davis, A.Y. and Rodriguez, D. (2000) 'The challenge of prison abolition: A conversation', *Social Justice*, 27(3): 212–218.

Donzelot, J. (1979) *The Policing of Families*, New York: Pantheon.

El-Enany, N. (2020) *(B)Ordering Britain: Law, Race and Empire*, Manchester: Manchester University Press.

Elliott-Cooper, A. (2021) *Black Resistance to British Policing*, Manchester: Manchester University Press.

Eubanks, V. (2018) *Automating Inequality: How High-Tech Tools Profile, Police, and Punish the Poor*, New York: St Martin's Press.

Gilmore, R.W. (2022) *Abolition Geography: Essays Toward Liberation*, London: Verso.

Gorz, A. (1987) 'Strategy for labor', in S. Larson and B. Nissen (eds) *Theories of the Labor Movement*, Michigan: Wayne State University Press, pp 41–56.

GOV.UK (2011) 'Prevent Strategy', Home Office. Available at: https://www.gov.uk/government/publications/prevent-strategy-2011

Hayes, K. and Kaba, M. (2023) *Let This Radicalize You*, Chicago: Haymarket Books.

Hillyard, P. (1993) *Suspect Community: People's Experience of the Prevention of Terrorism Acts in Britain*, London: Pluto Press in association with NCCL/Liberty.

Holmwood, J. and Aitlhadj, L. (2021) 'The people's review of PREVENT'. Available at: https://peoplesreviewofprevent.org/prop-report/

Holston, J. (2007) *Insurgent Citizenship: Disjunctions of Democracy and Modernity in Brazil*, Princeton: Princeton University Press.

Kaba, M. (2021) *We Do This 'Til We Free Us*, Chicago: Haymarket Books.

Kundnani, A. (2023) *What is Antiracism? And Why It Means Anticapitalism*, London: Verso.

Lister, S. (2006) 'Painting the town blue: the pluralisation of policing', *Criminal Justice Matters*, 63(1): 22–23.

Mauer, M. (1995) *Young Black Men and the Criminal Justice System: Five Years Later*, Washington, DC: The Sentencing Project.

Moran, D. (2015) *Carceral Geography: Spaces and Practices of Incarceration*, London: Routledge.

Neocleous, M. (2014) *War Power, Police Power*, Edinburgh: Edinburgh University Press.

Neocleous, M. (2020) *A Critical Theory of Police Power: The Fabrication of the Social Order*, London: Verso Books.

Nijjar, J.S. (2022) 'Racial warfare and the biopolitics of policing', *Social Identities*, 28(4): 441–457.

Pestaña, J.L.M. (2012) 'Jacques Donzelot's *The Policing of Families* (1977) in context', in R. Duschinsky and L.A. Rocha (eds) *Foucault, the Family and Politics*, London: Palgrave Macmillan, pp 121–141.

Robinson, C.J. (2019) in H.L.T. Quan (ed), *Cedric J. Robinson: On Racial Capitalism, Black Internationalism, and Cultures of Resistance*, London: Pluto Press.

Schenwar, M. and Law, V. (2020) *Prisons By Any Other Name*, New York: The New Press.

Tucker, R.B. (2017) 'The color of mass incarceration', *Ethnic Studies Review*, 37–38(1): 135–149.

Wastell, D. and White, S. (2017) *Blinded by Science: The Social Implications of Epigenetics and Neuroscience*, Bristol: Policy Press.

Yuval-Davis, N., Wemyss, G. and Cassidy, K. (2019) *Bordering*, Cambridge: Polity Press.

15

Harm reduction in the opiate crisis: non-carceral, community-led services and compassion

Donna Baines and Mohamed Ibrahim

Introduction

The use of psychoactive drugs has a long history of criminalisation, with policing of this activity focused in poor and racialised communities (Aykanian and Fogel, 2019). In contrast, those who use drugs and their allies have long called for community-led, harm reduction interventions including decriminalisation and regulation of a safe supply of drugs, testing illegal drugs to avoid poisonings, supervised consumption and overdose prevention, and low barrier, inclusive and supportive, social housing (Lupick, 2017; Csete and Elliott, 2021). The province of British Columbia (BC), Canada, continues to have one of the worst toxic drug deaths crises in the world especially fentanyl contamination of street drugs, and hence previously unthinkable solutions became not only thinkable but actionable. The arguably slow adoption of community-led, non-carceral, compassionate approaches has saved many lives, though the crisis continues and evidence suggests that deaths from drug poisoning continue to rise (BC Gov News, 2024). This chapter explores what compassionate, community-led harm reduction and non-carceral approaches mean for the marginalised and highly vulnerable groups of people living in Canada's poorest neighbourhood, Vancouver's Downtown Eastside (DTES). Drawing on abolitionist and community accountability theoretical insights and the concept of radical love, this chapter re-analyses some of our previously published research to ask in a carceral context, what can be learned about solidarity, deep compassion and meeting people where they are.

Contexts and literature

The Downtown Eastside

Occupying a small, five-block space on the unceded, ancestral lands of the Indigenous Coastal Salish people, the DTES was initially neighbourhood for the middle and merchant classes (Lees et al, 2013). Reflecting an economic shift to seasonal industries including lumber extraction, fishing and mining, by the early 1900s, the DTES provided high density, single room occupancy (SROs) housing for men made unemployed during the cold months of winter (Ivsins et al, 2019; Masuda et al, 2020). This pool of seasonally unemployed and bored men was seen as a market by those seeking easy profits from gambling, alcohol, drugs and sex work. The DTES began to be seen as an undesirable and dangerous neighbourhood.

The economy shifted downward again during the Great Depression, and many unemployed and stigmatised populations moved into the SROs of the DTES (Lees et al, 2013). This consisted of survivors of many kinds of trauma, including young adults discharged from the cacerality of the Indigenous Residential Schools, people formerly institutionalised for mental health and/or disabilities, people who had been in prison, and many others struggling with issues of chronic pain, mental health and addictions (Ivsins et al, 2019; Masuda et al, 2020). Rather than a pleasant middle-class neighbourhood, the DTES became an area known for mental health problems, addictions, poverty, homelessness, sex work and crime (Lees et al, 2013).

With the highest density in Canada, the DTES remains under-resourced and impoverished, with an average income of CAD23,359/year compared to CAD65,325/year for larger Vancouver (Provincial Health Services Authority, 2023). Vancouver's DTES is currently the poorest urban neighbourhood in Canada (Lupick, 2017; Provincial Health Services Authority, 2023). Residents of the DTES are disproportionately male, 35 per cent Indigenous (compared to 5 per cent in Canada), a higher proportion of people living alone, and a growing number of seniors (Mauboules, 2020; Canham et al, 2022). The DTES contains a myriad of public, private and non-profit organisations aimed at addressing the issues of the residents, though the largely top-down solutions have met with little success.

The crises

The interwoven crises of poverty, mental health, trauma and addictions in the DTES are exacerbated by homelessness and substandard housing, few employment opportunities, and an increasingly toxic drug supply embedded in crime gangs. Despite the presence of numerous service organisations, services often fail to meet people where they are (Jozaghi and Yake, 2020; Kerman et al, 2021). Despite this, Lupick (2017) argues that drug users and their allies in the DTES shifted the public discourse to view addictions as a health issue best addressed by services rather than by ongoing criminalisation. Community members effectively lobbied for policy change and the adoption of a Four Pillars Policy of prevention, treatment, enforcement and harm reduction (Lupick, 2017; Jozaghi and Yake, 2020). As part of the Four Pillars

Policy, Canada's first supervised safe injection site and needle exchange opened more than 20 years ago in the DTES with community members with lived experience of drug use forming a central part of the workforce (Jozaghi and Yake, 2020; Jordan, 2023). Their work includes a non-judgemental approach to welcoming those seeking a safe space to use drugs, and where possible, ensuring drugs are safe (not toxic) and used safely, providing companionship and a safe place to resurface after using psychoactive drugs, and referring to services as appropriate to each individual's situation and need.

Despite these measures, the death rate continued to climb, with 474 deaths in 2015 from toxic street drugs (Jannou, 2023). In April of 2016, the government of British Columbia declared a Public Health Emergency (BC Gov News, 2016), which meant that additional safe and supervised injection and overdose services opened, and data was actively collected on the breadth of the problem. The death rates showed no sign of slowing and by 2022 the number of deaths was over 2,300, with numbers continuing to rise in 2023 (BC Gov News, 2023).

In common parlance, the problem is generally presented as drug overdose; however, most of the deaths happen because the drug supply comes from criminal gangs and it has a high level of toxicity (Milaney et al, 2021). Drug poisonings are currently the leading cause of unnatural death in BC, surpassing homicides, suicides and motor vehicle collisions combined, and having the overall impact of lowering life expectancy in the province (Ivsins et al, 2022). Tragically, during the COVID-19 pandemic people could not access safe injection, treatment or overdose prevention sites, so people used and died alone as the drug supply grew more toxic (Ibrahim, 2020).

Responses that have helped: community-led strategies

People who use drugs and their allies advocate for far-reaching social interventions including the full decriminalisation of drugs and drug use, safe supply, and 'housing first', a no-barrier policy framework for comprehensive supportive housing (Kerman et al, 2021; Milaney et al, 2021). These policies are aimed at removing the stigma and coercion related to psychoactive drug use by ending the criminalisation of drug use and also removing the production and distribution of drugs from crime gang control (Jozaghi and Yake, 2020). For some, this means bringing the supply of drugs under the production and regulatory framework of the state, similar to alcohol, cannabis or gambling (Bertie and Somers, 2021). However, distrust of the state is high and others favour small-scale private production and community distribution (Jozaghi and Yake, 2020). Though far from comprehensive, the government of BC has decriminalised the possession of small amounts of certain drugs (BC Gov News, 2021; Jannou, 2023). However, the police continue to shut down compassion clubs, unregulated drug purity testing sites, and join right-wing politicians in claiming that safe supply drugs are being resold by gangs and that decriminalisation is leading to more addictions and deaths (Bailey and Woo, 2023; Armstrong, 2024).

Harm reduction is a set of policy and practice approaches that have been advanced by people who use drugs and their allies, and is grounded in respect for human dignity, human rights and the lived experience of drug users (Jordan, 2023). Harm reduction is based on the premise that people who use drugs are worthy of respect, and that support and care should be provided in ways that reduce risks and facilitate people into productive lives (Kerman et al, 2021). This includes providing ways to access drugs that remove or limit the need to interact with criminal elements, which has an immediate virtuous benefit in reducing people's ongoing exposure to trauma, violence and risk of incarceration (National Harm Reduction Coalition, 2020). Harm reduction also involves: the provision of a regulated and clean supply of substances; educating users in safer use, managed use, reduced use and alternative use; as well as addressing the social and economic conditions of use and the user (Jordan, 2023).

Under harm reduction, the requirements for detox and abstinence are removed and those actively using drugs are viewed as eligible for services and support (Aykanian and Fogel, 2019). Though not the goal of harm reduction, as it is recognised that some people will continue to use drugs across their lives, many involved in harm reduction find their lives stabilised to the point that they choose to reduce or end their substance use.

In response to the escalating and unrelenting toxic drug deaths, in 2023 the BC government undertook the first steps to decriminalise people who use drugs. Under the Public Health Emergency in BC, harm reduction approaches include: the decriminalisation of possession for personal use of some formerly illicit drugs (opioids, cocaine, methamphetamine and ecstasy) of up to 2.5 grams for BC residents of 18 years old and above; the safe supply of pharmacological grade drugs in lieu of toxic street drugs; the expansion of prevention and safe use sites; and the development of social and health services that are low barrier. Humanism, pragmatism, individualisation, autonomy, incrementalism and accountability without termination are the pivotal concepts underlying low barrier, harm reduction approaches that meet people where they are, rather than waiting until they meet service criteria (BC Gov News, 2021; Csete and Elliott, 2021; Jordan, 2023).

Housing First is an example of comprehensive harm reduction, a low barrier policy that meets people where they are by removing the criteria that people be 'housing ready' and abstinent (Milaney et al, 2021). Housing First prioritises permanent housing for people experiencing chronic or episodic homelessness (Kerman et al, 2021). The Canadian federal government funded one of the largest scale Housing First research initiatives, dubbed the 'At Home/Chez Soi' project in 2010 in five Canadian cities (Vancouver,

Winnipeg, Toronto, Montreal and Moncton) with a focus on the complex issue of homelessness, mental health and addiction (Gaetz et al, 2013). This was soon followed by the adoption of Housing First policies in BC (BC Government News, 2021). The policy asserts respect for choice and self-determination and claims to be 'client-driven' (Milaney et al, 2021). It argues further that when the need for housing is met, people can often find sufficient stability in their lives so that they can reach out for services and supports appropriate to their unique needs and experiences (BC Government News, 2021). The literature argues that harm reduction provides the opportunity to heal and rebuild lives (Aykanian and Fogel, 2019; Jozaghi and Yake, 2020). Early research tends to view Housing First policies as a promising and important strategy in addressing the tragedies of homelessness and opioid poisonings (Kerman et al, 2021; Milaney et al, 2021).

Theoretical resources

In her classic abolitionist text, Angela Davis (2011: 96) argued for the end of the carceral system and '[t]he creation of an array of social institutions that would begin to solve the social problems that set people on the track to prison, thereby helping to render the prison obsolete'. Like Davis, many in the social work abolition tradition advocate for new institutional approaches advancing fairness and transformative justice (Jacobs et al, 2021; Kim, 2021; Murray et al, 2023). However, others argue the ties between social work and the capitalist state cannot be reformed and ask how to practice social work that is not 'steeped in cacerality, containment and control' (Fortier et al, 2024). They call for abolitionist approaches that are community-led, and non-institutionalised (Fortier et al, 2024: 1).

Recognising that many human activities that are currently criminalised are rooted in systems of structural harm that need to be changed in order for the criminalised activities to also be eradicated, Kim (2021: 169) calls for abolitionist approaches to embrace community accountability and transformative justice. Community accountability focuses on building alternative, non-state interventions aimed at healing all those harmed by an activity, while simultaneously advancing structural changes aimed at expanding equity and far-reaching social justice (Kim, 2021).

The tension of working within, against or outside the state underlies the abolitionist debates presented earlier (Galper, 1975; Corrigan and Leonard, 1978; London Edinburgh Weekend Return Group, 1980; Briskman, 2013; Baines, 2022). It overlaps with another long-standing debate about whether social work is a force for care, coercion or both (Galper, 1975; Feldman, 2020; Maylea, 2021). These tensions play out in numerous complex ways in the DTES among those developing services and seeking solutions to the carcerality and the toxic drug supply problem.

Though most approaches eschew love as part of formal social work practice, Morley and Ife (2002) argue that this reflects individualism, neoliberalism and much of social work's focus on purportedly objective and scientific professionalism (see also Godden, 2017; Tanner, 2020; Collins, 2024). Studying love and critical social work, Butot (2004: 9) argues that the 'profession's colonial history of missionary "benevolence"' meant that love was remade as a personal emotion that had no place in professional practice. However, Godden (2017) argues that radical love has emancipatory potential and can be seen as a political process to transform systems of injustice. She (Godden, 2017) draws on bell hooks' (2000) argument that love depends on and builds justice by identifying and transforming systems of power, and acts as a service to others that one can engage in with accountability and responsibility. hooks (2000) advocates a decisive move away from the current social relations of domination based in capitalism, racism and patriarchy, instead 'embracing a global vision wherein we see our lives and our fate as intimately connected to those of everyone else on the planet' (hooks, 2000: 87–88). This kind of solidarity and deep compassion for others underlies the community-led initiatives to which we now turn.

Common themes

Drawing on the authors' previously published qualitative data, the following themes will be discussed in this section: community-led, non-carceral, harm reduction approaches; low barrier, harm reduction approaches; and radical love.

Community-led, non-carceral, harm reduction approaches

Vancouver has a long history of lived/living experience and/or survivor movements. These groundbreaking community programmes have been the foundation of some of the most successful social and health interventions currently mainstreamed, researched and regarded as evidence-based interventions (Ibrahim, 2020). Examples of such survivor/lived experience movements include the highly successful radical community based Mental Patients Association (MPA), the Vancouver Drug Users Network (VANDU) and the Drug Users Liberation Front (DULF). In essence, 'over the years, the DTES has been a battle ground, so to speak, in the fight for progressive drugs and addiction policies. A struggle that led to the opening of the first North American supervised drug consumption site' (Ibrahim, 2020: 272).

Both MPA and DULF were created intentionally as radical, liberatory and emancipatory movements to free persons with lived experiences from the shackles of the carceral colonial systems (Ibrahim, 2020). MPA in its current form remains one of the largest providers of housing and community support for persons living with mental health and substance use challenges in Metro

Vancouver and the Fraser Valley, with over 30 social housing programmes (MPA, nd). MPA's initial housing model and legal services of the early 1970s and 1980s are regarded as pioneers in the areas of inclusive housing, including the Housing First Model and legal aid for those incarcerated under the coercive and punitive BC Mental Health Act (Madness Canada, nd).

VANDU and DULF remain at the forefront of the decriminalisation movement and the widely accepted and mainstreamed harm reduction programmes in place contemporarily (Crackdown Podcast, nd). One of the striking aspects of these liberatory movements is their power to narrate their stories through their own platforms, to amplify their voice, to provide alternatives and to address policy and practice issues. MPA shared their voices through *In the Nutshell* magazine that ran from 1971 to 1983, with an expansive readers' network reaching as far as New Zealand (Madness Canada, nd). VANDU members and allies created the now widely successful Crackdown Podcast: 'The Crackdown Podcast a monthly podcast about drugs, drug policy and the drug war led by drug user activists and supported by research' (Crackdown Podcast, nd). As a community-led initiative, this podcast provides a forum for voices seldom heard in public debate about poverty, homelessness and drug use.

Fortier et al (2024) argue that community-led, abolitionist-linked projects need to reflect proportionate power and solidarity between the various groups involved, and to be firmly grounded in the needs and leadership of the community. In the DTES, community-led harm reduction services, including groups like VANDU, MPA and DULF, used strategies that put community members at the centre of planning and building services. As one community member argued:

> We just kind of flipped everything on its head and told the funders, we're going to do this the way the community says. We are going to meet people where they are, and we are going to use the knowledge that's already here, and hire the people right here who are living with drug use and poverty, because everything else has failed, and people keep dying.

An important aspect of community-led services in the DTES was that the main workforce were peers, or people with current/and or past experience of using drugs. The following quote underscores the importance of this workforce in terms of meeting people where they are:

> We fought for this. This is ours. The service wouldn't work without us. People might come through the door but they would just walk back out. When they see us they get some hope that maybe they won't be judged, they might be safe. We're their neighbors and they can talk to us about what is going on.

Another community member added, 'I think the peer model is what made the outcomes at [the safe injection site] successful enough that they have now expanded the model across the country'.

Low barrier, harm reduction approaches

Community-led, low barrier, harm reduction projects in the DTES have fostered conditions for peer participation, mutual respect and inclusive care. This reflects Fortier et al's (2024) argument that abolitionist services promote more egalitarian, non-coercive relationships that emphasise accountability and care. As one community member put it, harm reduction approaches are 'recognition that it [drug use and challenging behaviors] comes from trauma and it comes from living in abject poverty, and not because somebody's necessarily mean or unreachable'. A peer worker argued that 'we meet all kinds of behavior with empathy and understanding. We never kick people out, period, not even for behavior that would get them banned in other places. The behavior isn't the person, and there's always a reason when someone acts out'. Another peer worker told us that 'when we see people living on the street and not coming into our service, we go ask them what we would need to do to remove barriers to them coming in'. Each of the quotes reflect an accountability to the community and those needing support, rather than to rigid standards of professionalism or biomedical diagnosis.

Decolonising approaches on the DTES dovetail with non-carceral, low barrier, community-led approaches, taking their lead from those with lived experience and Indigenous cultures (Sharma and Wright, 2008; Huntley and D'Arcangelis, 2024). The high proportion of Indigenous people in the DTES has seen the development of Indigenous-led, community-based, low barrier, harm reduction services. As one Indigenous activist noted, 'Indigenous people have been incarcerated in jails, Residential Schools and psych wards. There is a lot of trauma out there. Our approach is to start with people where they are at, and offer them Indigenous teachings and ways of caring for each other'. Another Indigenous peer noted, 'decolonisation in the DTES is a long process, and we are in it for the long haul'. These quotes highlight accountability to and solidarity with community members in ways that recognise trauma, minimise barriers to services and, in this case, emphasises a path to stabilisation and healing that respects Indigenous cultural practice.

Radical love

As noted earlier, Godden advocates a politics of radical love for social workers, a call to activism and a strategy of conscious politics in which social workers challenge 'systems of neoliberal capitalism, patriarchy, racism and environmental exploitation' (Godden, 2017: 413).

Commenting on what we would argue is solidarity, deep compassion and an aspect of radical love, one community member commented: 'This is obviously a very poverty-stricken, low-income community, but there is – when you work in the community and get to know the community – there is much respect and much compassion for each other in the community.' This solidarity, and struggle to be caring in the face of marginalisation and deprivation, was also noted by a peer worker:

> It's so amazing the sense of community here. It honestly, like mind-blowing. This is my favorite neighborhood in BC ... Like anytime I've had a bad day or been sad because we've lost someone or something, I've had people stop me on the street, like, 'Hey are you ok?' and like, 'No, really, are you ok?'. The community down here is really something else.

A community activist added, 'There's a kindness and generosity in the community. A depth of warmth and humor that defies the conditions people live in.'

Conclusion

Earlier in this chapter we asked, in a carceral context, what can we learn about solidarity, deep compassion and meeting people where they are? Though criminalisation and carceral approaches have been the main strategies for dealing with illicit drug use in many societies, our analysis suggests that community-led and engaged harm reduction approaches disrupt the vilification of drug users, instead providing opportunities for dignity, stability and mutual care. Our analysis suggests further that this care and dignity are undergirded by something akin to radical love, in its capacity to transcend the highly stressed and challenging circumstances of people's lives and to meet them where they are with deep compassion and respect. These strategies resist the 'othering', dehumanisation and stigmatisation that has long been the public discourse surrounding people who use drugs, and begins to build the 'array of social institutions that would begin to solve the social problems' (Davis, 2011) that can be part of abolitionist futures.

Though our analysis touches on the tension between reforming the carceral state so that it regulates and distributes a safe use of drugs versus supporting exclusively non-state production and distribution, we do not resolve this issue. The evidence suggests that government and public discourse has the capacity to shift and advance more emancipatory strategies around harm reduction and community accountability, but evidence also shows that these strategies are vulnerable to attacks from the right wing who favour further criminalisation of people who may be poor or homeless, and use psychoactive substances (Bailey and Woo, 2023; Armstrong, 2024). These emancipatory advances reflect an unstable equilibrium of groups seeking more socially just and compassionate outcomes, and those seeking to roll them back. This means that those supporting harm reduction and safe supply will need to continue to work in solidarity with the community to defend and expand these advances. Our chapter concludes with a call to further explore community-led and engaged harm reduction options that have the capacity to identify and transform systems of power, and, like radical love, to act as a service to others that advances solidarity, accountability and social justice (Godden, 2017).

References

Armstrong, J. (2024) 'War of words over diversion of "safe supply" drugs', *Global News*. Available at: https://globalnews.ca/video/10353098/war-of-words-over-diversion-of-safe-supply-drugs

Aykanian, A. and Fogel, S.J. (2019) 'The criminalization of homelessness', in H. Larkin, A. Aykanian and C.L. Streeter (eds), *Homelessness Prevention and Intervention in Social Work*, London: Springer, pp 185–205.

Bailey, I. and Woo, A. (2023) 'Pierre Poilievre is at war with safer supply programs. What does he hope to gain?', *The Globe and Mail*. Available at: https://www.theglobeandmail.com/politics/article-pierre-poilievre-is-at-war-with-safer-supply-programs-what-does-he/

Baines, D. (2022) 'Soft cops or social justice activists: Social work's relationship to the state in the context of BLM and neoliberalism', *British Journal of Social Work*, 52(5): 2984–3002.

BC Gov News (2016) 'Provincial health officer declares public health emergency', *BC Gov News*. Available at: https://news.gov.bc.ca/releases/2016HLTH0026-000568

BC Gov News (2021) 'B.C. introduces new prescribed safer supply policy, a Canadian first', *BC Gov News*. Available at: https://news.gov.bc.ca/releases/2021MMHA0035-001375

BC Gov News (2023) 'More than 1,000 lives lost to toxic unregulated drugs in first five months of 2023', *BC Gov News*. Available at: https://news.gov.bc.ca/releases/2023PSSG0052-000971

BC Gov News (2024) 'Nearly 200 British Columbians lost to toxic drugs in January 2024', *BC Gov News*. Available at: https://news.gov.bc.ca/releases/2024PSSG0013-000261

Bertie, M. and Somers, J. (2021) '"The streets belong to those who pay for them": The spatial regulation of street poverty in Vancouver, BC', in D. Crocker and V.M. Johnson (eds), *Poverty, Regulation and Social Justice: Readings on the Criminalization of Poverty*, Halifax: Fernwood Publishing, pp 60–73.

Briskman, L. (2013) 'Courageous ethnographers or agents of the state: Challenges for social work', *Critical and Radical Social Work*, 1(1): 51–66.

Butot, M. (2004) 'Love as emancipatory praxis: An exploration of practitioners' conceptualizations of love in critical social work practice', Master's thesis, University of Victoria, Victoria, BC.

Canham, S.L., Walsh, C.A., Sussman, T., Humphries, J., Nixon, L. and Burns, V.F. (2022) 'Identifying shelter and housing models for older people experiencing homelessness', *Journal of Ageing and Environment*, 36(2): 204–225.

Collins, S. (2024) 'Love and social work in the UK: A critical evaluation', *Practice*, 36(1): 69–86.

Corrigan, P. and Leonard, P. (1978) *Social Work Practice Under Capitalism: A Marxist Approach*, London: Springer.

Crackdown Podcast (nd) 'Episode 1: War correspondents'. Available at: https://www.crackdownpod.com/episodes/afy1d8goaoohcffebex5b2o4py105c

Csete, J. and Elliott, R. (2021) 'Consumer protection in drug policy: The human rights case for safe supply as an element of harm reduction', *International Journal of Drug Policy*, 91: 102976.

Davis, A.Y. (2011) *Are Prisons Obsolete?*, New York: Seven Stories Press.

Feldman, G. (2020) 'Social work and the state: Perspectives and practice', *Social Policy Administration*, 55(5): 879–890.

Fortier, C., Hon-Sing Wong, E. and Rwigema M.J. (2024) 'Introduction', in C. Fortier, E. Hon-Sing Wong and M.J. Rwigema (eds), *Abolish Social Work (As We Know It)*, Toronto: Between the Lines, pp 1–17.

Gaetz, S., Scott, F. and Gulliver, T. (2013) *Housing First in Canada: Supporting Communities to End Homelessness*, Toronto: Housing Hub. Available at: https://homelesshub.ca/sites/default/files/HousingFirstInCanada_0.pdf

Galper, J. (1975) *The Politics of Social Services*, Hoboken: Prentice Hall.

Godden, N.J. (2017) 'The love ethic: A radical theory for social work practice', *Australian Social Work*, 70(4): 405–416.

hooks, b. (2000) *All About Love: New Visions*, London: The Women's Press.

Huntley, A. and D'Arcangelis, C.L. (2024) 'Conversations in decolonizing justice', in C. Fortier, E. Hon-Sing Wong and M.J. Rwigema (eds), *Abolish Social Work (As We Know It)*, Toronto: Between the Lines, pp 134–1154.

Ibrahim, M. (2020) 'COVID-19 in the era of opioid overdose: A glimmer of hope in the midst of double whammy tragedy', *Child and Youth Services*, 41(3): 271–273.

Ivsins, A., Benoit, C., Kobayashi, K. and Boyd, S. (2019) 'From risky places to safe spaces: Re-assembling spaces and places in Vancouver's Downtown Eastside', *Health and Place*, 59: 102164.

Ivsins, A., MacKinnon, L., Bowles, J., M., Slaunwhite, A. and Bardwell, G. (2022) 'Overdose prevention and housing: A qualitative study examining drug use, overdose risk and access to safer supply in permanent supportive housing in Vancouver, Canada', *Journal of Urban Health*, 99(5): 855–864.

Jacobs, L.A., Kim, M.E., Whitfield, D.L., Gartner, R.E., Panichelli, M., Kattari, S.K., et al (2021) 'Defund the police: Moving towards an anti-carceral social work', *Journal of Progressive Human Services*, 32(1): 37–62.

Jannou, A. (2023) 'Seven years into public health emergency, B.C. seeing more overdoses than ever', *CTV News*. Available at: https://bc.ctvnews.ca/7-years-into-public-health-emergency-b-c-seeing-more-overdoses-than-ever-1.6355062

Jordan, A. (2023) 'Meeting people where they're at: Safety optimization in addiction treatment research', *Biological Psychiatry*, 93(9): S1.

Jozaghi, E. and Yake, K. (2000) 'Two decades of activism, social justice and public health civil disobedience: VANDU', *Canadian Journal of Public Health*, 111(1): 143–144.

Kerman, N., Polillo, A., Bardwell, G., Gran-Ruaz, S., Savage, C., Felteau, C., et al (2021) 'Harm reduction outcomes and practices in Housing First: A mixed-methods systematic review', *Drug and Alcohol Dependence*, 228: 109052.

Kim, M.E. (2021) 'Transformative justice and restorative justice: Gender-based violence and alternative visions of justice in the United States', *International Review of Victimology*, 27(2): 162–172.

Lees, L., Slater, T. and Wyly, E. (2013) *Gentrification*, Abingdon: Routledge.

London Edinburgh Weekend Return Group (1980) *In and Against the State*, London: Pluto.

Lupick, T. (2017) *Fighting for Space: How a Group of Drug Users Transformed One City's Struggle with Addictions*, Vancouver: Arsenal Pulp Press.

Madness Canada (nd) 'After the asylum'. Available at: https://madnesscanada.com/after-the-asylum/

Masuda, J., Franks, A., Kobayashi, A. and Wideman, T. (2020) 'After dispossession: An urban rights praxis of remaining in Vancouver's Downtown Eastside', *Environment and Planning D: Society and Space*, 38(2): 229–247.

Mauboules, C. (2020) *Homelessness and Supportive Housing Strategy* (Report). City of Vancouver. Available at: https://council.vancouver.ca/20201007/documents/pspc1presentation.pdf

Maylea, C. (2021) 'The end of social work', *British Journal of Social Work*, 51: 772–789.

Milaney, K., Passi, J., Zaretsky, L., Liu, T., O'Gorman, C.M., Hill, L., et al (2021) 'Drug use, homelessness and health: Responding to the opioid overdose crisis with housing and harm reduction services', *Harm Reduction Journal*, 18(1): 1–10.

Morley, L. and Ife, J. (2002) 'Social work and a love of humanity', *Australian Social Work*, 55(1): 69–77.

MPA (Mental Patients Association) (nd) Available at: https:mpa-society.org/

Murray, B.J., Copeland, V. and Dettlaff, A.J. (2023) 'Reflections on the ethical possibilities and limitations of abolitionist praxis in social work', *Affilia*, 38(4): 742–758.

National Harm Reduction Coalition (2020) 'National Harm Reduction Coalition builds evidence-based strategies with and for people who use drugs'. Available at: https://harmreduction.org/

Provincial Health Services Authority (2023) *Downtown Eastside*. Available at: http://communityhealth.phsa.ca/CHSAHealthProfiles/PdfGenerator/Downtown%20Eastside

Sharma, N. and Wright, C. (2008) 'Decolonizing resistance, challenging colonial states', *Social Justice*, 35(3): 120–138.

Tanner, D. (2020) '"The love that dare not speak its name": The role of compassion in social work practice', *British Journal of Social Work*, 50(6): 1688–1705.

16

'They see it as Big Brother watching at all times': lone mothers and their children in Ireland's 'Family Hubs'

Aoife Donohue and Paul Michael Garrett

Introduction

In this chapter our focus is on 'Family Hubs' (FH) established in 2017 by the Irish government to ostensibly respond to homelessness by providing short-term 'emergency accommodation' beyond the hotel and bed-and-breakfast sectors (Irish Human Rights and Equality Commission [IHREC], 2017). The first part of the chapter outlines the stated purpose and history of the FHs in Ireland. The second section concentrates on social workers' experience of receiving referrals from the FHs that are mostly dealing with marginalised and impoverished mothers who are subjected to intensive surveillance, monitoring and regulation within these establishments (Hearne and Murphy, 2017). The final part of the chapter locates the evolution of the FHs in the context of Ireland's history of modalities of quasi-incarceration alongside some of the book's concerns relating to abolitionist social work.

Family Hubs: evolution and stated purpose

FHs are a material and symbolic state response to a long-term housing and homelessness crisis (Holborow, 2024). They are being developed around the country and are designed to provide short-term housing while also, it is argued, furnishing families with better access to on-site support, such as cooking and laundry services, ordinarily lacking in emergency bed and breakfast or hotel accommodation.

Significantly, however, there is no compelling research or evidence foundation to support the utility of FHs:

> We find no international research or evidence base to justify the emerging family hubs model and note there have been no pilots to demonstrate how they might work. ... This type of institutional approach can lead to a form of 'therapeutic incarceration' and over

time may lead society to blame these families – predominantly lone parent mothers, working class, migrant and ethnic minority women – for something they did not cause. This follows a long Irish history of gendered forms of social violence inflicted on poor mothers and their children who were made invisible, incarcerated and excluded from society. (Hearne and Murphy, 2017: 32)

Indeed, the FH approach risks resulting, over time, in wider society blaming families installed within FHs – mostly lone-parent mothers, working-class, migrant and ethnic minority women – for what are seen as *their* problems, which demand tough solutions (Garrett, 2018). The Irish Traveller community is the most vulnerable to homelessness, accounting for 9 per cent of the homeless population in 2018 while constituting less than 1 per cent of the Irish population (Grotti et al, 2018: ix).

As already hinted, FHs have certainly been subjected to honed criticism, with the IHREC warning that such structures and ways of managing residents may give rise to homelessness and living in emergency accommodation becoming 'normalised' (IHREC, 2017: 3). As a distraught mother told an *Irish Times* journalist, in late 2019, 'it's our fourth homeless Christmas, our third in a FH' (Holland, 2019). Moreover, the IHRC recommends 'Service Level Agreements related to the provision of emergency accommodation should be amended to include commitments to human rights and equality as well as specific references to the rights to family life, autonomy and privacy' (IHREC, 2017: 11).

The Ombudsman for Children's Office (OCO) (2019: 30), while not entirely condemning the FH endeavour, states that 'measures must be devised and implemented not only to combat any stigma associated with family homelessness, but to support the inherent dignity and worth of children and parents experiencing homelessness'. The OCO statement was made following the completion of an investigation of five FHs in Dublin, two in Limerick and one in Cork over the period October 2018 to January 2019 (Dublin City Council, 2017). Hearne and Murphy assert:

> The real risk and danger of family hubs as 'temporary' solutions is that they will become a permanent feature with homeless families left for years in inappropriate and potentially damaging accommodation. The experience of direct provision centres ['temporary' provision for those seeking asylum] – now in existence for almost two decades – demonstrates the likelihood that these institutions, once formed, will not be easily dismantled. (Hearne and Murphy, 2017: 34)

One focal problem with the FHs is the heightened surveillance that families, especially mothers, are subjected to by staff. Difficulties in this regard are compounded by the ambiguous functions that the latter are expected to fulfil, in that the

> dual role of the accommodation manager/landlord and key support worker can present a conflict of interest as homeless families who find strong conditional co-living rules imposed and monitored by key workers who are also the first source of support to the families. In particular the imperative on management to implement child protection guidelines determines the dominant approach to management. It is common to have living behaviour monitored with strict curfews, no accommodation of visitors in any part of the building, overnight leave rules (with a maximum of three days per month permitted absence from the emergency accommodation), restrictions on movement (a ban on being in others bedrooms), and parental rules (including a ban on holding and/or minding each other's children). (Hearne and Murphy, 2017: 26)

Because of pervasive concerns with basic survival, it is incredibly challenging for homeless – and temporarily and precariously housed – mothers to adequately parent. Unsurprisingly, the physical, mental and financial constraints of their predicament limits their capacity to properly meet the needs of their children. This pressure is potentially exacerbated in the context of strict regulation and surveillance.

Moreover, such attitudes are often bound up with the politics of exclusion and the way in which hegemonic projects appear to pivot on the construction of pariah groups. This was apparent during the period of New Labour in the UK (1997–2010) when the governing Blair and Brown administrations excavated the whole notion, seemingly buried in the 1950s/early 1960s, of the 'problem family'. Here the argument was that such families were the cause of 'antisocial behaviour' plaguing the country. Related to this was the establishment of 'intensive family support' projects which the media dubbed 'sinbins' (Garrett, 2007). These projects are significant in the context of the concerns in this chapter because they can be interpreted as, perhaps, helping shape the FHs in Ireland.

Remaking Mother and Baby Homes with CCTV? Exploring the Family Hubs

The small-scale research project on which this chapter is based included six child protection social workers, interviewed in early 2023, practising in a city in the west of Ireland (see also Table 16.1). None were based in the FHs because it is not the policy to have social workers located within these establishments. All of them, however, had a good deal of

Table 16.1: Research participants

Pseudonym and gender	Age	Role	Experience
Joe (Male)	25	Child Protection Social Worker	3 years
John (Male)	36	Child Protection Social Worker	8 years
Angela (Female)	33	Child Protection Social Worker	4 years
Delia (Female)	28	Child Protection Social Worker	4 years
Mary (Female)	41	Child Protection Social Worker	12 years
Rachel (Female)	30	Child Protection Social Work Team Leader	6 years

experience taking and responding to child protection concerns emanating from FH staff.

Leaving aside questions related to the methodology in this particular contribution, we will explore, in turn, five interrelated, not easily separable, themes that emerged from the interviews. These are:

- social workers' perspectives on the operation of the FHs;
- child protection concerns and the FHs;
- policies and procedures adversely shaping parenting in the FHs;
- surveillance in the FHs;
- social workers' ideas for change.

Social workers' perspectives on the operation of the Family Hubs

All six research participants had similar understandings of how FHs operated. Three pointed out that FHs are supposed to be 'temporary' and solely 'emergency' accommodation (Dublin City Council, 2017). However, the research participants knew of families residing in FHs for years, with one stating that some children were practically 'growing up' in FHs: 'I think it's supposed to be short-term. It's supposed to be for I think up to six months ... but unfortunately what we're seeing is families growing up. Children are growing up in transitional housing now, they're there for 3–4 years at this stage' (Rachel).

This was echoed by John, who pointed out that restrictions in place in the FHs might be manageable for families if they were merely short-term, but the impact on lone mothers' mental health could be adverse because of the length of time many are spending there:

I suppose there seems to be a lot of restrictions, and while I can understand that, maybe if it was actually just 'emergency' and 'short-term' accommodation, but we're seeing families in these Family Hubs for years and I think that just impacts mental health and other stuff for them as well. (John)

All six research participants believed that there was a significant impact for lone mothers having to enter FHs with their children. They acknowledged that none of these mothers chose to be homeless and there were varied and complex reasons why each family arrived in a particular FH. Three of the research participants felt that mothers in the FHs appeared to have higher parenting expectations placed on them than those living in the community. This, despite the former not even having access to cooking facilities, eroding a significant part of their mothering role:

There's a lot of deskilling because they're not able to do a lot of the cooking that they want to do, and they're not able to do a lot of their washing. They are kept on such a tight schedule and critiqued and everything, so I feel it really does deskill and devalue a lot of the mothers now. (Delia)

Angela expressed her opinion as follows:

There would have been no cooking facilities inside of the FH, so their meals and all that would be provided for but that wouldn't cater to each kind of family's personal preferences and often in the FHs they wouldn't be allowed microwaves and kettles and things in their room because they'd be a safety matter. So, something as simple as making a cup of tea and stuff they couldn't do. (Angela)

When research participants were asked about the advantages of FHs for lone mothers and their children, all six appeared to initially struggle to respond. For instance, Angela stated 'Oh God, that's hard to answer because I don't know if there is any.' Delia and Rachel could only provide one advantage in so far as, after some thought, as they said 'the only real advantage I am viewing is that they have a roof over their head' (Delia). Rachel echoed this notion by claiming 'that's really the only advantage that actually jumps to mind is they are living under a roof'.

Joe and John spoke of the advantages that might be associated with having a project/link worker able to furnish assistance for mothers and aid their acquisition of independent living skills. Joe suggested: 'So obviously the advantages of going into a supportive FH are that you're actually getting actual, emotional, physical support if you ever need any assistance, you have project workers there to help you deal with and improve your daily independent skills and sometimes they can teach you parenting roles.' However, all six research participants viewed the restrictions in place as having a deleterious impact. Moreover, it was reported that there was a 'high staff turnover' in the FHs and this often resulted in mothers repeating their 'stories' to project/link workers: 'What mothers tell me is that it's quite disheartening because they have to keep saying their stories again and again to new workers. After all, they have such a high turnover of staff. So, some of the mother's mental health has got quite low' (Delia).

Two research participants also noted the fact that it is difficult for mothers and their children, unlike their counterparts with more liberty and freedom in the community, to form and sustain friendships. Often, mothers and families arrive in the FHs having experienced traumatic situations and having suffered on account of male violence. Emotional support from other residents, as well as staff, was clearly vital, but this often seemed to be lacking within the FHs. Furthermore, children residing in the FHs did not tend to be afforded sufficient opportunity to play with one another.

> I know that three single mothers were separated in the FH before Christmas because they [the staff] didn't like that they were going into each other's rooms chatting. And so, they [the mothers] were all moved to different areas of the house. That's it, they're all pretty negative, and it's just really the impact on the kids. They have no real facilities for them to play and interact, like they would if they lived in a housing estate, for example. (Delia)

Given the often suffocating social dynamics and surveillance practices within the FHs, two research participants avowed that these projects tended to mirror many of the operational modalities of the Mother and Baby Homes of the past (Garrett, 2016). The difference in the present day is the role played by CCTV within the FHs: 'It's the threat of being on CCTV. ... That is the stick they're beating these women with now. It might not be a physical stick, but mentally that's what they're beating them with' (Rachel).

Child protection concerns and the Family Hubs

The main types of child protection referrals the research participants received from FHs revolved around issues pertaining to neglect and supervision. However, all of them reported that the chief underlying prompt for such referrals was that a parent was not appearing to adhere to FH policies and procedures. For example, if a child was left unsupervised for longer than 15 minutes, this was likely to result in a neglect referral to child protection services (CPS). Frequently, the CPS was contacted by FH staff if a mother, having a cigarette outside a FH building, left their child/children unsupervised for longer than 15 minutes. There were also instances where a referral was made because a mother had left a child/children for the same period of time to activate a laundry wash. John remarked:

> Giving an example for you … a mother who is a smoker and you know left and went and stood outside and had a cigarette and was talking to another mother in the FH … then they were pulled up for leaving the room and leaving their kids unattended. But for me, if a parent was living at home and their children were upstairs asleep in their room then you wouldn't expect them to be sitting in the room next to their children … it feels a bit over the top and feels a bit controlling sometimes. (John)

The research participants spoke about needing to 'peel back' and interrogate the nature of FH staff concerns (Rachel). Important here, they avowed, was trying to assess what was occurring in terms of the social isolation that mothers had to cope with when living in a FH. Restrictions pertaining to extended family and friends not being allowed to visit risked making matters worse. John summed up the situation as follows:

> I suppose the most common referrals I see are linked with some mental health difficulties for parents. That ties in with the isolation and limited support and I suppose just the stresses and pressures maybe of the homeless crisis in Ireland at the moment, and not getting in and out of the services as quickly as maybe they should. (John)

Rachel highlighted the fact that many of the lone mothers should be entitled to 'go out and find' a partner, get married if they wish and 'do all the lovely things in their life'. Here, however, the difficulty these FH women face is that if they are seen to leave the premises or stay elsewhere it is frequently assumed that they no longer need 'emergency' accommodation. The same research respondent confided:

> I think we all have somebody in our life that you could count on to stay with for a night or two. It doesn't mean you can move in with them tomorrow and stay there, so it's ridiculous. [The restrictions placed on the female FH residents] also takes away their opportunity to move their lives on. (Rachel)

Mary recollected a lone mother experiencing mental health difficulties in a FH and this gave rise to her three small children being taken into 'care' as there was nobody to look after them: 'Granny offered to come in and mind the kids while Mum went to the hospital and this was not allowed. And Granny wasn't allowed to reside on the FH premises even though she was there and willing to help.'

Policies and procedures adversely shaping parenting in the Family Hubs

As we have seen, parents are not allowed to leave their children unsupervised for longer than 15 minutes and also are rarely given the chance to forge connections and, unlike those living in the community, to maintain meaningful connections with others. Strikingly, the fact that families are not allowed to do so appears to run counter to the CPS' own safety planning procedures given the emphasis placed on keywords such as 'support' and familial and other informal 'networks' when they are, at times, perhaps struggling (see also Garrett, 2015).

John and Angela commented on how, in very stark ways, policy and procedure in the FH settings tended to be wholly at odds with a wider policy recognition of the vital significance of encompassing ecologies of care. John asserted:

> Within the FHs you're not allowed to leave your children with another parent or you're not allowed to have somebody in to look after them. And, that for me is a big challenge because of how we advise parents about family support services and the advice and guidance we tell them to look at their natural supports. (John)

Research participants acknowledged that lone parenting is already an immensely stressful '24/7' job and that the mothers in the FHs needed 'breaks', but unfortunately they did not have this 'luxury'. Three shared the perception that the regnant procedures were simply failing to acknowledge that for many families, life in a FH was far from the 'temporary' and 'short-term' stop-gap envisaged in the relevant policy document and statements by government ministers. This is a discourse that is 'outdated' and does not 'reflect what emergency accommodation or what homelessness is like, or the crisis that the country is in at the moment' in respect of the housing situation (Mary). Even more emphatically, Rachel avowed that FH policies and procedures needed to be

> reviewed in line with family living. Actually, in line with the Constitution and the right to family life and the right to leave your children with an appropriate adult. The transitional housing model needs to be reviewed if it's going to be used for families, it needs to be adjusted. (Rachel)

Surveillance in the Family Hubs

As is clear throughout this chapter, surveillance is a pervasive theme relating to the 'conduct of conduct' impacting on mothers in the FHs (Foucault, 2009; see also Garrett, 2019). Joe recalled that prior to his social work career, he worked as a 'support worker' in homeless accommodation:

> [F]rom my experience working as a social care worker, I was waking up every morning to look at the cameras to see you know what does someone do wrong and how you could give out to someone. Looking for someone doing something wrong. Basically, that's all we're looking at and this undermines parents. (Joe)

Some of the research participants speculated that CCTV surveillance played only a minor role in ensuring the health and safety needs of the parents and children and, according to Delia, it was deployed in a somewhat 'punitive' way. She went on to recollect how occasionally child protection referrers in FHs would provide very precise times at which mothers were alleged to have left children alone; for example, '2.37pm a parent left their room and then came back at 2.55pm'. She went on to say:

> I know from the parents inside [the FHs] that they do not see the CCTV as a comfort. They see it as Big Brother watching at all times. Not every parent is perfect and we have single mothers here who are put into a very difficult and high-stress environment in the FH with other families that they have to live in close confines with. And they can't even make a mistake without it being recorded. (Delia)

According to Rachel, intensive modalities of surveillance and constant watching and monitoring might

> actually impact the health of families more so because everything is so scrutinised, like I was saying when you're getting every detail like oh, they left at 11.57 and arrived back at 12.05 and you can count there's eight minutes there that the parent was not with their children and that instigates then a referral to the social work department which instigates conversations, which heightens stress and anxiety and things for the parents. ... [It then becomes almost] a spectator sport [because] you go down and you watch this video of two children ... like that's their whole right to privacy massively impacted on. (Rachel)

Joe claimed that the heavy reliance on CCTV surveillance within FHs was, to some extent, an invasion of privacy of residents. Certainly, parents who were not homeless and living in the community would not, he asserted, to be 'videotaped 24/7'. Families in the FHs are advised to treat these facilities 'like their home', but this is clearly far from the case.

According to the research participants, parents frequently arrived at the FHs partly fleeing relationships characterised by domestic violence and so they are already at a low point in their lives. They were on 'high alert' all the time and struggling to relax for fear their parenting was deemed not 'good enough parenting' by FH staff (Adcock and White, 1985).

Social workers' ideas for change

Joe and Delia avowed that communication between the staff in FHs and parents needs to be improved and this might reduce the apparently incessant surveillance. This might include more regular contact and conversational interactions with families, 'linking in' to better establish what support they may require. Perhaps, it was maintained, undue reliance on CCTV was functioning as a major obstacle to more fully engaged and trust building interaction. Delia volunteered the view that

> they [the parents in the FHs] should be able to go up and just talk to them [the FH staff]. I think if they had that bit of a connection, and they felt that they weren't going to be judged and punished for every mistake they make you know even to say like some parents, when they go up to the workers and say 'Look, I'm struggling with something, I feel a bit low. My five-year-old is running around, bouncing off the walls and not listening to me'. (Delia)

Presently, however, because of unequal power dynamics parents felt afraid to communicate for fear they risked being referred to CPS and being deemed incapable of looking after their children. Rachel believed 'the relationship piece is often missing' within the lived environment of the FHs:

> I think more relationship work needs to be done as opposed to monitoring and supervision. ... So actually, you need to change the way of working. I think there needs to be more relationship-based work with the workers in the place and less scrutinising and CCTV and monitoring CCTV all the time. (Rachel; see also Garrett, 2022)

John and Mary also expressed the view that the degree of intensity of surveillance in the FHs needed to be reviewed and this exercise had to be rooted in a clearer understanding as to why it was thought necessary. In this context it is important to recall that the FH for many families was something of a long-term home, yet they were not there because this was their preferred option. What is more, such families should not be viewed as subject to ambiguous processes of rehabilitation; neither did they present, perhaps unlike some in actual prisons, a potential threat to the wider community.

In what follows, we will aim to bring our findings on the FH into dialogue with some of the book's focal and recurring themes.

Discussion

A central contention of 'abolitionist' social work is that the profession is often enmeshed in policing with the child 'care' system functioning as a 'pipeline' frequently leading, especially for those in minority ethnic communities, straight into the prison system (Roberts, 2014). Drawing attention to the 'invisible ways in which carcerality remains deeply infused with social work', a good deal of the sense-making on this theme is persuasive and compelling (O'Brien et al, 2020: 5; see also Dettlaff et al, 2020). Although the 'abolitionist' perspective is arguably mostly entangled with the particularities of US racism (Kim, Chapter 11, this volume) this book makes a contribution to extending abolitionist approaches to other countries.

The call from feminists to 'consider abolition is not new' given that US figures such as Angela Davis, Julia Oparah, Beth Richie and Ruthie Gilmore have 'spent years working to shift paradigms within feminist spaces like journals, conferences, and grassroots movements' (Lawston and Meiners, 2014: 4; see also Gilmore, 2007). O'Brien et al (2020: 6) argue that 'feminist abolition' within social work gives rise to a feminist politics and practice that 'explicitly rejects any form of arrest and incarceration as legitimate'. What is more, this is an approach that 'aims not to reform but rather dismantle jails, prisons and policing' (O'Brien et al, 2020: 6). Toraif and Mueller (2023: 4) assert that like 'abolitionism generally, abolitionist social work calls for the dismantling of carceral institutions as a necessary step toward the goal of the abolition of oppressive structures as such and for the creation of alternative conditions, policies, and institutions that would displace carceral institutions'.

However, the idea that the police and prisons should be abolished is complex in a world of competing and unequal power interests, as many 'abolitionists' note. Revolutionary change needs to be defended and prisons, and related carceral forms, may continue to fulfil a purpose even though the longer-term aspiration is to entirely extinguish them (Lenin, 2024 [1932]). Alongside abolition, what is required is more reflection on new forms of policing and imprisonment (and social work) which might be repurposed, with new priorities and democratic/accountable structures. In short, while the state is not neutral, nor is it necessarily a mechanism to be simply condemned. We may be better served by questioning the social forces controlling it.

This chapter has dwelt on how social work and, more broadly, social care is increasingly at risk of becoming corroded in that, in certain settings such as the FHs, the users of services experience 'help' and assistance in a way that resembles, in fact, the experience of prisoners. Indeed – historically – Ireland has a long tradition of placing ambiguously 'troublesome' populations in quasi-incarcerative settings. Drawing on Foucault, we can maintain that the country maintained a 'whole series of institutions which, well beyond the frontiers of criminal law, constituted what one might call the carceral archipelago' (Foucault, 1991 [1977]: 297). In the 1950s there were only five prisons within the jurisdiction and the prison population was small in comparative historical terms. This might, therefore, be suggestive of a relatively benign social and economic cultural disposition within the Republic. However, such a comparison is complicated because of the relatively large populations residing, beyond the walls of the prison, in multifarious forms of 'coercive confinement' (O'Sullivan and O'Donnell, 2007). For example, 'unmarried mothers' were apt to find themselves located in Mother and Baby Homes or Magdalen Institutions.

The perspective of O'Sullivan and O'Donnell also encourages us to look at contemporary and evolving patterning of 'coercive confinement', including the so-called 'direct provision system', mentioned earlier, introduced to provide temporary accommodation for asylum seekers. Originally designed to 'support' them for up to six months, many have spent three years in this situation (Marovatsanga and Garrett, 2022). Indeed, we concur with Hearne and Murphy (2017: 4) that FHs may become the state's next 'direct provision' and an 'addition to Ireland's long lamentable experience' of quasi-penal institutional responses to social problems.

The question becomes, therefore, can the FHs be reformed? Alternatively, must progressives, within and beyond social work, seek the wholesale abolition of such structures. In this context, we are influenced by Karlene Faith, who posed the question at the century's outset:

> Every reform raises the question of whether, in Gramsci's terms, it is a revolutionary reform, one that has liberatory potential to challenge the status quo, or a reform, which may ease the problem temporarily or superficially, but reinforces the status quo by validating the system through the process of improving it. (Faith, 2000: 164; see also Garrett, 2024)

Seeking to interrogate such questions in a Gramscian way is tremendously helpful and it orientates us to conclude that the FHs, as presently constituted, cannot be reformed (see also Engler and Engler, 2021). These appear to be a good example of a particular form of intervention that demand abolition.

Conclusion

We align ourselves with Lawston and Meiners (2014: 5) and their articulation of what is termed the 'carceral state' in order to illuminate the 'multiple and intersecting state agencies and institutions that have punishing functions and regulate poor communities'. For us, the FHs are best understood, and their purposes and modalities articulated, in the glow of this analysis. Merely tampering with such structures may also serve to reinforce and validate FHs which can be perceived as programmes of 'gender therapeutic governance' embedding the oppression of impoverished homeless women and their families (Lawston and Meiners, 2014: 11).

More politically, we also need to keep in mind the 'bigger picture'; in early 2024 it was revealed that Ireland's richest two billionaires have more wealth than the bottom half of the entire population. Indeed, the richest 1 per cent hold 35.4 per cent of Irish financial wealth (Oxfam International, 2024). Our conclusion is that the avoidable plight of the women at the centre of this chapter can ultimately only be satisfactorily addressed by a political programme intent on a fundamental social and economic restructuring of Irish society that aims to redistribute income, wealth and opportunities.

References

Adcock, M. and White, R. (1985) *Good Enough Parenting*, London: BAAF.

Dettlaff, A.J., Weber, K., Pendleton, M., Boyd, R., Bettencourt, B. and Burton, L. (2020) 'It is not a broken system, it is a system that needs to be broken: the upEND movement to abolish the child welfare system', *Journal of Public Child Welfare*, 14(5): 500–517.

Dublin City Council (2017) 'Family Accommodation hubs across the Dublin Region for 624 families'. Available at: https://councilmeetings.dublincity.ie/documents/s11540/4%20Homeless%20Update.pdf

Engler, M. and Engler, P. (2021) 'André Gorz's non-reformist reforms show how we can transform the world today', *Jacobin*, 22 July. Available at: https://jacobin.com/2021/07/andre-gorz-non-reformist-reforms-revolution-political-theory

Faith, K. (2000) 'Reflections on inside/outside organizing', *Social Justice*, 27(3): 158–167.

Foucault, M. (1991 [1977]) *Discipline and Punish*, London: Penguin.

Foucault. M. (2009) *Security, Territory, Population: Lectures at the College de France 1977–1978*, Houndmills: Palgrave Macmillan.

Garrett, P.M. (2007) '"Sinbin" solutions: The "pioneer" projects for "problem families" and the forgetfulness of social policy research', *Critical Social Policy*, 27(2): 203–230.

Garrett, P.M. (2015) 'Words matter: deconstructing "welfare dependency" in the UK', *Critical and Radical Social Work*, 3(3): 389–406.

Garrett, P.M. (2016) 'Unmarried mothers in the Republic of Ireland', *Journal of Social Work*, 16(6): 708–725.

Garrett, P.M. (2018) 'Ending the "cruel rationing of human love"? Adoption politics and neo-liberal rationality', *British Journal of Social Work*, 48(5): 1239–1256.

Garrett, P.M. (2019) 'Revisiting "The Birth of Biopolitics": Foucault's account of neoliberalism and the remaking of social policy', *Journal of Social Policy*, 48(6): 469–487.

Garrett, P.M. (2022) 'Surveillance capitalism, COVID-19 and social work', *British Journal of Social Work*, 52(3): 1747–1764.

Garrett, P.M. (2024) *Social Work and Common Sense*, London: Routledge.

Gilmore, R.W. (2007) *Golden Gulag*, Berkeley: University of California Press.

Grotti, R., Russell, H., Fahey, E. and Maître, B. (2018) 'Discrimination and inequality in housing in Ireland'. Available at: https://www.ihrec.ie/app/uploads/2022/08/Discrimination-and-Inequality-in-Housing-in-Ireland.pdf

Hearne, R. and Murphy, M. (2017) 'Investing in the right to a home: Housing, HAPs and hubs'. Available at: https://mural.maynoothuniversity.ie/12056/1/RH_Investing.pdf

Holborow, M. (2024) *Homes in Crisis Capitalism*, London: Bloomsbury.

Holland, K. (2019) 'It's our fourth homeless Christmas, our third in a "family hub"', *The Irish Times*, 21 December. Available at: https://www.irishtimes.com/news/social-affairs/it-s-our-fourth-homeless-christmas-our-third-in-a-family-hub-1.4116749

IHREC (Irish Human Rights and Equality Commission) (2017) 'The provision of emergency accommodation to families experiencing homelessness'. Available at: https://www.ihrec.ie/app/uploads/2017/07/The-provision-of-emergency-accommodation-to-families-experiencing-homelessness.pdf

Lawston, J.M. and Meiners, E.R. (2014) 'Ending our expertise: Feminists, scholarship, and prison abolition', *Feminist Formations*, 26(2): 1–25.

Lenin, V. (2024 [1932]) *The State and Revolution*, London: Verso.

Marovatsanga, W. and Garrett, P.M. (2022) *Social Work with the Black African Diaspora*, Bristol: Policy Press.

O'Brien, P., Kim, M., Beck, E. and Bhuyan, R. (2020) 'Introduction to special topic on anticarceral feminisms', *Affilia*, 35(1): 5–11.

Ombudsman for Children's Office (2019) 'No place like home: Children's views and experiences of living in Family Hubs'. Available at: https://www.oco.ie/app/uploads/2019/04/No-Place-Like-Home.pdf

O'Sullivan, E. and O'Donnell, I. (2007) 'Coercive confinement in the Republic of Ireland', *Punishment and Society*, 9(1): 27–48.

Oxfam International (2024) 'Wealth of the five richest men doubles since 2020 as five billion people made poorer, 15 January'. Available at: https://www.oxfamireland.org/press/wealth-of-five-richest-men-doubles-since-2020-as-five-billion-people-made-poorer

Roberts, D.E. (2014) 'Child protection as surveillance of African American families', *Journal of Social Welfare and Family Law*, 36(4): 426–437.

Toraif, N. and Mueller, J.C. (2023) 'Abolitionist social work', in C. Franklin (ed), *Encyclopedia of Social Work*, New York: Oxford University Press. Available at: https://oxfordre.com/socialwork/display/10.1093/acrefore/9780199975839.001.0001/acrefore-9780199975839-e-1553

PART III

Facing the challenges of abolitionism: critical engagement with the state

17

Abolition, decolonisation and public health approaches to child protection: convergence, divergence and the new neoliberalism

Emily Keddell

Abolitionist perspectives are gaining prominence in US child protection. These perspectives provide a critique of the child protection system, with reference to social harms, administrative burdens and the racist legacy of targeting Black and Brown families living in poverty, while doing little to address the social causes of harm. This movement draws on the rich vein of abolitionist thinking in criminology, arguing that the carceral logics of surveillance and imprisonment in child welfare revolve around punitive risk and reputation management, rather than improving the lives of children, parents and communities (Roberts, 2002). How do these perspectives intersect with calls to decolonise child protection in other settler states, or compare to the movement to establish a public health model of child protection based on tiered, community-centred prevention? Importantly, how does each respond to deep inequities within child protection systems set up to address harm, yet disproportionately affecting Indigenous, racialised, poor women? Alternately, how does each respond to the harm inflicted on children within family life? Finally, how do the wider political projects of nation-states intersect with these perspectives?

This chapter will describe the key tenets of these distinct paradigms – abolition, decolonisation and public health – then analyse their areas of congruence and divergence. This mapping will explore each perspective's ways of conceptualising the causes of the problem they are trying to solve, and their solutions. I then comment on if, and on what basis, alliances can be built between these key movements. With reference to the new neoliberal political environment many nation-states find themselves enmeshed in, I contend that strategic alliances can be built between movements despite their differing ideological bases and 'end point' aims, if only to hold on to the basic building blocks of a child welfare web of supports, protections and services in the face of state withdrawal.

The initial proposal for this book noted that '[t]here has been an unravelling legacy of colonisation and racism in welfare state care systems ... notions of community devolution, decolonisation and calls to de-fund state surveillance mechanisms intersect with loss of trust in the liberal political system and the capacity of the state to progress a social justice agenda'. This direction of travel is particularly evident in child welfare systems in settler-colonial contexts, where the harms inflicted on Indigenous communities, and calls to abolish or decolonise child welfare systems, resonate not only with progressive efforts to restore authority to Indigenous people and the traditional left, but also with rising hyper-libertarian movements that perceive all state action as intrusive. Neoliberal governments reduce state oversight and resourcing from social services of all kinds, renouncing responsibility for child welfare without recognising Indigenous rights and jurisdiction, or providing the resources for communities to reclaim child protection services. These systems of hyper-individualism and populist politics, creating new alliances between traditional foes, I term the 'new neoliberalism'.

In Aotearoa (New Zealand) there has been a burgeoning decolonial project in child protection, emphasising Māori rights through legislation, state–iwi (tribal) partnerships, and an increase in resources for Māori child welfare agencies from 2018 to 2023 (Waitangi Tribunal, 2021; Cleaver, Chapter 10, this volume). However, with the election of a hard-right government in 2023, the state child protection agency lost around 10 per cent of its staff, while funding has been reduced to both Māori and non-Māori community services (Miller, 2024). Despite this contraction, there has been an undertaking that half of the current Oranga Tamariki (statutory agency) budget will be devolved to community organisations, including many Māori organisations, over the next few years, alongside a welcoming of Māori and non-Māori community organisations to 'take responsibility' for child welfare by the relevant minister (Morrah, 2024). Simultaneously the new government is repealing the specific sections of legislation implementing the relevant Treaty rights (creating high level partnerships between iwi [tribal networks] and the state that enabled devolution of legal powers, and requiring measurement of, and commitment to, disparity reduction). This is part of a wider project to remove all specific Treaty rights in legislation (Hurihanganui, 2024). So, the state is devolving responsibility and cutting the central agency workforce, while reducing the statutory vehicles for enforcing Indigenous-specific rights and reducing funding for community services. Alongside this, legislated child poverty reduction targets have been quietly reduced, and social protections such as income support, housing access and equitable healthcare remain deeply challenging in the face of a cost of living crisis (Radio New Zealand, 2024). From this brief outline, it is clear that, as in many national contexts, child protection system practices no longer align neatly with traditional political divisions, if they ever did.

Against these complex political and nation-specific changes, frameworks for understanding how child protection systems can be transformed to respond to the inequities they reflect, while also creating ways that children and families can be meaningfully supported to reduce real harms, are multiple. The remainder of this chapter examines three of the most popular: abolition, decolonisation and public health approaches, and considers them in light of these shifting political sands. Key questions traversed are: What are their key tenets? What are their logics and pathways to reduce inequities? What are the areas of convergence and divergence? And, finally, are there points of strategic solidarity between them, given the new neoliberalism?

Abolition in and outside of the US context

The abolitionist movement has its roots in intersectional approaches to social justice. Intersectionality draws attention to injustices resulting from multiple forms of oppression, and the complexity this generates for individual social locations. People may obtain privilege from one identity and suffer oppression from another, or face cumulative oppressions (Hill Collins and Bilge, 2020; Nayak and Robbins, 2020). In particular, the critique led by African American feminists drew attention to the concerns of women who identified neither with white feminism nor social critique based solely on racism. Such concerns are relevant to the child protection systems of many countries, where the combination of oppressions based on ethnicity/race, gender and class coalesce to target poor women of colour (Roberts, 2002, 2014; Roberts and Sangoi, 2018). Women, especially women of colour, are stereotyped as irresponsible, promiscuous and inherently criminal, and are hyper-surveilled as a result (Roberts, 2014).

Abolitionist approaches take as their starting point the conjoint child welfare and criminal justice systems, and the stark intersecting inequities of both, pointing out that '[t]he populations in both are disproportionally poor and African American, and both systems are particularly burdensome to poor Black mothers' (Pendleton, 2021: 1). The system situates parents and communities as discrete failures while ignoring 'the damage done to families and individuals by capitalism or in the lack of commitment to meet children's material needs' (Pendleton, 2021: 1). Kelly (2021) traces these effects in the child welfare system, also called the family policing system, arguing that it generates stigma, stress and unfairness in assessment and investigation, putting children at risk in unsafe foster care, and inflicting trauma through removal and subsequent abuse. She points out this creates a foster care to prison pipeline, along with the loss of community, family support and identity.

To address this, abolitionist approaches focus on creating 'new conditions of possibility'; an ambitious liberatory project that requires making a society free of all systems of oppression (Pendleton, 2021). While this may seem idealistic, a deeper reading of abolition shows that short-term aims can coexist with more aspirational long-term goals, building on Gorz's concept of 'non-reformist reforms'. His work argues for the acceptability of short-term reforms that do not require revolutionary transformation; reforms that 'could both make immediate gains and build strength for a wider struggle' (Engler and Engler, 2021: np). He defines these as reforms not constructed to accommodate the current system, but to reflect human demands and needs, and connected to a 'wider vision for change, rather than an end in and of themselves' (Engler and Engler, 2021). Gorz promoted partial reforms and 'stepping stone' objectives, as long as they reflect a growing power and control of people over their own lives. Importantly, Gorz promoted solidarity and allyship between more and less radical social movements, considering this productive as long as the differences in end goals were clear. In this formulation, abolition is not about immediately closing down child protection institutions, but a strategic redirection, redistributing power and resources 'away from the current systems so that those resources can be used to begin designing, planning and creating better anti-racist alternatives … to redistribute power and resources towards these important causes, instead of constantly giving millions of dollars to (CP systems)' (Asafo, 2022).

Criticisms of abolition often fail to grasp this nuance, or intentionally misread it. Garcia et al (2024: np), for example, argue that abolition must be taken at its word, not as a 'metaphor' or allegory; as 'complete eradication of federal, state, and local policies and practices related to child protection and out-of-home care services … and the entire infrastructure for child maltreatment prevention, intervention, foster care placement, reunification and adoption services is ended'. However, abolition approaches argue for resource and power redistribution to occur first, in a graded way, so communities can establish what is effective for them. This requires reimagining and risk-taking to trust affected communities and releasing resources to enable capacity building and design. Abolitionist perspectives emphasise the role of lived experience, arguing that those who should be central to redesigning systems of care are those who have experience of the current system (Pendleton, 2021). An ethics of care, as an overarching relational principle, is contrasted with a focus on risk detection, investigation and legal remedies. Responding to material needs such as housing and income, and centring those who are socially marginalised, are key aims (Dettlaff and Boyd, 2021). These are translated into practice in various ways, including provision of critical safety nets, affordable housing, the use of informal kinship care and concrete supports needed to care for children without intervention from Child Protective Services. This prescription includes eliminating 'policies that use arbitrary timelines to terminate parental rights' (Detlaff et al, 2020).

These elements may not directly translate across national contexts. The United States is at the forefront of the abolition movement, and this list is in many ways evoked by an archaic system with draconian rules, operating within a highly punitive and regulated environment (Roberts, 2022). This may not be a good fit in other countries, because the nature of inequities, levels of social protections and the drivers of disparities may differ. For example, in Aotearoa, while there is reference to children's timeframes in the legislation, there are no specific timelines for terminating parental rights, and absolute termination is very rare. More than half the children in care in 2022 were either in the care of their parents or in kinship care (3,623 out of 6,625). Residential care accounts for a tiny proportion of children in foster care (Oranga Tamariki, 2023). Aotearoa does not adopt children out of the care system, preferring to use alternative remedies such as long-term foster or kinship care with additional legal guardianship. The focus is on maintaining whakapapa (lineage/identity) connections for children, and many other Māori concepts are included in the relevant legislation (Oranga Tamariki, 2024). While Aotearoa does have marked inequities in system contact, with 65 per cent of children in care being Māori, the overall rates of children entering care over the last five years have reduced by more than half, as the country moves towards a more devolved system, focused on family preservation (Keddell, 2024). In this context, an abolitionist agenda has considerable overlap with the decolonial agenda already somewhat underway, though with some differences, which I now turn to describe.

Decolonisation

Another framework for progressing fundamental change to the child protection systems of many nations is decolonisation (Elkington et al, 2020; Paki Paki et al, 2023). The impact of colonisation on Indigenous people via child protection systems is profound. The combination of racial, cultural and religious superiority, the imposition of economic systems that impoverished Indigenous people, land theft and the use of force to undermine Indigenous systems of care, laid the ground for generations of damage (Wharewara-Mika and Copper, 2011). Colonisation damaged health, destabilised gender and relational roles and for some 'destroyed the nurturing protective environments required for child-rearing' (Smith and Wirihana, 2019: 3). These forces created the preconditions that justified the removal of Indigenous children. Entangled with this was the diminishing of the roles and status of Indigenous women, heightening racism and leading to the disproportionate removal of children (Cleaver, 2023). Disparities became entrenched, perpetuated by intergenerational trauma, poverty, disparate surveillance, racist risk assessment tools and Western psychological theories (Jenkins, 2021; Wright et al, 2024). Notions relating to parenting and attachment were used to justify removal, despite their basis in European relational systems that were completely inappropriate for Indigenous people (Choate and Lindstrom, 2017). Systems established to respond to need within Indigenous communities were often ineffective because they were based on Western knowledge and designed and offered by non-Indigenous bodies and professionals. This perpetuated inequities in system contact (Choate and Lindstrom, 2017; Paki Paki et al, 2023). State child protection agencies were experienced as surveillant and judgemental, resulting in multiple harms to Indigenous children who were removed, often on flimsy or racist reasoning, into abusive care environments, supported by assimilationist logics (Roberts, 2014; Robertson et al, 2021; Chamberlain et al, 2023). Decolonisation focuses on restoring family systems, reasserting cultural norms and regaining the authority and resources needed to claim back children and their parents (Fitzmaurice, 2022).

Decolonisation also involves legislative and constitutional arrangements to enable this reclamation of power. Napoleon (2014: 230) argues that Indigenous law 'and all it entails is a fundamental aspect of being collectively and individually self-determining as peoples'. Others argue that constitutional change is needed to enable the necessary rebalancing of power (see Charters et al, 2019). Decolonisation involves analysing the impact of colonisation and institutional racism, combined with political action to support Indigenous sovereignty. As a recent Tribunal[1] hearing into the child protection system in Aotearoa found, 'unless the core precepts of the care and protection system are realigned, with power and responsibility returned to Māori, disparity will be a persistent feature of the system' (Waitangi Tribunal, 2021: 4). This self-determination agenda has been pursued in every ANZUS country by Indigenous people and their allies over hundreds of years (Paki Paki et al, 2023).

Public health approaches

A third response to the deep inequities within child protection systems is a 'public health approach', although, as with the other two, this contains a number of internal diversities. This approach frames the problem within child welfare as not one of power, but that much child abuse and neglect is never detected, and when it is, many services are ineffective at addressing the causes of harm (Herrenkohl et al, 2020). Public health reformers acknowledge that there are structural drivers of system contact, and take a whole of population approach, emphasising the role of universal and secondary family and community supports as responses to structural inequalities (Bywaters et al, 2018). Community-based systems are fundamental to providing 'helpful help' and prevention (Scott et al, 2016; , 2018; Gray and Schubert, 2019; Higgins et al, 2024). They point out that systems focused on investigation, removal and care syphon the bulk of resources to administration, risk averse processing and foster care. Instead, they recommend a redistribution of resources to tiered primary, secondary and tertiary interventions; universal and secondary prevention, with investigation and removal as a last resort (Scott et al, 2016). The aim is to address known risk factors such as poverty, poor housing, lack of informal family supports and social cohesion. Supportive services should be offered to specific populations, at 'high receptivity points' such as key life-course events (Herrenkohl et al, 2020). Importantly, all services should be evidence-based programmes that deliver best practice:

> The need for child welfare reform and a radical re-orientation towards prevention ... raises the dual question: who is best placed to deliver such prevention-oriented services, and in delivering them, what does best-practice look like? ... [T]he model emphasizes the need for non-stigmatizing support provided at the right time, in the right measure, and to the right people. (Higgins et al, 2022: 447)

Despite the emphasis on universal supports, public health approaches do embrace the targeting of specific sub-groups for services, utilising linked datasets to identify high priority groups. This targeting is heightened if the quantum of service resources is reduced, for example in highly neoliberal environments where the focus of government is to reduce the 'fiscal spend' attached to family support. The language of social investment can be used to justify this targeting and rationing, and distorts the basic premises of a public health approach (Keddell, 2015).

Divergence, convergence and overlap?

Each approach has strengths and critiques. Abolitionism has been criticised for not taking enough account of harm to children and the need for legal protection. Nor does it provide any detail about how 'communities' will be defined (membership, location, religion, ethnicity?), or how fairness in resource access and decision-making outcomes would be determined (Garcia et al, 2024). Decolonisation perspectives in child protection may not take enough account of the reparative community and organisational capacity building needed before full legal responsibility could be restored (Cleaver, 2023). Issues in relation to 'fairness' have also been raised, as they have been in relation to abolition; for example, how can variations in responses by different tribal groups within a single nation-state be fair to all children, while also respecting tribal sovereignty?

Public health models are built on a need to identify 'at risk' populations for secondary and tertiary service provision. The line between this identification and increasing surveillance of marginalised communities is often thin. The use of linked datasets to predict populations 'at risk' and the intertwining of statutory services and community services potentially widens systems of surveillance (Keddell, 2015; Gerlach et al, 2017; Gray and Schubert, 2019). The application of evidence-based models favours acceptance of specifc types of positivist 'evidence', which may minimise or discount Indigenous ways of knowing, models of family and wellness, or community defined effectiveness. The age-old debates around social control or support are also at play. If implemented in a risk-dominated way, using Western-based models, such approaches may further disenfranchise poor families and those from racialised groups (Gray and Schubert, 2019). The roots of public health in epidemiological risk identification can create tensions between 'increasing push for more accurate risk assessment against concerns relating to greater social surveillance' (Gray and Schubert, 2019: 221). Within a public health model, those who offer services are cast as experts in service design, population identification and correct implementation. Finally, while public health models take account of the conditions and effects of poverty, they do not explicitly address causation, wrapped up in capitalism, colonisation and lack of distributive income mechanisms.

Despite these critiques, at a pragmatic level these different models, with differing assumptions and theoretical geneologies, have considerable overlap. While there is concern around the potential for the two more radical approaches – abolition and decolonisation – to be watered down by conservative state-centric approaches, there is also room to consider the intersections. Some solidarity over strategic change could emerge, particularly in the face of the neo-neoliberal ascendancy at play in many countries. Just as Gorz saw the opportunities for alliances between reformist and more radical movements, these three approaches have significant areas of convergence. To claim that small gains are merely tinkering at the edges does not take account of the need to build a movement in stages, with initial small gains needed to build legitimacy, momentum and capacity (Engler and Engler, 2021).

All three perspectives agree that poverty, racism and colonisation are at the root of inequities in the child protection system, increasing community damage and intergenerational trauma. All accept that the share of resources currently invested in investigatory approaches and care need to be redistributed, with a much greater share invested at the universal level and primary prevention (Featherstone et al, 2018; Keddell et al, 2019; Detlaff and Boyd, 2020; Herrenkohl et al, 2020; Waitangi Tribunal, 2021). All three agree that addressing social factors and rejecting an individualistic approach is important, as is shifting power and resources away from traditional child protection organisations towards community-based services, with an emphasis on adddressing the harms of poverty (see Child Welfare Inequalities Network, 2024). They also all promote kinship care and family preservation as the most important priorities, with child removal as a last resort.

Divergence on causes and solutions are evident on several fronts. The political nature of inequities is more clearly articulated by abolitionist and decolonial scholars, who apply a more radical analyis of the power relations intrinsic to settler states and racialised capitalism. Their critique is sourced from this basis, careful to avoid being recruited into more conservative approaches that do not take cognisance of the carceral, surveillant, punitive logics underpinning the current systems. Public health responses start at a different point, arguing that abuse incidence is high in the community, with little explaination of why, apart from reference to poverty. Decolonial scholars accept increased incidence is partly the case for Indigenous people but link this to colonial processes that subjugated familial norms, protective relationships and economic bases (Cram et al, 2015). Abolitionists say little about the incidence of abuse and harm within racialised, impoverished communities, pointing instead to racism and lack of helpful supports.

Decolonial and abolition frameworks emphasise that racism contributes to disparities in system contact through unequal and unfair surveillance practices, racist assessment tools rooted in white and Western middle-class knowledge bases, and the racism of workers within the system (Dettlaff and Boyd, 2020; Keddell, 2022). This is not prioritised in public health responses, which implicitly emphasise a 'risk/need' logic to explain disproportionality. However, public health responses have a detailed rationale about when to offer services, how to maximise service access and normalise help-seeking; something not as developed in abolitionist or decolonisation approaches. Abolitionist responses and some decolonial responses have more developed tools for building community capacities to respond to harm when it does occur, through restorative and relational processes, for example, working with perpretrators at the community level without involving formal authorities (see Hayden et al, 2014; Kaba and Hassan, 2019).

Decolonial and abolition perspectives also differ. Abolitionists state all child protection systems should end, with power devolving to lived experience communities, while decolonial perspectives emphasise power returning to Indigenous tribal authorities, not communities based on ethnicity, location, socioeconomic or family status. Decolonisation may also result in the recreation of child protection organisations within tribal jurisdictions, with the possibility of leadership by conservative, middle-class tribal leaders, not the grassroots bodies envisaged within abolitionist perspectives. Neither approach deals well with the real differences within any community, including power differences, nor how a fair and equitable spread of services and resources across a whole population would occur within and between communities (Garcia et al, 2024).

While all three approaches emphasise community-based services that offer support rather than surveillance, public health aproaches emphasise an expert-led approach underpinned by evidence-based services, derived from positivist research methods and aimed at populations categorised by predictive tools and other forms of expert-led determination of who is 'at risk' (Scott et al, 2016). Decolonisation, conversely, emphasises the return of power, including legal power and resources to Indigenous bodies to re-establish systems of care for Indigenous children. This is not the same as a central state body delivering in-home services, even if they are developed for Indigenous families according to 'evidence-based practice'. This process almost inevitably relegates Indigenous forms of knowledge to a 'lesser' category which may not conform to Western criteria for acceptable 'evidence', replicating colonial oppressions (Smith, 1999; Blackstock, 2019). Practice frameworks and theories of well-being based on Indigenous knowledges are a powerful way to reclaim definition over family forms, gender roles and what a good/healthy childhood consists of. This element of epistemic justice is key to decolonial approaches (Paki Paki et al, 2023).

Abolitionist approaches also take a grassroots stance, with communities who have lived experience of the current system in charge. This includes a strong critical gender analysis, pointing out the intersecting inequities facing women, especially women of colour. This is less prominent in decolonisation thinking (with some notable exceptions – see Cleaver [2023]), and invisible in public health approaches. However, some abolitionists object to 'services' at all – instead proposing that addressing material factors and drawing on peers to create communities of care based on lived experience inevitably reduce harm. Accordingly, abolitionist approaches have a much stronger emphasis on advocacy and empowerment for the mostly women of colour who are the subjects of the child protection system. They argue that this group should be to the fore in leading system re-design (Roberts, 2014).

How can we build solidarity in the face of neoliberal governments?

A final question is how these intertwining approaches, with deep political differences, can respond to the new neoliberalism. I define neo-neoliberalism as a political rubric with an extreme emphasis on the withdrawal of supportive services, a 'small state' ideal, and the reinscription of economic arrangements that exacerbate inequities, reduce Indigenous rights, and forment populist and extreme right-wing ideologies. These ideas tend to promote hyper-individualism dressed up in notions of 'freedom', resulting in residualist child protection policy. This consists of a protectionist policy orientation with few supports for families or children apart from removal, combined with a deflection of state responsibility to community groups (Gilbert et al, 2011). Those groups have few resources to meet the needs generated by the widening inequalities that arise from an economic system set free from regulation, even the basics promoted under liberal democracies (Hyslop, 2022).

Creating solidarity around key aspects is possible. First, poverty reduction for families must remain in the spotlight. The fundamental connections between poverty and the needs of children is basic to all three approaches. The language of public health and inequalities may be most effective at garnering bipartisan policy change, with its emphasis on prevention, evidence and effectiveness. Indeed, key projects centred on inequalities have been remarkably successful at reducing care entries in some countries (Child Welfare Inequalities Network, 2024). Resistance to the encroachment on Indigenous rights, including sovereignty and resources, is another aspect where all three could find common ground, recognising that when these are protected, Indigenous inequities are reduced. Promoting kinship as a key plank of alternative care approaches is fundamental to all three positions, as is rebalancing the focus on supportive prevention, with the use of coercion as a last resort. Using the language of one approach to further the aims of all three is possible. Public health is most likely to be taken up, especially by neo-neoliberal governments. The language of fiscal prudence and social investment (cost-saving) can be used to argue for redistribution of power towards community services and prevention. Such discourses can be utilised to enact subversive aims, but they must be applied strategically and with an appreciation of the risks as well as the positive possibilities; to engage in 'non-reformist reforms'.

Conclusion

Each of these perspectives offers valuable analyses of child protection systems, furthering debates regarding how best to respond to the pressing issue of child abuse and neglect, and the inequities and harms within the systems established to respond to it (Featherstone et al, 2018). Each makes similar general claims about causation, but significant differences emerge when aims and mechanisms are examined in more detail, particularly their ideological bases and 'end point' objectives. However, in times of grave political challenge to notions of progressive politics and Indigenous rights, with a swing towards a hardened 'new' neoliberalism, alliances may be valuable. Areas of convergence create opportunities for solidarity, even if only for initial changes or merely holding back the tide of reaction. Exploring these aspects of divergence and convergence, while broad brush, assists all parties to broker strategic alliances for specific policy purposes, while respecting important differences.

Nāku te rourou, nāu te rourou, ka ora ai te iwi – With my food basket, and your food basket, the people will thrive.

Note

[1] The Waitangi Tribunal is an extra-governmental body established in 1975 to hear claims relation to breaches of the Treaty of Waitangi (now extended back to 1840).

References

Asafo, D. (2022) 'Freedom dreaming of abolition in Aotearoa New Zealand', *Legalities*, 2(1): 82–118.

Blackstock, C. (2019) 'The occasional evil of angels: Learning from the experiences of Aboriginal peoples and social work', *First Peoples Child and Family Review*, 14(1): 137– 152.

Bywaters, P., Brady, G., Bunting, L., Daniel, B., Featherstone, B., Jones, C., et al (2018) 'Inequalities in English child protection practice under austerity: A universal challenge?', *Child and Family Social Work*, 23(1): 1365–2206.

Chamberlain, C., Gray, P., Herrman H., Mensah, F., Andrews, S., Krakouer, J., et al (2023) 'Community views on "Can perinatal services safely identify Aboriginal and Torres Strait Islander parents experiencing complex trauma?"', *Child Abuse Review*, 32(1): e2760.

Charters, C., Ruru, J., Olsen, T., Pryor, J., Kingdon-Bebb, K., Ormsby, W., et al (2019) 'He Puapua: Report of the working group on a plan to realise the UN Declaration of the rights of Indigenous people', *Te Puni Kōkiri*. Available at: https://natlib.govt.nz/records/45416887

Child Welfare Inequalities Network (2024) 'Understanding and identifying inequalities in child welfare intervention rates', Child Welfare Inequalities Network, Coventry University. Available at: https://www.coventry.ac.uk/research/research-directories/current-projects/2014/child-welfare-inequality-uk/

Choate, P. and Lindstrom, G. (2017) 'Parenting capacity assessment as a colonial strategy', *Canadian Family Law Quarterly*, 37(1): 41–56.

Cleaver, K. (2023) 'He whare takata: Wāhine Māori reproductive justice in the child protection system', *Aotearoa New Zealand Social Work*, 35(4): 16–30.

Cram, F., Gulliver, P., Ota, R. and Wilson, M. (2015) 'Understanding overrepresentation of Indigenous children in child welfare data: An application of the Drake risk and bias model', *Child Maltreatment*, 20(3): 170–182.

Dettlaff, A. and Boyd, R. (2020) 'Racial disproportionality and disparities in the child welfare system: Why do they exist, and what can be done to address them?', *The ANNALS of the American Academy of Political and Social Science*, 692(1): 253–274.

Dettlaff, A.J. and Boyd, R. (2021) 'Towards an anti-racist child welfare future', in A. Dettlaff (ed), *Racial Disproportionality and Disparities in the Child Welfare System*, Cham: Springer International Publishing, pp 441–445.

Dettlaff, A.J., Weber, K., Pendleton, M., Boyd, R., Bettencourt, B. and Burton, L. (2020) 'It is not a broken system, it is a system that needs to be broken: The upend movement to abolish the child welfare system', *Journal of Public Child Welfare*, 14(5): 500–517.

Elkington, B., Jackson, M., Kiddle, R., Mercier, O.R., Ross, M., Smeaton, J., et al (2020) *Imagining Decolonisation*, Wellington: Bridget Williams Books.

Engler, M. and Engler, P. (2021) 'Andre Gorz's non-reformist reforms show how we can transform the world today', *Jacobin*, 22 July. Available at: https://jacobin.com/2021/07/andre-gorz-non-reformist-reforms-revolution-political-theory

Featherstone, B., Gupta, A., Morris, K. and White, S. (2018) *Protecting Children: A Social Model*, Bristol: Policy Press.

Fitzmaurice, L.S. (2022) 'Te rito o te harakeke: Decolonising child protection and children's participation', PhD thesis, University of Otago. Available at: http://hdl.handle.net/10523/13625

Garcia, A., Berrick, J.D., Jonson-Reid, M., Barth, R.P. Gyourko, J.R., Kohl, P., et al (2024) 'The stark implications of abolishing child welfare: An alternative path towards support and safety', *Child and Family Social Work*, 1–13.

Gerlach, A.J., Browne, A.J., Sinha, V. and Elliott, D. (2017) 'Navigating structural violence with Indigenous families: The contested terrain of early childhood intervention and the child welfare system in Canada', *The International Indigenous Policy Journal*, 8(3).

Gilbert, N., Parton, N. and Skiveness, M. (eds) (2011) *Child Proetction Systems: International Trends and Orientations*, Oxford: Oxford University Press.

Gray, M. and Schubert, L. (2019) 'Critiques of a public health model in child maltreatment', in B. Lonne, D. Scott, D. Higgins and T. Herrenkohl (eds), *Re-Visioning Public Health Approaches for Protecting Children*, Cham: Springer International Publishing, pp 221–234.

Hayden, A., Gelsthorpe, L., Kingi, V. and Allison, M. (eds) (2014) *A Restorative Approach to Family Violence: Changing Tack*, Surrey: Ashgrove Publishing Limited.

Herrenkohl, T., Lonne, B., Higgins, D. and Scott, D.A. (2020) 'The personal security of children demands bold system reform', *International Journal on Child Maltreatment: Research, Policy and Practice*, 3(1): 9–17.

Higgins, D.J., Lonne, B., Herrenkohl, T.I., Klika, J.B. and Scott, D. (2022) 'Core components of public health approaches to preventing child abuse and neglect', in R.D. Krugman and J.E. Korbin (eds), *Child Maltreatment: Contemporary Issues in Research and Policy* (2nd edn), Cham: Springer, pp 445–458.

Higgins, D., Herrenkohl, T., Lonne, B. and Scott, D. (2024) 'Advancing a prevention-oriented support system for the health and safety of children', *Children and Youth Services Review*, np.

Hill Collins, P. and Bilge, S. (2020) *Intersectionality* (2nd edn), Cambridge: Polity.

Hurihanganui, T.A. (2024) 'Govt moves to replace or repeal Treaty principles clauses from laws', *One News*, 27 May. Available at: https://www.1news.co.nz/2024/05/27/govt-moves-to-replace-or-repeal-treaty-principles-clauses-from-laws/

Hyslop, I. (2022) *A Political History of Child Protection: Lessons for Reform from Aotearoa New Zealand*, Bristol: Policy Press.

Jenkins, B. (2021) 'Measuring the equity of risk assessment instruments used in child protection', *Children and Youth Services Review*, 131: 106266.

Kaba, M. and Hassan, S. (2019) *Fumbling Towards Repair: A Workbook for Community Accountability Facilitators*, Chico, CA: AK Press.

Keddell, E. (2015) 'The ethics of predictive risk modelling in the Aotearoa/New Zealand child welfare context: Child abuse prevention or neo-liberal tool?', *Critical Social Policy*, 35(1): 69–88.

Keddell, E. (2022) 'Mechanisms of inequity: The impact of instrumental biases in the this child protection system', *Societies*, 12(3): Article 83.

Keddell, E. (2024) 's7AA works just as intended', *Newsroom*, 2 July. Available at: https://newsroom.co.nz/2024/07/02/section-7aa-works-as-intended-to-reduce-child-protection-disparities-for-maori/

Keddell, E., Davie, G. and Barson, D. (2019) 'Child protection inequalities in Aotearoa New Zealand: Social gradient and the "inverse intervention law"', *Children and Youth Services Review*, 104: 104383. https://doi.org/https://doi.org/10.1016/j.childyouth.2019.06.018

Kelly, L. (2021) 'Abolition or reform? Confronting the symbiotic relationship between "child welfare" and the carceral state', *Stanford Journal of Civil Rights and Civil Liberties*, 17(2): 255–320.

Miller, C. (2024) 'Social service provider Family Start losing $14m in funding', One News, [online] 2 August. Available from: https://www.1news.co.nz/2024/08/02/social-service-provider-family-start-losing-14m-in-funding/

Morrah, M. (2024) 'Children's Minister Karen Chhour apologises to abuse survivors as officials eye major shake up of Oranga Tamariki funding model' New Zealand Herald, [online] 24 July. Available from: https://www.nzherald.co.nz/nz/cchildrens-minister-karen-chhour-apologises-to-abuse-survivors-as-officiails-eye-major-shake-up-of-oranga-tamariki-funding-model/OGWGM5DERH7JPLYUMRYE3RU/#ggoogle_vignette

Napoleon, V. (2014) 'Thinking about Indigenous legal orders', *Derecho & Sociedad*, 40: 207–222.

Nayak, S. and Robbins, R. (2020) *Intersectionality in Social Work: Activism and Practice in Context*, London: Routledge.

Oranga Tamariki (2023) 'Safety of children in care report'. Available at: https://www.orangatamariki.govt.nz/assets/Uploads/About-us/Performance-and-monitoring/safety-of-children-in-care/2022-23/J000093_SOCIC-Report-2023_v4.pdf

Oranga Tamariki (2024) 'Family and Whānau care'. Available at: https://www.orangatamariki.govt.nz/support-for-families/how-we-support-whanau/family-and-whanau-care/

Paki Paki, N., King, P.T., Lewis, L., MacKay, H.T.U., Anderson, D., Amante, E. and Kemp, S.P. (2023) 'Identifying key dimensions of indigenous led child welfare services: A qualitative literature review', *Child and Family Social Work*, 29(2): 465–481.

Pendleton, M. (2021) 'Making possible the impossible: A Black feminist perspective on child welfare abolition', *Columbia Journal of Race and Law* [blog], 20 February. Available at: https://journals.library.columbia.edu/index.php/cjrl/blog/view/311

Radio New Zealand (2024) 'Minister defends lowered child poverty targets as "achievable"', *RNZ*, 26 July. Available at: https://www.rnz.co.nz/news/political/523167/minister-defends-lowered-child-poverty-targets-as-achievable

Roberts, D. (2002) *Shattered Bonds: The Color of Child Welfare*, New York: Basic Books.

Roberts, D. (2014) 'Child protection as surveillance of African American families', *Journal of Social Welfare and Family Law*, 36: 59–65.

Roberts, D. (2022) *Torn Apart: How the Child Welfare System Destroys Black Families – and How Abolition Can Build a Safe World*, New York: Basic Books.

Roberts, D. and Sangoi, L. (2018) 'Black families matter: How the child welfare system punishes poor families of color', *Injustice Today*, 26 March. Available at: https://theappeal.org/black-families-matter-how-the-child-welfare-system-punishes-poor-families-of-color-33ad20e2882e/

Robertson, S.C., Sinclair, C. and Hatala, A.R. (2021) 'Indigenous mothers' experiences of power and control in child welfare: Families being heard', *Journal of Social Work*, 22(2): 303–322.

Scott, D., Lonne, B. and Higgins, D. (2016) 'Public health models for preventing child maltreatment: Applications from the field of injury prevention', *Trauma, Violence, and Abuse*, 17(4): 408–419.

Smith, L. (1999) *Decolonizing Methodologies*, London: Bloomsbury Publishing.

Smith, R. and Wirihana, C. (2019) 'Historical trauma, healing and well-being in Māori communities', in C.S. Tinirau (ed) *He Rau Murimuri Aroha: Wāhine Māori Insights into Historical Trauma and Healing*, Whanganui: Te Atawhai o te Ao.

University of Otago. Available at: http://hdl.handle.net/10523/13625

Waitangi Tribunal (2021) 'He Pāharakeke, he rito whakakīkinga whāruarua oranga tamariki urgent inquiry WAI 2915', Wellington: Waitangi Tribunal. Available at: https://forms.justice.govt.nz/search/Documents/WT/wt_DOC_171027305/He%20Paharakeke%20W.pdf

Wharewara-Mika, E. and Copper, J. (2011) 'Healing, towards an understanding of Māori child maltreatment', in T. McIntosh amd M. Mulholland (eds), *Māori and Social Issues*, Wellington: Huia Publishers, pp 223–245.

Wright, A., Gray, P., Selkirk, B., Hunt, C. and Wright, R. (2024) 'Attachment and the (mis)apprehension of Aboriginal children: Epistemic violence in child welfare interventions', *Psychiatry, Psychology and Law*, 1–25.

18

Haunting, abolition and Finnish child welfare

Kris Clarke and Mwenza Blell

Introduction

All children need love and security to thrive. Child welfare systems have statutory powers to safeguard children. Contested issues in child welfare are often centred on where the line between the family and the state lies, especially in socially unjust structures that cause harm to oppressed populations. Located on the periphery of Europe, Nordic nations have deployed their welfare state model since the Second World War as a global branding strategy (Marklund, 2017). This image has influenced international opinion to view Nordic societies as exceptional: uniquely egalitarian, practical, peaceful and almost utopian (Browning 2007; Marklund and Petersen, 2013). However, as Loftsdóttir (2019) has argued, the liminal quality of margins can reveal the messiness and complexities of the European project, both as a colonial enterprise and ideological construct. Similarly, taking an abolitionist lens to Nordic contexts can unveil how seemingly benevolent and efficient neoliberal approaches to care can be haunted by the legacies of colonialism and eugenics through the carcerality of state interventions and institutions.

Globally, Finland has some of the lowest child mortality rates, has long outlawed corporal punishment, and has been at the forefront in enhancing the participatory rights of children. Yet, this country with such a strong foundation of children's rights and support systems has more children than ever in contact with child welfare authorities (Finnish Institute for Health and Welfare, 2023). This represents a paradoxical state of affairs. While national welfare states are complex and multilayered, the Finnish welfare state has long stood for solidarity and equality. Emerging in the postwar era through compromise and consensus, the welfare state centred state interests, along with the accompanying values of unity and uniformity rather than conflict and rights (Kettunen, 2018). Still, this consensus was constructed on a false homogeneity that privileged the visibility, interests and needs of some over others in the organisation and practice of social and healthcare services (Keskinen et al, 2019). As Foucault observed, modern institutions discipline diverse bodies in specific and often carceral ways, whether unmarried, queer, racialised or differently abled, to enforce a hierarchal and exclusionary sense of 'normalcy' in society (Foucault, 2012). Many studies show that children removed from home are far more likely than peers raised in their own homes to face significant challenges in adulthood, including substance misuse, mental health issues and unemployment (for example, Gypen et al, 2017; Kääriälä and Hillamo, 2017). As a political project, abolitionist social work seeks to dismantle punitive and carceral social interventions, such as family separation, which create cognitive, psychological and spiritual violence disproportionately targeted at racialised, poor and marginalised people (Toraif and Mueller, 2023).

Since the Great Recession of the 1990s, when Finland faced a dramatic economic contraction due to the dissolution of its largest trading partner, the Soviet Union, there has been an exponential rise in the number of Finnish children living outside of their homes, representing a surge of 180 per cent (SOS-Children's Villages, 2024). This rise has been attributed to changes in legislation, the reduction of the welfare state, and the growing governance of families and children by the state (Pösö, 2015). The majority of child removals are 'in-home care', where child protection services have been engaged as a result of a report or at the request of the family. In this case, parents generally do not lose custody of their children, even if they are removed, because the placement is voluntary (Pösö and Huhtanen, 2016). The 2017 Child Welfare Act requires that good administrative practice and transparency prevail when making decisions on children, however, as Pösö and Huhtanen (2016: 33–34) underline, there is a lack of research into the decision-making process of social workers and how consent is obtained in 'voluntary' placements. While children have a right to express their views on matters that concern them, there is little research on how social work discretion is used, and therefore the danger that child protection interventions are disproportionately implemented with certain populations due to social worker bias or inadequate information for families, remains.

As neoliberalism has taken root in Finnish policy making, children's care homes have been largely outsourced to limited companies, providing a lucrative profit stream similar to how care in the United States and UK has been monetised and privatised. The expansion of the carceral state often comes after a period of austerity when essential resources to strengthen communities have been cut and carceral policies are targeted at certain communities (such as racialised or gendered groups) perceived as threatening to the national body (Richie and Martensen, 2020). Despite a 2013 Finnish public inquiry that examined the traumatic and abusive historic legacy of out-of-home care (Malinen et al, 2020), where ethnic groups such as the Roma were over-represented, the aim of building a transitional justice process that would lead to change is blocked by the logics of neoliberal care which monetises carceral approaches to child welfare and so these practices continue.

This chapter employs an abolitionist lens to explore how the afterlives of colonialism and eugenics haunt the Finnish welfare state in children's residential care, in the wake of the New Public Management (NPM) of 21st-century neoliberal capitalism. It proceeds by first presenting emerging abolitionist perspectives on social work, and then outlining the history of eugenics and its significance to the Finnish welfare state. Using Avery Gordon's (2008) notion of haunting as developed by Blell and Sudenkaarne (Sudenkaarne and Blell, 2022; Blell and Sudenkaarne, 2024), we explore how child welfare is haunted by uniquely Finnish iterations of ideologies of coloniality and eugenics, which have morphed, via neoliberal privatisation schemes, into the current situation of residential care.

Abolitionist perspectives on social work

Abolitionists articulate a fundamental critique of how social work is theorised and practised as a profession, seeking to assume the mantle of social justice advocacy while often individualising social issues as personal problems requiring licensed professional intervention. Abolitionist social work is a theoretical orientation and political project informed by guiding principles that seek to dismantle oppressive systems and carceral approaches to care, as well as to envision emancipatory social liberation that is grounded in decolonised and life-affirming institutions and relationships (The Network to Advance Abolitionist Social Work, 2024: 24–27). Abolitionist thought is informed by the work of Black feminist scholars such as Angela Davis (2011), Ruth Gilmore (2022), Andrea Ritchie (2017) and Dorothy Roberts (2002, 2023), who have provided detailed analyses of how caring systems have evolved within the structures of colonialism, racial capitalism and the prison-industrial complex. Abolitionist theory also draws on anti-colonial theorists such as Franz Fanon (1963/2004) and Edward Said (1978) who have identified how social work knowledge production has been stamped by Eurocentric and colonial ontologies and epistemologies. Abolitionist theory views carceral systems as rooted in racial capitalism and aimed at maintaining oppression. Social transformation therefore requires accountability and transformational justice which responds to harm by not causing further harm (Mingus, 2022).

As a statutory field, social work is immersed in systems that have deep roots in universalising coloniality, the pseudoscience of eugenics, and colonial-capitalist structures built on racism, patriarchy and extractivism, which have the capacity to dispose of life. Nigel Parton (2016) defined 'authoritarian neoliberal' systems of care as those which emerged in the wake of the financial crises of the early 2000s as politicians sought to realign the state's relationship to social welfare and 'the family' by contracting out services and using coercive paternalism to enforce labour discipline and control social behaviour. Yet, these very same care systems are some of the last lines of defence left to deal with the multitude of problems created by austerity measures and withdrawal of the state from communities. In the neoliberal political world, contemporary systems of care are thus constructed as 'carceral systems of care', which emphasise surveillance, punishment and separation/confinement as well as expertise often constructed as existing outside of the community. Dorothy Roberts (2002: vi–viii) has pointed out that many discussions of child welfare use a Manichaean political rhetoric of bad parents and innocent children or bad government and innocent parents. Rarely is the structural racism, classism, homophobia and sexism that permeates state social policies and the politics of social work practice a focus of analysis.

In grappling with the significance of the past on the present, many theorists have used the notion of haunting to understand the 'living ghosts' (Bhaba, 1996) that populate our contemporary systems, yet remain invisible through the lens of colonial epistemologies. Confronting these hauntings requires an ethical engagement with the continuities of violent pasts in order to build an emancipatory future (Blell and Sudenkaarne, 2024). The historical legacy of colonialism, Indigenous genocide, racial capitalism and class oppression are structural phenomena that have informed tactics like family separation, incarceration and surveillance, serving to enforce hegemonic power relations and repress diverse sociocultural identities and solidarities. These social structures thus create psychic structures by normalising racial capitalism and coloniality through eugenicist diagnoses and interventions that are actively embedded in state policies of containment and control by, for example, removing children and denying benefits (Nayak, 2015: 51). Abolitionists argue that oppressive structures haunt social care through the prevailing carceral techniques of managing clients in social and healthcare systems, which cause disproportionate harm to racialised, disabled, migrant, queer and poor people, among many other marginalised communities. These systems of violence, in other words, function as they are intended to and therefore meaningful reform from within is not possible (Murray et al, 2023).

With their reputation for comprehensive care and universal welfare, Nordic societies might seem incongruous places to explore abolitionist perspectives on social work. However, a closer examination of how the legacy of colonialism and eugenics haunts Finnish social work shows that the shift from a high level of state involvement in children's institutions to the current form of the most highly privatised system of children's care homes in the Nordic states demonstrates a familiar pattern of social violence, coercive control and carcerality, particularly in regard to certain children often seen as not belonging to the nation. Creating emancipatory social work thus requires memory work to exorcise the afterlives of colonialism and eugenics in contemporary policy and practice; to make possible new social work visions of an emancipatory future for all children resident in Finland.

Manufacturing the family in the Finnish nation

Notions of family have changed in Europe over time and are entwined with the emergence of colonialism. With origins in repression of women during the rise of capitalism (Federici, 2004), the 'traditional' family ideal that emerged during industrialisation replaced extended kinship systems with a heterosexual couple with biological children. The family, the market and the state ensured the reproduction of capitalist society through unequal power relations (between men and women as well as social classes) upon which capitalist society depends. As Patricia Hill Collins (1998: 63) noted: 'The power of this traditional family ideal lies in its dual function as an ideological construction and as a fundamental principle of social organisation.' Families have also been a central site of patriarchal and heteronormative oppression, intimate partner violence, coercive control and child sexual abuse.

Settler-colonialism relied on white families to fill the space of seized lands. As Phillips (2009) points out, the hegemonic nuclear family was key to defining reproductive and conjugal rights and privileges in colonial society via regulating marriage, legislating rights over children and the right to inheritance, all of which assigned privilege and constructed the borders between respectability and legitimacy and the illicit and immoral. In Finland, a self-defined white settler state established on Sámi territory, as elsewhere, fears about maintaining white dominance over colonised populations fed anxieties about maintaining the racial hygiene of white settler-colonists, thus prompting population control interventions directed at Indigenous[1] and racialised groups, such as coercive sterilisation and family separation (Blell and Homanen, 2025). Informed by Social Darwinist theories that were circulating the late 19th century, fears about the degeneration of nations translated into racial hygiene ideologies. As in other nations, in Finland nationalist self-definitions of good citizens emphasised sobriety, physical fitness and hard work. Carceral state measures thus targeted the undeserving and those seen to need correction.

Eugenics, an international 20th-century pseudoscientific social movement strongly linked with emerging professional social and healthcare policies and practices, was influenced by theories of racial hygiene and shaped by the values of white supremacy. Rising in influence in Nordic countries as the forces of industrialisation, mass emigration and rapid social change became felt (Weßel, 2018), the aim of eugenics was to 'improve' the genetic, physical, intellectual and social qualities of specific human populations (called 'races' before the Second World War) through various interventions, such as sterilisation, the promotion of marriage and reproduction, immigration restrictions, and the separation of children from their families in boarding schools and other institutions. In Finland, social workers played an essential role in eugenic sterilisation practices, as Mattila (2018) notes, in the ways that they were exhorted to encourage so-called anti-social persons, such as unmarried mothers, women in prison and Roma women, to be sterilised because of the presumed association between these characteristics and criminality, receipt of social benefits, immorality, poor parenting and cognitive disability.

There was no reckoning in Nordic societies, as in postwar Germany, with the horrific local legacy of eugenicist theorisations and practices until the late 20th century (Broberg and Roll-Hansen, 2005). Thus, the legacy of eugenics and colonialism continues to haunt the contemporary welfare state in how people perceived as non-Finns are narrated in reproductive healthcare, mental health and child welfare, for example: services which are considered merely neutral by those on the inside (Blell and Homanen, 2023; Dayib and Clarke, 2024; Blell and Homanen, 2025). Indeed, one aspect of the haunted Finnish health and care system is that it seems to repeatedly find ways to 'care' for society in a way that is directly at the expense of the rights of marginalised individuals, such as those disabled by society, migrantised or minoritised (for example, Sámi and Roma people) (Blell and Homanen, 2025), including the rights of children they claim are beneficiaries of its interventions. Contemporary social structures are thus deeply embedded in particular ways of organising social reproduction that have become normalised and culturalised through ideologies about the family, ability, gender and ethnicity. Following abolitionist scholars such as Richie and Martensen (2020), any form of social work that supports carceral systems is no longer providing 'social' services but delivering carceral services which reinforce systems of oppression.

Finnish child welfare: from consensus to neoliberalism

Finnish child welfare emerged in a context where national independence in 1917 was quickly followed by a civil war that led to thousands of children being orphaned. As Hämäläinen (2023: 996) points out: 'Early discussions around child welfare were conducted mainly by a small, cosmopolitan, predominantly Swedish-speaking scholarly elite in what was essentially a developing country experiencing economic and political instability.' Child welfare was viewed as a scientific and civil society field, especially as prominent bourgeois women became involved in charity work. Early concepts of child welfare were firmly embedded in notions of the nation and good citizenship, hygiene and health, the scientific thinking of the time, and the population policies of eugenics (Hämäläinen, 2023). Early child welfare focused on the family, as described above, as key to the notion of Christian patriarchal morality rather than individual children's rights.

By the 1990s, the geopolitical circumstances of Finland changed with the fall of the Soviet Union and membership in the European Union. A condition of entry to the European Union was agreeing to many international human rights laws and treaties. Still, the Finnish welfare state employed bordering practices as a larger wave of migration came to Finland in the 1990s, which Guentner et al (2016: 391) define as 'measures taken by state institutions – whether at territorial frontiers or inside them – which demarcate categories of people so as to incorporate some and exclude others, in a specific social order'. Bordering practices exist on a spectrum that ranges from detention and deportation to subordination. In Finland, these practices followed the historical tradition of othering directed towards Sámi and Roma people; populations that have been more subject to coercive and carceral 'care' practices. As Alaattinoğlu (2023: 149) asserts: 'In comparison to Norway and Sweden, Finland has a weak tradition of questioning and remedying oppression in its modern history.' This may be because the emphasis on consensus has often occluded an understanding of the importance of respecting difference and diversity.

NPM was widely implemented in Finland in the wake of the Great Recession of the 1990s. NPM is a set of strategies and practices that aim to reduce the role of the state in providing public services through outsourcing to private entities in the 'nonpolitical' neoliberal belief that publicly run services were inherently inefficient and in need of the innovation intrinsic to privatisation. A key aspect of the neoliberal political project was to deny that it was political so that it could be presented solely as a rational, economic plan. Neoliberalism, with its willingness to accept survival of the fittest, should require a massive moral and cultural change for a Nordic welfare state like Finland. However, if we accept the premise that the Finnish welfare state and social work has long been haunted by the ghosts of eugenics and institutionalisation, then the absence of these discussions is not surprising. Blell and Homanen (2023) identify the individualisation of misfortune and ideological closure as factors leading to a total acceptance of the NPM logic of scarcity of resources, and this acceptance acts as a barrier to making demands for justice for many Finns.

The afterlives of colonialism and eugenics in Finnish child welfare

The afterlives of colonialism and eugenics continue to haunt Finnish child welfare via what Patricia Hill Collins (2017: 1464) has termed 'intensified points of convergence' where the 'conceptual glue' of social structures moulds distinct types of interpersonal and systemic violence that 'facilitate the naturalisation and normalisation of political domination' at all levels of society. The deep structures of social work, its epistemologies, policies and practices (haunted as they are by colonialism and eugenics) dovetailed with neoliberal managerialism which blamed inefficient public administration and personal irresponsibility for social distress, thus individualising and privatising social problems, and enhancing carceral approaches to 'problem' clients through austerity measures and the commodification of care (Kantola, 2002). The presumption of professional neutrality fails to recognise how policies and practices are rooted in political decisions.

In recent years, there has been a rise in contacts with child welfare services and an increase in the number of children and youth placed in residential or foster care. According to the Finnish Institute for Health and Welfare (2023), in 2022, child welfare notifications were made concerning 9.1 per cent of children living in Finland, comprising 15.8 per cent of 12–15-year-olds. The children of immigrants are over-represented in educational disadvantage, criminal sentencing and prescribed psychotropic medications (Ansala et al, 2016). Despite having a relatively generous welfare system, Finland continues to have the highest number of children in voluntary out-of-home care in the Nordics (Hestbæk et al, 2020). This may seem paradoxical until we consider the way that structural problems are addressed increasingly in solely individualising ways within Finland's welfare state.

Finnish child protection services state that they step in when the universal child welfare supports are insufficient, and children are assessed as needing safeguarding. As Hestbæk et al (2020) point out, the consensus between parents and social workers about 'voluntary' removals in family-oriented social services can be questioned as the lines between consent and coercion are not always clear. A recent study of child removals indicates that structural issues such as living in a deprived area or having previous contact with child welfare authorities increases the chances of being removed from the home, while enhanced income support may decrease the need for intervention (Toikko et al, 2024). Arguing for a structural approach to child welfare, Timo Toikko et al (2024) criticise the individualistic approach to child welfare in Finland, arguing that such a narrow focus cannot address the structural issues that drive child removals. Hiitola et al (2020: 189) further analyse the manifold ways that Finnish welfare services use 'bordering' practices in everyday life where service providers act as gatekeepers, enacting practices that attempt to mould service users into respectable citizens. As welfare supports are continuously eroded and carceral 'care' in for-profit facilities is seen as a solution, growing numbers of families in crisis leads to increased business profits.

Shanks et al (2021) is one of the few systematic studies of the privatisation of Nordic residential care for children. It argues that there were several factors that led to the current situation in Finland where residential care is dominated by for-profit companies. The administration of Finnish care shifted in the late 1980s from centralised state control to growing municipal autonomy and control over the provision of care. The main funding mechanism for Finnish non-governmental organisations and foundations in the 1990s used the profits from state-run gambling to fund third sector activities. In 2001, a new Finnish law prohibited it from using public funding to support associations that could distort market competition (Shanks et al, 2021: 134). These structural changes systematically placed associations and non-profits at a disadvantage at the same time that there were growing economic opportunities for for-profit companies to insert themselves into and eventually dominate the market for children and youth residential care. Care homes thus became receptacles for individualised social problems that were monetised from the top down.

A search of the Finnish trade register in June 2024 showed 300 registered companies providing residential and professional care activities for children and young people. The categories of ownership are shown in Table 18.1.

The carcerality and harm of family separation and the institutionalisation of children has been examined in Finland. An inquiry into the treatment of children in care was initiated by the Ministry of Social Affairs and Health in 2013, as part of a transitional justice project that sought to come to terms with historical wrongs and to make amends for carceral harms. Academics were commissioned to research the prevalence and extent of abuse and neglect in institutions, though no specific actions were taken in response. The failure to right wrongs of this nature may be, as legal scholar Alaattinoğlu (2023: 147) argues, because Finland has 'an austere remedial culture with a stalled grievance formation process, in which victims have generally refrained from mobilisation, lacking a common identity as well as a sense of wrong to be remedied'. Public apologies can be performative, deflecting attention from related violence in the present, but they also serve the purpose of delegitimising historical mistakes, enhancing awareness of

Table 18.1: Ownership of Finnish children's homes

Non-profit association	17 (6%)
Foundation	7 (2.3%)
Government-owned	1 (0.3%)
Joint municipal authority	1 (0.3%)
Private person	21 (7%)
Company (partnership)	20 (7%)
Limited company	233 (78%)

Note: The total does not match 100 per cent due to rounding up.

social injustice and opening up dialogue around remedies (Dolan, 2021). The Finnish state has been more resistant to admitting guilt and being held accountable, whether it comes to issues surrounding its Indigenous Sámi population or disabled people who were targets of eugenicist policies. This stance has allowed discrimination to continue under the cover of neutral professional practice.

Finally, it is difficult to assess disproportionality in Finnish child welfare because research is not allowed to take into account the race or ethnicity of children. Doctoral student Amiirah Salleh-Hoddin (Ruotsalainen, 2024) has studied racial equality data, which is disaggregated data that compares the situations of diverse groups at risk of discrimination, that can be used as a tool to measure the extent of discrimination in society. Rather than self-identification, Finnish data relies on proxies such as citizenship and language spoken at home, which are intended to approximate racial identity but does not give clear information about identity groups. These euphemistic and colour-evasive data categories contribute to stigma and disparities. Further, Salleh-Hoddin (Ruotsalainen, 2024) points out that reliance on population registers and migration-based information affirms institutional definitions rather than self-identification. While this is often explained as being due to laws regarding confidentiality, it can also be seen as an official policy of colour-blind universalism which makes it impossible to gauge whether there is disproportionality in child removals and family separation, though anecdotal evidence would suggest that.

The origin of this prohibition on recording race is apparently the fear of repeating the violent racism of the Third Reich (which Finland doesn't acknowledge it had anything to do with, even though it did) and yet this fearful decision allows racism to continue. This is very much a haunted phenomenon (under Gordon's theorisation, specifically). Finland's policies are based on a desire not to repeat what it never admitted involvement with (things now over and done with but which also never happened) and their effect is to conceal, rather than protect against, that thing. Following Gordon, we are able to 'comprehend the living effects, seething and lingering, of what seems over and done with, the endings that are not over' (Gordon, 2008: 195) because they cannot be over while these haunted techniques of truth concealment still stand.

Conclusion

The Finnish myth of homogeneity silences histories of the personal cost of nation-building processes in the late 19th and early 20th centuries where disability, migration and ethnic diversity were seen as threatening to the integrity of the emerging nation-state (Blell and Homanen, 2023). This myth, along with the (false) belief that official colour-blindness immunises society against racism, means that Finns do not have to acknowledge the ghosts of the colonial or eugenicist past, nor recognise ongoing harms to racialised families: nor are they faced with evidence of whom the systems might unfairly target. The haunted lack of understanding of class or race as enduring structures in Finland (Sudenkaarne and Blell, 2022) and deflected focus on associated characteristics which are represented as individualised problems (that is, alcohol use, inability to communicate in Finnish) also allows the roles of discrimination and deprivation to remain unrecognised.

Mythic white homogeneity is also understood to be causally linked to the welfare state because diversity is considered incompatible with the social cohesiveness that legitimises the welfare state. The discourse that Finns have no obligation to care for foreigners (as a result of not having colonised them) and the notion that Finns and their welfare state are under threat from diversity coalesce here. Ethnic diversity can be represented as a new and unwieldy reality for Finnish systems and excuse any claims that the systems serve white (cis and heterosexual) Finns better, since these people are cast as temporally prior and most deserving (Blell and Homanen, 2023). Thus, discrimination can be recast as fairness or, at worst, an excusable lag in getting to grips with something new. As Richie and Martensen note:

> Continued carceral expansion to capture [im]migrants, transgender and gender-non-conforming people, people with disabilities, young people, and people with physical and mental health challenges illustrate both the power of carceral expansion and the ways that the carceral state is motivated by political instincts to control groups that threaten the status quo. (Richie and Martensen, 2020: 13)

It is key that research, policy and practice challenge the entrenchment of continuing bordering practices that are often haunted by the ghosts of the eugenicist past.

As Finnish child welfare and integration services face huge cuts in resources, the ground is being laid for increasingly carceral approaches to well-being. Contemporary abolitionist social work is a response to the tightening grips of the neoliberal carceral state, which has emerged from racial capitalism and coloniality. The individualisation of structural problems, use of bordering practices and reinforcement of hierarchies, all of which are haunted by the social violence that is allegedly in the past, but which has never really been acknowledged or remedied, inevitably leads to ghostly repetitions. Finally, as severe neoliberal cuts loom and increasingly carceral child welfare practices prevail, the question arises of how a country that is supposed to be fair finds it so difficult to admit to the possibility of unfairness. Until these hauntings are recognised, confronted and redressed, then social justice will continue to remain elusive in Finnish society. Abolitionist perspectives resolutely oppose all carceral methods in the fundamental belief that the remedy to harm is not causing further harm. Abolitionists call for social work to hold state institutions to account for harms caused by discrimination and privatisation and to create practical emancipatory visions to liberate all people.

Note

[1] The Sámi are the only officially recognised Indigenous group in the European Union.

References

Alaattinoğlu, D. (2023) *Grievance Formation, Rights and Remedies: Involuntary Sterilisation and Castration in the Nordics, 1930s–2020s*, Cambridge: Cambridge University Press.

Ansala, L., Hämäläinen, U. and Sarvimäki, M. (2016) *Slipping through the Cracks of a Welfare State: Children of Immigrants in Finland* [No. 06/16]. CReAM Discussion Paper Series.

Bhaba, H. (1996) 'Unpacking my library ... again', in I. Chambers and L. Curti (eds), *The Post-Colonial Question: Common Skies, Divided Horizons*, London: Routledge, pp 199–211.

Blell, M. and Homanen, R. (2023) 'Justice reproductive en Finlande? Le mythe de l'homogénéité dans une social-démocratie nordique 1', *Travail, genre et sociétés*, 2: 79–95.

Blell, M. and Homanen, R. (2025) 'Haunted data: Data politics as reproductive politics in Finland', in S.B. Franklin and M.C. Inhorn (eds), *The New Reproductive Order: Changing Infertilities across the Globe*, New York: New York University Press.

Blell, M. and Sudenkaarne, T. (2024) 'Ghosts in the machine: Black feminist and queer critiques of reproductive justice in Finland', *Journal of Lesbian Studies*, 28(4): 1–19.

Broberg, G. and Roll-Hansen, N. (2005) *Eugenics and the Welfare State: Sterilization Policy in Denmark, Sweden, Norway, and Finland*, Lansing: Michigan State University Press.

Browning, C.S. (2007) 'Branding Nordicity: Models, identity and the decline of exceptionalism', *Cooperation and Conflict*, 42(1): 27–51.

Collins, P.H. (1998) 'It's all in the family: Intersections of gender, race, and nation', *Hypatia*, 13(3): 62–82.

Collins, P.H. (2017) 'On violence, intersectionality and transversal politics', *Ethnic and Racial Studies*, 40(9): 1460–1473.

Davis, A.Y. (2011) *Abolition Democracy: Beyond Empire, Prisons, and Torture*, New York: Seven Stories Press.

Dayib, F. and Clarke, K. (2024) 'Transcultural mental health as the colonisation of racialised bodies: A personal insight', in K. Clarke, L. Lee-Oliver and S. Ranta-Tyrkkö (eds), *Decolonising Social Work in Finland*, Bristol: Policy Press, pp 161–181.

Dolan, E. (2021) *Gender and Political Apology: When the Patriarchal State Says 'Sorry'*, London: Routledge.
Fanon, F. (1963/2004) *The Wretched of the Earth*, New York: Grove Press.
Federici, S. (2004) *Caliban and the Witch*, Brooklyn: Autonomedia.
Finnish Institute for Health and Welfare (2023) 'Child welfare 2023', 15 August. Available at: https://thl.fi/en/statistics-and-data/statistics-by-topic/social-services-children-adolescents-and-families/childwelfare
Foucault, M. (2012) *Discipline and Punish: The Birth of the Prison* (2nd edn), New York: Vintage Books.
Gilmore, R.W. (2022) *Abolition Geography: Essays towards Liberation*, London: Verso Books.
Gordon, A. (2008) *Ghostly Matters: Haunting and the Sociological Imagination* (2nd edn), Minneapolis: University of Minnesota Press.
Guentner, S., Lukes, S., Stanton, R., Vollmer, B.A. and Wilding, J. (2016) 'Bordering practices in the UK welfare system', *Critical Social Policy*, 36(3): 391–411.
Gypen, L., Vanderfaeillie, J., De Maeyer, S., Belenger, L. and Van Holen, F. (2017) 'Outcomes of children who grew up in foster care: Systematic review', *Children and Youth Services Review*, 76: 74–83.
Hämäläinen, J. (2023) 'Constructing child welfare science in the early development of child welfare in Finland', *Paedagogica Historica*, 59(6): 994–1015.
Hestbæk, A.D., Höjer, I., Pösö, T. and Skivenes, M. (2020) 'Child welfare removal of infants: Exploring policies and principles for decision-making in Nordic countries', *Children and Youth Services Review*, 108: 104572.
Hiitola, J., Turtiainen, K., Gruber, S. and Tiilikainen, M. (2020) *Family Life in Transition: Borders, Transnational Mobility, and Welfare Society in Nordic Countries*, London: Routledge.
Kääriälä, A. and Hiilamo, H. (2017) Children in out-of-home care as young adults: A systematic review of outcomes in the Nordic countries', *Children and Youth Services Review*, 79: 107–114.
Kantola, A. (2002) 'Markkinakuri ja managerivalta: poliittinen hallinta Suomen 1990-luvun talouskriisissä', Doctoral dissertation, University of Helsinki, Department of Communication Studies.
Keskinen, S., Skaptadóttir, U.D. and Toivanen, M. (2019) 'Narrations of homogeneity, waning welfare states, and the politics of solidarity', in S. Keskinen, U.D. Skaptadóttir and M. Toivanen (eds), *Undoing Homogeneity in the Nordic Region*, London: Routledge, pp 1–17.
Kettunen, P. (2018) 'Wars, nation, and the welfare state in Finland', in H. Obinger, K. Petersen and P. Starke (eds), *Warfare and Welfare: Military Conflict and Welfare State Development in Western Countries*, Oxford: Oxford University Press, pp 260–289.

Loftsdóttir, K. (2019) *Crisis and Coloniality at Europe's Margins: Creating Exotic Iceland*, London: Taylor & Francis.

Malinen, A., Markkola, P. and Hytönen, K.M. (2020) 'Conducting commissioned research: The Finnish inquiry into the failures of child welfare, 1937–1983', *Scandinavian Journal of History*, 45(2): 202–220.

Marklund, C. (2017) 'The Nordic model on the global market of ideas: The welfare state as Scandinavia's best brand', *Geopolitics*, 22(3): 623–639.

Marklund C. and Petersen, K. (2013) 'Return to sender – American images of the Nordic welfare states and Nordic welfare state branding', *European Journal of Scandinavian Studies*, 43(2): 245–257.

Mattila, M. (2018) 'Sterilization policy and Gypsies in Finland', *Romani Studies*, 28(1): 109–139.

Mingus, M. (2022) 'Transformative justice: A brief description', *Fellowship*, 84(2): 17–19.

Murray, B.J., Copeland, V. and Dettlaff, A. J. (2023) 'Reflections on the ethical possibilities and limitations of abolitionist praxis in social work', *Affilia*, 38(4): 742–758.

Nayak, S. (2015) *What Can We Learn from Black Feminist Thought?*, New York: Routledge.

Parton, N. (2016) 'An "authoritarian neoliberal" approach to child welfare and protection?', *Aotearoa New Zealand Social Work*, 28(2): 7–8.

Phillips, R. (2009) 'Settler colonialism and the nuclear family', *The Canadian Geographer/Le Géographe canadien*, 53(2): 239–253.

Pösö, T. (2015) 'How the Finnish child protection system meets the needs of migrant families and children', in M. Skivenes, R. Barn, K. Kriz and T. Pösö (eds), *Child Welfare Systems and Migrant Children: A Cross-Country Study of Policies and Practices*, Oxford: Oxford University Press, pp 19–39.

Pösö, T. and Huhtanen, R. (2016) 'Removals of children in Finland', in K. Burns, T. Pösö and M. Skivenes (eds), *Child Welfare Removals by the State*, Oxford: Oxford University Press, pp 18–39.

Ritchie, A.J. (2017) *Invisible No More: Police Violence against Black Women and Women of Color*, Boston: Beacon Press.

Richie, B.E. and Martensen, K.M. (2020) Resisting carcerality, embracing abolition: Implications for feminist social work practice. *Affilia*, 35(1): 12–16.

Roberts, D. (2002) *Shattered Bonds: The Color of Child Welfare*, New York: Basic Books.

Roberts, D. (2023) 'Why abolition', *Family Court Review*, 61(2): 229–241.

Ruotsalainen, N. (2024) (audio podcast) 'Race, bordering and disobedient knowledge. Episode 3: Amiirah Salleh-Hoddin: Towards developing racial equality data', 15 August. Available at: https://www.helsinki.fi/en/swedish-school-social-science/studio-sockom/race-bordering-and-disobedient-knowledge

Said, E. (1978) *Orientalism*, New York: Pantheon.

Shanks, E., Backe-Hansen, E., Eriksson, P., Lausten, M., Lundström, T., Ranta, H., et al (2021) 'Privatisation of residential care for children and youth in Denmark, Finland, Norway, and Sweden', *Nordisk Välfärdsforskning*, 6(3): 128–141.

SOS-Children's Villages (2024) 'Finland', 15 August. Available at: https://www.sos-childrensvillages.org/where-we-help/europe/finland#:~:text=Children%20are%20at%20risk,on%20at%20least%20one%20occasion

Sudenkaarne, T. and Blell, M. (2022) 'Reproductive justice for the haunted Nordic welfare state: Race, racism, and queer bioethics in Finland', *Bioethics*, 36(3): 328–335.

The Network to Advance Abolitionist Social Work (2024) 'Conceptualizing social work, in Kim, M., Rasmussen, C. and Washington, D. (eds), *Abolition and Social Work*, Chicago: Haymarket Books.

Toikko, T., Gawel, A., Hietamäki, J., Häkkilä, L., Seppälä, P. and Zhu, N. (2024) 'Macro-level predictors of child removals: Do social welfare benefits and services reduce demand for children's out of home placements?', *Children and Youth Services Review*, 160: 107554.

Toraif, N. and Mueller, J. (2023) *Abolitionist Social Work*, Encyclopedia of Social Work. Available at: https://oxfordre.com/socialwork/view/10.1093/acrefore/9780199975839.001.0001/acrefore-9780199975839-e-1553

Weßel, M. (2018) 'An unholy union? Eugenic feminism in the Nordic countries, ca. 1890–1940', Doctoral dissertation, Faculty of Arts, University of Helsinki.

19

Beyond 'doing harm' and 'doing nothing': creating generative alternatives to psychiatric carcerality

Emma Tseris

Alongside many mental health systems across the globe, the Australian mental health system is carceral. Carcerality refers to not only the physical spaces in which mental health treatment occurs, but a logic that underpins how distress and difference are understood and responded to within mental health settings (Ben-Moshe, 2018). Mental health legislation in Australia and in many other countries allows for the detention and treatment without consent of people labelled with psychiatric diagnoses in certain circumstances (Gooding et al, 2018). Involuntary mental health treatment involves an array of experiences, including detention in mental health facilities, forced medication, seclusion, restraint, among many other practices, including the confiscation of belongings. There is also an increasing recognition of the serious harm caused by police acting as first responders in situations of crisis and distress (Randall et al, 2023).

Social work has been slow to grapple with the ethical questions raised by the profession's involvement in involuntary mental health treatment and its clear inconsistency with the profession's espoused social justice values (Maylea, 2017). There is a growing body of scholarship that challenges the ethics of mental health service provision and calls for an elimination of at least some forms of mental health treatment (Suslovic, 2024). While some research has focused on the abolition of mental health law and involuntary treatment, other scholars have called for a much more wide-scale rejection of psychiatry (Burstow, 2014). One of the reasons for this broader agenda is an acknowledgement that coercive practices extend far beyond legal parameters; informal coercion, force, threats, persuasion, inducement and clinical power underpin many voluntary mental health interventions (Gooding et al, 2018; Paradis-Gagné et al, 2021). Further, the persistent use of pathologising paradigms for understanding distress – for example, the imposition of a biomedical perspective irrespective of the views of people accessing services – can also be viewed as a form of psychiatric coercion, especially considering the extensive critiques of psychiatric diagnosing practices (Burstow, 2014).

Despite such strong criticisms, mental health systems in Western contexts are rarely discussed or understood in terms of carcerality or psychiatric harm. Instead, mental health services are most often positioned as overstretched and yet benevolent institutions, desperately requiring more funding in order to extend their reach into the lives of people experiencing mental distress and crisis. Such perspectives rest upon an assumption about the benevolence and usefulness of mainstream services, while ignoring the often devastating and enduring harms of mental health service involvement (Daley et al, 2019). The dominance of positive perspectives regarding mental health services may also be shaped by the now widely available first-hand accounts of people with social privileges and resources, who can sometimes find desired and helpful forms of support through private services, in ways that are usually not available to people accessing the public system (Daya et al, 2020). This chapter seeks to move beyond the assumption of psychiatric benevolence, and the justification of psychiatric coercion on the basis of 'risk' and 'best interests'. Informed by the substantial scholarship documenting the harms of psychiatric coercion, including by psychiatric survivors (Daya, 2022), the chapter discusses what it might mean for social workers to pursue the reduction or elimination of psychiatric power, and further, what additional considerations might be required in pursuing an anti-carceral mental health paradigm in the neoliberal era.

Engaging with simplistic and more nuanced arguments against abolition

Psychiatric coercion is characterised by the use of force and threats in the context of mental health service provision (Gooding et al, 2018). It includes such practices as involuntary hospital admissions in locked facilities, forced medication, seclusion and restraint. Despite its documented harms (Paradis-Gagné et al, 2021), psychiatric coercion has been described as a 'moral responsibility' and a 'necessary evil' in mental health crisis work (Strickland et al, 2019), and recent research demonstrates that many mental health workers continue to position coercion as an indispensable and beneficial practice (Morandi et al, 2021). In a renowned turn of phrase, the attempt to reduce the powers of mental health legislation has been described as leading to people 'dying with their rights on' (Treffert, 1979). The notion that eliminating psychiatric coercion will lead to exploitation, neglect and death is used to justify the continuation of involuntary mental health treatment (Wilson, 2018). Such arguments are frequently imbued with notions of 'risk', and concerns about the impacts of rolling back psychiatric powers on both the individual and society, underpinned by the dichotomous positions of 'using force' and 'doing nothing'. Despite immense evidence regarding its harms, psychiatric coercion is justified on the basis of medicalised beneficience (Morandi et al, 2021), which leads to the commonly accepted idea that its absence is not only inconceivable, but also, irresponsible and uncompassionate. Such arguments are further cemented by discriminatory statements about the supposed risks to 'public safety' in eliminating coercive psychiatry. They are also fuelled by moral panic and discriminatory media coverage, which draws problematic connections between distress and dangerousness (Daley et al, 2019).

In these framings of coercion, it is evident that the use of force has been normalised to such a significant extent within the mental health field that there is a lack of imagination among both professionals and the broader community about any other possible alternative responses to distress and despair, or other emotions, thoughts, or behaviours deemed socially unacceptable. We can also see the influence of neoliberalism on contemporary understandings of mental health, such that there is an acceptance of the role of the state in the surveillance of 'risky' individuals (Daley et al, 2019), and a complacency about a stripped-back welfare state that leaves people without supports, outside the scope of coercion (Brown, 2021). In short, there is a lack of imagination about the possibilities that lie beyond the dichotomy of coercion and neglect. It is important to consider the intertwining of arguments about the continuation of the psychiatric project, based in coercion–neglect binary thinking, and vested interests in keeping professional power intact and in attempting to silence a much-needed community conversation about the lived experiences of psychiatric harm (Daya, 2022).

However, not all concerns about abolition arise solely out of professional defensiveness. The aim to eliminate mental health legislation has been criticised by professionals, researchers and some people with lived experience as potentially leading to a withdrawal of support (Wilson, 2022). Indeed, such concerns reflect what already happens to people who access mental health services in a present-day, neoliberal context (Brown, 2021), wherein the current mental health system is a site of neglect and abandonment for many who access, or attempt to access, support – a system that is deeply enmeshed in carcerality and coercion, but that also routinely cruelly withdraws or denies support, telling people that their distress is not severe enough to warrant a response, or is not the right kind of distress, or is being expressed in such a way that the system deems to be 'attention-seeking', or that things have been tried and there is nothing else to be done. It is understandable that, without clear alternatives, some people may have fears about losing access to services, even when they are harmful or not meeting their needs. This is not an argument for funding more oppressive services because they are 'better than nothing', but rather, it is an argument for critical social work to avoid the pitfalls of a performative activism and to move beyond simply critiquing coercion, in order to attend sincerely to the daily, long-term work of developing alternatives and pathways for a transformed paradigm. It has been noted that abolition has been misinterpreted as a negative project that only involves critique of the current paradigm, and that instead, 'abolition is not just an agenda for demolishing but also for building' (Ben-Moshe, 2018: 353). This generative perspective shifts the focus from a narrow agenda of only 'tearing down' the carceral mental health system, towards building alternatives.

Maylea (2017: 340) argues that removing state powers to involuntarily treat a person does not remove other accountabilities, including a responsibility 'to provide voluntary, timely, appropriate and high quality treatment, and to uphold their social citizenship'. There is a risk that the dismantling of mental health services, in the absence of other actions, could play into the hands of a neoliberal state that seeks to withdraw support, engage in the surveillance of 'risky' individuals, and disseminate a message of 'individual responsibility'. As argued by Brown (2021), neoliberal approaches lead to a situation where an 'individual's capacity for resilience and recovery is championed while resources and care are limited, efficiency-based, and economically managed'. Spandler (2016) describes this approach as 'market madness' – 'each to their own, with no collective responsibility for those in need'.

We can therefore ask the question: Beyond biomedical neoliberalism, how else might we understand distress and madness, and what might social work's contribution be to building a world in which psychiatric coercion ceases to exist? This is not about creating a new, monolithic system to replace the current one, but it is a much more in-depth process of going to the root cause of issues, in order to create myriad 'new conditions of possibility', beyond the carceral state (Ben-Moshe, 2018: 353).

The entwinement of coercion and neglect in mental health services

Although the concern about neglect is frequently drawn upon as a reason why psychiatric abolition is unrealistic, it is well-documented that neglect and structural abandonment are core experiences in carceral settings, co-existing with coercion (Schliehe, 2021). In this section, interview excerpts from a study (Tseris et al, 2024) exploring experiences and understandings of involuntary mental health treatment, including the perspectives of people with direct experiences of unwanted treatment, and of social workers in these settings, are used to explore the ways in which coercion and structural abandonment are interconnected oppressions in mental health. A social worker explained how the two seemingly contradictory dynamics of coercion and neglect are interconnected oppressions:

> I don't think we consider human rights as such. We mask it as duty of care ... the 'patients' don't always feel they can talk to the doctors.

That they don't get listened to. They don't get considered, they just get told, well that's a side effect [of the medication] you have to deal with. ... And I think it's wilful neglect. ... We know [the service] isn't working but we're trying to put the onus on the clients, to [imply] they're 'too broken'. ... Rather than looking at the service and saying what aren't we doing, what aren't we providing. What is it about our service that isn't safe or isn't engaging or isn't meaningful to this person ... those aren't the conversations that are happening.

This excerpt describes an interplay between coercion and neglect in mental health services, whereby it is common for people to experience co-occurring difficulties in both navigating coercive interventions, and in struggling to access meaningful forms of support.

Risk assessment frameworks are used to justify force and detention, as well as a means to turn people away from support on the basis that they do not meet a 'threshold of risk' (Sawyer, 2008). The social worker noted that 'duty of care' is used to justify unwanted treatment and to override the right to liberty, but this principle does not shape an obligation on the part of the service to provide meaningful supports and resources; rather, psychiatrised people are blamed when they do not find a service useful. This leads to the intersecting oppressions of a denial of liberty and a denial of a right to support (Stone et al, 2020). Even when people receive involuntary mental health treatment, they may experience abandonment and force concurrently, through a medicalised approach that provides an extremely narrow response, including little or no support post-discharge, regarding experiences such as homelessness and gendered violence (Tseris et al, 2024). Failing to recognise and address the sociopolitical contexts of people's lives can lead to a dispiriting cycle of further admissions and experiences of further unwanted treatment (Whitaker et al, 2021).

Some would understandably argue that the experience of being turned away from services is better than the immense harms of pathologisation and forced treatment (Ussher, 2017). However, the experience of service denial can also be extremely detrimental. As described by a social worker reflecting on her time in an Emergency Department:

A younger woman ... she was expressing a lot of distress and suicidal thoughts, and ... this woman actually wanted to stay for a few days because of that, because she didn't feel safe. And when I spoke with her psychiatrist in the mental health unit, the first thing he said was, 'She's borderline,' and ... I learnt that it's not uncommon, women seem to just be really judged, they're pathologized, but then when they ask you for help, they're pathologized in a different way to say that, 'Oh, they don't need that help'. ... I didn't see them really finding the proper supports in the community when they then sent these women home, so they were basically not left with anything when they were discharged.

In the context of scant alternatives to mainstream mental health services, there can be few alternative pathways for support, other than returning to the mental health system. A psychiatric survivor discussed the experience of being turned away from a service – an experience which occurred after previously receiving a harmful involuntary mental health admission:

> I hadn't tried to kill myself so they're not going to help me ... I went to hospital, and I said, 'I need help.' And they said, 'We're not going to admit you.' And that's when I realised that they're not going to help me unless I do something, and that's a horrible message to learn. ... All I wanted was to be contained for maybe a night or two days because I thought it would give me a safe place to plan what to do. ... And also, I didn't have in my head any good alternatives because I didn't want to put pressure on my parents. ... And I went to hospital because of that ... I thought it would be good this time and this time it will be voluntary, and I'll only be there for a short period. ... I was very angry because I thought, what are you teaching me? ... I have to do something horrible to myself before I'm taken seriously.

When people do meet a threshold of 'risk' and become subject to involuntary mental health treatment, the devastating injustice of psychiatric violence is now well-documented, and reflected in a psychiatric survivor's words:

> I think the longer you spend in those systems, the more negative experiences you build. It just reached a breaking point of ... I don't think I can even survive the trauma of that again. I couldn't think of anything worse in the world than going back to hospital. Even if that meant not getting help or not [staying] alive. Nothing could be worse than that.

It is troubling that the social work profession has not taken a stronger stance in critiquing the human rights violations that occur within contemporary mental health systems (Ross, 2018).

It is also important to note that even seemingly emancipatory concepts can be co-opted by neoliberal agendas. For example, in the context of de-institutionalisation policies and the closure of most large-scale psychiatric institutions, Community Treatment Orders act as an alternative carceral strategy, allowing for the extension of psychiatric coercive powers far beyond an inpatient setting (Brophy and McDermott, 2003). Conversely, the alternative to coercion in hospital or the community is sometimes a situation of no support, wherein the supposedly empowering notion of 'recovery-oriented practice' can be 'used as a justification *not* to provide support and services' (Spandler, 2016: 8). This demonstrates a perverse misuse of a concept that originated in mental health activism to justify the withdrawal of services.

In sum, people in distress and crisis can be caught between the harmful impacts of coercive mental health treatment, or conversely, the harms of living without support:

> There's not a lot of options ... even if we acknowledge that those inpatient systems aren't ideal, there's really not anywhere else to turn sometimes. Sometimes I do need an increase in support and it just doesn't really exist ... which is really frustrating and sometimes quite frightening when you get to that point and it's like, do you choose to continue without the support that you need and take that risk, or be traumatised? I wish I didn't have to choose that.

Moving beyond rhetorical commitments to 'social justice'

As seen in the earlier examples, mental health systems are often profoundly ill-equipped to respond to mental distress, where it is not uncommon to experience harmful and over-medicalised interventions, or to be denied support altogether. There is a clear need for the social work profession to speak out about the ethical compromises involved in our role in involuntary mental health treatment settings (Maylea, 2017). For too long, the social work profession has adopted a limited imagination regarding the kinds of transformations that might be possible in the mental health field, adopting an unambitious approach to reform (Sapouna, 2022). Social work has been rightly critiqued for 'tinkering' with the dominant approach; for example, being too preoccupied with changing the ways in which we talk about our work rather than actually transforming our worldviews and practices, as is evident in the rise of 'trauma-informed' language, which arguably has achieved little material benefit for people experiencing services that continue to use force and a biomedical paradigm.

At the same time, it is perhaps not very surprising that some social workers are calling for increased resourcing and a more accountable and compassionate system, given the failings of the current system at the intersections of coercion and neglect. It has been noted that mental health services are under attack, but 'psych-thinking' is on the upsurge (Beresford, 2016), leading to circumstances whereby more and more of our distress is being understood through an 'illness' paradigm, while avenues to receive support are diminishing. This produces a paradox (Papadopoulos and Maylea, 2020), whereby social workers may find themselves simultaneously defending against the withdrawal of mental health services, even as they lament the pathologising effects of mental health services on people's lives and their failure to address social inequalities.

This is a more complex positioning than what might be contained within a 'negative' approach to mental health abolition that is focused on critiquing the current system, without positing alternatives. We should also be cautious about the limits of lofty academic theorising about the need for an end to psychiatric power, in ways that are disconnected from the complexities of lived experience. Indeed, with the neoliberalisation of research and education, there is a tide towards 'apathetic intellectualism' (Whynacht et al, 2018). Within this milieu, the pursuit of 'social justice' can become overly rhetorical and intellectualised. However, abolition is not simply an intellectual or ideological commitment to the absence of carcerality; rather it is an all-encompassing world-building project (Burns et al, 2020; Dobchuck-Land and Dolby, 2021). We need to avoid the hazards of aloof theorising and performative activism; at the same time, it is essential that we are aware of the problematic invitations to hollow, quick-fix and tokenistic reform agendas in response to psychiatric oppression (Sapouna, 2022). Some ideas for navigating these complexities, and the potential contributions of social workers in pursuing an anti-carceral mental health paradigm, are discussed in what follows.

Messy, creative, transformative everyday practices and activism

Abolition has been described both a negative and a positive project, including the creation of new arrangements in social life (Chua, 2020). For anti-carceral mental health activism, this helps us to move beyond a coercion–neglect dichotomy, in order to consider the hazards of neoliberal ideologies seeping into actions aimed at eliminating psychiatric harm. An anti-carceral paradigm in mental health cannot be based upon an uncaring void of support, built upon individual responsibility, rampant social inequalities, new forms of coercion and structural abandonment. We need to be attuned to when liberatory concepts are co-opted for political agendas that are misaligned with collectivist values; for example, when desired forms of mental health support are withdrawn on the basis of a 'recovery' orientation (Spandler, 2016). At the same time, we need to avoid the temptations of adopting a performative stance on abolition that takes a position of righteousness about the need to end the current system, while being disconnected from practical actions.

Abolition can be defined as actions aiming to 'shrink the system into non-existence' (Critical Resistance, 2012, in Bell, M., 2021). Non-reformist reforms are defined as actions aimed at the eventual dismantling of the carceral state, in comparison to reformist reforms, which aim to improve the current system (Bell, M., 2021). In day-to-day practice, the distinctions are less clear-cut (Morgan, 2023). This analysis opens up opportunities for anti-carceral mental health practices to commence within imperfect contexts, moving 'beyond protesting the current circumstances, to creating new conditions of possibility by collectively contesting the status quo' (Ben-Moshe, 2018: 353). There is, perhaps, the potential for dialogue between social workers who hold a dedicated position to eliminating psychiatric coercion, and those who are critical of psychiatric power while being hesitant about an ever-rising tide of neoliberalism that is reducing the already limited support provided by mental health services. Indeed, responding to the inequalities in neoliberalism is a core issue explored by the psychiatric survivor movement, as noted by Recovery in the Bin (2017): 'We want a robust "Social Model of Madness & Distress" building upon the Social Model of Disability and Independent Living meaning support where needed and not perpetual pressure towards unattainable self-sufficiency. Capitalism and inequality can be bad for your mental health!'

Far from seeking to expand upon the current system, such activism is grounded in developing transformative practices, beyond both carceral and neoliberal paradigms, towards justice and collective care. There are immense opportunities for social work, in connecting with and contributing to the consumer/survivor/ex-patient social movement, rather than a narrow and depoliticised approach to developing and deploying skills and knowledge in the mental health field. Iterative processes of risk-taking, creativity, messiness and reflection (Davis et al, 2022) are needed to create new conditions for a world without the coercive powers of psychiatry, where biomedical mental health interventions are not the only place to turn during times of crisis.

Transforming what we call 'mental health social work'

It has been argued that 'mental health is not about mental health' (Brossard and Chandler, 2022). For the social work profession, this means stepping beyond the frameworks offered by diagnosis, medicalisation, surveillance and individual-focused treatment protocols, towards recognising the ways in which mainstream mental health paradigms often conceal social inequalities and justify social control. This requires a significant reconsideration of mental health social work, away from the current push towards social workers as 'therapeutic experts' and towards a much more politicised agenda of working in solidarity with psychiatric survivors. To achieve this, social workers will need to exercise humility and know when to 'get out of the way', to make space for survivor-led paradigms of care, including peer support, organised resistance and grassroots alternatives (Suslovic, 2024). Our role should nonetheless be active rather than absent, pushing for the reallocation of funding and resources currently poured into the biomedical mental health system, making space for lived experience perspectives on the importance of non-carceral approaches, and being clear about the limits of medicalised, paternalistic interventions with our colleagues and the broader public. Indeed, while much attention has been given to how social workers can mitigate the impacts of involuntary mental health services, this is not our only potential contribution (Maylea, 2017). There are myriad actions that social workers can take to de-carcerating mental health from outside mental health contexts, and certainly outside mental health social work roles, as traditionally defined. Through addressing a raft of inequalities and oppressive social conditions, social workers are not limited to questioning the current mental health system, but can also contribute to 'material conditions, institutions, and forms of community that facilitate emancipation and human flourishing and consequently render prisons, police, and other carceral systems obsolete' (Toraif and Mueller, 2023: 1).

This is not about introducing more mainstream mental health social work roles, so that more and more people come to be understood as 'mentally unwell', contributing to the growth of the mental health system. Rather, it is about the significant possibilities that exist for social workers to contribute their skills, outside and beyond the mental health system, to weaken the relevance and perceived necessity of psychiatric power as a primary response to distress. Social work could start to reconsider the importance of community building (Spade, 2020), which has been marginalised in neoliberal times and in contexts of rising therapisation (Ecclestone and Brunila, 2015). Within these actions, it is crucial that social workers operate in a way that is not about self-interestedness and bolstering the profession, but rather, is centred on a community-led approach (Toraif and Mueller, 2023). Principles of mutual aid are very helpful in considering the diverse ways in which communities care for and protect each other, while addressing the root causes of injustice (Bell, F.M., 2021).

Positioning anti-carceral mental health as relevant to all social workers

Social workers who see psychiatric coercion as ethically compromising may opt to not work within the mental health system, especially avoiding involuntary mental health services. This is a perfectly understandable position, and could be a strategic decision about where to place limited energy and skills – after all, there are robust critiques regarding the limits of 'mental health reform' from within the mental health system (Pilgrim, 2018). However, social workers cannot shirk the responsibility for transforming the mental health field by simply opting out of particular job roles, or by claiming that psychiatric coercion is based upon medical and legal decisions made by other professionals. There is almost no area of practice where social work is not interfacing with the mental health system in some way – making or accepting referrals to or from mental health services; describing people's 'needs' in ways that invoke mainstream diagnostic language. Thus, all social work practice could be viewed as explicitly or implicitly located on the carceral mental health continuum (Whynacht et al, 2018).

Despite the need for far greater reflexivity regarding the social work role in psychiatric coercion, in contemporary social work practice there is a notable ongoing focus on diagnosis and individual-focused interventions, coupled with a persistent acceptance of coercive practices (Maylea, 2017). In addition, contemporary social work curriculum content in 'mental health' is contested, particularly in terms of its capacity to address the social and political dimensions of mental health practice and to move beyond a 'risk' orientation (Whitaker et al, 2023; Suslovic, 2024). Moving beyond a clinical level, there is so much for social work to learn through meaningful engagement with the consumer/survivor/ex-patient movement (Sinclair et al, 2023), in contesting conservative and pathologising understandings of 'mental health'. Through engaging with the *politics* of mental health, rather than only the *clinical* dimensions of mental health, social workers will be much better equipped to explore more radical understandings of psychiatrisation (Coppock, 2020) and to re-examine our relationship to 'helping' (Bell, F.M., 2021). This includes understanding the importance of peer-led alternatives to carcerality, and focusing on the social contexts of distress and crisis, instead of a persistent adherence to medicalised, coercive and neoliberal grand narratives.

References

Bell, F.M. (2021) 'Amplified injustices and mutual aid in the COVID-19 pandemic', *Qualitative Social Work*, 20(1–2): 410–415.

Bell, M. (2021) 'Abolition: A new paradigm for reform', *Law and Social Inquiry*, 46(1): 32–68.

Ben-Moshe, L. (2018) 'Dis-epistemologies of abolition', *Critical Criminology*, 26(3): 341–355.

Beresford, P. (2016) 'From psycho-politics to mad studies: Learning from the legacy of Peter Sedgewock', *Critical and Radical Social Work*, 4(3): 343–120.

Brophy, L. and McDermott, F. (2003) 'What's driving involuntary treatment in the community? The social, policy, legal and ethical context', *Australasian Psychiatry*, 11(sup1): S84–S88.

Brossard, B. and Chandler, A. (2022) *Explaining Mental Illness: Sociological Perspectives*, Bristol: Policy Press.

Brown, C. (2021) 'Critical clinical social work and the neoliberal constraints on social justice in mental health', *Research on Social Work Practice*, 31(6): 644–652.

Burns, D., Dominguez, L., Gordon, R., McTighe, L., Moss, L. and Rosario, G. (2020) 'The ground on which we stand: Making abolition', *Journal for the Anthropology of North America*, 23(2): 98–120.

Burstow, B. (2014) 'The withering away of psychiatry: An attrition model for antipsychiatry', in B. Burstow, B.A. LeFrancois and S. Diamond (eds), *Psychiatry Disrupted: Theorizing Resistance and Crafting the (R)evolution*, Montreal and Kingston: McGill-Queen's University Press, pp 34–51.

Chua, C. (2020) 'Abolition is a constant struggle: Five lessons from Minneapolis', *Theory and Event*, 23(5): S-127.

Coppock, V. (2020) 'Psychiatrised childhoods', *Global Studies of Childhood*, 10(1): 3–11.

Daley, A., Costa, L. and Beresford, P. (2019) *Madness, Violence, and Power: A Critical Collection*, Toronto: University of Toronto Press.

Davis, A.Y., Dent, G., Meiners, E.R. and Richie, B.E. (2022) *Abolition. Feminism. Now.*, Chicago: Haymarket Books.

Daya, I. (2022) 'Russian dolls and epistemic crypts: A lived experience reflection on epistemic injustice and psychiatric confinement', *Incarceration*, 3(2). Available at: https://journals.sagepub.com/doi/10.1177/26326663221103445

Daya, I., Hamilton, B. and Roper, C. (2020) 'Authentic engagement: A conceptual model for welcoming diverse and challenging consumer and survivor views in mental health research, policy, and practice', *International Journal of Mental Health Nursing*, 29(2): 299–311.

Dobchuk-Land, B. and Walby, K. (2021) 'Police abolition as community struggle against state violence', *Social Justice*, 48(1): 1–30.

Ecclestone, K. and Brunila, K. (2015) 'Governing emotionally vulnerable subjects and "therapisation" of social justice', *Pedagogy, Culture and Society*, 23(4): 485–506.

Gooding, P., McSherry, B., Roper, C. and Grey, F. (2018) *Alternatives to Coercion in Mental Health Settings: A Literature Review*, University of Melbourne. Available at: https://socialequity.unimelb.edu.au/__data/assets/pdf_file/0012/2898525/Alternatives-to-Coercion-Literature-Review-Melbourne-Social-Equity-Institute.pdf

Maylea, C. (2017) 'A rejection of involuntary treatment in mental health social work', *Ethics and Social Welfare*, 11(4): 336–352.

Morandi, S., Silva, B., Mendez Rubio, M., Bonsack, C. and Golay, P. (2021) 'Mental health professionals' feelings and attitudes towards coercion', *International Journal of Law and Psychiatry*, 74: 101665.

Morgan, J. (2023) *Abolition in the Interstices*. Available at: https://lpeproject.org/blog/abolition-in-the-interstices/

Papadopoulos, A. and Maylea, C. (2020) 'Medicare funded mental health social work: Better access to what?', *Australian Social Work*, 73(2): 137–148.

Paradis-Gagné, E., Pariseau-Legault, P., Goulet, M.-H., Jacob, J.D. and Lessard-Deschênes, C. (2021) 'Coercion in psychiatric and mental health nursing: A conceptual analysis', *International Journal of Mental Health Nursing*, 30(3): 590–609.

Pilgrim, D. (2018) 'Co-production and involuntary psychiatric settings', *Mental Health Review Journal*, 23(4): 269–279.

Randall, R., Bashfield, L., Kennedy, H., Nguyen, F., Karanikolas, P., Martin, R., et al (2023) 'Police apprehension as a response to mental distress'. Available at: https://opal.latrobe.edu.au/articles/report/Police_apprehension_as_a_response_to_mental_distress/25256512

Recovery in the Bin (2017) 'Key principles'. Available at: https://recoveryinthebin.org/ritbkeyprinciples/

Ross, D. (2018) 'A social work perspective on seclusion and restraint in Australia's public mental health system', *Journal of Progressive Human Services*, 29(2): 130–148.

Sapouna, L. (2022) 'Inclusion paradoxes in mental health: Critical reflections on knowledge, (in)justice and privilege', PhD thesis, University College Cork.

Sawyer, A.M. (2008) 'Risk and new exclusions in community mental health practice', *Australian Social Work*, 61(4): 327–341.

Schliehe, A. (2021) *Young Women's Carceral Geographies: Abandonment, Trouble and Mobility*, Bingley: Emerald Publishing Limited.

Sinclair, A., Mahboub, L., Gillieatt, S. and Fernandes, C. (2023) '"You just treat me like a human being": Using lived experience to (re) imagine boundary practices in mental health settings', *British Journal of Social Work*, 53(3): 1408–1425.

Spade, D. (2020) *Mutual Aid: Building Solidarity During This Crisis (And The Next)*, London: Verso Books.

Spandler, H. (2016) 'From psychiatric abuse to psychiatric neglect', *Asylum Magazine*, 23(2): 7–8.

Stone, M., Kokanovic, R., Callard, F. and Broom, A.F. (2020) 'Estranged relations: Coercion and care in narratives of supported decision-making in mental healthcare', *Medical Humanities*, 46(1): 62–72.

Strickland, N., Luke, C. and Redekop, F. (2019) 'When people lose autonomy: The case for coercion and the moral responsibility crisis clinicians have to society', *International Journal on Responsibility*, 3(2): 9–26.

Suslovic, B. (2024) 'Abolition of involuntary mental health services', in C. Franklin (ed), *Encyclopedia of Social Work*, Oxford University Press, pp 1–21.

Toraif, N. and Mueller, J.C. (2023) 'Abolitionist social work', in C. Franklin (ed), *Encyclopedia of Social Work*, Oxford University Press, pp 1–23.

Treffert, D.A. (1979) 'Dying with your (or somebody else's) rights on', *Wisconsin Medical Journal*, 130(9).

Tseris, E., Franks, S. and Bright Hart, E. (2024) *Psychiatric Oppression in Women's Lives: Creative Resistance and Collective Dissent*, Cham: Palgrave.

Ussher, J.M. (2017) 'A critical feminist analysis of madness: Pathologising femininity through psychiatric discourse', in B.M.Z Cohen (ed), *Routledge International Handbook of Critical Mental Health*, London and New York: Routledge, pp 72–78.

Whitaker, L., Smith, F.L., Brasier, C., Petrakis, M. and Brophy, L. (2021) 'Engaging with transformative paradigms in mental health', *International Journal of Environmental Research and Public Health*, 18(18): 9504.

Whitaker, L., Smith, F., Petrakis, M. and Brophy, L. (2023) 'Teaching mental health social work: What are we preparing students for?', *Australian Social Work*, 76(4): 428–440.

Whynacht, A., Arsenault, E. and Cooney, R. (2018) 'Abolitionist pedagogy in the neoliberal university', *Social Justice*, 45(4): 141–162.

Wilson, K. (2018) 'The call for the abolition of mental health law: The challenges of suicide, accidental death and the equal enjoyment of the right to life', *Human Rights Law Review*, 18(4): 651–688.

Wilson, K. (2022) 'The CRPD and mental health law: The conflict about abolition, the practical dilemmas of implementation and the untapped potential', in F. Felder, L. Davy and R. Kayess (eds), *Disability Law and Human Rights: Theory and Policy*, Canberra: Springer, pp 171–197.

20

Twin births, twin abolitions: abolishing the capitalist, carceral state and the liberal individual – and, with them, conventional social work

John Fox

The abolitionist movement has grown from calls to abolish slavery, to the abolition of the state and the prison-industrial complex, and now the kind of society that renders the carceral state legitimate. However, abolitionist literature has not considered the state's twin development: the repeated, violent reconstruction of relational, collective, forms of the self into the state's ideal subject – the liberal individual. Prior to the 16th century, relational, collective, forms of self characterised feudal society. Most people's livelihoods depended on common, communally managed, access to lands and waterways for food, fuel and building materials. Their lives were governed by a moral economy where need took precedence over private property and the market. From the 16th century, the emergence of capitalism, particularly in the form of the enclosure (privatisation) of the commons, reduced the former, more relational, self to the limited, liberal self: the self with an inner locus of being, separate to and pre-existing any relationships, including those that secured the means of life.

Both the modern, carceral state and the liberal self called each other into existence as part of capitalism's rise to dominance. The accumulation of wealth necessary to capitalism's emergence – the enclosure movement – and the elimination of alternatives to wage labour met with extensive resistance, which was only overcome by the growth of the state's reach and power. The carceral state emerged to subdue and reduce the pre-capitalist relational self to the limited, 'free', liberal self. If the carceral state is to be abolished, so too must its twin, the liberal self.

Social work emerged as the capitalist, carceral state consolidated its domination in the 19th century. It reflects the tensions of those times – the extension of state power (control) and the emerging profession's desire to relieve the resulting suffering (care). Social work literature evidences a vigorous debate about that tension: whether social work is so corrupted by its ties to state control that it, too, needs to be abolished. However, that debate, while it critiques the liberal self, does not contest its foundation – an inner locus or foundation of being. In caring for that reduced form of being, contemporary social work maintains the damage done by the capitalist, carceral state: care becomes control. If social work is to sever its ties with that state, it, too, must abandon those foundations.

Alternatives already exist. The network of relations that comprise the self continue, notwithstanding their restriction, in the forms of communally held wealth – commons – that capitalism has long sought to exploit. Commons are continually created, defended and repaired because they are the stuff of life: the basis on which any person exists. They provide strategies for living 'outside' the capitalist, carceral state – that is, living in accordance with different values – and suggest approaches to reconstruct social work as a form of service to those commoning communities, as forms of living and care that render conventional social work redundant.

This chapter considers: the neglect of the liberal self in abolitionist literature; the twin births of the carceral state and the liberal self; the links between conventional social work, the state and the liberal self; the possibilities suggested by Autonomist Marxism and commoning; and, through them, the abolition of conventional social work. This discussion is preceded by an outline of the relational self, drawing on Marxist and post-anthropocentric theory, to capture the ensemble, network or aggregate of relations that the capitalist, carceral state reduced to the limited, supposedly 'free', liberal self. This sets the ground for considering commoning as the means to release the self from those restrictions.

While enclosures occurred, and continue to occur, throughout the world (Perelman, 2000; Federici, 2014; Linebaugh, 2014), this chapter focuses on England. The enclosure movement there involved state violence beyond that experienced elsewhere (Linebaugh, 2008). This chapter also focuses on class. It does not consider all who suffer under the capitalist, carceral, state, including the vital histories of resistance and loss by reason of gender (Federici, 2014) and race (Linebaugh and Rediker, 2000).

The relational self

Marx's conception of the self has two key foundations: materialism and dialectics. He drew on Hegel's (1975: 179) dialectics in which 'existence is the indefinite multitude of existents ... which ... are co-relative, and form a world of reciprocal dependence and ... infinite interconnection'. Unlike the conventional view that treats relations as connecting distinct beings, dialectics sees those relations as part of – internal to – being (Ollman, 1976; Fox, 2015). Being is constituted relationally.

Being, then, includes the human body and its relations to the material world: 'nature is [man's] [sic] ... body ... man is a part of nature' (Marx,

1975a: 328). Human beings have a distributed body: the organic or integrated body bounded by skin, and the inorganic or unintegrated body constituted by the balance of the material world (Marx, 1975a; Fox, 2015). However, matter's character means that relation is unstable. Drawing on the ancient Greek philosophers concerning matter, Marx (1975a) held that matter was active and volatile – difficult to secure. Nature and the self were in the 'absolute movement of becoming' (Marx, 1975b: 570). Dealing with this instability rendered cooperation with others – social relationships – necessary. So central were these relationships, Marx (Marx and Engels, 1998: 37) first called them the 'mode of life' (this later became the mode of production). This made 'the essence of man [*sic*] ... the ensemble of social relations' (Marx, 1975b: 846, 570).

These two elements have been revisited within post-anthropocentric theory, drawing on feminist, post-structuralist and other literature. Post-anthropocentric theory expands our grasp of matter's active character, presenting it not only as a negative force but a positive one, as resistant and recalcitrant (Bennett, 2010) and vital, generative, exuberant and effervescent (Barad, 2007). This literature also enriches conceptualisations of the relational self in terms of assemblages, networks (Bennett, 2010), congealments, condensations and entanglements (Barad, 2007).

Together, Marx's theory and post-anthropocentric theory present the self as intimately bound up with the material world and with other people. This self had to be stripped down in a process that created both a new form of self – the limited, 'free', liberal self – and a new form of state, the capitalist, carceral state.

Abolitionism, the carceral state and the liberal self

Abolitionism's origins lie in the movement to outlaw slavery. It now extends beyond carceral apparatuses and practices and challenges the ways in which race, class and other structures render some people undesirable and criminalises their ways of being (Davis, 2003; Kaba, 2021; Davis et al, 2022; Branson et al, 2023). Abolitionism now takes as its object 'the abolition of a society that could have prisons ... and therefore not abolition as ... elimination ... but ... as ... founding ... a new society' (Moten and Harney, cited in Kaba, 2021: 24).

Abolitionists like Angela Davis and Miriame Kaba have recognised the ties between capitalism and the origins of the police and prisons as part of the violent transformation of 18th-century England (Davis, 2003). The continuing relevance of those ties has also been recognised, with the United States' extraordinary expansion of prisons linked to the neoliberal resurgence of capitalism (Davis, 2003; Kaba, 2021). However, the calls for change remain focused on the environment within which the self is situated and not the self itself.

While some challenge is implied in the abolitionist literature, it does not explicitly address the liberal self. Key influences on contemporary abolitionist literature – anti-racist, feminist and queer politics – all include commitments to more relational conceptions of the self. The society envisaged in abolitionism's goals also contradicts the liberal self's self-interested independence: a 'society built on co-operation instead of individualism, mutual aid instead of self-preservation' (Kaba, 2021, 17; Davis, 2003); 'a world based on ... desire ... joy ... mutual aid, love and care' (Branson et al, 2023: 2, 3). However, absent explicitly challenging the liberal self and explicitly promoting a more relational model, there remains the risk that the liberal self will survive abolition and, with it, the relations of domination and exploitation upon which it is founded.

Twin births: the liberal self and the carceral state

The modern, carceral state and the liberal self were both shaped by the emergence of capitalism, particularly through the enclosure movement. The state grew to repress the resistance of the dispossessed, and, in that antagonism, they radically transformed each other: carceral practices became central to the state and the relational self of the middle ages became the 'free' liberal self.

At the beginning of the 16th century England remained a feudal state. Two key elements of that state needed to be demolished before capitalism could become dominant: access to the commons and restrictions on the free operation of the market. Together, these formed the foundations of a moral economy: 'a popular consensus as to what were legitimate and what were illegitimate practices ... grounded upon a consistent traditional view of social norms and obligations, of the proper economic functions of ... parties in the community' (Thompson, 1993: 188; Bohstedt, 2010). In such an economy, need took precedence over private property and the freedom of the market (Linebaugh, 2008; Bohstedt, 2010).

Within feudal relationships, peasants' ability to subsist depended upon access to the commons: shared pastures and resources within local woods and waterways. These provided essential sources of food, fuel and building materials (Linebaugh and Rediker, 2000; Perelman, 2000; Federici, 2014). Commoning rights were so significant that they were expressly recognised in the Magna Carta in 1215 and in the less well-known, but more extensive, accompanying treaty, the Charter of the Forest (Linebaugh, 2008).

Another central element of the reciprocal relations that characterised feudal society involved the regulation of markets to ensure a fair price for essential goods (principally food) (Linebaugh, 2008). Wage labourers also enjoyed a range of customary rights entitling them to take portions of workplace materials, such as offcuts of wood or cloth, to supplement their wages.

These, like access to the commons, were vital, as wages were paid infrequently and often in arrears (Linebaugh, 2006).

From the 16th century that moral economy and the relational form of self it supported came under assault. This began with the enclosure of common lands, with more than 4,000 enclosure acts passed by the 19th century (Angus, 2023). By 1830 almost 'one quarter of all cultivated land ... all open field farms and most common land' had been privatised (Perelman, 2000; Angus, 2023: 111–112). The effect was 'catastrophic ... a matter of life and death' (Angus, 2023: 48, 62). It forced a radical transformation of the peasantry, forcing them off the land and towards waged labour (Thompson, 1963; Linebaugh, 2008; Federici, 2014).

These changes were fiercely resisted. Riots and uprisings were frequent, widespread and often on a significant scale (Thompson, 1963; Linebaugh and Rediker, 2000; Angus, 2023). In the mid-17th century that resistance coalesced into prominent, organised, social movements – the Levellers and the Diggers – who sought to maintain the commons and opposed wage labour as a form of slavery (Linebaugh and Rediker, 2000). So hated was wage labour, that many took to the road as vagabonds and highwaymen (Linebaugh, 2006; Federici, 2014).

Even as wage labour was accepted, workers resisted the unrestrained operation of a market economy, particularly the replacement of workers with machinery. By the early 19th century, this resistance was led by the Luddites who destroyed machines when they were used to undermine working conditions and the established way of life (Thompson, 1963; Linebaugh, 2014). This rebellion ceased when the destruction of factory machinery was made a capital offence (Thompson, 1963; Linebaugh, 2014).

There were over 700 separate food riots between 1550 and 1820 (Bohstedt, 2010). They sought to maintain the moral economy, and often succeeded, forcing bread to be sold at customary prices (Thompson, 1993; Bohstedt, 2010). These, too, came to an end when made a capital offence in the early 19th century.

This resistance was likened to the 'many-headed hydra' – the monster fought by Hercules in Greek myth, where cutting one head off only triggered more to arise (Linebaugh and Rediker, 2000). The state grew to meet this challenge, introducing a regime of terror through the 17th and 18th centuries: one characterised by 'periodic massacres at the gallows' and 'a massive prison construction program' (Linebaugh and Rediker, 2000; Linebaugh, 2008: loc. 98), which transformed England into a 'thanatocracy' (a regime 'that ruled by the frequent use of the death penalty') (Linebaugh, 2006: 330, 50).

From the earliest interventions in support of enclosure and dispossession, legislation criminalised vagrancy and unemployment, with penalties ranging from whipping and imprisonment to execution (Perelman, 2000; Angus, 2023).

By the 1570s over 300 people were hung annually pursuant to these laws (Federici, 2014).

From the late 17th century, the hunting of game on enclosed lands was criminalised, with penalties ranging from fines, imprisonment and transportation to death (Perelman, 2000; Angus, 2023). Private gamekeepers were given powers analogous to those later granted to the police (Angus, 2023). Convictions ranged from approximately 5,000 annually in the 1840s to over 12,000 in 1877 (Angus, 2023).

From the late 16th century, customary wage supplements were criminalised (Linebaugh, 2014). By the late 17th century they, too, became subject to capital penalties (Linebaugh, 2006) and, in 1798, saw the introduction of the Marine Police Office, which established the model for the Metropolitan Police (Linebaugh, 2006).

Capitalism's rise to dominance over the moral economy could not have taken place without extensive, aggressive, state support. The resistance to the rise of capitalism forced the development of key elements of the modern carceral state: the police, new crimes and new forms of punishment. This expansion of the state transformed most of England's population. It stripped ordinary people of the means of pursuing their former way of life and reduced them to the limited, liberal self. The capitalist, carceral state and the liberal self were twin births, borne of, and maintained by, violence.

Social work, the carceral state and the liberal self

Social work developed in the wake of the consolidation of the capitalist, carceral state, when the damage to the relational self had already been done. The 1834 Poor Laws formed a key part of this consolidation. Its principles were embraced by social work's predecessor, the Charitable Organisation Society (Lavalette, 2019). The development of this work – particularly casework, as captured in Mary Richmond's (1917) writings – provided one foundation from which social work emerged.

Capitalism's consolidation, however, was resisted. The late 19th century, when social work first emerged, was marked by extensive industrial action. These upheavals contributed another dimension to social work, as reflected in the community-based work of Jane Addams and others who embraced the 'age of ... association' and collective action (Addams and Scott, 1964: 137).

Many (including Olson, 2007; Jones and Lavalette, 2013; Brady et al, 2019; Maylea, 2021; Ioakimidis and Wyllie, 2023; Pease, 2023) see these two conflicting commitments of social work – control and care (regulation and liberation) – as irreconcilable, as evidenced by social work's repeated intrusions into vulnerable people's lives on behalf of, or promoting principles shared with, the state. Social workers' ambition for professional recognition is also cited as giving them an interest in control: securing the right to exclusively deal with particular people or needs, and thereby secure a source of income, itself involves a claim to some control over those people and relies on the state's support (Olson, 2007; Brady et al, 2019; Maylea, 2021; Pease, 2023).

However, the focus of these conflicting commitments takes the limited, liberal self for granted. Both ultimately treat the liberal individual as the focus of their work and differ mainly in the range of external – rather than internal – relations they consider. Both retain a focus on an inner locus of being, separate to and pre-existing relationships, rather than a being that only ever exists as an intersection, ensemble or network of relationships. The distinction between care and control then becomes tenuous as social work then preserves the restraints that were violently imposed on the relational self: care becomes control. If social work is to sever its ties to the capitalist, carceral state, it must sever its ties to the limited, liberal self.

The radical tendencies within social work have sought to weaken, if not sever, these ties. Radical social work prioritised addressing social structures through community work and activism, but still retained a place for individually focused casework (Brake and Bailey, 1980; Galper, 1980). Radical social work's conception of the self continued to treat the relations affecting the self as external to, rather than constituting, the self. This tendency continues within critical social work, particularly as shaped by post-structuralist thought. While the latter destabilises and opens the modernist unified self and charts the intimate influence of the social through language, its application in casework – still social work's most prominent activity – retains a focus on the self, as exemplified by Fook (2016).

More recent approaches better engage with the relational self. Post-anthropocentric social work, founded in revitalised conceptions of materialism and of being, provides one promising approach (Bozalek and Pease, 2021). Popular social work – social work undertaken by community members and social movement participants as a form of mutual aid, and not by independent professionals – is another. It is not only founded in relational conceptions of the self but removes the conflict of interest that has long dogged social work (Lavalette and Ioakimidis, 2011, 2019; Jones and Lavalette, 2013). It points to places, organisations and movements that rarely figure in definitions of social work, such as working-class mutual aid initiatives in the midst of strikes, programmes organised by people in refugee camps, and community responses to natural disasters. This chapter, in considering commoning, also looks to the work of those not usually considered to be social workers.

Beyond the carceral state and the liberal self

Autonomist Marxism and commoning evidence the potential to recover the relational self. They reveal this immanent, partly realised potential by focusing on people's repeated efforts to collectively put their own values into effect – to assert a new moral economy – most recently through practices of commoning. Autonomists point to the long history of the autonomous creation, recovery and repair of social ensembles and networks; to relations of solidarity, support and care that can realise the abolitionist vision of a life without carceral institutions and conventional social work.

Autonomist Marxism

Autonomist Marxism developed from the Italian workerist movement in the 1960s and 1970s. It has, and continues to, inspire new engagements with Marxism and commoning (see, for example, Midnight Notes, 2001; De Angelis, 2007; Federici, 2014; Holloway, 2019). It takes its name from the actions of factory workers, women and students, taken autonomously of any form of leadership (Wright, 2017). It seeks to learn from those struggles, and the relationships and resistance they involve (Eden, 2012; Wright, 2017).

These initiatives are treated as demonstrations of the working class's ability to 'base itself on use values' (Negri, 2005: 214). Negri (2005: 47, 271) calls this 'invention power', reframing Marx's concept of labour power to emphasise its creative potential to shape different forms of life. This goes beyond resistance: it includes the construction and protection of alternatives to capitalism and '[overturns] the historical priority between capital and labour' (Tronti, 2019: 224).

Autonomists consider each capitalist restructure as a response to working-class initiatives: initially, the concentration of work in factories in response to the control exerted by workers in the 'putting out' system; and then, in response to the successful organisation and resistance of workers in factories, neoliberalism's fragmentation and dispersion of work (Negri, 2005; Caffentzis, 2013). Autonomists see capitalism as seeking to spread so far beyond the factory as to make all society a factory (Negri, 2005; Murphy, 2012; Tronti, 2019), 'all those who are subordinated to, exploited by, and produce under the rule of capital' part of the proletariat, and all the relations of self-valorisation and alternatives to capitalism locations of ongoing contest (Hardt and Negri, 2000: 256; Murphy, 2012; Caffentzis, 2013; Wright, 2017; Barbagallo et al, 2019).

Autonomists see both capitalists and working people as seeking to 'valorise' – express in practice – their values, making the contest one between working people developing alternate ways of life and capitalists seeking to colonise those relationships. For Marx, this contest – which he called 'primitive accumulation' – provided the foundation from which capitalism first developed (Marx, 1976). Building from Marx, Autonomists treat self-valorising relationships and attempts to privatise or enclose those relationships as constituting a key, ongoing feature of capitalism. They see the efforts to promote and expand alternate spaces as best represented in commoning (Hardt and Negri, 2000; De Angelis, 2007; Barbagallo et al, 2019).

Commoning

The term commons originally referred to communities sharing common lands and resources in pre-capitalist societies (De Angelis, 2007; Federici, 2019). Today commoning ranges from activities that might be called hobbies, such as outlaw bicycling, pirate programming and community gardening (Carlsson, 2008), to substitutes for services usually provided by the state or commerce, such as healthcare, education and accommodation (Sitrin, 2006, 2012; Taylor and Brehmer, 2023).

Two contemporary examples are the Zapatista in Mexico and Horizontalists in Argentina. Both arose in response to the violent neoliberal expansion of capitalism. In 1994 the Zapatista sought to prevent the state from allowing the sale of Indigenous people's communally owned lands as part of Mexico's entry into the North American Free Trade Agreement (Midnight Notes, 2001; Henck, 2018). In 2001, the Argentinian government's efforts to comply with the International Monetary Fund's neoliberal funding requirements led to millions taking to the streets and the fall of five governments (Sitrin, 2006, 2012). The actions in Mexico and Argentina both centred on upholding different values to those of capitalism. The Zapatista protected local Indigenous communities' way of life, have held 250,000 hectares of land, and built five autonomous regional commons (Fitzwater, 2019). Argentinian Horizontalists sought to recover the relational self in the wake of violent authoritarian and neoliberal regimes, with hundreds of thousands since engaged in commoning.

Commoning involves two dimensions: first, common wealth (property); and, second, community (De Angelis, 2003; Federici, 2019). The verb 'commoning' ties these together and indicates how commoning expresses the relational self – 'networks of mutual aid and solidarity' (De Angelis, 2003). It is radically inclusive (Hardt and Negri, 2000, 2004, 2009; De Angelis, 2007; Federici, 2019), primarily by means of collective decision-making processes in the form of assemblies in which all participate (Midnight Notes, 2001; Sitrin, 2006, 2012; Fitzwater, 2019).

Commoning's potential resides in its creation of spaces 'outside' the capitalist, carceral state: not in absolute terms, but as relationships enacting different values (Sitrin, 2006, 2012; De Angelis, 2007). This potential is widespread: for the relational self commoning 'is an irreducible aspect of ... life ... a necessity of ... existence' (De Angelis, 2007; Federici, 2019: 147). Community gardening and squatting illuminate its potential: they can free participants from securing food and housing from the market and, in turn, free them from the need to sell their labour.

This potential is not limited to 'external' restraints; it also frees relational subjectivity from liberal limitations (Sitrin, 2012; De Angelis, 2019). The experience of participating in assemblies is transformative: so much so as to be described in terms of love and affection (Sitrin, 2006, 2012; De Angelis, 2007, 2019; Hardt and Negri, 2009; Federici, 2019). Martin, a Horizontalist cited in Sitrin (2006: 232), spoke of 'a certain sensibility ... something affective ... a desire for transformation ... that generated a ... new interpersonal relationship ... a ... sense of "we", or oneness'.

Assemblies promote an affective politics. Affect refers to the capacity to act and to be acted on that precedes and exceeds rationality and emotion and even individuation: contagions – like the mood one feels on entering a room. Affect points to a politics of encounters and their unpredictable, powerful promotion (or limitation) of convergence and synchronicity (Gregg and Seigworth, 2010). Commoning's affective politics points to the kind of society abolitionists strive for. It works against a society that requires some to be excluded and incarcerated. This is not love in the sentimental, romantic sense, which involves likeness or identity rather than difference and change. That love, together with the patriarchal family, commercial corporations and the nation-state, are corrupted forms of commoning: they '[impose] ... hierarchy and control' (Hardt and Negri, 2009: 162), introduce 'closures or limitations – enclosures or privatisations – [on] ... the human capacity to relate to others' (De Angelis, 2017), and restrict the assembly's openness and authority.

The Zapatista's good government principles provide guidance as to how an affective politics can be implemented (how the openness and authority of the assembly can be protected). Fitzwater (2019: xxv) describes these principles as 'not only a form of service but ... a form of awakened or mindful care ... perhaps the deepest expression of the politics of care in the world today'. The principles are:

1. To serve others not oneself;
2. To represent not supplant;
3. To build not destroy;
4. To obey not command;
5. To propose not impose;
6. To convince not defeat; [and]
7. To go below not above (Lower yourself, don't raise yourself up). (Fitzwater, 2019: 2)

These principles shape their approach to justice. The Zapatista have no judges, police or prisons. Instead, they apply a restorative approach to justice, with those in office acting as mediators rather than judges, seeking to secure the collective agreement of all those affected to some form of work that benefits the broader community (Fitzwater, 2019). They suggest how commoning might replace the carceral state.

These principles also suggest how social work might be freed of its contradictions. The principles limit the accumulation of privilege and power by those in office. Those positions are unpaid and filled by regular rotations of community members. The Zapatista do not promote specialisation and accept the resulting losses in efficacy and efficiency, aiming for knowledge and skill to be accumulated in the broader community (Henck, 2018; Fitzwater, 2019).

Commoning severs the connection between social work and the liberal self, and thereby a key link with the carceral state. In its place, social work can be embedded in the community it seeks to serve and free itself of the need to secure its sustenance from the state. Social work can become a richer expression or form of affective politics – of love and care – and, 'leading by obeying', realise its aspirations to be a value-centred profession, rooted in the values of the communities it serves. Social work can learn from the Global South, and from the experience of commoning, that radical subjective change can best be effected through participation in assemblies and other collective activities, reinforcing social work's re-orientation to community rather than individual work.

Conclusion

Abolitionism now not only seeks to address the state and its carceral institutions, but the social relations that make such institutions appear necessary. To effect that aim, the movement also needs to abolish the liberal self, as that form of the self and the modern carceral state mutually constituted – and continue to constitute – each other. Capitalism initially rose to dominance through the enclosure and exploitation of the commons. In so doing, it repeatedly assaulted the moral economy – the ensemble or network of social relations – that constituted the dominant form of self in feudal England, working to reduce that web of supports and reciprocity to the impoverished, 'free', liberal self. The resistance to these assaults prompted the expansion of the state and its powers, making the modern carceral state and the liberal self's twin births. The latter was produced by state violence and continues to justify the maintenance of that state.

Social work developed following the consolidation of the capitalist, carceral state's dominance. It too remains focused on the limited, liberal self. As such, it is beset by contradictions: as an agent of, or at least dependent on and profoundly shaped by, the state, social work has too often enacted and extended its reach in ways that limited, if not overrode, its capacity to pursue its commitments to care. While these contradictions have been challenged by radical forms of social work, those alternatives have had limited influence, in part because they have continued to prioritise care for the limited, liberal self and, in so doing, maintain the very violence that produced it.

There are alternatives that may enable social work to reinvent itself and operate free of the capitalist, carceral state and the liberal self. Autonomist Marxism and commoning suggest approaches that may realise the abolitionist vision of replacing both the carceral institutions of the state and the social relationships that produce them. Both recognise that commoning – relations of interdependence and mutual support – are a necessary feature of human life and that the history of capitalism is that of their construction, colonisation and destruction, and re-construction. Commoning, as evidenced by the experiences of the Zapatista in Mexico and Horizontalists in Argentina, demonstrates one way in which the relational self has contested and supplanted the liberal self, and how their experience might be drawn on elsewhere. They suggest how conventional social work might be abolished by reforming the social relations that support it – by freeing the relational self from the limited, liberal self through commoning.

Neither Autonomist Marxism nor commoning provide comprehensive guides to achieving these ends. Rather, they provide a pathway along which we can, like the Zapatista, 'walk by asking questions' (Midnight Notes, 2001: 91) – advance through discussion and experiment – tentatively exploring new forms of society and social work.

References

Addams, J. (1964) 'Industrial amelioration', in J. Addams and A.F. Scott (eds), *Democracy and Social Ethics*, Cambridge, MA: Harvard University Press, pp 137–156.

Angus, I. (2023) *The War Against the Commons: Dispossession and Resistance in the Making of Capitalism*, New York: Monthly Review Press.

Barad, K. (2007) *Meeting the Universe Halfway: Quantum Physics and the Entanglement of Matter and Meaning* [Kindle 3.4.2 version]. Available from: https://www.amazon.com.au/Meeting-Universe-Halfway-Quantum-Entanglement-ebook/dp/B00EHNU7UY.

Barbagallo, C., Beuret, N. and Harvie, D. (eds) (2019) *Commoning with George Caffentzis and Silvia Federici*, London: Pluto Press.

Bennett, J. (2010) *Vibrant Matter: A Political Ecology of Things* [Kindle 3.4.2 version]. Available from: https://www.amazon.com.au/Vibrant-Matter-Political-Ecology-Franklin-ebook/dp/B00EHNZM9U

Bohstedt, J. (2010) *The Politics of Provisions: Food Riots, Moral Economy, and Market Transition in England, c. 1550–1850*, Abingdon: Routledge.

Bozalek, V. and Pease, B. (eds) (2021) *Post-Anthropocentric Social Work: Critical Posthumanism and New Materialist Perspectives*, Abingdon: Routledge.

Brady, S., Sawyer, J. and Perkins, N. (2019) 'Debunking the myth of the "radical profession": Analysing and overcoming our professional history to create new pathways and opportunities for social work', *Critical and Radical Social Work*, 7(3): 315–332.

Brake, M. and Bailey, R. (eds) (1980) *Radical Social Work and Practice*, London: Edward Arnold.

Branson, S., Hudson, R. and Reed, B. (eds) (2023) *Surviving the Future: Abolitionist Queer Strategies*, Oakland: PM Press.

Caffentzis, G. (2013) *In Letters of Blood and Fire: Work, Machines, and Crisis of Capitalism*, Oakland: PM Press.

Carlsson, C. (2008) *Nowtopia: How Pirate Programmers, Outlaw Bicyclists and Vacant-Lot Gardeners are Inventing the Future Today!*, Oakland: AK Press.

Davis, A. (2003) *Are Prisons Obsolete?*, New York: Seven Stories Press.

Davis, A., Dent, G., Meiners, E.R. and Richie, B.E. (2022) *Abolition. Feminism. Now.*, Dublin: Penguin Books.

De Angelis, M. (2003) 'Reflections on alternatives, commons and communities or building a new world from the bottom up', *The Commoner*, 6: 1–14.

De Angelis, M. (2007) *The Beginning of History: Value Struggles and Global Capital*, London: Pluto Press.

De Angelis, M. (2017) *Omnia Sunt Communia: On the commons and the transformation to postcapitalism*, London: Zed Books.

De Angelis, M. (2019) 'The strategic horizon of the commons' in C. Barbagallo, N. Beuret and D. Harvie (eds), *Commoning with George Caffentzis and Silvia Federici*, London: Pluto Press, pp 209–221.

Eden, D. (2012) *Autonomy: Capitalism, Class and Politics*, Abingdon: Routledge.

Federici, S. (2014) *Caliban and the Witch: Women, the Body and Primitive Accumulation*, New York: Autonomedia.

Federici, S. (2019) *Re-Enchanting the World: Feminism and the Politics of the Commons*, Oakland: PM Press.

Fitzwater, D.E. (2019) *Autonomy is in Our Hearts: Zapatista Autonomous Government Through the Lens of the Tsotsil Language*, Oakland: PM Press.

Fook, J. (2016) *Social Work: A Critical Approach to Practice* (3rd edn), London: SAGE.

Fox, J. (2015) *Marx, the Body, and Human Nature*, Basingstoke: Palgrave MacMillan.

Galper, J. (1980) *Social Work Practice: A Radical Perspective*, Englewood Cliffs: Prentice-Hill.

Gregg, M. and Seigworth, G.J. (eds) (2010) *The Affect Theory Reader*, Durham, NC: Duke University Press.

Hardt, M. and Negri, A. (2000) *Empire*, Cambridge, MA: Harvard University Press.

Hardt, M. and Negri, A. (2004) *Multitude: War and Democracy in the Age of Empire*, New York: Penguin Books.

Hardt, M. and Negri, A. (2009) *Commonwealth*, Cambridge, MA: The Belkap Press of Harvard University Press.

Hegel, G. (1975) *Logic*, Oxford: Oxford University Press.

Henck, N. (ed) (2018) *The Zapatista's Dignified Rage: Final Public Speeches of Subcommander Marcos*, Chico: AK Press.

Holloway, J. (2019) *Change the World Without Taking Power: The Meaning of Revolution Today*, London: Pluto Press.

Ioakimidis, V. and Wyllie, A. (2023) 'Learning from the past to shape the future: uncovering social work's histories of complicity and resistance', in V. Ioakimidis and A. Wyllie (eds), *Social Work's Histories of Complicity and Resistance: A Tale of Two Professions*, Bristol: Policy Press, pp 3–28.

Jones, C. and Lavalette, M. (2013) 'The two souls of social work: Exploring the roots of "popular social work"', *Critical and Radical Social Work*, 1(2): 147–165.

Kaba, M. (2021) *We Do This Til We Free Us: Abolitionist Organizing and Transforming Justice*, Chicago: Haymarket Books.

Lavalette, M. (2019) 'Popular social work', in S. Webb (ed), *The Routledge Handbook of Critical Social Work*, Abingdon: Routledge, pp 536–548.

Lavalette, M. and Ioakimidis, V. (2011) *Social Work in Extremis: Lessons for Social Work Internationally*, Bristol: Policy Press.

Linebaugh, P. (2006) *The London Hanged: Crime and Civil Society in the Eighteenth Century*, London: Verso.

Linebaugh, P. (2008) *The Magna Carta Manifesto: Liberties and Commons for All*, Berkeley: University of California Press.

Linebaugh, P. (2014) *'Stop Thief!': The Commons, Enclosures, and Resistance*, Oakland: PM Press.

Linebaugh, P. and Rediker, M. (2000) *The Many-Headed Hydra: Sailors, Slaves, Commoners, and the Hidden History of the Revolutionary Atlantic*, Boston: Beacon Press.

Marx, K. (1975a) 'Economic and philosophical manuscripts', in K. Marx and L. Colletti (ed), *Early Writings*, London: Penguin Books, pp 279–400.

Marx, K. (1975b) 'Concerning Feuerbach', in K. Marx and L. Colletti (eds), *Early Writings*, London: Penguin Books, pp 421–423.

Marx, K. (1976) *Capital, Volume 1*, London: Penguin Books.

Marx, K. and Engels, F. (1998) *The German Ideology*, Amherst: Prometheus Books.

Maylea, C. (2021) 'The end of social work', *British Journal of Social Work*, 51: 772–789.

Midnight Notes (2001) *Auroras of the Zapatistas: Local and Global Struggles of the Fourth World War*, New York: Autonomedia.

Murphy, T.S. (2012) *Antonio Negri: Modernity and the Multitude*, Cambridge: Polity Press.

Negri, A. (2005) *Books for Burning: Between Civil War and Democracy in 1970s Italy*, London: Verso.

Ollman, B. (1976) *Alienation: Marx's Conception of Man in Capitalist Society* (2nd edn), New York: Cambridge University Press.

Olson, J. (2007) 'Social work's professional and social justice projects: Discourses in conflict', *Journal of Progressive Human Services*, 18(1): 45–69.

Pease, B. (2023) 'Facing the legacy of social work: Coming to terms with complicity in systemic inequality and social justice', in V. Ioakimidis and A. Wyllie (eds), *Social Work's Histories of Complicity and Resistance: A Tale of Two Professions*, Bristol: Policy Press, pp 219–232.

Perelman, M. (2000) *The Invention of Capitalism: Classical Political Economy and the Secret History of Primitive Accumulation*, Durham, NC: Duke University Press.

Richmond, M. (1917) *Social Diagnosis*, New York: Russell Sage Foundation.

Sitrin, M. (ed) (2006) *Horizontalism: Voices of Popular Power in Argentina*, Oakland: AK Press.

Sitrin, M. (2012) *Everyday Revolutions: Horizontalism and Autonomy in Argentina*, London: Zed Books.

Taylor, M. and Brehmer, N. (eds) (2023) *The Commonist Horizon: Futures beyond Capitalist Urbanisation*, Brooklyn: Common Notions.

Thompson, E.P. (1963) *The Making of the English Working Class*, New York: Vintage Books.

Thompson, E.P. (1993) *Customs in Common*, New York: The New Press.

Tronti, M. (2019) *Workers and Capital*, London: Verso.

Wright, S. (2017) *Storming Heaven: Class Composition and Struggle in Italian Autonomist Marxism*, London: Pluto Press.

21

After social work?

Chris Maylea

Introduction

As this book demonstrates, abolitionist perspectives are growing in popularity in a number of areas. Primarily, the term refers to carceral systems of policing and prisons, although it has roots in anti-slavery movements. More recently, the term has been applied to the end of war (Ryan, 2024), whiteness (Gregory, 2021), state borders (Tazzioli and De Genova, 2023), criminalisation of sex work (Harris, 2008) or the use of animals for human purposes (Marks, 2013). Shackelford defines abolitionism as follows: 'Abolitionists aim to create a society free from oppression and exploitation, with complete economic, political and social equality. Abolition often centres on dismantling carceral institutions, limiting the power and scope of their influence and shifting resources away from carceral institutions and towards investments in marginalised communities' (Shackelford et al, 2024: 1405). This chapter uses this definition, including sites of detention such as forced mental health and disability, immigration, policing and correctional detention facilities, and incorporeal institutions that use carceral approaches, such as systems of child removal. Iwai et al write on abolition medicine:

> Abolition medicine invokes W E B Du Bois's 1935 notion of 'abolition democracy', a vision based not only on breaking systems down but also on building up a new, healthier, and more just society. Abolition has subsequently been championed by activist–scholars like Angela Davis and Mariame Kaba who have argued that the abolition of slavery was but one first step in an ongoing process of abolitionist practices to address racialised systems of policing, surveillance, and incarceration. Medicine can perhaps be added to this list. (Iwai et al, 2020: 159)

Social work, certainly, should also be added to this list. As Rasmussen and James (2020) write, '[s]ocial workers have a long and troubled history as partners to the state, more often serving as carceral enforcers than as collaborators toward liberation'. Lown (2023: 1) writes that '[a]bolitionist social workers believe that a world without police and incarceration are not only possible, but necessary'. If social workers are as inherently carceral as police, should we not also believe that a world without social workers is equally possible, equally necessary?

Social work does have a long, if rarely implemented, theoretical strand of anti-oppressive approaches that are aligned with abolition (Pollack, 2004; Dominelli, 2010a; Esquao and Strega, 2015; Nipperess and Clark, 2016). More recently, a range of authors have argued for an 'abolitionist social work' (see, for example, Gregory, 2021; Jacobs et al, 2021; Nourie, 2022; Hunter and Wroe, 2024; Kim et al, 2024; Shackelford et al, 2024). In general, social work's engagement with abolition views social work as an *alternative*, as a *solution*, to oppression – although there is no lack of literature identifying social work's role in maintaining and sustaining carceral institutions (Kennedy, 2008; Johnson and Moorhead, 2011; Fortier and Wong, 2019; Okpokiri, 2020). This chapter questions this approach, proposing that, rather than being part of the solution, social work *is* a carceral institution and should be abolished. This is not to say that all social work is carceral, but that social work – the professional and academic discipline – is an inherently carceral institution that cannot be reformed or converted.

Few non-social work academics spend much time considering social work at all, which means that virtually all academic scholarship on social work is done by social workers with a vested interest in maintaining their professional identity. Largely, in this scholarship, the need for social work goes unquestioned, and the profession's potential for harm is rarely investigated. When social work is interrogated, and found lacking, the answer seems always, curiously, to be *more social work*. In the entire social work canon, there are vanishingly few critiques that do not reach this self-serving conclusion. Even studies that specifically identify the ways in which clients may *hate* their social workers advocate for increased training for social workers rather than their abolition (see, for example, Ferguson et al, 2021). Analyses that identify the carceral functions of social work attempt to reimagine an abolitionist social work (see, for example, Shackelford et al, 2024), or abolish particularly carceral elements of social work (see Maylea, 2017; Jacobs et al, 2021; Nourie, 2022; Murray et al, 2023). Fortier and Wong (2019: 437) perhaps come the closest, arguing for deprofessionalisation – 'the restructuring of the "helping" practices of social work back under the control of communities themselves'. Even the most radical social work writers, demanding change of such proportions that 'social work become unrecognisable from its current form' (Rasmussen and James, 2020), are *still talking about social work*. The authors of the new journal *Abolitionist Perspectives in Social Work* or the recent book *Abolition and Social Work* (Kim et al, 2024) and *Abolish Social Work (As We Know It)* (Fortier et al, 2024) take the same approach.

The key problem with this is that social work is not capable of heeding these calls for reform. Social work is a profession in constant crisis, with repeated and consistent calls for reform throughout its existence (Wootton, 1959; Pemberton and Locke, 1971; Beresford and Croft, 2004; Dominelli, 2010b; van Ewijk, 2010; Marston and McDonald, 2012; Reisch, 2013; Jones, 2014; Maylea, 2021). In the nebulous, indefinable noise that is social work, the one clear and consistent voice is self-critical, calling for urgent root and branch reform. Despite generations of calls for such reform, there is little that can be shown in terms of coherent strategic direction for the profession. An 'abolitionist social work' assumes that shifting social work is possible. Yet Pease and Nipperess (2016: 12) note that 'critical social workers can aim to resist the most harmful effects of state control, while acknowledging that they cannot escape its coercive dimensions completely'. As such, this chapter asks if it is not time to abandon the social work project entirely, much as others have abandoned police and prisons as fundamentally counterproductive. Calling for an 'abolitionist social work' makes as much sense as calling for an 'abolitionist police force' or 'abolitionist prison system'.

Other arguments for the abolition of social work have been made elsewhere (Maylea, 2021), and responded to robustly with scholarly rigour (Garrett, 2021; Whelan, 2021; Steggall and Scollen, 2024). This chapter will not relitigate all those arguments, but instead will ask what a post-social work world could look like. However, it is necessary to first briefly highlight the inherently carceral nature of contemporary social work to illustrate its unsuitability as a vehicle of abolition.

This chapter explores this process in three parts: first, discussing how the carceral elements of social work may be laid to one side, removing them from the shielding provided by the social work brand, then examining two ways in which social work's failed mission could be better achieved through other approaches. These two approaches are peer-run services and advocacy services, although there are many more approaches than could be covered here, such as transformative justice or mutual aid.

What are we abolishing anyway?

Before proceeding, it is necessary to be clear about the scope of what is to be abolished. In this chapter, for clarity, I refer to social work as the discipline and profession in the Anglophone world – primarily the United States, Canada, the UK, Australia and New Zealand. Each of these jurisdictions have social work bodies and accredited social work university degrees, and the reader may use the shorthand of abolishing these professional bodies and university disciplines.

I do not include social work in other jurisdictions as the context as application of the discipline in places such as India or the Philippines is wholly different. I strongly suspect that transhipping Anglophone concepts such as social work to those settings is mere colonialism which will require endless decolonisation (Tusasiirwe, 2023; Garrett, 2024), but that is not considered in this chapter.

All of Anglophone social work is, to some extent, carceral, because it inevitably links back to carceral functions. However, the elements of social work that directly participate in involuntary mental health treatment, child removal, coercive disability, immigration detention and prisons are inexorably carceral and have no place in an 'abolitionist' social work. For example, Bergen and Abji (2020) illustrate the facilitation role that social workers play in funnelling children from child protection systems to gaol and deportation, and Berger (2019) tracks the way mental health institutions replaced prisons. As our societies have become reliant on these carceral roles, they will certainly continue. However, without the shielding of social work's brand, they may be more thoroughly and critically interrogated and eventually dismantled.

For those less inherently carceral roles, there are few that are unlinked to carceral functions. For example, virtually every client-facing social work interaction begins with explaining to clients that their confidentiality will be violated if they are assessed, by the social worker, to pose a risk of harm to themselves or others. In many jurisdictions, social workers are mandatory reporters, legally required to breach confidentiality and inform child protection or other authorities (Gruber, 2023). Increasingly, this extends to adult safeguarding (Donnelly, 2019) and intimate partner violence (Vatnar et al, 2021). Inevitably, reporting to authorities raises the spectre of the carceral state – be it police 'welfare checks' for suicidality (Randall et al, 2024), child protection involvement or straightforward criminal investigation.

It is irrelevant that the social worker feels that it is 'necessary' to breach confidentiality, or that they envisage a non-carceral response from the relevant authorities who are subsequently notified. This is no different, no less carceral, than a police officer or a judge explaining that a person 'needs' to be incarcerated to protect society. There should be no false doubt that the implied threat to breach confidentiality, as heard by the client, is that the social worker poses a carceral risk to the client.

Compounding this is that social work, as a concept, has such poor definitional quality that it has been adapted and used in so many different settings as to be unrecognisable. An abolitionist social work may be, in fact, so far distant from social work as actually practised in hospitals and homes as to be a conceptually different, unrelated profession.

Social work has, over time, claimed everything from individual counselling to community work and policy advocacy. Teater and Lopez-Humphreys (2019: 616) write that '[t]he social work profession lacks a single unified definition of social work practice, which has implications for solidarity in the profession, identification as a social worker, and the public's understanding of social work'. Social workers are expected to be able to work in child protection, mental health, family violence, mediation, hospitals, policy, community, immigration, government services, youth services, family services, counselling and any number of other areas. With this incredibly broad reach, social work conceals its carceral features behind a veil of human rights and social justice. Those elements of social work which may lay claim to non-carceral status, such as policy advocacy or community development, shield the carceral roles with the broader social work brand.

It is necessary, therefore, to abolish the broader social work brand and let these discrete elements of the profession stand on their own. For the foreseeable future, people in distress will continue to require assistance. Abolishing social work does not require the reduction of this assistance, and there is no evidence that social work has succeeded in reducing the degradation of the welfare state or contributed meaningfully to a society that is more community focused and supportive. Therefore, the title of social worker can be abolished, leaving behind specific functions of counsellor, child protection worker, family violence worker, mental health clinician, community worker or policy advocate. Some of these roles may be salvageable, from an abolitionist perspective.

Indeed, counsellors, although regularly collaborating with carceral institutions, are already an entirely distinct profession with their own discipline, training and accreditation in many jurisdictions. They may contentedly deploy technical cognitive therapies on the despairing masses of capitalist modernity without, in inherently doing so, being in conflict with their espoused value system. There is no – absolutely none – empirical evidence that social workers are 'better' at counselling than counsellors who are not social workers as a result of their alleged human rights or social justice orientation. Similarly, policy advocates who are not social workers are not inherently inferior to policy advocates who are social workers.

Similarly, there is no evidence that the alleged human rights and social justice training that social work academics and discipline leaders tout as central to social work practice leads to improved human rights or social justice in practice. For a First Nations person, having their child removed by a worker with human rights training feels much the same as by one without. There is no evidence that mental health social workers are, in practice, less likely to detain and forcibly treat people than their nursing or psychology trained colleagues. The human rights and social justice framing and the consideration of broader structural issues that differentiates social work from other professions *has no tangible value for clients in carceral systems.*

It may be argued that less-carceral elements of social work, such as community-based feminist sexual assault support, are free of these issues, or that in those roles social workers' human rights and social justice frameworks are beneficial for clients. These are excellent arguments for training human rights and social justice oriented professionals for these roles, but this is not what contemporary social work training does.

Instead, social work courses attempt to prepare graduates for such a wide range of potential employment opportunities as to leave virtually no room for the kind of specialisation that might make a social work degree useful. This production line of barely qualified graduates is not the major concern from an abolitionist perspective. However, the abolition of social work may result in graduates who are genuinely qualified for their prospective roles. These roles may, or may not be, abolitionist in their framing, but they will at least have that potential.

The remainder of this chapter explores two roles that have this abolitionist potential. The first, instructional advocacy, is open to post-social workers. The second, peer work, will largely not be. Both, however, provide a model for replacing social workers with roles consistent with human rights and genuinely working towards abolitionist outcomes.

Instructional advocacy

Instructional advocacy is largely found in the mental health and disability spheres, with some emergence in child protection and other arenas. In England, Wales and the Australian states of Victoria and Western Australia, independent mental health advocacy is well established and widespread (Newbigging et al, 2015; Maylea et al, 2019). The key tenet of this approach to individual advocacy is that the advocate acts on instructions, rather than in the best interests of the person. The role of the advocate is to give voice to the person, not to get what the social worker thinks is best for them.

Advocates are commonly, but not universally, trained in social work. I have argued elsewhere that this approach to advocacy *is* a social work model of advocacy (Maylea et al, 2020). Insomuch as social work is focused on human rights and social justice, instructional advocacy *is* consistent with the definition of social work, and is also abolitionist. Curiously, however, social workers who have come from best interests roles such as mental health or child protection have a very difficult time adjusting and require substantial retraining to take on this way of working.

In the case of independent mental health advocacy, the advocate is most often working to get the person out of an inpatient unit in which they are detained – although the setting of advocacy goals sits entirely with the person detained, not the advocate. Advocates will often advocate for clients to be released from inpatient units when all other involved professionals are arguing for their continued detention. In the child protection sphere, instructional advocacy attempts to give voice to parents who are at risk of having their children removed. In the case of parents with disabilities and First Nations parents, this is a question of human rights and epistemic justice (Atkin and Kroese, 2021; Maylea et al, 2023). Instructional advocates are inherently anti-carceral although not inherently abolitionist.

In our quest for an 'abolitionist' social work, the challenge is that other, non-abolitionist social workers are routinely complicit or actively engaged in the detention and forced treatment of people in disability and mental health facilities, and in systems that facilitate child removal, particularly removal of First Nations children from their communities. Instructional advocates are often advocating *at other social workers*.

Rather than showing a way in which social work can become abolitionist, social workers working as instructional advocates highlight the way in which the profession cannot extract itself from carceral institutions. Only by abolishing the discipline and separating the carceral and non-carceral elements apart can those who wish to be abolitionists, such as by working as instructional advocates, achieve this goal.

While instructional advocacy aims to empower individuals by ensuring their voices are heard, the systemic context within which advocates operate often limits their capacity to effect real change. By working within established frameworks of mental health and child protection systems, advocates, with or without social work training, may inadvertently reinforce the very structures they seek to challenge. This paradox arises because these systems are deeply rooted in carceral logics that prioritise control and compliance over genuine emancipation and self-determination. As such, the advocacy efforts, though well-intentioned, risk being co-opted by institutional agendas that uphold the status quo. For advocates to truly embody abolitionist principles, there must be a radical reimagining of the system itself, moving beyond the confines of existing systems to foster alternative, non-carceral forms of support and community care. Peer work provides one of these opportunities.

Peer work as abolition

Peer work in mental health involves individuals with lived experience of mental health issues providing support, education, advocacy and research within mental health systems. The goal of this inclusion is to transform how mental health services are provided by leveraging the unique insights and empathy that come from personal experience. Peer work is its own profession, own discipline, and not simply work done by people with lived experience. Peer work is also common in other settings, such as drug and alcohol work, but I will focus on mental health peer work here.

Peer work (or peer support), a variant of lived experience work, has a coherent theoretical perspective which aligns with abolitionism, and has done for over 20 years (Mead et al, 2001). In this context, an abolitionist approach seeks to dismantle traditional psychiatric systems that are seen as oppressive or harmful, advocating for alternative methods of support that do not rely on coercion, medicalisation or pathologisation of distress. Instead, it promotes practices rooted in human rights, social justice and self-determination. An abolitionist position is not uniform in lived experience movements, with many divergent perspectives (Daya et al, 2020). Peer work is an *option* for abolitionist approaches, not a guaranteed pathway for abolition.

In the context of Anglophone mental health policy in Australia, Canada, the United Kingdom and the United States, peer work is framed within existing mental health systems and is often seen as both a solution to improving individual mental health outcomes and as a way to support incremental reform of the mental health system itself.

However, in practice, the implementation of peer work within existing mental health systems often falls short of even these reformist (as opposed to abolitionist) goals. While peer workers bring valuable lived experience perspectives that can challenge traditional psychiatric practices, they are frequently integrated into the same structures they aim to reform. Sinclair et al (2024: 1673) write that peer workers can be 'assimilated into pre-existing systems and ways of working, creating contradictory and potentially harmful effects for peer workers and peer work practice'. This integration can result in peer workers reinforcing the existing system rather than transforming it.

As with advocates, the inclusion of peer workers in policy can sometimes position them as complicit in maintaining 'psy-regimes of governance', which reinforces traditional psychiatric authority (Adams, 2020). This limits their ability to promote alternative representations of mental health and achieve broader structural changes. The transformative potential of peer work is thus constrained by the systemic and institutional frameworks within which it operates.

To align more closely with its abolitionist roots, peer work needs to push beyond mere integration into existing systems and advocate for fundamental changes that address the root causes of mental distress. This would involve redefining mental health problems and solutions from a lived experience perspective, promoting non-coercive, non-medicalised forms of support, and advancing self-determination and social justice. Peer work services need to be peer-run, to ensure that they are not captured by the system. Kaufman-Mthimkhulu (2020), who runs Project LETS, writes: 'We are accountable to the people we work with. Not the institution. Not the police.' Other examples include peer-run Alternative to Suicide programmes, Open Dialog and peer-run crisis services – but these are limited in number, scope and availability (Radford et al, 2019; Davidow and Mazel-Carlton, 2020). However, only through such approaches can peer work fully realise its abolitionist principles in practice.

Conclusion

The discourse surrounding the abolition of social work is a provocative yet necessary endeavour that compels us to critically examine the foundational structures and practices of the profession. As highlighted throughout this chapter, social work is deeply entangled with carceral systems, often perpetuating the very oppressions it purports to dismantle. The call for abolition is not merely a radical repudiation but a considered response to the persistent failures and harms enacted by social work.

Abolitionist perspectives underscore the need to move beyond reformist tweaks and instead envision a transformative approach that dismantles oppressive structures. This entails recognising and severing the carceral ties inherent in social work practices, particularly those involving involuntary mental health treatment, child removal and mandatory reporting. Such practices, regardless of their intent, align social work with systems of control and punishment rather than liberation and justice.

In exploring alternatives, the chapter details the potential of instructional advocacy and peer work as abolitionist practices. Instructional advocacy, when grounded in genuine human rights principles, can empower individuals by ensuring their voices are heard and respected within oppressive systems. However, this advocacy must navigate the paradox of operating within the very systems it seeks to transform. Similarly, peer work, rooted in lived experience, offers a radical reimagining of support and care in mental health. Yet, its transformative potential is often constrained by its integration into existing psychiatric frameworks. Neither instructional advocacy nor peer work are, nor should be, regulated by the state. They must resist the lure of professionalism that has so confounded social work, and maintain connection and obligation to the communities they serve, not to the carceral systems they exist within.

The abolition of social work as a profession does not signify the end of care and support for people who need it. It does not pander to those on the right to seek to dismantle the welfare state, as Paul Michael Garrett (2021) warns. Instead, it invites the creation of new, non-carceral forms of support that genuinely embody the principles of human rights, social justice and self-determination. This reimagining requires the deconstruction of the social work brand, allowing discrete roles such as counselling and advocacy to stand independently, unshackled from carceral associations.

Ultimately, the abolitionist call challenges us to envision and enact a world where support and care are disentangled from coercion and control. It is a call to build systems rooted in community, mutual aid and genuine liberation. By embracing this vision, we can work towards a society where the well-being of individuals is prioritised over the maintenance of carceral structures, paving the way for a truly just and equitable future.

References

Adams, W.E. (2020) 'Unintended consequences of institutionalizing peer support work in mental healthcare', *Social Science and Medicine*, 262: 113249. Available at: https://pubmed.ncbi.nlm.nih.gov/32768773/

Atkin, C. and Kroese, B.S. (2021) 'Exploring the experiences of independent advocates and parents with intellectual disabilities, following their involvement in child protection proceedings', *Disability and Society*, 37(9): 1456–1478.

Beresford, P. and Croft, S. (2004) 'Service users and practitioners reunited: The key component for social work reform', *British Journal of Social Work*, 34(1): 53–68.

Bergen, H. and Abji, S. (2020) 'Facilitating the carceral pipeline: Social work's role in funneling newcomer children from the child protection system to jail and deportation', *Affilia*, 35(1): 34–48.

Berger, D. (2019) 'Finding and defining the carceral state', *Reviews in American History*, 47(2): 279–285.

Davidow, S. and Mazel-Carlton, C. (2020) 'Alternatives to suicide: Myths and new choices', in *The Broader View of Suicide*, Newcastle upon Tyne: Cambridge Scholars Publishing, pp 107–123.

Daya, I., Hamilton, B. and Roper, C. (2020) 'Authentic engagement: A conceptual model for welcoming diverse and challenging consumer and survivor views in mental health research, policy, and practice', *International Journal of Mental Health Nursing*, 29(2): 299–311.

Dominelli, L. (2010a) 'Anti-oppressive practice', in M. Gray and S. Webb (eds), *Ethics and Value Perspectives in Social Work*, Houndmills: Palgrave Macmillan, pp 160–172.

Dominelli, L. (2010b) 'Globalization, contemporary challenges and social work practice', *International Social Work*, 53(5): 599–612.

Donnelly, S. (2019) 'Mandatory reporting and adult safeguarding: A rapid realist review', *The Journal of Adult Protection*, 21(5): 241–251.

Esquao, S.A. and Strega, S. (2015) *Walking this Path Together: Anti-Racist and Anti-Oppressive Child Welfare Practice*, Nova Scotia: Fernwood Publishing.

Ferguson, H., Disney, T., Warwick, L., Leigh, J., Cooner, T.S. and Beddoe, L. (2021) 'Hostile relationships in social work practice: Anxiety, hate and conflict in long-term work with involuntary service users', *Journal of Social Work Practice*, 35(1): 19–37.

Fortier, C. and Wong, E.H-S. (2019) 'The settler colonialism of social work and the social work of settler colonialism', *Settler Colonial Studies*, 9(4): 437–456.

Fortier, C., Wong, E.H-S. and Rwigema, M.J. (eds) (2024) *Abolish Social Work (As We Know It)*, Toronto: Between the Lines.

Garrett, P.M. (2021) '"A world to win": In defence of (dissenting) social work – a response to Chris Maylea', *British Journal of Social Work*, 51(4): 1131–1149.

Garrett, P.M. (2024) 'What are we talking about when we are talking about "decolonising" social work?', *British Journal of Social Work*, 54(5): 2027–2044.

Gregory, J.R. (2021) 'The imperative and promise of neo-abolitionism in social work', *Journal of Social Work*, 21(5): 1203–1224.

Gruber, T. (2023) 'Beyond mandated reporting: Debunking assumptions to support children and families', *Abolitionist Perspectives in Social Work*, 1(1). Available at: https://apsw-ojs-uh.tdl.org/apsw/article/view/12

Harris, V. (2008) 'In the absence of empire: Feminism, abolitionism and social work in Hamburg (c. 1900–1933)', *Women's History Review*, 17(2): 279–298.

Hunter, D. and Wroe, L.E. (2024) '"Already doing the work": Social work, abolition and building the future from the present'. Available at: https://bristoluniversitypressdigital.com/view/journals/crsw/12/3/article-p312.xml

Iwai, Y., Khan, Z.H. and DasGupta, S. (2020) 'Abolition medicine', *The Lancet*, 396(10245): 158–159. Available at: https://pubmed.ncbi.nlm.nih.gov/32682471/

Jacobs, L.A., Kim, M.E., Whitfield, D.L., Gartner, R.E., Panichelli, M., Kattari, S.K., et al (2021) 'Defund the police: Moving towards an anti-carceral social work', *Journal of Progressive Human Services*, 32(1): 37–62.

Johnson, S. and Moorhead, B. (2011) 'Social eugenics practices with children in Hitler's Nazi Germany and the role of social work: Lessons for current practice', *Journal of Social Work Values and Ethics*, 8(1): 1–10.

Jones, R. (2014) 'The best of times, the worst of times: Social work and its moment', *British Journal of Social Work*, 44(3): 485–502.

Kaufman-Mthimkhulu, S.L. (2020) 'We don't need cops to become social workers: We need peer support + community response networks', *Medium*, 22 June. Available at: https://medium.com/@stefkaufman/we-dont-need-cops-to-become-social-workers-we-need-peer-support-b8e6c4ffe87a

Kennedy, A. (2008) 'Eugenics, "degenerate girls," and social workers during the progressive era', *Affilia: Journal of Women and Social Work*, 23: 22–37.

Kim, M., Washington, D. and Rasmussen, C. (eds) (2024) *Abolition and Social Work: Possibilities, Paradoxes, and the Practice of Community Care*, Chicago: Haymarket Books.

Lown, J. (2023) 'Informal social control and the endorsement of police legitimacy: A confirmatory factor analysis', *Abolitionist Perspectives in Social Work*, 1(1). Available at: https://apsw-ojs-uh.tdl.org/apsw/article/view/6

Marks, J. (2013) 'Animal abolitionism meets moral abolitionism: Cutting the gordian knot of applied ethics', *Journal of Bioethical Inquiry*, 10(4): 445–455.

Marston, G. and McDonald, C. (2012) 'Getting beyond "heroic agency" in conceptualising social workers as policy actors in the twenty-first century', *British Journal of Social Work*, 42(6): 1022–1038.

Maylea, C. (2017) 'A rejection of involuntary treatment in mental health social work', *Ethics and Social Welfare*, 11(4): 336–352.

Maylea, C. (2021) 'The end of social work', *British Journal of Social Work*, 51(2): 772–789.

Maylea, C., Alvarez-Vasquez, S., Dale, M., Hill, N., Johnson, B., Martin, J., et al (2019) *Evaluation of the Independent Mental Health Advocacy Service (IMHA)*, Melbourne: RMIT Social and Global Studies Centre.

Maylea, C., Makregiorgos, H., Martin, J., Alvarez-Vasquez, S., Dale, M., Hill, N., et al (2020) 'Independent mental health advocacy: A model of social work advocacy?', *Australian Social Work*, 73(3): 334–346.

Maylea, C., Bashfield, L., Thomas, S., Kuyini, B., Fitt, K. and Buchanan, R. (2023) 'Advocacy as a human rights enabler for parents in the child protection system', *Ethics and Social Welfare*, 17(3): 275–294.

Mead, S., Hilton, D. and Curtis, L. (2001) 'Peer support: A theoretical perspective', *Psychiatric Rehabilitation Journal*, 25(2): 134–141.

Murray, B.J., Copeland, V. and Dettlaff, A.J. (2023) 'Reflections on the ethical possibilities and limitations of abolitionist praxis in social work', *Affilia*, 38(4): 742–758.

Newbigging, K., Ridley, J., McKeown, M., Machin, K. and Poursanidou, K. (2015) '"When you haven't got much of a voice": An evaluation of the quality of Independent Mental Health Advocate (IMHA) services in England', *Health and Social Care in the Community*, 23(3): 313–324.

Nipperess, S. and Clark, S. (2016) 'Anti-oppressive practice with people seeking asylum in Australia: Reflections from the field', in B. Pease, S. Goldingay, N. Hosken and S. Nipperess (eds), *Doing Critical Social Work: Transformative Practices for Social Justice*, Crows Nest: Allen and Unwin, pp 195–210.

Nourie, A.E. (2022) 'Child welfare abolition: Critical theories, human rights, and heteronormativity', *Journal of Human Rights and Social Work*, 7(1): 3–12.

Okpokiri, C. (2020) 'Parenting in fear: Child welfare micro strategies of Nigerian parents in Britain', *British Journal of Social Work* [preprint]. Available at: https://doi.org/10.1093/bjsw/bcaa205

Pease, B. and Nipperess, S. (2016) 'Doing critical social work in the neoliberal context: working on the contradictions', in B. Pease, S. Goldingay, N. Hosken and S. Nipperess (eds), *Doing Critical Social Work: Transformative Practices for Social Justice*, Sydney: Allen and Unwin, pp 3–24.

Pemberton, A.G. and Locke, R.G. (1971) 'Towards a radical critique of social work and welfare ideology', *Australian Journal of Social Issues*, 6(2): 95–107.

Pollack, S. (2004) 'Anti-oppressive social work practice with women in prison: Discursive reconstructions and alternative practices', *British Journal of Social Work*, 34(5): 693–707.

Radford, K., Wishart, E. and Martin, R. (2019) *'All I need is someone to talk to': Evaluating DISCHARGED Suicide Peer Support*, Perth: Curtin University.

Randall, R., Kennedy, H., Karanikolas, P., Bashfield, L., Rayner, A., Nguyen, F., et al (2024) '"I was having an anxiety attack and they pepper sprayed me": Police apprehension in mental health contexts in Australia', *Policing and Society*, 35(1): 85–100.

Rasmussen, C. and James, K. 'Jae' (2020) 'We need to defund police entirely – not turn social workers into cops', *Truthout*, 17 July. Available at: https://truthout.org/articles/trading-cops-for-social-workers-isnt-the-solution-to-police-violence/

Reisch, M. (2013) 'What is the future of social work?', *Critical and Radical Social Work*, 1(1): 67–85.

Ryan, C. (2024) *Pacifism As War Abolitionism* (1st edn), New York: Routledge.

Shackelford, A., Rao, S., Krings, A. and Frances, K. (2024) 'Abolitionism and ecosocial work: Towards equity, liberation and environmental justice', *British Journal of Social Work*, 54(4): 1402–1419.

Sinclair, A., Fernandes, C., Gillieatt, S. and Mahboub, L (2024) 'Peer work in Australian mental health policy: What "problems" are we solving and to what effect(s)?', *Disability and Society*, 39(7): 1656–1681.

Steggall, D. and Scollen, R. (2024) 'Clown-based social work as dissent in child protection practice', *British Journal of Social Work*, 54(5): 2124–2141.

Tazzioli, M. and De Genova, N. (2023) 'Border abolitionism', *Social Text*, 41(3): 1–34.

Teater, B. and Lopez-Humphreys, M. (2019) 'Research note: Is social work education a form of social work practice?', *Journal of Social Work Education*, 55(3): 616–622.

Tusasiirwe, S. (2023) 'Disrupting colonisation in the social work classroom: Using the Obuntu/Ubuntu framework to decolonise the curriculum', *Social Work Education*, 43(8): 2170–2184.

van Ewijk, H. (2010) 'Positioning social work in a socially sensitive society', *Social Work and Society*, 8(1): 22–31.

Vatnar, S.K.B., Leer-Salvesen, K. and Bjørkly, S. (2021) 'Mandatory reporting of intimate partner violence: A mixed methods systematic review', *Trauma, Violence, and Abuse*, 22(4): 635–655.

Whelan, J. (2021) 'On your Marx…? A world to win or the dismantlement of a profession? On why we need a reckoning', *British Journal of Social Work* [preprint]. Available at: https://doi.org/10.1093/bjsw/bcab132

Wootton, B. (1959) *Social Science and Social Pathology*, Oxford: Macmillan.

Index

References in **bold** type refer to tables. References to notes show both the page number and the note number (95n1).

'60's Scoop' 131–132, 134

A

ABC television 168
Abji, S. 302
abolition
  and abandonment 32–33
  criticisms 242
  decolonial perspectives 247
  defining 7–8, 277
  'dismantling' and 'rebuilding' 82–83
  dismantling systems of oppression 76, 307
  food justice and poverty 16
  negative and positive projects 277
  reproductive justice framework 16
  resource and power redistribution 242
  in social work 7
'abolition democracy' (Du Bois) 43–44
abolition ecology 16
abolition feminism 157–158, 160–161, 171
Abolition. Feminism. Now (Davis, Dent, Meiners and Richie) 161
abolitionism 4–6, 294
  defining 299
  harm to children 245
  origins 286
  and social work 73, 257–259
abolitionist approaches 6–10, 195, 212, 241–242, 248
abolitionist futures 60–61
abolitionist literature 284, 285
abolitionist social work 7–8, 47–48, 68–69, 231, 257, 265, 300–302
abolitionist social workers 7, 47–48, 69, 72–73, 86, 305
abolitionist theory 257
abolitionist thinking 10
abolition medicine 299
abolition movements 42–46, 157, 241, 243, 284
abolition politics 16, 113
abolition social work 91
Aboriginal and Torres Strait Islanders 67–68, 81–82
Aboriginal children 70, 81–2, 88
Aboriginal Peoples 70
Aboriginal prisoners 85–86
Aboriginal women 66, 82, 83–85
Aboriginal youths 87

absorbing knowledge 72
accountability 186, 192
Acheson, R. 170
activist profeminist men's networks 174
Addams, Jane 41, 128, 289
'administrative violence' 172
adoption 27, 145
  see also foster care
advocates 304–305
affective politics 293–294
affirmative strategies 60
African American feminists 241
African Americans 197–198
Aitlhadj, L. 201
Akay, L. 58
Alaattinoğlu, D. 261, 263
Alberta 130, 133, 136
Ali, Idil 181–190
aloof theorising 277
Alternative to Suicide programmes 306
Althusser, L. 121
Anglophone social work 301–302
Angus, I. 288
anti-capitalist emancipatory social science thinking 123
anti-carceral approaches to feminist practice 165
anti-carceral mental health 277–280
anti-colonial practices 74
anti-colonial theorists 257
anti-migrant rhetoric 59
anti-oppressive approaches 143, 300
'anti-oppressive practices' (AOP) 3, 4, 82
anti-patriarchal activism 164
anti-racist protests 59
'anti-state state' (Gilmore) 199
anti-violence feminists 13, 156, 158–160
te Ao Māori (Māori world/worldview) 147
Aotearoa 142–154
  abolition agenda 151
  child poverty reduction targets 240
  child protection 119–121, 148–150, 152, 240
  constitutional reform 150–151
  Crown/Māori partnerships 148–149
  Declaration Working Group 151
  decolonising child protection 119, 240
  ethic of restoration 146–147
  'He Puapua' report (Charters) 151, 152
  legal frameworks 152

Index

logic of elimination 145
long-term foster/kinship care 243
Native School Act 1867 145
neoliberal social investment policies 116
Office of the Commissioner for Children 121
Oranga Tamariki 148, 149, 153n6, 240
Oranga Tamariki Act 1989, Section 7 AA 148–150, 151, 153
'Puao te Ata Tu' report 120–121
Royal Commissions 2–3
Royal Commission of Inquiry into Historical Abuse in State Care and in the Care of Faith-Based Institutions 119–120, 145–146
terminating parental rights 243
Tiaki Taoka caregiver services 149
Te Tiriti o Waitangi 147
unconditional material help 117
Waitangi Tribunal report 121, 148
Te Whakaputanga o te Rangatiratanga o Nu Tireni framework 147
see also Māori
'apathetic intellectualism' (Whynacht) 277
apologies 46, 81, 134, 263
Applin, S. 170
Are Prisons Obsolete? (Davis) 160
Argentinian Horizontalists 292, 295
Arons, Anna 32–33
Asafo, D. 242
Asian children 56, 57
assemblies 292–294
Assembly of First Nations 130–131
'At Home/Chez Soi' project (Canada) 211–212
'at risk' populations 245–246
attachment (bonding) 133
Australia 81–91
  African 'gangs' 89
  age of criminal responsibility 88, 89
  built on genocide 70
  child imprisonment 86
  Community Treatment Orders 275
  Human Rights and Equal Opportunity Commission (HREOC) 81
  juvenile justice system 87
  mental health system 270
  National Apology to the Stolen Generations 81
  National Inquiry into the Separation of Aboriginal and Torres Strait Islander Children from their Families 81
  National Plan to End Violence Against Women 2022—2032 85
  out-of-home care (OOHC) 81-2, 88
  positive masculinities 168
  racialisation of crime 88–89
  'Raise the Age' campaign 89
  Royal Commissions 2–3
  Royal Commission into Aboriginal Deaths in Custody 81, 82
  section 28 orders 88
  social work 69–70
  Stolen Generation 70
  Australian Association of Social Workers (AASW) 81, 82, 83
  Australian Social Work (journal) 83
'authoritarian neoliberal' systems of care 257–258
authoritarian relationships 105
Autonomist Marxism 285, 290–292, 295

B

Bailey, R. 47
balance of power 136
Ballantyne, N. 123
Bangladesh 56
'battered-child syndrome' (Kempe) 95
being (Marx) 285–286
Bell, M. 277–278
Ben-Moshe, L. 8, 278
Bennett, D. 54
Bergen, H. 302
Berger, D. 302
Bernard, C. 61
Bernstein, Elizabeth 158
Bhaba, H. 258
Bierria, A. 8
Bilson, A. 54
biomedical neoliberalism 273
biopolitics of gender 165–166
Black Americans 41–42, 44
Black Caribbean 56
Black children 26, 29–30, 31, 42, 44
Black families 26, 28
Black Lives Matter 5, 118, 189
Black men 41, 198–199
Black power movement 5
Black Reconstruction in America 1860–1880 (Du Bois) 43–44
Blackstock, Cindy 131, 144, 149
Black young people 30, 57
Blell, M. 261
Bohstedt, J. 287
borders and bordering 202
Bourdieu, P. 117
Brace, Charles Loring 40
Braithwaite, J. 106
Brake, M. 47
breaching confidentiality 302
Bringing them Home (HREOC) 81
British Columbia (BC) 208, 211
British Empire 200
  see also colonialism
'British Values' 196
Brockmann, O. 7, 114, 122

Brodie, I. 117
Brossard, B. 278
Brown, C. 273
Brown, S. 167–168
Brown v Canada (ONSC) 134
Brown, W. 164, 167, 172
Bumiller, K. 165
Burrell, S. 168
Burstyn, V. 164
Butot, M. 213
Bywaters, P. 54

C

Canada 128–136
   '60's Scoop' 131–132
   An Act respecting First Nations, Inuit and Métis children, youth, and families 131, 135
   apologies 134
   assimilation of 'Indians' 129
   attachment versus culture 133
   child protection (CP) 128–131, 134, 135–136
   child welfare laws on reserves 131
   class action lawsuits 133–134
   colonial policies 134
   Constitution Act 1867 129
   Day Scholar Compensation Payments 133–134
   denialism agenda 134
   Directive 20-1 130
   Hawthorne Report 1967 129
   'At Home/Chez Soi' project 211–212
   Indian Act 1951 129, 130
   Indian Day Schools 131
   Indian Residential Schools (IRS) 131
   Indian Residential Schools Settlement Agreement (IRSSA) 133
   Indians as "wards" 129
   Indigenous aspirations 149
   Indigenous children in care 129–130, 132
   intergenerational legacies 131–133
   Millennium Scoop 132
   Nisga Nation (First Nation) 151
   reforms 136
   Royal Commissions 2–3
   Royal Commission on Aboriginal Peoples (RCAP) 130, 136
   safe injection sites 210
   Supreme Court of Canada (SCC) 131
   Truth and Reconciliation Commission (TRC) 129, 130, 135, 136
Canada v Gottfriedson (FCA) 133
Canadian Association of Social Workers 129
Canadian Broadcasting Corporation (CBC) 133
Canadian Human Rights Commission 130–131
Canadian Human Rights Tribunal (CHRT) 131, 136
capitalism 69, 114, 284, 286–287, 289, 291–292, 294
capitalist 'realism' (Brockmann) 122
carceral creep 158–159, 161–162
'carceral feminism' (Bernstein) 5, 158, 161, 166
carcerality 67–68, 165, 263
carceral logic 47, 59, 87, 95, 97, 196, 199
carceral policing 201
carceral punishment 198
carceral state
   and abolitionist movements 284
   coercive arms of the state 199
   expansion 61, 256
   and the liberal self 287–294
   racism 198
   resistance to 157–158
   social services 6
   social workers 87
'carceral systems of care' 258
care 54, 115–116, 173
care and control 290
Care Coordinators 107
caregivers 104–105
Caribbean children 56
Cartesian dualism 118
case plans 105
Caulfield, Lauren (Loz) 182–190
Chandler, A. 278
Charitable Organisation Society 289
Charter of the Forest 287
Charters, C. 151, 152
Chester, P. 72
child abuse and neglect
   deaths 31
   public health approaches 244
   Texas 31
   United Kingdom 58
   United States 28, 95–96, 97, 98, 99, 101, 104
child maltreatment 31, 54, 95, 99, 102
child protection 239–249
   Aotearoa 119–121, 148–150, 152, 240
   Canada 128–131, 134, 135–136
   child abuse and neglect 58
   decolonisation 243–244, 245, 247
   deprivation and poverty 54–55, 60
   England 52–55
   Family Hubs 226–228
   gendered approaches 5
   instructional advocacy 304–305
   Māori 142–144, 150, 240
   'risk' discourses 57
   shaming and blaming 55
   and youth justice 88

Index

Child Protective Services (CPS) 95–107, 242
  Black children 26
  carceral logic 97
  Care Coordinators 107
  coercion and intimidation 101
  contacting collaterals 103–104
  decision making 104–106
  failing to keep children safe 31
  family assessments 96
  government databases 98–99
  'home visits' 102
  interviews 102, 103
  investigations 96–102, 107
  parents' rights 100
  reforms 105–107
  surveillance 33
  see also United States (US)
child removal practices
  Aboriginal people 70, 84
  Canada 130
  Finland 256, 262, 264
  foster care industry 106
  Indigenous settler colonial experiences 144
  Māori 145, 148
  United States 27, 34, 44, 96
children
  foster care 28
  homelessness 88
  killed by parents 31
  rescuing from poverty 40
  social model for protecting 55
  socioeconomic circumstances 54
Children's Aid Society 40
The Child Savers (Platt) 41
child-saving movement 40–41
child sexual exploitation 56–57
child welfare agencies 27, 29
Child Welfare Inequalities Project (CWIP) 54, 56, 60
child welfare systems 25
  Aotearoa 119–121
  assessing safety and risk 103
  carceral logic 59
  and criminal legal system 29–30
  designed to oppress 26
  destroying families 27
  Finland 262
  marginalised families 26
  neoliberal cuts 265
  social workers 41
  United States 42
  visibility of adolescents 57
  see also family policing (family regulation system)
Circles of Care (CoC). 107
Clarke, K. 128

Class, Capital and Social Policy (Ginsberg) 116
classifying service users 205
Cleaver, K. 248
close accompaniment principle 185
coercion and neglect 272, 273–276, 277
'coercive confinement' (O'Sullivan and O'Donnell) 232
collective action 71
collective knowledge mapping 150
Collins, Patricia Hill 261–262
colonialism
  child protection inequities 243, 246
  and eugenics 258, 260
  gender as a prison 168
  and social work 69–70
  violence of law 203
  Western knowing 119
  see also decolonisation
colonial warfare 86
Color of Violence conference (Santa Cruz 2000) 160
colour-blind universalism 264
Colvin, E. 88
Colwell, Maria 53
commoning 173–174, 285, 287–288, 290–295
communities of colour 41, 67, 157–158
community accountability 160, 182, 185, 212
community alternatives 9
community-based care organisations 8
community-based feminist support 5, 303
community-based support 8, 33, 61, 120, 186–187, 244–248
community cultural wealth perspectives 61
community devolution 240
community expertise 90–91
community-led strategies 210–215
community responses to harm 183–188, 191
comprehensive harm reduction policies 211–212
confidentiality 302
Connelly, Peter ('Baby P') 53
consensual policing 200
contemporary abolitionism 5, 287
Contextual Safeguarding 57
control and care 289–290
Convention on the Rights of Children (CRC, UN) 147
Cooke-Stanhope, Judge 133
Cook, Len 119–120, 145
Coppock, V. 205
counter-insurgency/terrorism 199–200, 205–206
'county lines' criminal networks 56–57
COVID-19 pandemic 32–33, 210

Crackdown Podcast 214
CrazyBull, Brandy 132–133
Crenshaw, Kimberlé 159–160
criminal exploitation 56–57
criminal justice 59, 168
criminal law enforcement 29
critical reflection and reflexivity 72
Critical Resistance 48, 160, 162, 277
critical social work theorists 4
cultural and familial knowledge 191
Cunneen, C. 86–87
Cuomo, D. 9

D

Dacquino, M. 170
The Dangerous Classes of New York (Brace) 40
Davis, Angela Y. 5, 48, 231, 257, 287
  abolition feminism 160–161
  abolition of slavery 44
  abolition transforming society 82–83
  American carceral system 197–199
  Are Prisons Obsolete? 160, 212
  capitalism, police and prisons 286
  race and racialisation 202
Davis, S. 8
De Angelis, M. 293
decolonisation 119, 215, 240, 243–244, 245, 247–248
  see also colonialism
Dent, Gina 161
de-radicalising extremists 199
Dettlaff, A.J. 58
Diggers 288
Dimou, E. 119
'direct provision systems' 232
disenfranchised working class 122
disparity defenders 31
'disruptive social work' (Feldman) 7
'dissenting social work' (Garrett) 115
Don Dale Youth Detention Centre, Northern Territory 89
Donzelot, Jacques 204–206
Douglass, Frederick 43
Downtown Eastside (DTES, Vancouver) 208–210, 213–215
Doyle Jr, Joseph 30
drugs 56–57, 208–212
Drug Users Liberation Front (DULF) 213–214
Du Bois, W.E.B. 43–44
Duggan, Mark 200
Durie, Mason 146, 147
'duty of care' 274
'dying with their rights on' (Treffert) 271

E

economic relations of power 119
Elizabethan poor laws 27

Elliott-Cooper, Adam 199–201
emancipatory social work 258–259
El-Enany, Nadine 202–204
enclosure of common lands 284, 288–289
'end of social work' debate 115
engaging with failure 187, 188
England 52–61
  Black and mixed children 58
  child protection 52–55
  Department for Education 54, 55
  deprivation 54
  far right violence 59
  feudalism 287
  Metropolitan Police 289
  poor laws 27, 128, 289
  poverty 54, 55
  'thanatocracy' 288
  see also United Kingdom (UK)
Engler, M. 242
Engler, P. 242
Enlightenment reason 118
environmental harms 170
'epistemicide' (Dimou) 119
epistemic justice 118–119
essentialist feminism 159–160
ethic of care 173–174, 242
'ethic of restoration' (Jackson) 146
eugenics 259–262
Eurocentric culture and worldview 66, 70, 128–129
evidence-based models 246
exclusion 4, 188, 192, 223
exploitation 8
extended kinship systems 259
externalising shame 192–193
'extra-familial risks/harms' 56–57

F

'fairness' 245
Faith, Karlene 232
families 47, 55
family assessments 96–97
family destruction 27
Family Hubs (FH) 221–233
  CCTV surveillance 229–230
  child protection 226–228
  'emergency' accommodation 224, 227
  and lone mothers 225–226, 227
  policies and procedures 228
  referral to CPS 226–227
  reforming 232–233
  and social workers 224–226
  surveillance 222–223, 229–231
  unsupervised children 226–227
  see also Ireland
family policing (family regulation system) 25–34, 95, 106
  abolition 32–34

incarcerating parents 29–30
marginalised communities 26–27, 28
and poverty 26
racism 27–28, 31
separating families 30, 44
stigma, stress and unfairness 241
surveillance 28–29
trauma from investigations 30
see also child welfare systems; United States (US)
family regulation agencies 100
family violence 180–181, 189
Fanon, Franz 257
far right violence 59
Fayter, R. 8
Featherstone, B. 55, 61, 115
Federique, K. 8
Feldman, G. 7
feminist abolitionists 5
feminist anti-carceral social work 164–165
feminist anti-violence movements 13, 156, 158–160
Ferguson, I. 3
feudalism 287–288
Finland 255–266
  bordering practices 261
  child protection services 256, 262
  child removals 256, 262, 263
  child welfare 262
  Child Welfare Act 2017 256
  colonialism and eugenics 258, 261–264
  colour-blind universalism 264
  Great Recession 256
  Institute for Health and Welfare 262
  manufacturing the family 259–260
  myth of homogeneity 264–265
  neoliberalism 256–257, 261
  New Public Management (NPM) 257, 261
  out-of-home care 262
  public inquiry 2013 256–257
  racial equality data 264
  recording race 264
  residential and professional care 263, **263**
  Roma 256
  welfare state 255
First Nations Child and Family Caring Society (FNCFCS) 130–131
Fitzwater, D.E. 293
flax (harakeke) 144, 152–153
Floyd, George 45, 46, 118, 180
food justice 16
food riots 288
Fook, J. 72
Fortier, C. 214, 215, 300
foster care 26, 27–28, 30, 44
  see also adoption
foster-industrial complex 27

Foucault, M. 229, 232, 255–256
Fraser, Nancy 60
freedom and hyper-individualism 248
#FreeHer campaign 90
Fronek, P. 72

G

gamekeepers 289
Garcia, A.R. 59, 242
Garrett, P.M. 6–7, 115, 117, 307
Garthwaite, K. 53
gender abolition 170–173
gender-based violence 8, 85, 159–161, 169–170
  see also violence
gender binaries 165–166, 167, 170, 171–172
gendered approaches 5
gendered power relations 166
gender equality 167, 170–171
gender identity 166
gender-less societies 171
gender training 168
genocidal colonial conquest 118–119
Gilmore, Ruth Wilson 169, 199, 231, 257
Ginsberg, N. 116
Global North 16
Global South 16, 294
Godden, N.J. 213, 215
good government principles (Zapatista) 293–294
Gorz, André 9, 162, 242, 246
Gove, Michael 53
governmentality framework 166
Guentner, S. 261

H

Hämäläinen, J. 260
hapū (Māori extended relational/social structures) 143–144, 148, 150, 152, 153, 153n4
harakeke (flax) 144, 152–153
Hardt, M. 293
harm reduction interventions 208–217
  community-led strategies 210–215
  low barrier approaches 215
  radical love 215–216
Harney, S. 286
Harper, Stephen 134
Harvey, D. 117
Hassan, S. 9
Hastings, Aotearoa 121
Hatcher, D. 27
haunting 258
'the Hawkes Bay Uplift' (2019) 121, 148
Hawthorne Report (1967) 129
Hayes, K. 201
health and social services 84–85

healthy and toxic masculinities 164, 166
Hearne, R. 221–223, 232
'hearts and minds' counter-insurgency tactics 200–201
HeForShe 164, 167
Hegel, G. 285
hegemonic masculinity 170
hegemonic nuclear family 259
hegemonic power 158
Hélie, S. 130
'He Pāharakeke, He rito, Whakakīkīnga Whāruarua' (WAI 2915) 121, 148
'He Puapua' report (Charters) 151, 152
Hestbæk, A.D. 262
Higgins, D.J. 245
'high receptivity points' 245
Hillyard, P. 200
Holmwood, J. 201
Homanen, R. 261
homelessness 222–223
hooks, bell (Gloria Jean Watkins) 213
Horizontalists, Argentina 292, 295
Housing First 211–212, 214
'How white is social work in Australia?' (Walter) 83
Huata, Donna 149
Hull House, Chicago 128
human rights 122, 303
human subjects 118
Hunter, D. 8, 74
hunting game 289
hyper-individualism 248
Hyslop, I. 120–121

I

ideas of community 191
ideas of failure 191
Ideological State Apparatus (Althusser) 121
Ife, J. 213
'illness' paradigm 276–277
immigration detention centres 203
immigration law 203
incarcerated parents 29–30
incarcerated women 85
INCITE! Women of Color Against Violence 5–6, 156–157, 160–161
income inequality 58
incremental reforms 76
independent mental health advocacy 304
Indian Residential Schools (IRS) 131
Indigenous children
  in care/CP services 129–130
  foster care 26
  removal from families 131–132, 144
Indigenous Coastal Salish people 208
Indigenous communities 144, 292
Indigenous cultural parenting practices 129
Indigenous flourishing 146–147

Indigenous Governing Bodies 135
Indigenous knowledges 10, 248
Indigenous peoples
  carcerality and social control 67–68
  care systems 115–116
  colonial processes 247
  DTES 215
  gaslighting 134
  intrusion into familial lives 131
  laws and jurisdiction 135
  logic of elimination 118
  neoliberal expansion of capitalism 292
  social determinants of health 136
  social structures and colonial project 144–145
  state regulation 149
Indigenous Residential Schools 209
Indigenous rights 147, 249
individualised problems 265
Industrial Revolution 39–40
informal processes 90–91
'information is power' 99
'innocence' of childhood 86
Inquiry Commissions *see* Royal Commissions
institutional racism 57
instructional advocacy 304–305, 307
'intensive family support' projects ('sinbins') 223
internalising carceral logics 191
International Federation of Social Workers (IFSW) 1, 115
International Monetary Fund 292
interpersonal violence 5, 183–184
intersecting harms 118
intersectionality 4, 76, 159–160, 241
interviewing children 102
In the Nutshell magazine 214
intimate partner violence 180, 185, 191
  see also sexual violence; violence
involuntary mental health treatment 270, 273, 275
Ioakimidis, V. 71–72
Ireland 221–233
  child protection services (CPS) 226–227
  homelessness 222–223
  Mother and Baby Homes 226
  Ombudsman for Children's Office (OCO) 222
  prisons 232
  see also Family Hubs (FH)
Irish Human Rights and Equality Commission (IHREC) 221, 222
Irish Times 222
Irish Traveller community 222
Islamophobic rhetoric 59
Iwai, Y. 299
iwi (Māori tribal structures) 119, 121, 143–144, 148, 150–153, 153n4, 240

J

Jackson, M. 146
Jacobs, L.A. 72
James, K. 299, 300
Jamieson, Sacha 83–86
Jinibara Peoples, Australia 66
JMacForFamilies 32
Johnston, A. 58
Jones, C. 3
juvenile crime 87–88

K

Kaba, Chris 200
Kaba, Mariame 157, 201, 286, 287
Te Kāika hub service model 149–150, 152
'kāinga' (Māori home, land and community) 148, 152, 153
Kāi Tahu 142
Kaufman-Mthimkhulu, S.L. 306
Keddell, E. 121
Kelly, L. 241
Kelsey, J. 118
Kempe, C.H. 95, 98
Kenya 200
Kilroy, Debbie 69, 70, 76, 90
Kim, M.E. 212
King, P. 147–148
Kirk, J. 7
Kitson, Frank 200
Kivel, P. 169
'know your rights' legislation 100
Korea 157
Kulin Nations, Australia 66

L

Lamble, S. 9–10, 60
Lamusse, T 69
land possession 68
Lavalette, M. 7
law and racial capitalism 202
law enforcement 159
Lawston, J.M. 233
Law, V. 59, 199
Lean, T. 69
Leonard, [initial required] 116
Levellers 288
Lewis, L. 149
liberal capitalism 122, 123
liberal feminists 170, 171
liberal reforms 158
liberal self 284–295
  Autonomist Marxism 290–292
  carceral state 286–289
  commoning 292–294
  materialism and dialectics 285–286
  social work 289–290
liberal states 166–167
liberationist social work 113
Liberty 61
life-affirming relationships and institutions 8
Lindstrom, Desi 132
lived-experience abolitionists 69, 242
lived experience movements 213
'living ghosts' (Bhaba) 258
Loftsdóttir, K. 255
lone mothers and parenting 224–227, 228
Lopez-Humphreys, M. 302
love 213, 293
'loving' adoptive homes 53
low barrier, harm reduction approaches 215
Lown, J. 299–300
Luddites 288
Lupick, T. 209

M

MacAlister, J. 55
Magna Carta (1215) 287
maltreatment 104–105
Man Box 164
Man Up (ABC television programme) 168
Māori 142–153
  te Ao Māori (world/worldview) 147
  child protection 142–144, 150, 240
  child removals 121, 145, 148
  coalition government reforms 150
  experience of racism 151
  hapū (extended relational/social structures) 143–144, 148, 150, 152, 153, 153n4
  iwi (tribal structures) 119, 121, 143–144, 148, 150–153, 153n4, 240
  'kāinga' (home, land and community) 148, 152, 153
  mauri noho (languishing) 146, 153
  mauri ora (flourishing) 146–147, 150, 152–153
  mokopuna (grandchildren/children) 142, 144–148, 152, 153n1
  mokopuna rights 147
  Oranga Mokopuna 147–148, 150
  Pā harakeke (social support structure) 142–150, 152–153
  'Puao te Ata Tu' report 120–121
  restoring social structures 142
  state regulation 149
  struggle for justice 120
  urbanisation 145
  wāhine (woman/women) 144, 153n5
  whakapapa (genealogical lineage/identity) 144, 147, 243
  whānau (broad family structure/system) 121, 143–144, 146–147, 150, 153n3
  see also Aotearoa

Māori-driven transformation 121
marginalised communities 2
　child welfare oppressing 26, 27–28
　empowerment 71
　family policing 29
　Finland 260
　identification and surveillance 245–246
　persecution 115
　prisons subjugating 68, 143
　'small state' ideology 53
　state-sponsored violence 180
　trust in social workers 59
Martensen, K.M. 61, 260, 265
Martin (Horizontalist) 293
Martin, K.E.C. 54
Marx, K. 285–286, 291–292
masculinist states 164, 166–168
masculinity 166, 170
Mason, W. 61
Massey, R. 168
mass incarceration 198–199, 202
Masson, A. 8–9
Matahaere-Atariki, Donna 149
material needs and support 117, 242
Mattila, M. 260
Mauer, M. 198
Maylea, C. 6–7, 113, 115, 121–122, 273
McClain, A. 45–46
McCook, S. 168
McFarlane, S. 72
McGovern, M. 205
McLean v *Canada* (FC) 133–134
McMillan, Joyce 100
Meiners, Erica R. 87, 161, 233
men
　abolitionist practices against violence 173–174
　anti-patriarchal activism 164
　rationalist masculinity 167
　violence against women 165, 169
　violence prevention 168, 169
Menezes, Jean Charles de 200
mental health 88, 270–280
　alternative carceral strategies 275–276
　Anglophone policies 306
　coercion and neglect 273–276
　de-carcerating 279
　instructional advocacy 304–305
　involuntary treatment 270, 273, 275
　and neoliberalism 272, 273
　overstretched services 271
　peer work 305–306, 307
　service denial 274–275
　and social justice 276–277
　women 274–275
mental health social work 278–279
Mental Patients Association (MPA) 213–214
Metallic, Naiomi 131

Midnight Notes 295
militarism 170
military industrial complex 169
Miranda v *Arizona* (US Supreme Court) 100
Missing and Murdered Indigenous Women and Girls Report (MMIWG) 130
'mode of life' (Marx) 286
mokopuna Māori (grandchildren/children) 142, 144–148, 152, 153n1
moral economy 287–289, 294
Morgan, J. 90
Morley, C. 72
Morley, L. 213
mortality statistics 28
Moten, [initial required] 286
Movement for Black Lives 46
Mueller, J.C. 47, 231
multidisciplinary alliances 90
multigenerational losses 132–133
Murphy, M. 221–223, 232
Muslims 199, 203, 205
mutual aid 8, 32–33, 61
mythic white homogeneity 265

N

Napoleon, V. 244
National Apology to the Stolen Generations 81
National Association of Social Workers (NASW) 39, 41, 45–46
National Inquiry into the Separation of Aboriginal and Torres Strait Islander Children from their Families 81
National Plan to End Violence Against Women 2022—2032 (Australia) 85
native children 27
neglect 26
Negri, A. 293
neoliberal biopower 166
neoliberalism 117, 119
　abolitionist social work 265
　building solidarity 248–249
　disenfranchised working class 122
　emancipatory concepts 275
　Finland 256–257, 261
　gendered power relations 166
　IMF funding requirements 292
　inequalities 278
　and mental health 272, 273
　professionalisation of skills and knowledges 192
　research and education 277
　UK 58
　US 58, 286
network of relations 285
Network to Advance Abolitionist Social Work 162

Index

Newfoundland and Labrador 133
New South Wales (NSW) 82, 89
  Department of Communities and
    Justice 85
New York City 32–33, 159
  Administration for Children's Services
    (ACS) 32–33
New Zealand *see* Aotearoa
Ngāi Tahu Te Kaika hub model 151–152
Ngāi Tahu tribal authority 149
Nipperess, S. 301
Nisga Nation (First Nation Canadian) 151
non-abolitionist social workers 305
non-binary people 166
non-carceral community-led approaches 215
non-government social services
  sector 168–169
non-profit industrial complex 123,
  168–169, 190
non-reformist reforms (Gorz) 9, 32, 97,
  106, 195, 242, 277–278
  see also reformist reforms
non-state responses to violence *see*
  transformative justice
Nordic nations and societies 52, 255, 258,
  262–263
North American Free Trade
  Agreement 292
North Korea 157
not-for-profit industrial complex 188–189

O

Oakland, California 159
O'Donnell, I. 232
Okpokiri, C. 56
Ollman, B. 285
Ontario 130
Oparah, Julia 231
Open Dialog 306
oppression 8, 69, 114
optimism of the penitentiary 198
Oranga Tamariki 148, 149, 153n6, 240
Orphan Train Movement 40, 41
O'Sullivan, E. 232
out-of-home care (OOHC) 81–82, 88

P

pacification approaches 200
Pā harakeke (Māori social support
  structure) 142–150, 152–153
Pain, R. 8, 173
Pakistan 56
Palestine 17
parent advocacy programmes 55
Parent Legislative Action Network (PLAN,
  JMacForFamilies) 32
parents 26, 54–55, 56, 243–244, 304
partnership-based family services 52

Parton,, Nigel 257
patriarchy 168, 204
Pease, B. 116, 301
peer work in mental health 305–306, 307
Pelton, L.H. 97, 105
Pendleton, M. 241
Perelman, M. 288
performative activism 272, 277
Phillips, R. 259
Philpott, Jane 136
Platt, Anthony M. 41
police and policing 6, 41
  abolition 231
  child safeguarding processes 57
  and inter ethnic problems 186
  maltreatment reports 29
  militarised paradigm 200
  and prison-industrial complex 67
  role of social work 45
  United Kingdom 199–201, 289
  US anti-violence movement 158
  Victoria, Australia 189
police social work 41
The Policing of Families (Donzelot) 204
popular social work 7, 290
post-anthropocentric social work 290
post-anthropocentric theory 285, 286
post-social work world 301
poverty 26, 46–47, 54–55, 114, 246, 249
'poverty porn' (Garthwaite) 53
power and control wheel 169
Pratt, M. 171
'pre-criminal space' 201
preventative family support services 59
PREVENT policy 196–197, 199, 201,
  203–206
  see also United Kingdom (UK)
'Prevent Strategy' (Home Office,
  GOV.UK) 196
Price, J. 169
'primitive accumulation' (Marx) 291
prison abolition 69, 157, 160, 162,
  168, 231
prison-industrial complex (PIC) 9, 67–68,
  118, 168, 169, 197
prison reform 199
prisons
  Australia health of women 84–85
  and the carceral system 199
  and child welfare 29–30
  colonial legacies 68–69
  'criminogenic effects' 86
  as harsh and dehumanising 44
  as penitentiaries 198
  structural violence 5
private companies 27, 202
privatisation of social services 117
problem families 223

problem poor 115
professionals 86, 105
Progressive Era 27
Project LETS 306
promoting kinship 249
protector roles 166–167
psychiatric abolition 273
psychiatric coercion 271–272, 273, 279–280
psychiatric power 277
psychoactive drugs 208, 210
'psych-thinking' 276
'psy-regimes of governance' 306
'Puao te Ata Tu' report (Aotearoa) 120–121
public health 86, 244–249
'punishment disguised as help' 83, 89
punishment, exclusion and demonisation 4–5
punitive models 204–205
punitive sentencing policies 197

Q

Québec 130
Quinn, A. 130

R

race
  and class-based oppression 119
  and ethnicity 55–57
  and poverty 58
  and settler-colonialism 128
racial bias 26–27
racial capitalism 118, 202
racial hygiene ideologies 259
racially minoritised families 56
Racine v *Woods* (SCC) 133
racism 71, 84, 143, 198, 246, 247
radicalisation 57, 114
radicalism 71–72
radical love 213, 215–216
radical reflections 72–73
Radical Safeguarding (Johnston and Akay) 58
radical social work 4, 47, 71, 290
radical transformation 73–74, 115
'Raise the Age' campaign 89
Rasmussen, C. 7, 299, 300
rationalist masculinity 167
Reauthorization of VAWA 161
Recovery in the Bin (RITB) 278
'recovery-oriented practice' 276
Redden, J. 135
redistribution of power 249
reformist reforms 9, 48, 83
  see also non-reformist reforms
rehabilitation 198
Rein, M. 71

relational self 285–286, 290–291
rendition 203
Repo, J. 165–166
reproductive justice frameworks 16
rescuing children 53
resource and power redistribution 242
responsive regulation 106
restorative approaches to justice 293–294
restorative practices initiative (Reauthorization of VAWA) 161
re-storying shame 193
Review of Children's Social Care (MacAlister) 55
revolutionary social work 74–76
Richie, Beth E. 61, 161, 231, 260, 265
Richmond, Mary 289
rights-based frameworks 90
right-wing populism 59
risk assessment frameworks 274
risk determination processes 87–88
'risk' discourses of child protection 57
'risks of reoffending' 87–88
Ritchie, Andrea 257
Roberts, Dorothy 25, 58, 59, 100, 143, 257, 258
Rodriguez, D. 168–169, 173
Royal Commissions 2–3
Royal Commission into Aboriginal Deaths in Custody (Australia) 81, 82
Royal Commission of Inquiry into Historical Abuse in State Care and in the Care of Faith-Based Institutions (Aotearoa) 119–120, 145–146
Royal Commission on Aboriginal Peoples (Canada) 130, 136
Rwanda 203

S

safeguarding practices 57
safe injection sites 210
Said, Edward 257
Salleh-Hoddin, Amiirah 264
Sámi territory, Finland 259
Sandbeck, S. 166
Schenwar, M. 59, 199
seasonal employment and industries 209
'second Stolen Generation' (AASW) 82
the self (Marx) 285
Serious Case Reviews of Black children 56
settler colonialism 120, 152, 157, 168, 259
settler colonies 115–116, 190
sex categories 166, 171–172
sexual violence 180, 191
  see also intimate partner violence; violence
Shackelford, A. 299
'shadow state' (Gilmore) 169

Index

'shadow state' (Wilson) 5
Shalleck-Klein, D. 101
shame 192–193
Shanks, E. 262
Shattered Bonds (Roberts) 25
Shepherd, L. 170
Sherwood, Juanita 83
Silver, E. 123
single room occupancy housing (SROs) 209
Sitrin, M. 293
slavery 5, 27, 43, 118, 198
slow violence 170
'small state' ideology 53
Smith, R. 243
social control 39, 41, 68, 200, 246
Social Darwinist theories 259
social determinants of health (SDH) 84–85, 128–129, 135, 136
social harms 1–2, 61
social justice 1, 2, 3–4, 113–123, 303
  Aotearoa 119
  Canada 128
  and mental health services 276–277
  and social work 39, 69, 73, 113–114
social justice workers 123
social safety net 117
social services 2, 6, 47, 117, 122, 129, 168–169
social work 1–2
  abolitionist perspectives 6–10, 48, 257–259
  Anglophone concepts 301–302
  anti-oppressive approaches 89, 300
  as carceral 300, 302–303
  and the carceral state 7, 87, 289–290
  care and coercion 212
  contradictions 116, 294
  control and care 289
  defining 115, 302
  deprofessionalisation 7, 300
  development 2, 289–290
  future 46–48
  golden age 2–3, 117
  as a moral profession 121–122
  and the 'problem poor' 115
  professional recognition 289–290
  reinventing 295
  social power and domination 69
  as 'soft police' 66
  and the state 116–117
  training 303–304
  Western Eurocentric worldview 66
social workers
  'agents of the state' 81, 84
  areas of work 302–303
  building a new society 47
  carceral policing 41, 201
  challenging injustice and oppression 39
  child welfare system 41
  identity 83–84
  removing Indigenous children 132
  and social justice 69
social work literature 284–285
societal problems 46–47
sociological traps 10
softer masculinities 167
'soft police' 6
solidarity 216, 249
South Korea 157
Spade, D. 8, 9, 73, 172
Spandler, H. 276
'Staircase of Accountability' 74
Stanley, E.A. 73
Starr, Ellen Gates 128
state–iwi (tribal) partnerships 240
state violence 81, 85, 157, 160, 294
Stolen Generations 70, 81, 84
Stop G20 conferences 184
striking mine workers 117
strip-searching 85
structural abandonment 273
structural problems 262, 265
structural racism 199
structural violence 5, 9, 76, 169–170, 183–184
supportive assistance myth 96
surveillance 6, 41, 205, 222–223
survivor insider knowledge 191
survivor movements 213
system harm 90
systems of oppression 68–69

T

Teater, B. 302
terminating parental rights 32, 243
Texas 31
Think of Us 30
Thomasson, Anita (Ani) 182–190
Thompson, E.P. 287
Thompson, J.L. 72
Tiaki Taoka caregiver services 149
Tinirau, R. 151
Toikko, Timo 262
Toraif, N. 47, 231
Torn Apart (Roberts) 25
'tough and smart' justice measures 85
toxic drug deaths 208, 211
toxic masculinity 164, 166
'traditional' family ideals 259
transformative justice 6, 74, 160, 180–194
  abolitionist approaches 190–191, 212
  and community accountability 182
  and family policing 33
  and family violence 181
  non-state responses to violence 180–181

radical anti-capitalist approaches 193–194
responding to violence 173
transformative praxis 74
transformative strategies 60
transgender people 166, 171–172
"transmitted deprivation" (Leonard) 116
Treaty of Waitangi (Te Tiriti o Waitangi) 147
Treffert, D.A. 271
trust 59
Truth and Reconciliation Commission (TRC, Canada) 129, 130, 136
  Calls to Action 135
Tucker, R.B. 198

U

unconditional material help 117
'Undoing racism through social work' (NASW) 46
unemployment 209, 288–289
United Kingdom (UK)
  abolitionist futures 60–61
  'austerity' financial cuts 53
  Black resistance to policing: 199–201
  borders 202
  British Nationality Acts 202–203
  child protection system 52, 58, 61
  child rescue project 53
  Conservative-led coalition 53
  Counter-Terrorism and Security Act 2015 196
  disadvantaged neighbourhoods 56
  immigration laws 202–203
  income inequality 58
  New Labour 53, 223
  new social settlement 60
  PREVENT policy 196–197, 199, 201, 203–206
  race and ethnicity 55–57
  right-wing populism 59
  social and political contexts 58
  socio-legal approaches to extremism 196
  welfare state 58
  see also England
United Nations Declaration on the Rights of Indigenous Peoples (UNDRIP) 81, 147
United Nations Standard Minimum Rules for the Treatment of Prisoners (the Mandela Rules) 85
United Nations (UN), Convention on the Rights of Children (CRC) 147
United States (US) 39–48, 95–107, 156–162, 181
  abolitionist debates 57–59, 239, 241–3
  'abolitionist' social work 231
  abolition movement 42–46, 243
  Adoption and Safe Families Act 1997 32
  anti-violence sector 156

authoritarian system 52
carceral system 29–30, 95, 197–198
CARES Act 2020 33
child abuse and neglect 28, 95–96, 97, 98, 99, 101, 104
childhood poverty 34, 40
child welfare agencies 29, 58, 97–98
child welfare system 29–30, 44, 95
Civil War 27, 43
community support groups 61
criminal legal system 157
Department of Justice 161
European immigrant children 41
expansion of prisons 286
Fourth Amendment 28, 99, 101
George Floyd Justice in Policing Act 46
imprisoning Blacks 29–30, 41, 198
income inequality 58
Industrial Revolution 39–40
NASW 39, 41, 45–46
permanency plans 29
punitive sentencing policies 197
removing children from families 27, 44, 58, 101–102
right-wing populism 59
Violence Against Women Act (VAWA) 1994 156, 160, 161
see also Child Protective Services (CPS); family policing (family regulation system)
universal structuring template 118
universal supports 245
unwanted treatment 273, 274
upEND movement 48, 59
URM (2018 ABPC) 133

V

vagrancy 288–289
Vancouver
  Downtown Eastside (DTES) 208–210, 213–215
  Four Pillars Policy 209–210
  lived experience/survivor movements 213
Vancouver Drug Users Network (VANDU) 213–214
Vaughn, L. 57
Victoria, Australia 189
violence 76, 180–194
  against Black Americans 44
  carceral responses 182
  community responses to harm 188
  failure to care 173–174
  individual and collective responsibility 182–183
  interpersonal and structural violence 183–184
  law and colonialism 203

utopian future 187
  see also gender-based violence; intimate partner violence; sexual violence
violence against women 5, 9, 85, 167, 169
violence prevention 5–6, 164–165, 168–172
violent communities 184–185

W

wage labour 287–288
wāhine (woman/women) 144, 153n5
Waitangi Tribunal 121, 145, 148–150, 244
  'He Pāharakeke, He rito, Whakakīkīnga Whāruarua' (WAI 2915) 121, 148
Wald, M.S. 98
Wallace, J. 116
Wall Street Journal 45–46
Walter, M. 83
'war on crime' 159
Wastell, D. 205
Watkins, Gloria Jean (bell hooks) 213
Watson, I. 70
welfare politics 117–118
welfare states 9, 58, 255
whakapapa (genealogical lineage/identity) 144, 147, 243
Te Whakaputanga o te Rangatiratanga o Nu Tireni framework (Aotearoa) 147
'Whakatika' report (Tinirau) 151
whānau (Māori broad family structure/system) 121, 143–144, 146–147, 150, 153n3
Whelan, J. 6–7
white children 56
white privilege 72, 83
White, R. 86–87
white racial groupings 198
White Ribbon Campaign 164, 167
White, S. 205
white settler states 259
white supremacy 72, 168, 202
Whynacht, A. 277
Wilkins, K. 129
Williams, A. 167–168
Wilson, Marie 136
Wilson, R. 5
Wirihana, C. 243
women
  ill-health and incarceration 84–86
  mental health services 274–275
  stereotyping 241
  violence against 5, 9, 85, 167, 169
Wong, E.H-S. 300
Woodly, D. 173
working class 117, 204–205
World Health Organization 85
A World Without Sexual Assault collective 184
Wright, Eric Olin 123, 171
Wroe, L.E. 8, 57, 61, 74
Wurundjeri People, Australia 66

Y

Yassine, Lobna 86–89
Yellow Bird, M. 128
Young, I. 167
youth justice 57, 88

Z

Zapatista, Mexico 292–295
zines 190
Žižek, S. 122

www.ingramcontent.com/pod-product-compliance
Lightning Source LLC
Chambersburg PA
CBHW070802040426
42333CB00061B/1790